Snow on the Cane Fields

Snow on the Cane Fields

Women's Writing and Creole Subjectivity

Judith L. Raiskin

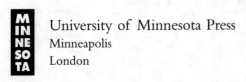

University of Minnesota Press
Minneapolis
London

The following publishers have given permission to use quotations from copyrighted works: From *Sans Souci,* by Dionne Brand. Copyright © 1989 by Dionne Brand. Used by permission of Firebrand Books, Ithaca, New York. From G. Buelens/E. Rudin, *Deferring a Dream: Literary Sub-Versions of the American Columbiad.* Volume published within ICSELL Series edited by the English Seminar of the University of Basel. Copyright © 1994 by Birkhäuser Verlag AG, Basel, Switzerland. Used by permission of the publisher. From *The Land of Look Behind,* by Michelle Cliff. Copyright © 1985 by Michelle Cliff. Used by permission of Firebrand Books, Ithaca, New York. From *No Telephone to Heaven* by Michelle Cliff. Copyright © 1987 by Michelle Cliff. Used by permission of Dutton Signet, a division of Penguin Books USA Inc. From *The Lesbian Postmodern,* edited by Laura Doan. Copyright © 1994 by Columbia University Press. Reprinted by permission of the publisher. From *ARIEL: A Review of International English Literature,* vol. 22, no. 4 (October, 1991), for "Jean Rhys: Creole Writing and Strategies of Reading," by Judith Raiskin. Copyright © 1991 The Board of Governors, The University of Calgary. Reprinted by permission of the publisher. From "The Day They Burned the Books," "Let Them Call It Jazz," and "Again the Antilles" by Jean Rhys. From *The Collected Short Stories by Jean Rhys.* W. W. Norton, 1987. Reprinted by permission of the Wallace Literary Agency, Inc. British rights: from *Tigers Are Better Looking* (Penguin Books 1972, first published by André Deutsch) copyright © Jean Rhys, 1960, 1962, 1927. Reprinted by permission of the publisher. From *The Letters of Jean Rhys,* by Jean Rhys, edited by Francis Wyndham and Diana Melly. Copyright © 1984 the Estate of Jean Rhys. Introduction copyright © 1984 by Francis Wyndham. Selection copyright © 1984 by Francis Wyndham and Diana Melly. Used by permission of Viking Penguin, a division of Penguin Books USA Inc. From *The Letters of Jean Rhys 1931–1966,* edited by Diana Melly (Penguin Books, 1985) copyright © the Estate of Jean Rhys, 1979. Reprinted by permission of the publisher. From *Smile Please,* by Jean Rhys (Penguin Books, 1981, first published by André Deutsch) copyright © the Estate of Jean Rhys, 1979. Reprinted by permission of the publisher. From *Voyage in the Dark,* by Jean Rhys. W. W. Norton, 1969. Reprinted by permission of W. W. Norton and Company, Inc., and the Wallace Literary Agency, Inc. British rights: Penguin Books 1969 (first published by André Deutsch), copyright © Jean Rhys, 1934. Reprinted by permission of the publisher. From *Wide Sargasso Sea,* by Jean Rhys. W. W. Norton, 1982. Reprinted by permission of W. W. Norton and Company, Inc., and the Wallace Literary Agency, Inc. British rights: Penguin Books 1968 (first published by André Deutsch), copyright © Jean Rhys, 1966. Reprinted by permission of the publisher. From "The Schooner Flight," in *The Star-Apple Kingdom,* in *Collected Poems, 1948–1984,* by Derek Walcott. Copyright © 1986. New York: Farrar, Straus and Giroux, Inc.; London: Faber and Faber Ltd. Reprinted by permission of the publishers. From *You Can't Get Lost in Cape Town,* by Zoë Wicomb. Copyright © 1987 by Zoë Wicomb. Reprinted by permission of Pantheon Books, a division of Random House, Inc.

Every effort has been made to obtain permission to reproduce copyright material in this book. The publishers ask copyright holders to contact them if permission has inadvertently not been sought or if proper acknowledgment has not been made.

Published by the University of Minnesota Press
111 Third Avenue South, Suite 290, Minneapolis, MN 55401
Printed in the United States of America on acid-free paper

Library of Congress Cataloging-in-Publication Data
Raiskin, Judith L.
    Snow on the cane fields : women's writing and Creole subjectivity / Judith L. Raiskin.
        p.   cm.
    Includes bibliographical references and index.
    ISBN 0-8166-2300-7 (hc)
    ISBN 0-8166-2301-5 (pbk.)
        1. South African literature (English)—Women authors—History and criticism.   2. West Indian literature (English)—Women authors—History and criticism.   3. Women and literature—South Africa— History—20th century.   4. Women and literature—West Indies—History—20th century.   5. Schreiner, Olive, 1855–1920—Political and social views.   6. Rhys, Jean—Political and social views.   7. Cliff, Michelle—Political and social views.   8. Wicomb, Zoë—Political and social views.   9. Subjectivity in literature.   10. Creoles in literature.   I. Title.
    R9358.R35   1996
    820.9
viilmathoneS9287–dc20   95–35095

The University of Minnesota is an equal-opportunity educator and employer

In memory of my mother,
Helen Cutler Raiskin, Ph.D.

Contents

Acknowledgments

I have written this book while commuting between two states and am grateful for the support of academic communities in both places.

A summer grant in 1991 from the Humanities Center at the University of Oregon provided me with space and time to begin work on this book. Whenever I returned to Oregon over the next several years, Sandra Morgen, Cheris Kramarae, and Diana Sheridan at the Center for the Study of Women in Society and Barbara Corrado Pope in women's studies found me office space and welcomed me into a vibrant intellectual community where I was able to share this work in its early stages; I thank them for their care and generosity. My appreciation is also due to the women's studies program at the University of California at Santa Barbara and especially to the chairs of my program, Sarah Fenstermaker, Patricia Cline Cohen, and Sharon Farmer, for assigning me a teaching load that made it possible to continue my research and writing. I was further assisted in this project by a Faculty Career Development Award from the university.

My work has been enriched by my discussions with the graduate students in the women's studies doctoral emphasis program and by those who engaged so thoughtfully and enthusiastically in my seminars. I am particularly indebted to Rachel Adams, who provided careful and imaginative research assistance for this book, often at short notice; Madelyn Detloff and Patricia Ingham offered me intellectual and institutional support as graduate students and teaching assistants in women's studies. For their friendship and their help with computers, office machines, and university bureaucracies in both Santa Barbara and Eugene, I thank Claire Flynn, Ann Wainwright, Agnes Curland, Elizabeth Archers, Robin Cochran, and Ruthann Mcguire.

I am deeply grateful to all those who so carefully read and commented on earlier drafts of these chapters: Steven Kruger, Margo Horn, Randall McGowen, Marilyn Farwell, Anthony O'Brien, Julie Carlson, and Claudine Michel. As I have asked new questions for this book, I have remained guided by the scholarship and advice of Mary Louise Pratt, Lucio Ruotolo, and Barbara Charlesworth Gelpi, who directed my dissertation at Stanford University; the comments of Mary Lou Emery, Sidonie Smith, and the anonymous reader for the University of Minnesota Press have helped me immensely with my revisions. Biodun Iginla, Elizabeth Stomberg, and many whose names I do not know at the Press have contributed their expertise toward the production of this book. I greatly appreciate Hank Schlau's skill as a copyeditor and wish also to thank Do Mi Stauber, the indexer. This book has benefited from many stimulating conversations I have had with my colleagues and friends, among them Diana Abu-Jaber, Michael Clark, Maria Damon, Marylynn Diggs, Faye Hirsch, Linda Kintz, Regina Kunzel, Annie Popkin, Tres Pyle, Elizabeth Reis, Ellen Rifkin, Beth Schneider, Siobhan Somerville, Lynn Tullis, and Claudia Yukman.

For their ongoing emotional and intellectual support while I wrote this book, I thank Rebecca Mark, Jesse Gathering, Linda Gardner, Kathryn Cirksena, Meryl Shader, Nanci Clarence, Sara Garver, and Steven Kruger. I would also like to thank my father and stepmother, Gerald and Helen Raiskin; my sister-in-law Leslie Wood; and the rest of my family (Raiskins, Greenbergs, Bilovskys, and Woods) for their unconditional support over the years I wrote this work. In particular, I appreciate the encouragement of my oldest friend, my sister, Jordana Raiskin, who has always shown me important connections I might otherwise have missed.

Most of all, I thank my partner, Mary Elene Wood, who took time from her own writing to read and to respond to multiple drafts of every chapter of this book and to participate in an ongoing discussion about its subject for years; she has offered me the most thorough criticism with humor and love. In the face of the disruptions of commuting, the negotiations of parenting, and the limited number of hours per day, she has remained steadfast in her faith that we could both continue to teach, write, and maintain friendships. For this I will always be grateful. Finally, I thank my son, Eli, whose presence allows me to spend the afternoons in parks as well as in libraries and whose good humor gives me perspective on all things.

Introduction

This is a study of definitions, cultural fictions, and the lives lived through and against them. Most generally, this book suggests that literature by creole women writers constitutes an important transnational, multiracial category raising challenging questions about some of our basic terms of identity and the choices they permit. Because a central term of this category, "creole," itself defies easy definition, the boundaries of this literary class are conspicuously, and usefully, elastic. While the term "creole" has been used in all parts of the world to describe linguistic mixtures that develop from extended contact between different cultures, as a term designating people it has until recently been used primarily to describe only those born in the colonies of the Americas. The term, however, is a useful one for describing a variety of colonial and neocolonial social relationships throughout the world and for highlighting similar experiences and literary responses in different national contexts. Putting aside for a moment the value-laden connotations of the term "creole," its broadest reference is to something or someone originating in a colonial territory. The writers I examine in this study all share the status of "Creole" by virtue of their births in British colonies or ex-colonies and their cultural ties to England fostered either by the self-identifications of settler societies or by Anglocentric colonial educations. Their perspectives as "Creoles" share a great deal yet vary as dramatically as do the different racial and national meanings of their creole identities. Defining themselves either as English settlers or as racially or culturally "mixed" indigenes, these women writers further complicate the

1

colonial vocabulary by highlighting the gendered nature of race, citizenship, nationhood, culture, and the language of literature.

I have chosen to examine four writers whose works span the last century in order to highlight creole literary responses to dramatic changes in colonial politics in two imperial domains. Olive Schreiner and Zoë Wicomb were born in South Africa, and Jean Rhys and Michelle Cliff were born in the Caribbean. All received colonial educations stressing English literature and culture, and all moved to England to shore up their claim of British subjecthood. Their evaluations of the "mother country" vary depending on their historical moments, their relationships with the countries of their birth, and their racial and cultural identifications. While each has contributed to what has come to be called "postcolonial" literature and theory, the difference in their perspectives and their strategies highlights the important historical and national particularities that the overarching term "postcolonial" often obscures.[1] Unlike the term "postcolonial," which relegates the economic and social structures of colonialism to a vague and distant past, the indeterminacy of the term "creole" makes no temporal claims and permits a recognition of the different perspectives available to those born in British colonies or countries that once were British colonies.

Olive Schreiner (1855–1920), born in South Africa to English and German missionary parents, identified herself as an "English South African" yet objected to British colonial policies and insisted that any plan for national independence must support Afrikaner culture and grant universal suffrage regardless of race or sex. Less willing to claim specific national allegiance, Jean Rhys (1890–1979), a fourth-generation West Indian who lived most of her life in Europe, identified herself as a "white Creole." As the Caribbean colonies moved toward independence, she explored the historic complexity of colonial relationships between white Creoles and British colonists, between French and English settlers, and among Blacks, Whites, and "Coloreds." A generation later, Michelle Cliff reveals how these colonial legacies of racism and economic exploitation persist in postcolonial, or, more accurately, neocolonial, societies. While they share much with these earlier creole writers, Michelle Cliff and Zoë Wicomb, who are identified by colonial racial formations as "colored," also critique the white colonial literary history in which they are misrepresented as unfortunate and disconcerting "by-products" of sexual defilement. Born in 1948, the year the Nationalist government came to power in South Africa, Zoë Wicomb describes in her fiction the experience of being "coloured" under apartheid and the specificities of that legal status. Her analysis makes clear that such terms as "postcolonial" are tragically erroneous for understanding South African politics, society, or literature. Therefore, while these writers do respond to important moments of colonial history, from the "scramble for Africa" to the postapartheid "New South Africa," I am not suggesting a reading of colonial history that emphasizes progress but rather one that highlights the way colonialist and nationalist discourses are invoked in different ways at different times for different purposes.[2] By closely reading the works of these four writers, I mean to establish a dialogue across the centuries as these creole writers endorse, qualify, denounce, or rewrite the languages of racial, sexual, and national difference they inherit.

The guiding term of this study, "creole," itself manifests great fluctuations over time and place. Beyond the most generic definition referring to colonial origin (a definition including plants and animals), "Creole" generally refers to those of (some) European descent born in European colonies or in independent territories that once were colonies. However, depending on the time and the place of its use, the term can signify full European ancestry (implying a claim of "unsullied" whiteness), mixed "racial" ancestry resulting from colonialism (usually implying some European ancestry mixed with African, Amerindian, or other so-called racial groups, depending on the location), or syncretic cultural and linguistic practices (such as "creole" music, food, or language). The conflicting meanings embedded in this term consequently cast the surrounding colonial vocabulary of nationality and racial identity into confusion as well.

For instance, although race and nationality are often understood as discrete markers of identity, the history of the meaning of "creole" demonstrates the interdependence of these concepts. It is telling that the Spanish *criollo* was initially a term not of racial but of geographical and national distinction. One meaning of *criollo* (1590) was the child born to Spanish parents in the New World, as opposed to the *gachupín,* or Spanish-born immigrant. The tension that developed between the two positions was a political one between loyalists and advocates of independence.[3] Another early meaning of the Spanish *criollo* (1602) was "black slave born in America," as opposed to *bozal,* meaning "newly arrived slave." The distinctions here, while specifically referring to racial categories, are also national distinctions, conferring prestige or defamation depending on the speaker of the term. There is some evidence, for instance, that black slaves born in Africa *(bozales)* were highly insulted if called *criollos,*[4] while in racist colonial societies the designation has also conferred status to light-skinned individuals since it implies white and European ancestry.

Tracing the use of the term "creole" through Spanish, French, Italian, English, and Portuguese to show the shifting semantic manifestations of the word, Thomas M. Stephens finds that the racial significance of the term was tied first to the importation of slaves and then to the prohibition of the slave trade. The end of the slave trade in the nineteenth century made all American black slaves *criollos,* and therefore to call an American-born Black a *criollo* was redundant. Consequently, the Spanish *criollo* came to designate only "whites born in the colonies." The later connotation of racial purity, that is, "American of pure white European race," does not occur, according to Stephens, until 1883. For French and English, however, the connotation of "whiteness" in addition to "having been born in the Americas" is earlier and more consistent over time.[5] In this century, "creole" often takes a racial adjective ("white creole," "black creole"), although it is common that different communities attributing different meanings to "creole" will assume the term is racially self-evident. For instance, Stephens notes that whereas in Mauritius the term *créole* may mean a "black person" or a "native to the island," in Belize the term now denotes a "person of black-white parentage."[6] In her excellent study of the politics of racial labeling, *White by Definition,* Virginia R. Domínguez shows the current contradictory uses of the term "creole" by Whites (of French and Spanish ancestry) and "Coloreds" (of mixed European and African ancestry) in Louisiana:

> Two types of Louisianians consequently identify themselves today as Creole. One is socially and legally white; the other, socially and legally colored. The white side by definition cannot accept the existence of colored Creoles; the colored side, by definition, cannot accept the white conception of *Creole.* . . . There are, in fact, colored Creoles who are virtually ignorant of the existence of whites in Louisiana who call themselves Creole . . . [and] find the term *white Creole* to be a contradiction in terms.[7]

These variant, even contradictory, meanings make it clear that we cannot pursue an essentialist conception of a single "creole identity." Rather, we are examining the various cultural uses of a term that, in all its definitions, complicates racial or national binarisms (white, black; European, American). The plasticity of this term permits its usage as both broadly inclusionary and narrowly restrictive. For example, *Inside the Creole Mafia,* a play examining the psychology of racial and cultural identity in the creole community of Los Angeles, exposes the dangerous claims of racial exclusivity available, ironically, to contemporary mixed-race creole discourse. The playwrights, Mark Broyard and Roger Guenveur Smith, quote from an editorial in *Bayou Talk,* a newspaper for the "creole diaspora," which demands that "America and the rest of the world needs [*sic*] to wake up and except [*sic*] us as a separate ethnic race."[8] The editorial goes on to exhort creole youth to avoid "mixed ethnic" marriages. Comparing such rhetoric to that of white supremacist and neo-Nazi groups, Broyard and Smith highlight the deep ironies and ambiguities of "creole" identity as a category as well as the dangers of *any* essentialist conception of ethnicity or race.

While examining the contradictions and ambiguities of the numerous terms for people of so-called mixed race (creole, *métis, mestizo,* hybrid, half-breed, half-caste, *die Mischlingen, bambini de sangue misto,* and so on), it is imperative that we are not seduced by these fictional categories to believe that there exists any "unmixed" or "pure" race or ethnic group. These dangerous and injurious beliefs are the legacy of both colonial rhetoric, which had a vested interest in promoting such ideas as national purity, and nineteenth-century European "race science," which contributed the concepts of racial integrity and degeneration. That "creole" can connote both biological purity and mixture underscores the poverty of both concepts as categories of difference.

Recently, a broader, more metaphorical conception of "creole" has been in use, focusing not on the individual human body or on supposed biological difference but on cultural intersections and mixtures. Thus Ulf Hannerz calls for a "creolist" anthropological theory that can account for the complexities of "the world in creolisation."[9] This construction emphasizes that this cultural phenomenon is not static but is in constant process and that this process is universal. Similarly, Françoise Lionnet fruitfully describes *métissage* as an evolving emancipatory concept and practice emphasizing heterogeneity and solidarity and demystifying "all essentialist glorifications of unitary origins, be they racial, sexual, geographic, or cultural."[10] To these challenges made by the concept of *métissage, la créolité* (or "creoleness") adds a specifically national and political challenge where the "Creole" is juxtaposed to both the "metropole" and the "colonial."

"Creoleness" can be understood both as evidence of particular political histories and nationalist movements and as an ongoing practice of articulating those histories in the languages of the people they have shaped. These metaphorical meanings of "creoleness" turn attention from the body to the "consciousness"; from the iconographic vocabulary of physical "looks" to the oral stories, songs, and poetry of the largely nonliterate populous; from the colonial past to a future where racial distinctions are not understood as hierarchical.[11]

Like "creole," many of the terms used by the authors I examine in this book have universalizing tendencies that a comparison of their works disrupts. While broadening the contours of the category "creole," I have endeavored to accent important differences between South Africa and the Caribbean, between the nineteenth and twentieth centuries, and between the treatment of "white" and "colored" people in colonial and neocolonial societies. Reading these works together not only shows the similarities of "creole" experience but also reveals the way different stories can be told using the same words. For instance, while Michelle Cliff recognizes in Zoë Wicomb and Bessie Head a shared colonial history that identifies all three as "colored," the *meaning* of "colored" varies dramatically between Jamaica, South Africa, and Botswana. While both Cliff and Wicomb examine the ambivalences, self-betrayals, and perspicacity of light-skinned "colored" people, "colored" identity under apartheid was maintained by a historical and legal construction that was different from that in the Caribbean and southern United States. The usefulness of proposing the concept "creole subjectivity," or, for that matter, "women's writing," is contingent on such recognitions of both the similarities and the divergences of racial and sexual meanings in different places at different historical moments.

All four writers recognize the interdependence of colonial taxonomies of difference and use the analogies made between race, sex, and sexuality by racist and sexist scientific and nationalist discourses to ask entirely new questions. For instance, recognizing the conflation of race and sexuality in colonial rhetoric, Cliff deconstructs the physicality of each of these categories and insists that we comprehend such identifications as metaphorical and political. By creating mixed-race, transgender characters, Cliff challenges the historical race/sexuality conflation that interprets one taxonomy in terms of the other (attributing sexual characteristics to racial identities and supposed racial characteristics to sexual behaviors and identities) and reads any transgression of racial and sexual binarisms as evidence of degeneration. By emphasizing the characters' choices of these positions, Cliff underscores the metaphysical nature of these categories. Similarly, recognizing the racist underpinnings of nationalist discourse, Wicomb exposes the social constructions of "race" to unseat romantic ideas of "nation"[12] and allows her character Frieda's elderly, nonwhite relatives to redefine exclusionary nationalist symbols. Whereas Schreiner could appeal to the term "nation" to supersede racial difference as she envisioned a multiracial, independent South Africa,[13] after half a century of the National Party's use of "nation" and "homeland" to reify supposed racial and cultural difference (i.e., the "Colored Nation") and to deny the vast majority of South

Africans the basic rights of citizenship, Wicomb is much more suspicious of nationalist rhetoric.

As "Creoles" whose political relation with the state is always a question, all four of these writers also highlight the way women are citizens only secondarily to men who claim political rights (of voting and entering legal contracts) and economic rights (of ownership and access to education, trades, and professions) and are afforded dubious symbolic opportunities (of soldiering and governing) to prove their national allegiance. Since women's political identity is often determined by marriage (as it is for Jean Rhys's characters Sasha and Marya), citizenship for women is never the "given" Benedict Anderson claims it is in the modern world.[14]

Each of the women writers studied here critiques the uses of the ideological constructions of "the family" to support nationalist and imperialist enterprises, on the one hand, and to enforce women's subservience, on the other. It is ironic that women, particularly as mothers, have been deployed to symbolize national values when, in fact, the nationalist projects they represent ignore their needs.[15] To the extent that such national discourses are exclusionary, women have often been entrusted with maintaining the "purity" of the nation in question. In the name of national cohesion and noble motherhood, prohibitions against miscegenation and state-sponsored eugenics programs have justified the enforced control of women's sexuality.

It is quite striking that all four authors in this study deny many of their women characters both motherhood and mothers. The majority of the women characters in these novels are removed by their authors from their biological contributions to the "nation" or the "race." Schreiner's Lyndall dies from complications of childbirth after having a baby who lives only several hours; Rhys's Anna has an abortion from which she herself almost dies; Cliff's Clare is rendered sterile not by the effects of interracial sexuality (as imagined by colonial "race science") but by a miscarriage caused by Agent Orange; at a recent time in South Africa when interracial sexuality and marriage were illegal, Wicomb's Frieda, pregnant by her white lover, aborts the fetus. By removing their women characters from the colonial drama of racial progress or degeneration, these authors demand of them new ways of defining or redefining their national identities.

Equally notable are the deaths of mothers in all these texts. The main characters of each of the novels experience the painful loss both of their dreams of acceptance by the "mother country," England, and of their own mothers, who either are dead when the novels open or die, deserting their daughters when they need them most. That the daughters' political disillusionment, alienation, and loneliness are figured by this very personal and irreparable loss highlights the gap between the symbology of the national "family" and the lived experience of these women. Far from finding themselves the beloved daughters of the empire finally at "home," once in London, these characters are either imprisoned, rendered homeless and destitute, or immobilized by their own alienation in rented rooms. Despite their girlhood fantasies of marrying English men, almost all of these characters remain unmarried, many of them becoming mistresses or prostitutes afforded none of the economic or political rights of marriage.

By comparing the storybook versions of England with the Creole's experience of it, each of these authors reverses the colonial gaze and offers her own evaluations of an alien land, the metropolis. In Rhys's *Voyage in the Dark,* for instance, Anna expresses her shock and disorientation upon recognizing Britain's image of itself as a fiction:

> I had read about England ever since I could read — smaller meaner everything is never mind — this is London — hundreds thousands of white people white people rushing along and the dark houses all alike frowning down one after the other all alike all stuck together — the streets like smooth shut-in ravines and the dark houses frowning down — oh I'm not going to like this place I'm not going to like this place.[16]

Having been educated by a colonial curriculum that posited England as "home" for all British subjects of the empire, the characters of these creole texts experience conflicted relationships to British culture, the English language, and the geography and cultures of their native lands. They are both English and not English at the same time, regardless of their own desires or affiliations. Edward Kamau Brathwaite, a poet, historian, and theorist from Barbados, explores the effect of English education on Caribbean writers in particular:

> What our educational system did was to recognize and maintain the language of the conquistador — the language of the planter, the language of the official, the language of the Anglican preacher. It insisted that not only would English be spoken in the Anglo-phone Caribbean, but that the educational system would carry the contours of an English heritage. Hence . . . Shakespeare, George Eliot, Jane Austen — British literature and literary forms, the models that were intimate to Europe, that were intimate to Great Britain, that had very little to do, really, with the environment and reality of the Caribbean — were dominant in the Caribbean educational system.[17]

That this education was not only irrelevant but punitive is made clear by the Trinidadian writer Merle Hodge in her novel *Crick Crack, Monkey:*

> Once in a dictation nearly the whole class had either spelt "sleet" wrong or left an inglorious blank, and [Sir] had lined us up and given us each three with the tamarind-whip for not knowing how to spell it, and six more because none could offer any suggestion as to what "sleet" might be.[18]

As a result of this education, the Caribbean, in Brathwaite's view, was until recently a "cultural disaster area" where writers knew how to write about falling snow but not about the hurricanes that are their own lived experience. As an example of the ambivalent perceptual position of Caribbean writers and of their literary adaptations, Brathwaite cites Caribbean children's school essays:

> Now the Creole adaptation to [the English educational system] is the little child who, instead of writing in an essay, "The snow was falling on the fields of Shropshire" (which is what our children literally were writing until a few years ago . . .), wrote "The snow was falling on the cane fields." The child had not yet reached the obvious statement that it wasn't snow at all, but rain that was probably falling on the cane fields. She was trying to have both cultures at the same time. But that is creolization.[19]

The works of the four writers studied here are centrally concerned with the English and European literary models they have been given and the politics of determining a national language. The past twenty years have seen tremendous conflict in South Africa over the former National-ist government's brutal enforcement of Afrikaans as the national language. In light of this struggle, which led to the Soweto uprising and student protests in the 1970s and 1980s, Schreiner's defense of Afrikaans in a very different political moment is an especially interesting addition to South Africa's politico-linguistic history. Because we come to consciousness through language and our experiences are mediated by language, these authors recognize the political, psychological, and literary stakes involved in such debates. Each author highlights in her work the way landscape descriptions are not innocent but are projections of larger systems of belief. For exam-ple, Schreiner's conscious attempts to rewrite the African landscape as more than a treacherous foil to England challenges over three centuries of English representations of Africa; Jean Rhys's character Antoinette tries to explain to "Rochester," the visiting Englishman, that the Caribbean landscape is not the "green menace" he has read about and now experiences but is, in fact, indifferent to him.

Rhys's novel *Wide Sargasso Sea* is itself a powerful literary challenge to English imperial culture as it rewrites Charlotte Brontë's *Jane Eyre* from the point of view of the madwoman locked in the attic of Thornfield Hall whom few but colonial students remember is a white Creole from Jamaica. Describing herself as a sister of that madwoman, Bertha,[20] Cliff demands a reconstruction of history from multiple points of view to offset the colonialists' version that has been taught as part of the curriculum sent from the "home office" in London and taken for truth by the colonized people as well. By recasting the English material from their own experience, these writers hold such tales historically and morally accountable.

These kinds of challenges are not easily accomplished, particularly when one's credibility is weighed in cultural and linguistic terms. All of these writers recognize that race, culture, and national identity are intimately connected to language and work out in their writing their own versions of Frantz Fanon's equation that "the Negro of the Antilles will be proportionately whiter—that is, he will come closer to being a real human being—in direct ratio to his mastery of the French language."[21] Seduced by the "King's English," the creole writers studied here nevertheless recognize an alternative eloquence that has been banned from the classroom. By attempting to include oral languages in literary texts, that is, Caribbean patois or creole or rural Afrikaans in primarily English-language fiction, these authors present a challenge to English cultural and literary supremacy.

Perhaps, then, the colonial cultural situation is not quite a "disaster area." Out of the double consciousness produced by a British education and a Caribbean or South African environment, these creole writers, like the schoolchildren Brathwaite describes, produce creolized cultural products combining the oppressive British literary tropes with indigenous symbols and metaphors of rich oral traditions. Creole, then, can be seen as a form of cultural, national, and psychological resistance. The linguistic meaning of "creole" can shift the focus from the visual iconographies of imperial representations of non-Europeans to the oral interpretations of the colonized. For Rhys, Cliff, and Wicomb, these localized, vernacular articulations can defy the spectacle of racist valuation by which Rhys's character Anna views herself as a "fair baboon...worse than a dark one every time," Cliff's character Clare imagines herself an "albino gorilla," and both Clare and Wicomb's character Frieda describe themselves as doomed mules, members of an indeterminate and degenerate species. Defying the traditional view that all variations on the King's English are merely the gibberish of such nonhuman beings, Houston Baker Jr. has claimed such oral interpretations and linguistic experiments as "supraliterate," "maroon or guerrilla action[s] carried out *within* linguistic territories of the erstwhile masters, bringing forth *sounds* that have been taken for crude hooting, but which are, in reality, racial poetry."[22]

As one can well imagine, the creole position is highly ambivalent, situated as it is between national, racial, and linguistic identities.[23] The writings I examine in this book reveal this ambivalence, both that which the writer consciously examines and that which causes problematic contradictions in the writing itself. While all of the writers recognize the valuable perspective afforded the creole writer, the white writers, Schreiner and Rhys, tend to be less conscious of the ways their racial standing has compromised their portrayals. For instance, while Schreiner intends to defend various South African populations from Britain's colonial abuses, her education and social status as a white English South African lead her to pursue metaphors and arguments that rely on standard British racist evaluations of the competing white Afrikaner colonists, black South Africans, and Jews. Similarly, while Rhys recognizes in her fiction the complex ways English literature and culture are used to mark and protect racial identification, she nevertheless falls back at times on English portrayals of nonwhite Caribbeans as inarticulate or frightening.

The two later writers of color, Cliff and Wicomb, are not only conscious of their compromised perspectives but make that ambivalence the subject of their fiction. For instance, Cliff explains Clare's decision to pursue her education in London as "the logic of the creole" and, like Wicomb, blames English colonial education for the political passivity and confusions of her character. While all these writers claim a certain authority based on their specific national positions (an authority they must wrest from the traditional metropolitan suspicions and dismissals of the noncultured Creole),[24] Wicomb in particular publicly questions her own interpretations, warped, she suggests, by an education and a racist regime that seemingly rewarded the collusions and self-betrayals of "coloured" South Africans.

That Rhys's last novel, *Wide Sargasso Sea,* is consciously critical of the fantasies and desires of the white Creole in ways her earlier fiction is not suggests that it is not only racial identity but the development of a theoretical vocabulary that makes such analytical perceptions possible. Throughout this book I therefore place the novels and short stories by these four authors in the context of relevant theoretical debates and historical events that contribute to the perspective each text offers. Just as the scientific discourse of the nineteenth century certainly influenced Schreiner's portrayals of those she calls "half-castes," the theoretical debate regarding colonial relations after World War II and the process of decolonization has much to do with Rhys's fictional rendering of emancipation a century earlier.

How and why these authors or any of us create new stories that challenge the dogmas of our times are, in fact, the underlying questions of this study. What a reading of the works of these authors suggests is that their new stories are the result of cultural, ideological, and political dissonances. First, there are deep contradictions within and between the scientific, religious and political discourses through which these authors attempt to understand their situations. These conflicts allow for doubt and the attempted creation of systems of thought that more successfully answer troubling questions about the relation of the self to social structures.[25] Second, the political or social status of each of these authors is highly relational and also deeply fraught with contradictions and divisions. For example, recognizing herself as politically disenfranchised by virtue of her sex, Schreiner identified with rural Afrikaners and South African Blacks, an identification that, as we shall see, was clearly one-sided. And while Rhys may have longed for an affiliation with Caribbean Blacks and eloquently described the shared Caribbean culture of Blacks and white Creoles, she nevertheless occupied a privileged position racially and economically as she grew up in Dominica, a position that she knew made an easy affiliation impossible. Raised to "pass" as white, Cliff and Wicomb internalized racist systems of belief that both valued and stigmatized their "not quite white" status. These conflicts of identity and ambivalent loyalties as well as the gap between the "reality" offered to them in their English textbooks and their own geographical and social environments must have compelled all these authors to take some critical distance from the dominant colonial and neocolonial discourses of their times. If Michelle Cliff is more conscious in her writing of her own ambivalences or political shortcomings than is Olive Schreiner, it is not because as a woman of color she simply and already knows what the white woman does not, but because the gap between what is taught as truth and her own experience is perhaps greater and because an anti-imperialist vocabulary has developed over the last century that assists her articulation of her insights. That Schreiner herself made important early contributions to this vocabulary should not be overlooked.

I have written this book with several audiences in mind. For those primarily interested in colonial and postcolonial studies, the analysis of these four authors focuses on both the rhetoric of British imperialism and a variety of anticolonial theoretical perspectives advanced over the past century.

As individuals who have found themselves defined by both these discourses, these authors provide unique insights into the creole position and into "creoleness," a potentially liberatory perspective. Despite some excellent work by a handful of feminist scholars, there are still relatively few examples of postcolonial theory or studies of nationalism that take gender as a central question. In this study I have attempted both to map out how gender nuances national, cultural, and racial identities and to suggest when it is not the most salient component of identity in social and political relations.

Those interested in feminist literary criticism and women's writing will, I hope, find these four writers profoundly interesting in that they, as Creoles and as women, challenge the aesthetic fashions of their times, revealing the assumptions that belie each literary movement's claim to radical insight. Insisting that writers must attend to the "everyday life" that includes women and rejecting the adventure tale that misrepresented and exoticized Africa *and* women, Schreiner disparages the Victorian romance and offers an early description of the modernism Virginia Woolf was to pursue a generation later. Similarly, writing in Paris during the 1920s and 1930s about female alienation, colonial displacement, and economic destitution, Rhys challenges the "high" modernist view of history. Her representations of the fragmented personality (as in the paragraph cited above) suggest a style and perspective we have come to call "postmodern." And while Michelle Cliff and Zoë Wicomb experiment with nonlinear, nonchronological narratives and incorporate the detritus of contemporary culture into their fiction, they insist that this postmodern "play" does not offer a deliverance from the shackles of history. These challenges to canonical literary categories suggest that the terms "realism," "modernism," or "postmodernism" may have radically different meanings and connotations in colonial, postcolonial, or neocolonial societies.[26]

Finally, for those who come to this book for readings of the works of these specific authors, I have engaged with some of the major debates in "Schreiner scholarship" and "Rhys scholarship" while also offering readings of lesser-known writings by these authors in the context of their "creole" identities. Because we have the complete ouvre of Schreiner and Rhys and a large body of criticism on their writings, I have been able to trace both writers' literary and theoretical development over the course of their lives and the variety of critical responses to their work at different times and from different countries. Michelle Cliff and Zoë Wicomb are in the midst of their writing lives, and, as the bibliographical sections on them reveal, their work has not yet received diverse critical response. These chapters, then, are meant both to introduce these works to those who have not yet had the opportunity to read them and to claim them as important contributions to literary history.

In many ways the ambiguous etymology of "creole" suggests a starting point for this study. While most sources trace the root from the Spanish *criado* (one bred or reared) to *criar* (to breed) to the Latin root *creare* (to create), it is not immediately clear whether the Creole is the product or the agent of this creation. And, indeed, this tension figures in every work examined in this book. To the extent that the Creole's identity is formed by a politicized system of human difference that constitutes the backbone of colonial and neocolonial social structures, the Creole exists as an object of scrutiny and suspicion. But to the extent that the Creole expresses a decidedly different perspective than the metropolitan or the colonial, s/he is a creative subject.[27] The writers represented in this book, while certainly the products of colonial histories, are nevertheless clearly creating new sentences, new sounds, new stories. This is a profoundly powerful activity, for "snow on the cane fields" is a creation that even the Creator has not yet imagined.

Part I
Settler Discourse and Colonialism

1 / "An English South African"

Olive Schreiner's South Africa, Land and Language

After all anybody is as their land and air is. Anybody is as the sky is low or high, the air heavy or clear and anybody is as there is wind or no wind there. It is that which makes them and the arts they make and the work they do and the way they eat and the way they drink and the way they learn and everything.
— Gertrude Stein, What Are Masterpieces

Transnational Identity: An English South African

Doris Lessing says of Olive Schreiner's *The Story of an African Farm* that it was "the first 'real' book I'd met with that had Africa for a setting. Here was the substance of truth, and not from England or Russia or France or America, necessitating all kinds of translations, switches, correspondences, but reflecting what I knew and could see."[1] Like Schreiner, Lessing was born in a southern African country under colonial rule and therefore appreciates the significance of Schreiner's attempt to write about South Africa as a South African with only English colonial fiction and travel narratives to serve her as models. Identifying herself as a South African writer, Schreiner used for her pen name not only the well-known pseudonym "Ralph Iron" but also "A Returned South African" and "An English South African." While naming herself a national writer, Schreiner qualifies that identity insisting not only on her South African origins but on the colonial nature of those origins. She is both "not merely" South African and "not quite" South African. Her representation of South Africa in her fiction and essays is a fascinating struggle between claims of native authenticity and literary forms that depend on the alien status of both writer and reader. That Lessing should find in Schreiner's descriptions of South Africa a "truth" that reflected what she could "see" speaks to a tradition of what J. M. Coetzee calls "white writing" in South Africa, writing that, while grounded in European understandings of landscape, at times demands metaphorical and linguistic transformations of those traditions.[2] Whether these representations should be called South African or English South African or colonial or anticolonial is a question at the heart of this study. Given a language and a literary tradition that reflect a particular culture and set of political and social relations, how transformative can an individual's use of that language and tradition be? In Schreiner's case, how does the particular constellation of her political, racial, cultural, and sexual positions influence her ability and desire to struggle with and against the literary tradition she inherits?[3]

This chapter examines the way nineteenth-century conceptions of nationhood and Schreiner's own ambiguous national position influence her representations of South Africa at a sensitive moment in the history of European colonialism. I have focused this chapter on Schreiner's contribution to the national-language debate and to an Afrocentric rewriting of the African landscape because both are central to her critique of British cultural and political imperialism and both reveal her own ambivalent national identity.

Throughout her writing, Schreiner is constructing a new national identity at a time when such identification is of increasing political and psychological importance. In *Imagined Communities: Reflections on the Origin and Spread of Nationalism,* Benedict Anderson dates the normalization of national identity in the late nineteenth century. Whereas religious and dynastic affiliation had once constituted the political identity of an individual, Anderson argues, by World War I a particular nationality had become as central as gender to the modern idea of identity.[4] Nationhood came to be seen as an "unchosen" state, one that is not constructed but is "natural" to a complete self-identity.

Simultaneous with this naturalization of national identity, however, we can also see the growth of supposedly universal or antinationalistic discourses such as the international workers' movements, psychoanalytic theory, and, of particular interest to the works of Olive Schreiner, the international woman's movement. Women, who were denied the national citizenship rights granted men (particularly those of the vote, equal property and civil rights, and guaranteed rights of citizenship regardless of that of the marital partner),[5] saw their struggles in transnational terms.

Women in England, Europe, and America, by recognizing women's disen-
franchisement from national governments, sought to address the problems
of women, which were clearly not bounded by national borders, through
international organizations. The popular Social Purity movement — which
grew out of the abolitionist movement, the movement to repeal the English
Contagious Diseases Acts of the 1860s, and religious revivalism — was the
work of women from many countries who recognized the commonality of
their situations across national boundaries.[6] The suffrage movement was also
international, with members from twenty-six countries participating in the
International Woman Suffrage Alliance.[7] The organizations of the woman's
movement, such as the Women's Cooperative Guild and the International
Council of Women, were predominantly international or sent delegates to
international women's congresses.

As Anne Wiltsher has pointed out in *Most Dangerous Women: Feminist
Peace Campaigners of the Great War,* the transnational political ideology and
alliances of some of the women's organizations that had developed in the
second half of the nineteenth century did lead to a movement that opposed
the nationalism of colonial expansion and finally sacrificed what national
support it had in order to oppose World War I. The only international congress that met to try to resolve the hostilities immediately after the outbreak
of World War I was the Women's International Congress at The Hague
(at which Olive Schreiner was a committee member).[8] From this congress
came the outlines of what was to be the Covenant of the League of Nations in 1920.[9] In the face of increasing national jingoism and talk of an
imperialistic federation of British territories, many of the women leaders
with whom Schreiner was in contact in England sought such international
alliances with the hope of creating a truly international and representative
federation of nations in the future.[10]

Some of these international groups specifically addressed racial issues
such as slavery and lynching. Nevertheless, in her study of some of these
nineteenth- and early twentieth-century feminist projects, Vron Ware argues that while these projects were striking in their commitment to an
interracial and transnational "sisterhood," the rhetoric was at times "dangerously close to the imperialist ideologies of a universal womanhood"
and often partook of a rhetoric that emphasized the "civilising" benefits
of English civil law, education, and Christianity.[11] While Ware argues that
English feminism of the late nineteenth century was unable to connect a
critique of masculinist ideology with a critique of colonialism and racism,[12]
as an English South African Schreiner does forge a theory that seeks to

understand and expose the connections between sexism, colonialism, and racism. As I will argue in this section, it is precisely Schreiner's cultural and political position as a "creole" woman writer that both inspires and limits the boundaries of her imagination.

As a colonialist, a socialist, a pacifist, and a feminist, Schreiner adds new perspectives to this debate about the benefits and limitations of national identity with her insistence on her "South African" identity and, at the same time, on the transnational nature of that identity. As one of the first literary South African voices (in English or Afrikaans), Schreiner defines for England, and for South Africa itself, some of the contours of a territory on its way to nationhood. If nationalism is, as Anderson argues, the invention of nations where they have not existed,[13] what is the South Africa that Schreiner invents for her readers? If nations are in fact the "imagined communities" of political and literary discourse, Schreiner's works "imagine" a nation that is both part of European culture and distinct from it, a fulfillment of English colonial policy and a challenge to it. This complicated view is influenced by Schreiner's own complicated biography, which has intrigued her critics for the last century.

Schreiner began all three of her novels between 1873 and 1874, when as a young woman of eighteen she worked as a governess on Afrikaner farms. It is therefore striking that these novels shared much in common with two types of late-Victorian English novels: the novels that, incorporating the scientific and sociological debates of evolutionary theory, raised uncomfortable and exciting questions about faith, morality, and religion; and the "New Woman" novels that challenged the sexual ideologies and family politics of Victorian England. Given these debates at the time, *The Story of an African Farm* (the only one of the novels published in Schreiner's lifetime) made a sensation in England when it was published in 1883. Its appeal, however, was not only its uncompromising exploration of sexual and religious questions but also its colonial South African setting. As a native of South Africa, Schreiner became a spokesperson for the English South African upon her arrival in London in 1881. Although she came to England to study medicine and enrolled in nursing at the Edinburgh Royal Infirmary, her chronic asthma made it too difficult for her to continue. She stayed in England until 1889, writing allegories (eventually published as *Dreams* in 1900) and involving herself in the intellectual and political life of London. During these years she began her lifelong friendship with Havelock Ellis, who was then beginning his career as a professional sexologist. She became a member of the Men and Women's Club and of a larger intellectual circle including Karl Pearson, Eleanor Marx, Edward Carpenter, Elizabeth Cobb, and others. At this time and in such company, Schreiner was able to develop her thinking about women's economic position, the politics of prostitution, and the struggle of the working classes.[14]

These ideas she incorporated into her allegories and through their biblical style created visions of sexual and socialist utopias. Schreiner claimed to have written these allegories for the specific audience of "all Capitalists, Millionaires and Middlemen in England and America and all high and mighty persons."[15] In fact, they became widely read among the working classes as well. For instance, in the collection of writings by working-class women edited by Margaret Llewelyn Davies and introduced by Virginia Woolf, a Mrs. Scott, identified as "a Felt Hat Worker," refers to Schreiner's *Dreams* thirty-one years after it was first published.

Schreiner returned to South Africa in 1889, and in the decade culminating in the Anglo-Boer War, began to write a series of essays addressed to both English and English South African audiences, providing information about the geography, history, and policies of the colony. These eight essays, among them "South Africa," "The Boer," and "The Problem of Slavery," were later collected into a volume with several of Schreiner's earlier essays and published as *Thoughts on South Africa*. The essays provide naturalist descriptions of landscape, botany, and zoology; ethnographies of English, Afrikaner, and African peoples; and analyses of colonial history and its effect on social institutions. In these essays, which support a political perspective unique in the literature, Schreiner redefines the position of the South African "Creole" as an authority and adviser on European political policy.

Schreiner was intensely interested in South African politics and for a short while enjoyed a friendship with Cecil Rhodes, who became prime minister of the Cape in 1890. Although she respected his power and imagination, Schreiner curtailed their relationship as she became disillusioned with his politics, especially those pertaining to the rights of black Africans and to his involvement in the Jameson Raid, an attempt by the Chartered Company to take over the Transvaal Republic, a pursuit that set the stage for the Anglo-Boer War in 1899. During this decade Schreiner also sought to influence the political positions of her brother Will, then attorney general under Rhodes and later himself prime minister of the Cape Colony.[16] In 1896 Schreiner wrote what some critics believe to be one of the strongest antiwar pieces ever written, *Trooper Peter Halket of Mashonaland*. This is an extended allegory condemning Rhodes's Chartered Company's atrocities against Matabeles in Mashonaland. In it a young English trooper spends the night in conversation with a stranger he meets in the desert. The stranger turns out to be Christ, who, after listening to Peter naïvely recount the brutality and greed of the campaign, converts him to a more humane understanding of the rights of the black Africans. At the end of the story Peter is shot by his commanding officer when he frees a black prisoner.[17]

As tensions between the English and the Afrikaners reached a climax in 1899, Schreiner wrote *An English South African's View of the Situation: Words in Season,* which was published in both England and South Africa and translated into Dutch. It is a patriotic appeal to the English to avoid what she predicted would be a long and difficult war. During the ensuing hostilities, Schreiner's political position was complex. While Ruth First and Ann Scott point out that Schreiner's stance against British imperialism and her unreserved support of the Afrikaner "underdog" blinded her to the racial bigotry and brutality of the Afrikaner republics, Joyce Berkman argues that as a British subject Schreiner had more daily reminders of British abuse of Afrikaners and black Africans and had more of a commitment to address her own nation's failings.[18] Because of her support of the Boer cause, Schreiner was forced to spend the war under British guard in Hanover and returned to Johannesburg in 1902 to find her house looted and her manuscripts for a first draft of her major book on women burnt.

In 1911 she published *Woman and Labour,* a work that she described as a fragment of the longer work that had been destroyed. For Vera Brittain and many other early twentieth-century women it became the "Bible of the Women's Movement."[19] *Woman and Labour* concerns itself with the exclusion of women from the labor market and the tragic consequences not only for women but for society as a whole. Women, Schreiner argues, had been reduced to "sex parasites" in a society that prohibited them from working in most professions. The rallying call of the book — *"We take all labour for our province!"* — inspired feminists throughout England and the United States. In an excellent chapter on *Woman and Labour,* First and Scott place Schreiner's economic analysis and the feminist-pacifist arguments of the work in the context of both her earlier studies of female sexuality with Pearson and Ellis and the shifting politics of the suffrage movement just prior to the outbreak of World War I. When the war broke out in 1914, Schreiner was again living in England. As an uncompromising pacifist and supporter of conscientious objectors, she now found herself at odds with many of the leaders of the women's movement. Throughout the war years, Schreiner was increasingly isolated and suffered further estrangement as she was often forced to move from her lodgings because of her German name. After the war she returned to South Africa, where she died in 1920.[20]

Olive Schreiner's writings are important not only because of what they tell us about South African history and politics, British colonialism, and feminist thinking a century ago but also because they provide us with an example of an individual mind grappling with major ideological shifts in science, national politics, and gender relations. Schreiner played an active role in the intellectual debates of her time, and her work provoked as much as reflected the changes we can identify from our perspective almost one hundred years later. Similarly, from her unique position as a native South African white woman who wrote self-consciously about that political and psychological space, she provides us with portrayals of Africa, its land, people, and cultures, that both influence and are influenced by conventional English colonial renderings of a territory half the world away. The tensions between her self-conscious, reactive descriptions and theories of her native land and her acceptance of some ideas intimate to colonial rule make her work a fascinating example of what Mary Louise Pratt has called "creole self-fashioning." What we see in Schreiner's fictional and nonfictional representations of Africa is the attempt to forge a new nation independent from English military and economic control and a new South African creole subject who yet partakes of European culture and values.[21]

Creole Author/ity

As a "creole" woman whose life was divided between South Africa and England, Schreiner recognized with both frustration and pride that she was on the periphery of the British literary establishment. Yet she claimed her literary authority on this specific position as a white, first-generation, English-speaking South African woman — both inside and outside the structures of colonial power. Debunking traditional depictions of her homeland by British travel writers and reworking colonial/imperial adventure romances, Schreiner presents what she believes to be a more "realistic" portrayal, one that anticipates the modernist experimentation with form and character.

Schreiner's realism is rooted in her attempt to write from her creole national and literary identity, critical of, yet deeply dependent on, European forms. She introduces her first published novel, *The Story of an African Farm,* to both the English and South African readership with the warning that her depiction of life will not be according to "the stage method" that offers readers a false sense of satisfaction and completion. Rather, she will attempt to describe life as it is actually experienced, where "nothing can be prophesied.... When the curtain falls no one is ready." This kind of fiction, Schreiner anticipates, may not easily be understood by English critics because it describes in detail geographical settings and characters unfamiliar in literary representation and refuses to reproduce the romantic depictions of Africa created by English writers. As she writes in her introduction to *The Story of an African Farm*:

> It has been suggested by a kind critic that he would better have liked the little book if it had been a history of wild adventure; of cattle driven into inaccessible "kranzes" by Bushmen; "of encounters with ravening lions, and hair-breadth escapes." This could not be. Such works are best written in Picadilly or in the Strand: there the gifts of the creative imagination untrammelled by contact with any fact, may spread their wings.[22]

Describing "the scenes among which [the writer] has grown" is, to Schreiner, an enterprise that demands attention to "reality." Choosing for her pen name "Ralph Iron" and naming her hero "Waldo," Schreiner implicitly invokes Emerson and his celebration of a "new" literature: "The literature of the poor, the feelings of the child, the philosophy of the street, the meaning of household life."[23] By centering her fiction around such "ordinary" people (working-class characters, Afrikaners, women, children), Schreiner provides us with an excellent example of what Erich Auerbach sees as "the foundation of modern realism":

> The serious treatment of everyday reality, the rise of more extensive and socially inferior human groups to the position of subject matter for problematic-existential representation, on the one hand; on the other, the embedding of random persons and events in the general course of contemporary history, the fluid historical background.... [24]

This attention to the "insignificant" character or detail is a function not only of a literary movement to "modernism," however, but also of a feminist critique of androcentric literature and history. For Virginia Woolf, whom Auerbach selects as his example of the modern realist, the inclusion of "common" characters in fiction, biography, and history is a struggle, finally, for the inclusion of *women* as literary subjects. Educated by her father, Leslie Stephen, to value the more "obscure" or common figures in history,[25] Woolf, like Schreiner before her, recognizes that it is by foregrounding the lives of women that history, biography, or literature truly approaches a modernist depiction of everyday reality or reveals, as Emerson puts it, "the meaning of household life." In other words, what is seen as a "modernist" portrayal of reality in the writing of Schreiner and Woolf comes primarily from their desire to explore the subjectivity of female characters in particular. By turning her interest to women, who are relegated to the sidelines of political or historical discourse, particularly regarding English imperial policy, Schreiner admits into fiction the "common" characters and domestic scenes she realizes will be unfamiliar to her readers, English and South African alike.

Schreiner's portrayal is additionally "unfamiliar" to her readers because as "South African" literature, her work is a deliberate challenge to the dominant British imaginings of South Africa. Schreiner's realism, then, also expresses a nascent national consciousness. Her depictions of, for instance, specific topographies; non-English populations and languages; non-English customs, dress, and diet; and labor specific to South Africa (working in diamond mines, making roaster-cakes, tending ostriches) — all this complicated British claims on South Africa and suggested a possible nation in the making. Schreiner's challenge of British portrayals of South Africa came at a time of great political upheaval when South Africa's "identity" was, as it is today, the subject of political, economic, legal, and military struggle. In her writing Schreiner both invents a South Africa that partakes of traditional colonial language about Africa and draws different territorial markings that include new imaginings of what and who is South African.

Defining the Language of National Culture

Writing *The Story of an African Farm* while living on an Afrikaner farm, Olive Schreiner first called the book *Thorn Kloof.* The bilingualism of the original title, made up of the Afrikaans word *kloof* (ravine) and the English translation of the Afrikaans *doring,* points to a central issue in Schreiner's work: the role of language in national literature. Schreiner claimed her *English* South African nationality quite self-consciously and, as we shall see, believed that English, as opposed to Afrikaans, was the appropriate and inevitable language of an independent South African nation. And yet, as a self-proclaimed *South African* writer, Schreiner invests the English of her writing with some of the tension and richness critics are now appreciating in contemporary "New English" literatures. Although English was Schreiner's first language, it was an English studded with words and expressions from German, Afrikaans, and indigenous African languages. This English, apparent in Schreiner's three novels, is a new linguistic, political, and literary development.[26] Schreiner's creole articulations — that is, her Euroafrican perspective, use of language, and choices of genre and form —

reveal both the limitations inherent in creole writing and the revolutionary possibilities it opens up.

As one of the first native writers of South Africa, Schreiner confronts one of the most difficult and painful problems for a colonial writer: How does one portray experiences for which there is no vocabulary in the language of the colonizing "mother country"? Dan Jacobson, a contemporary South African writer, finds Schreiner's descriptions of the South African landscape almost heroic for daring to make literary that which is a "wordless" experience for the colonist educated by British books. In his introduction to *The Story of an African Farm,* Jacobson describes his own incredulity when reading the novel for the first time, for it was his first experience of reading descriptions of his native land in a work of fiction:

> For it isn't only the hitherto undescribed, uncelebrated, wordless quality of the life around him that makes it seem implausible to the colonial as a fit subject for fiction; it is also (no matter how bright the moonlight may be) its appearance of drabness, its thinness, its lack of richness and variety in comparison with what he has read about in the books that come to him from abroad.[27]

Nadine Gordimer also speaks of not having read literary descriptions of the South African landscape until she read Schreiner's novel when in her twenties.[28] If claiming a South African literary identity is difficult for even contemporary writers, Schreiner's insistence over a century ago on her South African subject and subjectivity is indeed remarkable.

Schreiner's position as a colonial writer, politically outside the literary sphere of English novelists both as a South African and as a woman, leads to her ambivalent relationship with English literature and the English language. On the one hand, she confronts British adventure and travel literature with her more "authentic" portrayals of South African experience; her descriptions of South African day-to-day life and her use of Afrikaans words instead of their English translations attest to the increasing separation of colonial South African experience from British experience. On the other hand, Schreiner's familial and political ties to England are also apparent in her nonfictional essays on South Africa and on the conflict between English and Afrikaans as the South African national language.

In 1891 Schreiner published "South Africa: Its Natural Features, Its Diverse Peoples, Its Political Status: The Problem," the first of a series of articles about South Africa. In this essay Schreiner asserts her South African identity and looks forward to a future when South Africa will produce artists and art distinctly South African. Schreiner's declaration of an increasing literary independence from England is the South African equivalent of Emerson's earlier call for a distinctly American literature:

> Our day of dependence, our long apprenticeship to the learning of other lands, draws to a close.... We have listened too long to the courtly muses of Europe.... We will walk on our own feet; we will work with our own hands; we will speak our minds.[29]

At the time that Schreiner's essay "South Africa" appeared in the *Fortnightly Review*, British magazines were full of articles that sought to justify Britain's political connection with its territories based on the shared English language and literature. W. T. Stead, for instance, opened the first issue of the *Review of Reviews* in January 1890 with an address "to all English-Speaking Folk." The express intent of the new review was to "help hold together and strengthen the political ties which at present link all English-speaking communities save one . . . [and] to promote by every means a fraternal union with the American Republic." Many of the articles in the British journals at this time attempt to assert England as a cultural, particularly a literary, center and to tie political and commercial territories in which English is spoken to the motherland. As Theodore Watts-Dunton writes in the June 1891 *Fortnightly Review*, a month before Schreiner republished (in the same journal) her prophecy of a distinctly South African literature:

> A poem written in the English language, whether produced in England or in some other part of the vast English-speaking world, is an English poem, no more and no less.... The poetry beginning with Piers Plowman, and ending, up to now, with certain English, American, Canadian, Australian and South African bards whose name is legion, is the birthright of every English-speaking man wherever he may be born.... Nor is there any reason why in the United States or in Canada or in Australasia or in Capeland or in Mashonaland English poetic genius should not in the twentieth century blossom as vigorously as it blossomed in the England of Shakespeare. But English poetry it will be — English poetry to be judged by the canons of criticism of the mother-land. In any one of these colonies the Shakespeare of the twentieth century may be born. But splendid as is the present glory of the United States — splendid as is the promise of Canada, Australasia and South Africa — these colonies can never produce a Shakespeare who is not an English poet.[30]

This insistence on Englishness is simultaneously a shoring-up of the traditional, archaic signs of the nation — what Homi Bhabha calls the pedagogical narrative of nationness — and an enactment of a new English identity whose performance might take place anywhere in the world.

Claiming "Englishness" as an a priori historical foundation whose signs are repetitive and predictable (Piers Plowman, Shakespeare), Watts-Dutton nonetheless uses these signs for a new national narrative of colonialism and expansion. As we shall see, it is this paradox that Schreiner is also able to exploit to split and reconstitute both the English and African national subject. Schreiner's designation and performance of the "English South African" can be seen as an excellent example of a "counter-narrative of nation" that necessarily "evokes and erases" the pedagogical narrative.[31] While Watts-Dunton and others writing similar pieces in the British press use the cultural icons of the past to consolidate a "pure" English identity, Schreiner's claim of a creole literary position calls upon and disrupts the myth of "English culture." Perhaps surprisingly, both moves, as I will argue, provide a rationale for colonial expansion.

Watts-Dunton's assumed cultural link between the colonies and England provides more than a justification for political and military presence in these regions, however. That race and language no longer assured similar political or cultural beliefs created an anxiety particularly noticeable in these articles on colonial culture, a culture that depends on an unambiguous knowledge of who is self and who is other. Lord Meath in a May 1891 article in the *Fortnightly Review* entitled "Anglo-Saxon Unity" appeals to literature, especially to novels, to help maintain understanding and sympathy "between members of the same large family." If colonials continue to read Trollope, Meath asserts, and Englishmen continue to read Bret Harte and Rider Haggard, then the Englishman born in England and the "Englishman" born in the colonies will always recognize each other as kin:

> The political union of the English-speaking races may be an impossibility. Imperial Federation may be a dream, but the future supremacy of the Anglo-Saxon race will *not* be a dream, if only the members of this wide-spread family be true to high ideals of life, to themselves and to each other.[32]

In other words, if South African–born colonials recognize themselves as essentially English and accept the foundational myth of an "Anglo-Saxon" race, their allegiance will presumably be to English as opposed to South African political and commercial pursuits. Benedict Anderson has pointed to an earlier similar anxiety in Europe regarding the allegiance of "fellow Europeans" born in the Americas. These Creoles were valuable to the European governments for the administration of the colonies, but because they shared European culture, "they had readily at hand the political, cultural, and military means for successfully asserting themselves" that the indigenes did not.[33]

Schreiner's contention in her 1891 article in the *Fortnightly Review* that South Africa would eventually produce artists of its *own* is a cultural as well as a political challenge to the "mother country," which views its literature and its language as the cornerstone of political dominance. A decade later, on the other hand, when Schreiner opposes British military suppression of the Boers, she switches tactics and argues that because English linguistic and literary dominance in the colony has *already* resulted in a shared culture between the English and the Boers, force is not necessary:

> Cultured Dutch and English South Africans alike are fed on English literature, and England is their intellectual home. They have — both Dutch and English — in many cases a deep and sincere affection for the English language, English institutions, and a sincere affection for England herself.[34]

Written with an English audience in mind, this bit of wishful thinking and blatant Anglophilism on Schreiner's part is politically motivated by the imminence of British military hostility against the Afrikaner settlers and of the ensuing Anglo-Boer War.

When Schreiner writes her novels, however, there is no such immediate political reason for her to so overemphasize the positive ties between the South African English and South African Dutch colonists. The place of the English language in South African life is a central issue in Schreiner's fiction, making her work particularly "colonial" as opposed to English in theme. The language of her literature, therefore, is not taken for granted but resonates with political meaning. Schreiner emphasizes the local colonial settings in her novels by including Afrikaner Dutch words and phrases that often remain untranslated in the text. In *The Story of an African Farm* Schreiner includes a glossary of "several Dutch and Colonial words occurring in this work." The list of twenty-three words is partial and is clearly for the benefit of an imagined English audience, and each word is marked by quotation marks in the text.[35] There are Afrikaans phrases, however, that Schreiner does not bother to translate, especially in conversations between two Afrikaner characters, such as Tant' Sannie and her niece Trana (*SAF,* p. 118). It is at moments such as these that Schreiner's text becomes unself-consciously South African. English (or English-speaking) readers who are not South African must recognize a side of experience determined by language and not easily translated. When the South African *kopje,* for instance, is translated to the English "hillock," it becomes something else, something that does not exist in South Africa.

The great humor in the courtship between Bonaparte Blenkins and Tant' Sannie revolves around their inability to understand each other's language, belying Schreiner's assertions in a later work (*An English South African's View of the Situation*) that Afrikaners knew and loved the English language. The relationship between Bonaparte and Tant' Sannie plays on the political complexities of British-Afrikaner relations in South Africa. Bonaparte is an English Mark Twain character, a scoundrel and imposter, who pretends to be descended from Napoleon and, as a travel writer, to have come to Africa to "open up the land." Tant' Sannie meets him with hostility and suspicion:

> "You vaggabonds se Engelschman!" said Tant' Sannie, looking straight at him.
> This was a near approach to plain English; but the man contemplated the block abstractedly, wholly unconscious that any antagonism was being displayed toward him.
> "You might not be a Scotsman or anything of that kind, might you?" suggested the German. "It is the English that she hates." (*SAF,* p. 52)

The relationship is mediated by the German overseer and the "Hottentot" (Khoikhoi) maid, neither of whom speaks either English or Dutch as their first language. Little Piet Vander Walt, whom Tant' Sannie woos after her disastrous affair with Bonaparte, also finds the English presence on the farm uncomfortable: "To young Piet Vander Walt that supper was a period of intense torture. There was something overawing in that assembly of English people, with their incomprehensible speech" (*SAF,* p. 201).

In the later book *An English South African's View of the Situation,* published just before the Anglo-Boer War, Schreiner reveals her ambivalent position regarding the Dutch creole language, "the Taal."[36] She speaks condescendingly about "low Dutch" yet defends it against British deprecations:

> The peculiarities which arose from [the Boers'] wild, free life were not always sympathetically understood; even their little language, the South African "Taal," a South African growth so dear to their hearts, and to all of those of us who love indigenous and South African growths, was not sympathetically dealt with. (*ESAV,* p. 20)

Like the South African landscape, Afrikaans represents for Schreiner both antiquity and youth. Like the colony, it is a new growth, unique in the world of old nations and old languages. But while Schreiner includes Boer language and customs in her novels because, as she says, the Boer is "the most typically South African,"[37] she insists that the literary expression of South Africa must of necessity be in English. Although Schreiner is in debate with those like Theodore Watts-Dunton who claim all literature written in the English language to be English culturally *and therefore* politically, she does assert that the South African literature she envisions will be in her own language, English. While the Taal flavors South African English with humorous or homey phrases, it is not, she claims, a language that can support complex ideas:

> So sparse is the vocabulary and so broken are its forms, that it is impossible in the Taal to express a subtle intellectual emotion, or abstract conception, or a wide generalization; and a man seeking to render a scientific, philosophic, or poetical work in the Taal, would find his task impossible. ("TB," p. 87)

This, of course, is and was completely untrue. In his 1976 introduction to the reprinting of this essay, Richard Rive points out that in 1892, when Schreiner wrote "The Boer," the following were already in existence: the Afrikaans newspaper *Die Afrikaans Patriot;* at least two collections of poetry in Afrikaans, *Afrikaans Gedigte* (1878) and *Vyftige Uitgesogte Gedigte* (1888); and a novel, *Catharina, die dogter van die Advokaat* (1879), by Hoogenhout.[38] Schreiner compares the Taal to "the 'pigeon' English of a Chinaman, or better still [to] the Negro dialects of the Southern American States" ("TB," p. 80).[39] Despite acknowledging a competing Afrikaner South African national identity, Schreiner underscores the marginality of Afrikaner culture from her English South African perspective.

What Afrikaans represents for Schreiner is another juncture at which nationalist and internationalist interests compete.[40] Schreiner's pride in Afrikaans as a language original to South Africa and as evidence of South African individuation from England is complicated by the terms she inherits from what Stephen Greenblatt calls "linguistic colonialism" and from over one hundred years of English debate on the relationship between language and class. In contrast to her depictions of Afrikaans, Schreiner views English as having the advantage of being an international language precisely because it is capable of articulating philosophical abstractions and poetry revealing the complexity of the English mind that developed it and now uses it. In his article "Learning to Curse: Aspects of Colonialism in the Sixteenth Century," Greenblatt connects English linguistic chauvinism both with a missionary desire to spread European languages as a gift to less fortunate people who were seen as speaking "gibberish" and with the recognition that language, as the bishop of Ávila explained to Queen Isabella in 1492, "is a perfect instrument of empire."[41] Cultural historians have noted the coincidence of the publication of the first grammar of a modern European language and the first voyage of Columbus in 1492.[42] That the value of the grammar was immediately apprehended in colonialist and imperialist terms supports the centrality of language as a theme in colonial and postcolonial fiction and theory. That this belief in the relationship between language and political control was current in Schreiner's time is obvious from an article by Hyde Clarke in the *Asiatic Quarterly* summarized in the August 1890 issue of the *Review of Reviews*. In this article, Clarke deplores "the lack of interest shown by the English [in India and in the East] in spreading their language," which he claims (and editor Stead agrees) "is a great instrument of civilization." Decisions regarding the spread of the English language in English-held territories are seen as central to political control: "Russia . . . appreciates the value of language as an instrument of dominion, while we are allowing our language to be suppressed in the State of the Congo."[43]

Greenblatt's readings of exploration and colonial writings of the New World point to the travelers' insistence that American Indian languages were incapable of eloquence. To acknowledge the eloquence, or even the intelligibility, of native languages would open the possibility that English colonization would not be providing barbarians with their *first* civilized language, social contracts, and religion, but, instead, would merely be forcing English language and culture on an already existing developed society with its own language and culture. Just as the former position protects the colonizers of the Americas from an uncomfortable acknowledgment of native culture, so Schreiner's acceptance of similar attitudes about the supposed simplicity and incomprehensibility of Boer and African languages thereby justifies the political and cultural predominance of the English language.

The connection Schreiner makes between language and complexity of mind is also rooted in eighteenth-century English linguistic theory, which was still influential in the nineteenth century. In her essay "The Problem of Slavery," Schreiner cites contemporary studies of "Bushman" (San) language that are similar to her own condescending analysis of the Taal:

> Their language is said by those who have closely studied it to be so imperfect that the clear expression of even the simplest ideas is difficult. They have no word for wife, for marriage, for nation; and their minds appear to be in the same simple condition as their language.[44]

Rather than recognizing that the language of the San might contain an alternative definition of power relations or even acknowledging the ideological underpinnings of these particular words ("wife," "marriage," "nation"), Schreiner accepts the androcentric and colonial analysis that posits the absence of these words as an indication of cultural and psychological underdevelopment. The tradition of this kind of European analysis in which indigenous languages are seen to reflect the state of the culture finds its roots in debates about the ability of Indians (and later Africans) to receive religious faith. Greenblatt cites a late sixteenth-century observation by Pierre Massée that "the Brazilian Indians lack the letters F, L, and R, which they could only receive by divine inspiration, insofar as they have neither 'Foy, Loy, ne Roy.' "[45]

In her study *The Politics of Language: 1791–1819,* Olivia Smith argues that into the nineteenth century "civilization" was, in fact, a linguistic concept.[46] Studies of grammar were highly political in that they inevitably linked languages to intellectual potential and moral development. Class struggles, particularly those regarding suffrage, were played out in debates about grammar and the relationship between "refined" and "vulgar" language. The study of universal grammar took these debates into the imperial arena. Smith finds that these studies asserted that although languages were alike in that they represented the mind, they were different in the "quality of mind and civilization that they represented":

> Grammar, virtue, and class were so interconnected that rules were justified or explained not in terms of how language was used but in terms of reflecting a desired type of behavior, thought process, or social status. James Buchanan, for instance, argues that the English verb system must be complex because the English people are wise and respectable. For grammarians to maintain that the English verb system might be simple "is manifestly affirming that the English language is nothing superior to that of the Hottentots."[47]

While Buchanan's outrage is really in reaction to the argument of radical thinkers that refined and vulgar English are indeed the same language, that class privileges are not therefore justified as natural, his use of the "Hottentot" example shows the similarity between the arguments for repression of the working classes within England and those for the suppression of natives in the expanding empire. In Schreiner's view the "simplicity" of Afrikaans is well suited to the "sheep-souled Boer" (*U,* p. 2) but too "poor" to serve as the literary language of a rising nation.

Although it is a relatively young linguistic development, Afrikaans appears to Schreiner as a production that has separated the Boers from the

European cultural developments of the preceding two hundred years. The Afrikaner language, then, is at once too new to have developed sufficiently for literary expression and too isolated to be able to render ideas of the modern world:

> Behind [the Boer], like a bar, two hundred years ago the Taal rose, higher and higher, and land-locked him in his own tiny lagoon. All that was common to the great currents of European life at the time of his severance from them, you will still find to-day in his tiny pool, if you take a handful of his mental water and analyse it, but hardly one particle of that which has been added since has found its way into him. His little speech, not only without literature, incapable of containing one, and comprehensible only to himself and his little band of compatriots, shut him off as effectively from the common growth and development of Europe as a wall of adamant. ("TB," p. 97)

Because Afrikaans represents South African isolation, it cannot, according to Schreiner, adequately express South African experience, which in the late nineteenth century is inextricably involved with European politics and commerce.

When this judgment was translated into political legislation, however, Schreiner was horrified. In May 1905, nine years after the publication of "The Boer," Schreiner's description of Afrikaans as a language of isolation was summarized and used by the London Daily Mail and the Cape Times to argue against a motion in the House Assembly for inclusion of the Taal as a compulsory subject in the South African civil service examination.[48] Schreiner, who during the Anglo-Boer War sided with Afrikaner resistance against the British, was outraged by this use of the earlier article she had written out of political sympathy with "the Boer." The May 10, 1905, issue of the Cape Times debates Schreiner on her support of the motion, claiming that she is refusing the inferences of her own previous description and that in her present response she romanticizes what she sees as seventeenth-century culture preserved by the Boer into the nineteenth century:

> The survival [of Boer culture] may be "wonderful," doubtless is wonderful: nor need we dispute that the Boer who shuts himself up within a taal-ringed fence may also shut himself off from some of the vices of civilisation. But all this is nothing to the point, [which is] . . . that the taal which kept him within the ringed fence, caused him to lose more than he gained.

Schreiner's refusal or inability to associate her condescending description of Afrikaans with the legislation that would discourage its widespread use points up most clearly the seductiveness and power of the British discourse on language for English-speaking colonials, even those most sympathetic to Afrikaner culture. Schreiner recognizes that the repression of national bilingualism as a political move of British domination in South Africa is as real as, if more subtle than, military force. As the author of the *Cape Times* article expresses it, the "decay" of the Taal "renders easier the spread of liberal ideas, and in the spreading may remove some of the deeply-rooted prejudices against British rule." What exasperates Schreiner's opponents in this debate about a national language is her simultaneous criticism of Afrikaner "narrowness" and her defense of the group as an oppressed people under British rule. Schreiner's contention that the opposition to official bilingualism is a suppression of Afrikaans and is politically motivated is dismissed as "undiluted rodomontade" by her opponents. After Schreiner's use of the colonial rhetoric in "The Boer," it is understandable that pro-English advocates would be surprised that while Schreiner does not recant her earlier position, her writing now encourages "certain patriotic Afrikander ladies in some towns of the Colony to attempt a boycott of the English language." Her defense of Afrikaans is seen as almost treasonous in this post–Anglo-Boer War period.

Schreiner defends Afrikaans in both liberal and nationalistic terms. She appeals to the nationalistic obsession with origins to argue that the institutions of (white) South Africa were built by Dutch, not British, settlers. Afrikaans, in Schreiner's view, is not in *opposition* to English, but both are the linguistic inheritance of every white South African. While it is of central importance to Schreiner to carve out a South African identity that is distinct from an English one, and to present sympathetically all that which is now native to South Africa, her desire to engage in Anglo-European philosophical debates on politics, feminism, religion, race, and economics leads her to align herself with English culture when that which is distinctly South African threatens to marginalize her too far from the metropolitan centers of discourse. She prophesies, incorrectly, that Afrikaans would soon disappear on its own, and her hope is that an English flavored by Afrikaans would come to serve as a distinctly South African language for distinctly South African literary production. Schreiner does not, however, even begin to imagine an indigenous African language as a candidate for a national language. This remains as a debate for the postapartheid South Africa of the next century.

"Painting in Grey":
Deexoticizing the African Landscape

*There is no neutral naturalism. The artist, no less than the writer, needs a
vocabulary before he can embark on a "copy" of reality.*
                                    —E. H. Gombrich, *Art and Illusion*

Alienation is the very bedrock of landscape's existence.
   —Doris Kadish, *The Literature of Images*

Although Schreiner partakes of the British chauvinism about the superiority of English as a language, as a creole writer she nevertheless critiques
the limitations of the English language in describing non-English localities.
She finds the language of British description particularly inept for a geo-
graphically and emotionally accurate representation of South Africa. One
advantage the English South African has over the nonnative visitor, according to Schreiner, is an understanding of the physical country inaccessible
to the traveler. While she believes that the visitor can offer a disinterested,
even objective, description of geography and human customs, Schreiner
argues that these descriptions, which lack "emotional sympathy" with the
land and people, do not yield coherent or correct analyses. In a series of
essays written between 1891 and 1901, Schreiner attempts to provide the
absent description of South Africa by a native to the land. Neither an artist
nor a politician, she argues, can understand the salient issues of a nation or
region unless s/he is of and "belongs" to that nation:

> There is a sense in which the people of a country are justified in their con-
> tempt of the bird's-eye view of the stranger. There is a certain knowledge
> of a land which is only to be gained by one born in it, or brought into
> long-continued, close, personal contact with it, and which in its perfection is
> perhaps never obtained by any man with regard to a country which he has
> not inhabited before he was thirty.[49]

Schreiner's argument in this 1891 essay that the separate regions of South
Africa could successfully be united, if not into a cohesive nation then into
united states, rests, in part, on her belief that all people born and raised in
South Africa "are bound by the associations of their early years to the same
vast, untamed nature" ("SA," p. 60). These "associations" form a shared
psychology that binds South Africans, be they English, Dutch, or Black,
not only to the geography but to one another (*ESAV,* p. 5).

   Because she writes as a native of South Africa, Schreiner claims that
her portrayal of the people, the politics, the very landscape, must necessarily be different, supposedly more "truthful," than the volumes written

by both visiting adventurers and colonialists, neither of whom could ever see the African landscape as "natural." I am not, however, suggesting that Schreiner's portrayal of the South African landscape and its people is necessarily a transparent description of social realities.[50] In part, her descriptive vocabulary necessarily depends on three and one-half centuries of British discourse about Africa. Her attempt to "reclaim" South Africa in literature allows us to see some of the ideological contexts, the sphere of possible meanings, in which she wrote. How Schreiner creates this "new" image of South Africa is the story of how a national culture creates itself and is created by those outside its borders. When reading landscape descriptions, Doris Kadish argues, we must make ourselves aware not only of the physical "point of view" of the description but also of the mental outlook of the narrative consciousness she calls the "focalizer" of the piece. Landscape descriptions offer as much political and cultural information as they do geographical or botanical knowledge.[51]

The description of the South African landscape, then, can be seen as central to Schreiner's project of claiming the colony as her home in the face of English renderings of it as an imperial territory. As much as her writing challenges some of the romantic English colonial definitions of South Africa that endorse colonial policies, however, her rejection also fits squarely with a new colonial rhetoric that increasingly describes a benign, livable South Africa. Each of her novels opens with a specifically African landscape that reveals some of the tension inherent in Schreiner's specific political "vantage point" as an English-speaking South African. Both *Undine* and *The Story of an African Farm* open on landscapes that for the reader accustomed to African travel narratives become difficult to "read." The first image in *Undine* is presented through the traditional travelogue device of piling up images and then concluding with an aesthetic evaluation:

> Karoo, red sand, great mounds of round iron stones, and bushes *never very beautiful to look at* and now almost burned into the ground by the blazing summer's sun.[52]

Everything in the passage that follows is old, dry, and broken. What is "typically" African is simultaneously homey and *un*-English, the debris of a Boer homestead: "an old Dutch farmhouse," "an old stone wall," "an old tent-waggon," "an old willow tree." Unlike the British literary tradition that sees Africa as "a world apart," as an anachronism from another era,[53] the age Schreiner invokes here is on a human and domestic scale. The old wall, house, and wagon, even the old willow tree, are at most several generations old. They are given as familiar, not as exotic relics. This is not an Africa that strains the imagination; rather, the description asks that we look at what "we" ("South Africans" while we read this section) know as familiar, notice its beauty, and, in the context of its familiarity, acknowledge the strangeness of the everyday.[54]

Undine is a novel divided between England and South Africa, in both subject and imagined audience. This is Schreiner's first novel, begun when she was between sixteen and eighteen years old, before she had ever been to England. The only descriptions of the South African landscape she had read had been written by English writers. In this, her earliest description of Africa, Schreiner is quite conscious of how the Karoo "looks" to the European, and the opening paragraph acknowledges the conventional bleakness before revealing the beauty. In the midst of this bleak scene, however, goats "delight" in "deformed" pear trees, and ducks happily "disport" themselves in a mud-thickened pond. An interesting disjuncture appears in this description between the satisfaction of the animals and birds in this country and the evaluative language used to describe it. That is, the pear trees are only "deformed" to the extent that they are compared unfavorably with hypothetical pear trees growing elsewhere, for instance in England or in English literature. The cultural location of the narrator increasingly becomes of issue as the passage proceeds.

Having composed this picture of blazing heat and precarious survival, a picture familiar to the European reader of African descriptions, Schreiner sets the reader in another scene altogether — the same scene by moonlight. Shedding a new light on the African setting, Schreiner reveals the beauty that she believes is accessible only to those who are born and raised here:

> All these parts compose a picture in which, when looked at by daylight, it were hard work to find the slightest trace of beauty; but tonight, penetrated in every nook and corner by the cold white light of an almost full moon, there is a strange weird beauty, a beauty which the veriest sheep-souled Boer that ever smoked pipe or wore vel-skoen, might feel if he had but one rag of light left in him. (*U,* pp. 1–2)

In this moonlight the African night is not a terrifying shroud or an entangling mystery, as it is in many travel narratives,[55] but rather is a surprising "way in" to an appreciation of not a domesticated Africa, but a domestic life within Africa.

The explicit contrast here is between an assumed daylight ugliness of the African Karoo and the beautiful nighttime scene that is less well known. But there is also a more embedded tension between the two "focalizers" of the landscape, the Boer and the narrator. On the one hand, the "sheep-souled" Boer is part of the description of the natural landscape, like the goats and ducks. On the other hand, he, like the narrator, is a separate observer of that beauty. The paragraph plays out a competition between the native and the stranger and between the two colonizing peoples, the Afrikaners and the British, for the true understanding of the African landscape. The Boer, although he appears almost indigenous to the landscape here, pays for that native status by a symbolic loss of "enlightenment" or consciousness. His appreciation of the beauty depends on the "one rag of light left in him," the consciousness that remains separate from the natural world.

In other words, although Schreiner claims her appreciation of the African landscape as a native of the country, she also resists an implied engulfing power of the African world that subsumes the human observer into itself. In order to *be* an observer at all, this passage implies, one must maintain to some degree the position of the stranger that Schreiner disdains. As Kadish puts it, "Alienation is the very bedrock of landscape's existence."[56] Schreiner's position as both native and stranger leads her to use descriptive terms such as "weird" and "beauty" that might seem contradictory.[57] As a native South African, she can recognize the beauty not emphasized in British travel writing; but as a young writer who has read only English literature, she nevertheless incorporates in her descriptions the English expectations implied by the vocabulary ("strange," "weird") of these models. Schreiner's two other novels similarly open with African landscapes. In *Story of a South African Farm* the ethereal "otherworldly" images of an African night give way to utterly banal descriptions of African homesteads by daylight, while in *From Man to Man* the African landscape offers the child-protagonist a comforting escape from the terrors of childbirth and the domestic life of the house.

For Schreiner, the experience of being born into this country sets South Africans apart from Europeans not only physically, since they are "shut off by vast seas and impassable forests from the rest of the world" ("SA," pp. 60–61), but also emotionally. What she calls the "South African condition" binds the Afrikaner, Briton, Jew, and black African, provided they all came of age in South Africa. This belief in a "national identity" or *Volksgeist* influenced by the geographical environment was certainly not a new one, but was quite popular, in fact, in the eighteenth century in relation to American Creoles, those of European descent born in the American colonies. But whereas writings by metropolitans such as Jean-Jacques Rousseau and Johann Herder stressed the effect of climate and geography on culture and character in order to deride those born in the colonies and to restrict their political power,[58] Schreiner uses this belief to argue for South African national cohesiveness and pride. In a footnote to *Woman and Labour* in which Schreiner vehemently refutes a deterministic conception of "difference" and a simplistic correlation of behavior with environment, she reverses the metropolitan belief in "creole" inferiority and contrasts the "successful" South African colonist with the poor Irish farmer:

> We have heard it gravely asserted that between potatoes, pigs, mud cabins and Irishmen there was an organic connection: but we who have lived in the Colonies, know that within two generations the pure-bred descendent of the mud cabins becomes often the successful politician, wealthy financier, or great judge; and shows no more predilection for potatoes, pigs, and mud cabins than men of any other race.[59]

While in other essays Schreiner partakes of the rhetoric of deeply embedded racial traits, her articulation of a new South African national subject assumes the environmental influence of a national landscape that predates humanity and draws together all those born and raised in it. Schreiner uses this landscape as a foundational myth much as Watts-Dunton uses Shakespeare. His myth, however, is a national narrative designed as a defense against claims — such as Schreiner's assertion of creole consciousness — that weaken the boundaries of Englishness. Schreiner's South African nationalism is both a refutation of an assumed creole inferiority and an idealistic construction of an inclusive South African "identity" and consciousness.

While each of Schreiner's novels focuses on the universality of the struggle for self-identity in childhood, her characters Waldo, Lyndall, Rebekah, and Undine find their identities through their relationship with a highly particularized South African world of nature. The section "Times and Seasons" in *The Story of an African Farm* describes the development of identity and self-consciousness as simultaneously a universal and an individual process. The central consciousness of the section, identified by the first person pronoun "we," is at once a universal "everyperson" and an individual character, Waldo, who, growing up on the South African Karoo, struggles with the mysteries of perception, power, religion, and nature. In addition to the *cultural* worlds in which her contemporaries Sarah Grand and May Sinclair, and later Virginia Woolf and James Joyce, explore a child's developing consciousness and personality, Schreiner grounds her exploration in a highly particularized *physical* setting as well.[60] Like the universal/particular character of "Times and Seasons," the physical settings in *The Story of an African Farm* are themselves both particular and hint toward a general and shared setting, what Benedict Anderson calls a "socioscape," an environment "described in careful, *general* detail."[61] This individual story and the particular descriptions of life on an upcountry farm imply not only autonomy from English nationality but a real South African community for whom the descriptions would be familiar. In telling the story of *an* African farm, Schreiner evokes thousands of similar farms and children like Waldo finding their identities in this countryside.

For Schreiner, it is finally "our" (Waldo's) recognition of the wonders of the Karoo and a methodical study of nature that lead to a unified sense of identity and selfhood (*SAF,* p. 152). Through Waldo's development, Schreiner fictionalizes Emerson's statement that "Know thyself" and "Study nature" are in the modern world the same maxim.[62] In Schreiner's writing, identity is formed not by the explorer's "commanding" overview[63] of the new and exotic landscape but by the close examination of what is taken for granted as "home." Waldo's identity in *The Story of an African Farm* and Rebekah's identity in *From Man to Man,* as Schreiner's own, are inextricably connected with the South African countryside, and it is for this reason that the native South African writer will, according to Schreiner, necessarily produce a literary geography quite different from that of the English writer. J. M. Coetzee argues that Schreiner recast the terms of landscape evaluation by originating the idea that the true South African landscape is of rock, not of foliage. The geological as opposed to the botanical gaze (for instance, Waldo's discussion of the stony kopje [*SAF,* 49]) demands a longer time line, acknowledging not only a precolonial history but a prehuman one as well.[64]

As a colonial child, however, Schreiner's assessment of her native environment was mediated by the travel narratives and romances written by writers from the imperial "home," England. By invoking the travel wonders she read as a child, Schreiner underscores the simple "realism" of her own descriptions:

> It is the land of Livingstone. Some of us remember on hot Sunday afternoons, as little children, when no more worldly book than missionary travels was allowed us, how we sat on our stools and looked out into the sunshine and dreamed of that land.... From there we believed the Queen of Sheba brought the peacocks and the gold for King Solomon.... The very names Zambesi and Limpopo drew us, with the lure of the unknown. ("SA," pp. 46–47)

Like any child reading Livingstone in England, she can dream of this "unknown" mysterious territory. But having the experience of living a daily and nonadventurous life in Africa, as opposed to in the mythical "land of Livingstone," she can also acknowledge the romance for what it is — a fantasy, most probably a fantasy even at the time of the writing, and most certainly one now:

> It is more than possible that if we went there now we would not find all we have dreamed of. Elephants are scarce; Selous says he has killed the last white rhinoceros; if we met a lion he might eat us; the hippopotami will soon be driven away from the Victoria Falls; the ruins may not be three thousand years old; boredom and Sunday afternoons may exist there as elsewhere. ("SA," p. 47)

Schreiner's expository description of the Karoo, in contrast, is notably lacking in colorful metaphor or association. As opposed to the poetic vocabulary of the travel writings, her descriptions are prosaic, she explains, because her first apprehension of the landscape is not comparative. What the European experiences as "otherworldly" and frightening is for the native-born South African natural and a matter of great pride:[65]

> This is the Karoo. To the stranger, oppressive, weird, fantastic, it is to the man who has lived with it a scene for the loss of which no other on earth compares. ("SA," p. 38)

And yet Schreiner seems almost reticent in articulating what the feelings of the native-born observer actually are. In both this and the following passage, the South African's emotions are presented only as a negation of the stranger's alienation from a "world apart." Although in the fictional descriptions of nature with which she opens her novels Schreiner uses the very words of the visitor to lend a sense of strangeness to the night landscape in order to deexoticize the *daily* landscape of the farm, in her nonfictional sketches Schreiner limits her use of this traditional literary vocabulary in order to convey the South African passion for "the land itself":

> The stranger sees the barren scene, but of the emotion which that barren mountain is capable of awakening in the man who lives under its shadow he knows nothing. ("SA," p. 29)

Of course, the "barrenness" that the stranger is supposed to see is itself metaphorical and comparative with something other than this "land itself." Schreiner's portrayal of Africa is constantly mediating between two audiences that require different, often incompatible, descriptive languages. The adjectives for Africa, "weird," "fantastic," and even "barren," are generated by the phantom antonymical concepts of the English "home" and their more evaluative corollaries: the African landscape that is "weird" contrasts with the English "commonplace" (normal, safe), the African "fantastic" with the English "realistic" (boring, honest), the African "barren" with the English "fertile" (productive, blessed). The description of that which is un-like "home" is fantastic or "uncanny" (as Freud translates *unheimlich*) and depends on a belief in and loyalty to its opposite, the *heimlich,* or "homey."[66]

The problem for Schreiner as a colonial subject is that because she writes for both an English and South African audience, the ground from which she can generate her metaphors, the phantom region of the "common/ place," is not stable. That Schreiner has both these audiences in mind is clear from her publishing of her essays in both South African and Eng-lish publications.[67] Her English audience requires a literary production that posits Africa as the "uncanny," a representation of all that "home" is not. This passage from Henry Stanley's *Through the Dark Continent* (1878) shows this comparison quite clearly:

> Yet Nature has not produced a soft, velvety, smiling England in the midst of Africa. Far from it. She is here too robust and prolific. Her grasses are coarse, and wound like knives and needles; her reeds are tough and tall as bamboos; her creepers and convolvuli are of cable thickness and length; her thorns are hooks of steel; her trees shoot up to a height of a hundred feet.[68]

Whatever Africa is, and the literature offers a varied and contradictory description,[69] it is dependent on a shared idea of home.

For Schreiner, whose home and much of whose audience are South African, the traditional descriptive terminology is problematic. For the colonialist born in South Africa, the landscape can be seen as *unheimlich* only to the extent that the British literary representation of it does not clash ridiculously with her/his experience or with the South African construc-tion of what the home-colony is. To assume that the colony's understanding of itself is identical to the British understanding of it belies the political and cultural tension between the English imaginings of empire and the day-to-day administration of it in the colonies. This is not to say that the colonial self-imaginings are a purely new discourse, "untainted" by the English vi-sion. Far from it. Stephen Gray's description of Schreiner's challenge to the structure of the traditional British novel set in Africa is equally enlightening in regards to her vocabulary:

> Schreiner has taken the outstretched glove of the hunter-adventure fiction and tried to turn it inside out. That some of the fingers remained stuck in the old positions, and that the glove does not look as polished on the inside, is part of the fascination of the work.[70]

What Olive Schreiner's essays and fiction show most clearly is both the irrepressible desire of those marginal to the dominant discourse to center themselves with a self-definition and the impossibility of constituting that definition in a vocabulary purified of the dominant rhetoric.

By calling visitors to South Africa "strangers," Schreiner can decenter the European view that has dominated the literary construction of Africa. Because Schreiner is "explaining" South Africa to itself as well as to England, she cannot "get away with" as much of the colorful vocabulary as she could if her work were for a strictly European audience. Eric Gombrich in his study of the relationship between art and psychology cites an old Chinese treatise that helps explain Schreiner's artistic problem when writing about her native land: "Everyone is acquainted with dogs and horses since they see them daily. To reproduce their likeness is very difficult. On the other hand, since demons and spiritual beings have no definite form and since no one has ever seen them they are easy to execute."[71] Because they are describing a land they know less well, British travel and adventure writers enjoy a creative freedom Schreiner cannot. She herself recognized the difference between her own representations of Africa and those that "are best written in Picadilly or in the Strand: there the gifts of the creative imagination untrammelled by contact with any fact, may spread their wings" (preface, *SAF,* p. 28).

Rider Haggard's works provide excellent examples of the highly metaphorical and symbolic descriptions of African landscapes that dominated the literature about Africa when Schreiner wrote and published *The Story of an African Farm*. In this passage from *She* (1886), an archaic and desolate landscape promises English adventurers the most spectacular, but possibly the last, view of their lives:

> To the right and left were wide stretches of lonely death-breeding swamp, unbroken and unrelieved so far as the eye could reach except here and there by ponds of black and peaty water that, mirror-like, flashed up the red rays of the setting sun. Behind and before us stretched a vista of the sluggish river.... To the west loomed the huge red ball of the sinking sun, now vanishing into the vapoury horizon, and filling the great heaven, high across whose arch the cranes and wildfowl streamed in line, square, and triangle, with flashes of flying gold and the lurid stain of blood. And then ourselves — three modern Englishmen in a modern English boat — seeming to jar upon and be out of tone with that measureless desolation...[72]

In *The Story of an African Farm,* Schreiner satirizes the freedom of such travel and pseudotravel writing; before Bonaparte Blenkins shares his "adventures" in Russia, he first guarantees that none of his audience has ever been there (*SAF,* p. 59). Bonaparte provides the English interpretation of Africa that attributes fantastic properties to everyday life on the farm. Unfamiliar with such common farmyard creatures as ostriches and tarantulas, Bonaparte becomes hysterical when an ostrich looking over the open door pecks him on the head. Because he is unable to account for this sensation by his English experiences of nature, he attributes it to spirits who choose this way to reprimand him for his sins against the old German, Otto (*SAF,* pp. 100–101).

Despite Schreiner's claims to the native, nonimperialist eye, the specter of the English audience, for whom Africa is necessarily *unheimlich,* influences her choice of descriptive vocabulary. The result is an inconsistency of presentation in which South Africa is both commonplace and fantastic, both an interesting but unremarkable landscape and a decipherable realm of symbolic meaning. This inconsistency is indicative not only of Schreiner's personal transnational experience but also of a European relationship with Africa that required by the last quarter of the nineteenth century a broader range of representations than the early Victorian insistences on African darkness and savagery.

For Schreiner, one of the important "meanings" of the South African landscape is liberation. While using many of the tropes of the British discourse about South Africa, Schreiner's descriptions are also an answer to them, a "defense" of her native land. In contrast to the English tourist's "almost inarticulate" reaction upon seeing the bush for the first time, "Oh! It's so terrible! There's so much of it! There's so much!" ("SA," p. 50), Schreiner paints the familiar and supposedly comforting image of "England, our home" only to reveal what is "terrible" in it for the South African tourist. As she did in the opening to *Undine,* Schreiner piles up descriptive images (this time ones that are traditionally comforting), but here she undercuts the expectations of the reader familiar with British literature by asserting a distinctly South African experience:

> The lane, the pond, the cottage with roses climbing over the porch, the old woman going down the lane in her red cloak driving her cow, the parks with the boards of warning, the hill with the church and ruin beyond, oppress and suffocate us. ("SA," p. 50)[73]

While much of the British writing about Africa stresses the "terror" inspired by the great size of the continent, Schreiner finds in that expanse a freedom she believes is unknown in the present-day English village or European salon: "There is nothing measured, small nor petty in South Africa" ("SA," p. 50).

Although Schreiner attempts to provide a uniquely "native" image of South Africa by undercutting the familiar British image of Africa as horrific and weirdly dangerous, her unique defense is, in fact, part of the larger late nineteenth-century discourse on South Africa in which the fear inspired by the "world apart" descriptions by Stanley and others is played down in favor of the country's promise of freedom and opportunity.

By 1891, when Schreiner wrote this description, South Africa had become a well-tried "land of opportunity" for speculators. Nearly twenty years before, Schreiner had experienced the great influx of speculators to New Rush diamond fields (renamed Kimberley in 1873). In 1873, while living with her brother Theo and sister Ettie at New Rush, she began *Undine,* her novel about a first-generation English South African woman who, renouncing the wealth she earned through a hypocritical marriage in England, returns to South Africa to earn her living in the diamond fields. By this time the fields had attracted speculators from across Europe and Africa. In *Undine,* Schreiner describes the peculiar community in the diamond fields made up of the Europeans who came to Africa to find wealth, the working classes that developed in the camps to serve the material needs of the speculators, and the black African servants who worked in the dangerous mines for the white so-called diggers. By the time Schreiner wrote her essays on South African geography and population (i.e., 1891 to 1902), almost all of Africa had been divided up between the European nations, and the British government was committed to protecting the economic interests it had encouraged for the previous twenty years in South Africa.

Schreiner's rhetoric of liberation and national youth, then, while contrasting with the literary tradition that represented Africa as a place of terror and prehistoric "timelessness," is part of an English shift in attitude toward Africa. It is ironic that Schreiner's very success in constructing a white South African identity and vocabulary understood as being no longer European depends in part on shifts in European economics and colonial policies. Schreiner's debunking of the dangers of the African interior, for instance, is historically coincident with England's economic expansion into new territories.

A combination of the changing political climate and Schreiner's emphatic feminism allows her to offer a refreshing critique of the gendered nature of British depictions of Africa written by the almost exclusively male writers

of travelogues and adventure tales.[74] Schreiner reworks the familiar image
of Africa as Dangerous Woman[75] into one of liberation:

> South Africa is like a great fascinating woman; those who see her for the first
> time wonder at the power she exercises, and those who come close to her fall
> under it and never leave her for anything smaller, because she liberates them.
> ("SA," pp. 50–51)

Although Schreiner's "woman" is seductive and powerful, like other "Africa
as woman" figures in male travel or adventure tales, her liberating power is
a deliberate rewriting of these figures as they appear in works such as *She*.
In Haggard's adventure story, the protagonists find in the heart of Africa
a two-thousand-year-old white woman whose superhuman powers, unlimited resources, two-thousand-year political isolation, and female hysteria
ultimately threaten the British Empire and the entire world. For Schreiner
as a white African woman this image and H. M. Stanley's image of the
monstrously fecund female jungle (quoted above) are absurd and dangerous. Schreiner's feminized Africa challenges the traditional male narrative of
conquest that demands that the monstrous female "other" be "controlled,"
most likely destroyed, in the pursuit of civilization.[76] Aligning this African
female image with liberation rather than with danger suggests a critique of
European constructions of Africa that call for the military subjugation of
the African continent and its people.[77]

Nonetheless, the theme of liberation in Schreiner's work is, of course,
particularly attractive to the British reader of the 1890s who looks to
Africa for adventure, economic gain, and what is Schreiner's own particular brand of "conquest." While in the passage on "Livingstone's Africa"
Schreiner attempts to counter the unrealistic representation of Africa so
common in the later adventure tales, her rhetoric of freedom and liberation is a particularly imperialistic one looking to a future of unlimited
cultural and economic expansion. Schreiner concludes her debunking of
the Livingstone description of the past with this hope for the future:

> But it is certain that in these auriferous regions will ultimately spring up
> dense populations. It is from the territories north of the Vaal and south of
> the Zambesi, in this moister climate, with its more navigable rivers, that civi-
> lization in its coarser proportions will first unroll itself. More Southern Africa
> may produce better men; our greatest poet may yet be born in the Karoo;
> our great artist in the valley of the Paarl; our great thinker among the keen
> airs of Basutoland; neither wealth nor dense population have a tendency to
> produce the finest individuals; but it is in the north-east of Southern Africa

that mineral wealth and vast populations with all that they signify for good and evil will probably first arrive. ("SA," pp. 47–48)

Although Schreiner prefers to see the possibilities Africa offers in terms of poetry, art, and culture, the credibility of her vision, according to the contemporaneous constitution of African landscape description, requires an economic assessment of Africa's potential as well. Having spent the last decade before she wrote this essay in England in a primarily socialist circle, Schreiner is less than enthusiastic about the British material exploitation of Africa for its own wealth. Her alternative vision of cultural and artistic production in the new landscape, however, partakes of the popular visionary formula of the exploration narratives that, as Mary Louise Pratt has shown, ignores the existing populations and projects onto the view a vision of future European production.[78] Although Schreiner is clearly ambivalent about the results of British economic exploits in South Africa, her own dream of cultural development similarly ignores the indigenous culture in favor of a "new" Western art. In *From Man to Man,* Rebekah's creation of the allegory of the advanced "white-skinned" extraterrestrials reveals the colonial cultural hierarchy of Western art over indigenous art: "They had beautiful and wonderful things we had not even dreamed of — musical instruments more wonderful and sweet than ours, *as our organs and violins are better than the gorra-gorras which the Bushmen and Hottentots play on.*"[79]

This ambivalence — which I have been attributing to the political conflicts inherent in Schreiner's position as a white South African woman — is revealed blatantly in passages like this one comparing European and African art and more subtly in passages about future African artists. The passage about Livingstone's Africa (quoted above) is particularly telling, for it is at once desirous and suspicious of British and colonial growth in South Africa. The version edited and published by S. C. Cronwright-Schreiner after Olive's death is a compilation of the version she wrote for the *Fortnightly Review* and the version she revised a month later for the *Cape Times* (August 18, 1891). In the South African paper, Schreiner adds a sentence about colonial expansion that does not appear in the British journal: "It is from this region that *central tropical Africa will be opened up;* in this moister climate with its more navigable rivers, that civilisation in its larger proportions will first unroll itself" (emphasis added). The next sentence is punctuated differently in the two publications and reflects, if not Schreiner's conscious change in meaning, then the reading that the expansionist tone of the added material inspired in her editors. The following sentence reads: "More

Southern Africa may produce better men," which she clarifies as artists, poets, and thinkers. The word "More" is not punctuated in either the *Cape
Times* or Cronwright-Schreiner's edition as an adverb (i.e., "More,"), as it is
in the 1891 version in the *Fortnightly Review,* but as an adjective emphasizing the desirability of colonial expansion. The spread of "civilization" into
these "deserted" areas, in other words, may render a new South African art
and poetry "of our own." That each reading was possible in the context
of the larger article points both to the ambivalence in Schreiner's own text
and to the interpretations of her writing that were possible for her different
audiences.

Native to a land that is misrepresented in her British cultural heritage,
Schreiner delineates the landscape in terms that can be variously interpreted.
Because she uses the same words and writes in the language of the "mother
country," the play she introduces between the word and its accepted meaning is not always apprehended by her readers. By recognizing her political
and cultural locality, we can appreciate the gap Schreiner opens between the
words of her text, such as "wealth," "adventure," even "South Africa," and
the meanings they held particularly for her British audience. Her "remap-
ping" of the colony as "home" while using the same language as that used
by English visitors both challenges British "readings" of South Africa and
fulfills the imperial project that claims the land of others as "home" for
English subjects. How Schreiner portrays these other groups who also claim
South Africa as home reveals the deep ambivalences of creole discourse in
general and of Schreiner's feminist creole perspective in particular.

2 / Seeking a Third Term

Schreiner's Representations of Jews, Boers, and Blacks

I believe that an attempt to base our national life on distinctions of race and colour, as such, will, after the lapse of many years, prove fatal to us.
— *Olive Schreiner,* Closer Union

Schreiner's project is not only the definition of a new nation but a new definition of a nation, one that recognizes the full citizenship of women and accounts for the vital existence of national "subgroups." Complicating the already confused English rhetoric that correlated "nation" with "race," the South African nation that Schreiner participates in constructing is multiracial, multiethnic, and multilingual. Her representations of these national subgroups (Briton, English settler, Boer, European immigrant, San, Khoikhoi, Xhosa, Zulu, and so on) are influenced by the overlapping and contradictory dominations and violent struggles among them. The admirable intent of her depictions is to challenge the national chauvinism of the British, the racism of the British and the Boers, and the anti-Semitism of both the antialienist imperialists and the anti-imperial left. Her purpose, as she describes it, is to show "the possible mental attitude of the members of one society towards each other if divided by race."[1] In this Schreiner anticipated a project that waited over half a century before writers like Lillian Smith, Jean Rhys, Minnie Bruce Pratt, and Barbara Deming would attempt to map out the psychological experience of white women who have been raised in and live in racist societies.[2]

Schreiner's interest in such questions, her remarkable prescience about

50

political developments in Europe and in Africa (she correctly predicted the protracted Anglo-Boer War, the Union of South Africa, and both world wars), and her early argument that women's subjection is based on economic and educational, not biological, disadvantages have earned her the reputation of a devastatingly accurate, even prophetic, social critic. And yet those who read the full body of her work — the fiction, allegories, essays, and political speeches — have not failed to notice problematic contradictions and inconsistencies in her representations and arguments. Some of those contradictions are the result of changing political conditions or Schreiner's intellectual growth. Margaret Lenta, for instance, argues that Schreiner's acute observations and open mind led her to outgrow the racist prejudices of her colonial upbringing, making her later arguments inconsistent with her earlier ones.[3] Joyce Berkman suggests that Schreiner's arguments suffered from the mistakes and limitations of the nineteenth-century race science that was available to her.[4] Schreiner's writing therefore reflects the contradictory arguments both within and among religion, science, and social Darwinism as she moves between these discourses to make sense of her physical and social world. Certainly her own diverse education — her isolated childhood in the veld and her early contact with Afrikaners and Africans, her intellectual relationships in London, and her political relationships in South Africa — led to her radical disjuncture with many accepted Victorian ideas. Yet she also clung to the forms of the academic knowledge she so coveted, forms such as anthropological ethnography or anatomical measurement that ultimately limited her analysis. Many moved by Schreiner's ambitious attempts to explain race relations, human history, or social evolution recognize her sometimes paradoxical positions as paralleling her own paradoxical and contradictory life.

Certainly her sense of herself as an outsider influenced her empathic and impassioned defenses of those she saw as vulnerable or abused by power: women, Blacks, Afrikaners, prostitutes, pacifists, children, and Jews. Her lifelong sense of alienation and aloneness was both familial and political. As an adolescent, Schreiner broke with her missionary family and announced herself to be a "freethinker," a position that she claimed made her forever an "outcast sister" in her family.[5] Due to the financial destitution of her family, Schreiner was farmed out to various households of her elder siblings and at fifteen became a governess with no home of her own. Her sense of homelessness was heightened by her lifelong struggle with illness and the search for a healthy environment.[6] Due in part to recurring bouts of asthma, Schreiner was not able to settle in either England or Africa and had to move within and between the two countries her entire adult life. In Africa, where she was denied the vote and access to formal education and to the professions, her alienation was both sexual and political. As a member of the English colonial settler class she nonetheless was an ardent critic of British colonial policy, and she maintained an embattled position as an English-speaking supporter of Afrikaners during the Anglo-Boer War. With even less support, she vehemently objected both before and after the war to the solidifying of policies and laws that laid the foundation for apartheid, laws such as the Native Land Act of 1913, which relegated black Africans to 8 percent of the country's land. To her dismay she also found herself isolated in South African feminist politics when she insisted that universal adult suffrage must include black Africans as well as white women. In England she led an isolated life as a single woman writer and intellectual in her first eight years there and was seen as a "foreigner," especially during World War I when her support of conscientious objectors and her German name made her suspect to her landladies and neighbors.[7]

And yet we have seen some of the ways Schreiner was also in a position from which she could demand recognition. Her English roots, her position as a white, native-born colonialist, and her celebrity recognition after the publication of *The Story of an African Farm* provided her with the political status of "belonging," however uncomfortable that might have been for her. As a sister of Will Schreiner, the attorney general under Rhodes and later prime minister of the Cape, and as the close friend of, for instance, Havelock Ellis, Edward Carpenter, Karl Pearson, and W. T. Stead in England, Olive Schreiner was "known" as a member of elite political and intellectual circles.

The contradictions that critics have identified in Schreiner's writing illuminate the conflicting ideologies and loyalties of the white creole position. For example, Schreiner's contradictory representations of Boers, Blacks, and Jews reveal her attraction to figures that might merge that which in colonial discourse are dichotomous identities. If, for example, the English South African Creole is a political impossibility in national terms, so is the mixed-race "half-caste" an impossibility in the colonial mythologies of racial difference. Schreiner's persistence in challenging colonial binarisms with such "third terms" can be interpreted as a creole awareness of identities and positions denied by the very political forces that create them. Schreiner's fascination with these particular figures is additionally informed by her feminism and her critique of the imperialist rhetoric that employs myths about the family and "home" to exact political, national, and racial loyalty. Schreiner's writing, I am arguing, exemplifies a feminist, creole consciousness that not only accidentally produces problematic contradictions but repeatedly seeks to uncover equally problematic contradictions inherent in Victorian and colonial discourse.

The Jew and Colonial Consciousness

Perhaps nowhere are the terms of national citizenship more fully articulated and deliberated than in the late nineteenth- and early twentieth-century English and European debate of "the Jewish Question." It is not surprising then that Olive Schreiner takes a particularly keen interest in the plight of Eastern European Jewish immigrants who, being deported or barred from England as "unassimilable" by the British Aliens Act of 1905, arrive in South Africa. "The Jew" in Schreiner's fiction and essays, like "the Boer" and "the half-caste," is a contradictory figure expressing the complexity of racial stereotypes, the ambivalence of Schreiner's own political position, and her desire to confound the dichotomies of colonial society. While Schreiner's portrayal is not singular, and indeed fits neatly with the contradictory images of the "good" Jew and the "demon" Jew of contemporaneous British literature and journalism,[8] her fascination with Jewish identity is certainly influenced by the ways mass immigration and transnational "racial" identity challenge the definitions of nationhood. Her creole position and sensibility find such challenges both validating and threatening.

It is striking that as the daughter of a strict Wesleyan Methodist missionary family, Schreiner often identified herself as a Jew and wrote her mother hoping for confirmation of a possible Jewish ancestor, to which her mother responded: "I have always heard . . . that we had Jewish blood in our composition, dating from my father's maternal grandfather."[9] In a letter to Havelock Ellis in 1900, Schreiner wrote of the "Jewish appearance" of many in her family, including herself.[10] That she might have been known as a Jew in the literary circles in London is suggested by Virginia Woolf's description of her as a "sumptuous Jewess."[11] Schreiner's ambivalence toward the Jew, her identification and her aversion, is obvious in a story her husband, S. C. Cronwright-Schreiner, tells of her "amusement" at being taken for a Jew in Cape Town:

> Olive related to me, with amusement, that once, as she was walking alone in a street of Cape Town, a seedy-looking Jew came up to her, and speaking with an obvious accent, said: "Excuse me, but are you of the House of Cohen?[12]

The amusement derives both from the Jew's apparent sincerity and from the obviousness of his mistake. The tension of this one sentence "story" hinges on the possibility of Jewish identity and the danger that such close proximity to Jewishness represents in gentile fantasy. Despite the increasing danger evoked as the story builds to its climax, we are cued to read it "with amusement." The story itself suggests a frightening experience: Schreiner is pointedly "alone" in the street when she is approached by the "seedy-looking Jew." The "obviousness" of his accent implies his attempt to hide it and alludes to the Anglo-European association of Yiddish with dishonesty and secrecy. Part of the humor of the story is the anticlimax in which the "alien" man approaches the unprotected woman merely to ask a question of acquaintance. But the horror of the possible alternatives to this climax (robbery, abduction, rape, murder) lends drama to the Jew's innocuous question. Indeed, the question itself, implying Schreiner's familial relation to Jews, becomes the assault the "plot" suggests. Two similar scenes appear in George Eliot's *Daniel Deronda*. In the first scene Daniel is horrified by the "claim" made by a Jew that he himself might be Jewish:

> He felt a hand on his arm, and turning with a rather unpleasant sensation which this abrupt sort of claim is apt to bring, he saw close to him the white-bearded face of that neighbor, who said to him in German, "Excuse me, young gentleman — allow me — what is your parentage — your mother's family — her maiden name?"
>
> Deronda had a strongly resistant feeling: he was inclined to shake off hastily the touch on his arm; but he managed to slip it away and said coldly, "I am an Englishman."[13]

Although the question referred to his family, not his nationality, David asserts his English origins to deny any Jewish ancestry. The second scene also takes place in a Jewish neighborhood where Daniel pursues his curiosity about and strange attraction toward all things Jewish. Mordecai's question of Daniel's background, "You are perhaps of our race?" again elicits the greatest confusion and feeling of aversion in Daniel.[14]

Schreiner's "story" serves as an introduction to the ambivalence of her identification with Jews that recurs in both her political writing and her fiction. While she longs to identify herself with Jews and to champion their cause against English jingoism and colonial nationalism, the subtext of much of her writing reveals her fear of the destructive power attributed to the Jew, no matter how powerless he appears. As we shall see, the Jew in Schreiner's work is both a frightening and dangerous stranger and a metaphor for the colonial woman herself. Like the white colonial woman's position, his dependent and marginal status in colonial society undercuts whatever power he may wield. Schreiner's ambivalent desire to identify herself with and distance herself from an oppressed group ultimately leads once again to a compromised liberal position.

The Stranger in a Strange Land

For the South African, even more pointedly than for the English citizen, the Jew in South Africa is from "abroad." In the colony anxious about its cultural independence, his European origins present a heightened sense of danger.[15] For Schreiner's South African characters who are raised in the upcountry, European culture offers a false and dangerous promise of freedom. As Stephen Gray reminds us, the children in *The Story of an African Farm* and *From Man to Man* are not settlers but first-generation native South Africans. While Otto's map of Germany comforts him with the memory of a faraway "home," Europe for Waldo, Lyndall, and Em is a mysterious realm.[16] Each of the children is seduced and disillusioned by an English- or European-identified "stranger."

In *From Man to Man* Schreiner dramatically highlights this theme of the dangerous European stranger in the character of "the Jew." The complexities of the relationship between the native South African character and the European stranger are at the heart of the plot of the novel. Schreiner worked on this novel throughout her life, beginning it in her youth as a governess and continuing it in England, where it was published posthumously. Like Lyndall and Em in *The Story of an African Farm*, Rebekah and Bertie, the two sisters in *From Man to Man*, are raised on an isolated South African farm, which in this case is English, not Afrikaner. While their father loses himself in the spiritualism of Swedenborg, their mother escapes the drudgery and isolation of the farm by her nostalgic reminiscences of an idyllic England she left twenty-five years before. Rebekah inherits this desire for England from her mother but adds to it the skepticism of the native-born Creole. An upcountry "innocent," Baby-Bertie is seduced by a traveling English tutor and flees to her aunt's house, where she is ultimately ostracized by women and men alike when rumors of her "immorality" reach them.[17] When her aunt turns her out of the house to protect her own daughters' reputations, Bertie realizes that there is no place in South Africa she can go, no home she can return to. The public knowledge of Bertie's sexuality is seen as a grave threat to the Victorian ideal of family, and in protection of this mythical hearth and home Bertie is made homeless. It is at this moment of Bertie's utter homelessness that Schreiner introduces her most complex fictional figure, "the Jew." This character, called only "the Jew" throughout the novel, simultaneously represents Bertie's salvation and the fulfillment of her ruin; in offering her a home, the Jew ensures her alienation. The Jew, as a symbolically "homeless" figure himself, functions in Schreiner's writing as a point both of identification and of danger.

The Jew in *From Man to Man* was created in a time of intense political debate about and literary redefinition of "the Jew." Between the mid-nineteenth century and World War II, the idea of "the Jew" shifted from the medieval "wandering Jew" to the more politically dangerous modern "international Jew," a *stateless* person. With the increasing global activities of European countries and the changing concept of "citizenship" in the late nineteenth century, the Jew comes to represent a challenge to the increasingly important political identity adhering in nationality. The conflict that Jewish identity represents for Europeans and for the English at this time is evidenced by the obsession with the Jews' transnational political existence and the confusion evinced by Yiddish, a renegade language limited neither by national borders nor by linguistic genus.

The so-called nation of Jews discussed in mid-nineteenth-century writing refers more to a racial distinction than to a political or geographical one. Robert Knox, whose *Races of Men* (1850) found race to be ultimately of greater historical influence than national politics, devotes several of his chapters to deciphering the "puzzle" of the Jew. Knox's recurring theme is the disturbing statelessness of the Jewish "race," which is "dispersed over the globe since very remote times, without a country, a home, a rallying point."[18] The Jews' homelessness, in this view, is not of political but of racial origin: "Wanderers, then, *by nature* — unwarlike — they never could acquire a fixed home or abode. Literature, science, and art they possess not. It is against *their nature* — they never seem to have had a country, nor have they any yet."[19]

George Eliot, on the other hand, while also disturbed by Jewish statelessness, looks for a political solution to this anomaly in *Daniel Deronda*. Daniel Deronda's utopian vision is therefore the creation of a Jewish state: "The idea that I am possessed with is that of restoring a political existence to my people, making them a nation again, giving them a national centre, such as the English have, though they too are scattered over the face of the globe."[20] Implicit in Eliot's equation of diaspora and empire is her idealistic nationalism and her opposition of "racial" mixture either abroad or at home.[21] Such metaphors of imperialism and of exile that converge in the meaning of the Jew in the late nineteenth century are especially significant as context to "the Jew" of colonial fiction and rhetoric.

Schreiner was writing at a time of both increasing colonial activity and increasing Jewish immigration from Eastern Europe to England and South Africa. The prevailing metaphor for immigration in the English newspapers and parliamentary debates was the Jewish "colonization" of the world, particularly of England. As the "antialienist" author Arnold White wrote to the *Times* in 1887 while en route to South Africa: "Will you permit me to fire a parting shot at the pauper foreigner? He is successfully colonising Great Britain under the nose of H. M. Government."[22]

The common image of the threatening Jewish diaspora, and later of the "international Jew," reveals a cultural anxiety or ambivalence among the English toward the ever-increasing British Empire. The simple and comforting definition of an "Englishman" as one who is born and lives his life in England becomes inadequate in the face of British imperialism, through which the English are "scattered over the face of the globe." The imperialist figure of the inherently honest and good Englishman, who maintains his "Englishness" wherever in the world he might find himself and under whatever "uncivilized" or exotic conditions, becomes a standard character in British imperial fiction at the same time that the character of the "wandering Jew" takes on a more ominous presence. In this figure of the deracinated Jew lies the complexity of modern nationhood and national identity that the simple figure of the "Englishman" does not admit.

Schreiner brings her heightened sensitivity regarding issues of colonialism and political exile to her recurrent portrayal of supposedly typical Jewish figures. While she uses many of the standard journalistic stereotypes of Jews in her fiction, she nevertheless defends Jewish immigration against the growing antialienist "England for the English" and South African protectionist sentiments of the time. Her own exclusion as a "foreigner" in England, her distaste for British jingoism, her friendship with Eleanor Marx, and her attraction to socialism, which was attributed at the time to Jewish activism[23] — all these contributed to her identification with the position of Jews in England and South Africa. Yet, at the same time, she projects her own anxiety about "belonging" onto the traditional image of the Jewish pariah, an image that serves as a contrast to her self-identification as one who is native to South Africa and therefore decidedly *not* a "stranger in a strange land."

The answer to the "Jewish question" in Schreiner's view is to offer the Eastern European refugees the national identity of South Africa. In 1906, in response to continuing reports of pogroms against Jews in Russia, Schreiner wrote "A Letter on the Jew," which her husband read to a protest meeting in Cape Town and which she published in the *Cape Times* (July 2, 1906).[24] The public meeting was called by the Cape Town branch of the Jewish Territorial Organisation and was chaired by the Jewish mayor, H. Liberman. In order to counter the pervasive anti-Semitic charges of Jewish wealth and financial corruption, Schreiner in this essay emphasizes the immigrant Jew, the exiled and wandering Jew, the victimized Jew.

The argument of Schreiner's letter is that Jews, far from endangering South African culture, offer the country the sophisticated culture and learning they have provided every other country in which they have been allowed to settle. In contrast to Robert Knox's thesis that Jews possess neither art nor science, Schreiner contends that all the great religious and ethical teachings of European culture come from the Jews. Claiming that Arabic and Spanish Jews were responsible for saving the classics lost to Europe in the Dark Ages and that they themselves have produced the greatest of modern Europe's philosophers and artists, Schreiner is "filled with astonishment that the entire civilised world is not dominated by the consciousness of the magnitude of the debt which it owes to the Jewish race." Instead of offering gratitude, Schreiner laments, gentiles have always made the Jew the scapegoat for any financial scandal. She argues that Jews are in business precisely because they are not granted equal citizenship rights: "For ages the Jew, persecuted and oppressed, allowed no social or political right, incapable in many countries of holding real property, and liable in all to have it torn from him, was driven to finance and the dealing in money as the one path open to him."

The Jew that Schreiner draws in this letter is not a guilty interloper but the victim of "racial envy and of greed." Arguments to exclude the Jew from South African immigration are, in Schreiner's terms, comparable to the centuries-old tradition of stoning defenseless Jews who ventured out of the ghetto. The three Jews she holds up for her audience's admiration are Heine, Marx, and Jesus — all exiles.[25] Although the Russian Jewish immigrant comes to South Africa "with his clothes bound up in a handkerchief and a couple of pence in his pocket — or no pence at all," his poverty is no reason to exclude him, for Jesus himself was a Jew in exile:

> Far off across the centuries, in a long ago past, I see a stable from whose open door the light streams out, and in it I see a young Jewish mother, the wife of a carpenter, bending over the head of her newly-born child — a head which often in the years which were to come should find no place of refuge.

Although this letter was originally delivered to a predominantly Jewish audience, Schreiner "Christianizes" the Jew in order to make what she calls her "impersonal" argument against the persecution of Jews. The "good" Jew Schreiner describes in the letter is finally the financially and politically *powerless* Jew and the *cultured,* scholarly Jew. While Schreiner, along with most other writers addressing "the Jewish question," obsesses on the transnational condition of Jews, she deliberately counters the contemporaneous depiction of Jews as omnipotent financiers and corrupters of European culture. By centering herself in this essay as a gentile South African citizen, Schreiner finds a way to contain the wayward identity of the "stateless" Jew by drawing him within the civic fold of South African "national life" — that is, the domestic, cultural, and economic life of South Africa.[26]

Schreiner shares this intense interest in the Jew with other exiled or expatriated writers such as Henry James, James Joyce, T. S. Eliot, and Ezra Pound, and provides the tradition to later South African writers such as Doris Lessing, Alan Paton, and Nadine Gordimer.[27] In spite of the different attitudes they articulate toward Jews, each of these writers presents Jewish characters as rootless outsiders whose internationalism or cosmopolitan tendencies are liberating and/or dangerous to the native sensibility.

It is striking that this theme recurs particularly in the writings of those authors for whom national identity is a personal question. Henry James, visiting New York from England in 1904–5 during the height of British "antialienist" agitation,[28] writes the New York chapters of *The American Scene* with controlled horror, focusing on the changed features of his native land where now "the alien was . . . truly in possession" and where "the fruit of the foreign tree [was] shaken down there with a force that smother[ed] everything else."[29] It is the Jewish ghetto in particular that represents an almost "otherworldly" ghoulish nightmare for James — "the Hebrew conquest of New York." Of all the immigrants in New York, it is ultimately the Jew in whom James locates his own sense of displacement, alienation, and "dispossession" from the desired "sweet and *whole* national consciousness" of his native land.[30] At the same time, the Jew is seen as an eternally deracinated figure who centers James, even as an expatriate living far from home, as the rightful inhabitant of the land. James projects the anxiety of the expatriate's "right" to live where he chooses onto the immigrant who chooses the country James himself has rejected.[31]

In an excellent study of the racial construction of "the Jew" in English "Semitic discourse," Bryan Cheyette argues that writers do not merely draw on fixed or mythic stereotypes of "the Jew" but actively construct them in different ways to express their own relation to other discourses such as nationalism, religion, or modernism. James Joyce, for instance, exploits the indeterminacy of Leopold Bloom's Jewish identity to question the cultural certainties of Irish citizenship and Catholic doctrine.[32] The position of the Jew as a figure always in exile, even in his native land, captures the imagination of the writer who feels him/herself also to be in exile. In *Ulysses,* Bloom is a wanderer in Dublin, a cipher for all the myths and paranoia projected onto his difference. The catch for the Jew is that, denied equal citizenship status (as "the citizen" denies Bloom his Irish identity), he has been traditionally accused of lacking patriotism and national feeling.[33]

Unlike Joyce, who works this question of Jewish identity to break down the binary oppositions between Jew and gentile, T. S. Eliot and Ezra Pound (both expatriates) employ the myth of the parasitic nationless Jew to reinforce religious, racial, and national boundaries.[34] T. S. Eliot focuses his more vitriolic anti-Semitism apparent in his poem "Burbank with a Baedeker, Bleistein with a Cigar" (1919) specifically on the Jew's lack of geographical locality:

> A saggy bending of the knees
> And elbows, with the palms turned out,
>   Chicago Semite Viennese.[35]

If, on the one hand, the Jew is suspect as a rootless, landless wanderer, as a settler he is more dangerous still. The landed Jewish immigrant in this literary tradition, as we shall see in Schreiner's *From Man to Man,* is almost necessarily a landlord whose economic exploitation of the "rightful" owners of the land leads to an erosion of the national culture. In Eliot's "Gerontion" the Englishman's proverbial castle decays under the ownership of its bestial and filthy Jewish owner:

> My house is a decayed house,
> And the jew squats on the window sill, the owner,
> Spawned in some estaminet of Antwerp,
> Blistered in Brussels, patched and peeled in London.[36]

In the poetry of the expatriates T. S. Eliot and Ezra Pound the "jew" becomes not merely another incarnation of the "wandering Jew," which Edgar Rosenberg admirably traces through English literature and source material,[37] but the "international Jew" so devastatingly developed in the *Protocols of the Learned Elders of Zion.*[38] Pound's obsession with "Jewsury," equating financial corruption with Jews, Judaism, and "the international racket" (Canto 52), derives from the gentile terror of the "Jew at large" in the world. It is not coincidental that this fascination with the contradictory and indeterminate construction of "the Jew" appears in writing by these authors who are themselves cosmopolitan travelers, whose national identities are problematic. The horror that "statelessness" holds for the modern consciousness is projected onto the symbolic Jew who threatens linguistic, national, and racial boundaries.

The Jew and the Colonial Woman

The Jew in Schreiner's *From Man to Man* is part of this literary and cultural tradition that posits "the Jew" as a nameless, alienated figure who exceeds cultural boundaries. In many ways Schreiner's portrayal is standard fare. "The Jew" is first introduced as a "shuffling little figure" who has arrived at Bertie's uncle's house to press for payment on a loan:

> He was a small man of about fifty, with slightly bent shoulders and thin, small limbs. His face was of a dull Oriental pallor, and his piercing dark eyes and marked nose proclaimed him at once a Jew; above a high square forehead rose a tower of stiffly curling, gray, upright hair. He spoke with a strong foreign accent. (*MM,* p. 306)

This is the cartoon image of the Jew that Hannah Arendt sees in Charlie Chaplin's nationless characters: the little man in oversized clothes who does not recognize the class order of the world and who is wily and impudent enough to thumb his nose at those who maintain social order. Schreiner's Jew, like Chaplin's character, is small, exotic, and weak, yet the desires of both these characters threaten familial and social stability; this threat both attracts and frightens Schreiner.[39] Throughout her writing Schreiner's treatment of the Jew exhibits the ambivalence found in Coleridge's famous description of the Jew as disturbingly both sacred and profane, holy and degraded: "The two images farthest removed from each other which can be comprehended under one term are, I think, Isaiah, — 'Hear O heavens, and give ear, O earth!' and Levi of Holywell-street — 'Old Clothes' — both of them Jews, you'll observe, *Immane quantum discrepant.*"[40]

Predictably, Schreiner's Jew is a wanderer, who, born and orphaned in north Germany, made his way to the East End of London as a teenager, where he bought and peddled old clothes. As an adult he travels between London, South Africa, and South America as a diamond merchant and moneylender. When imagining "the Jew's" possible family, Bertie's uncle sees him only as a wandering businessman from "Hamburg or England or wherever his headquarters may be," not a man with a home (*MM*, p. 313). And yet this "homeless" figure offers Bertie a home when she has nowhere to go. The "home" "the Jew" offers her, however, is an ironic perversion of the idea of the Victorian home, which Bertie's sexual history endangered. Bertie is not "the Jew's" wife but his mistress, and while she is no longer "homeless," she is alien in the English "home" of her parents. While "the Jew" provides her with an abundance of the domestic spoils of colonial speculation, he keeps her a prisoner in the upper stories of the house, which are lavishly furnished for her comfort. Given that "Bertie" is a close match with "Bertha," it is possible that Schreiner had *Jane Eyre* in mind when she created this colonial creole woman imprisoned in an English manor.

The figure of "the Jew" here primarily underscores Bertie's own alienation in London. Schreiner herself, like many native colonial writers "returning" to London a generation or more after their parents left, was shocked by the strangeness of the place so familiar in literature. Schreiner was perhaps the first creole writer to treat this theme of alienation that was so central to later postcolonial writers like Jean Rhys, Michelle Cliff, and Zoë Wicomb. The England of *Undine,* a novel Schreiner wrote before she had ever been there, is filled with the lovely rose-laden gardens of the literary pastoral tradition.[41] In this early novel the image of England is that from storybooks or from the nostalgic memories of English parents. In contrast to this "delicious dream" (*U,* p. 34)[42] the England of *From Man to Man* is drab, inhospitable, and wet, while the idyllic garden is now found in Rebekah's South African arbor. The chapter "How the Rain Rains in London" is a cityscape from the point of view of an outsider to whom urban distinctions are incomprehensible. The "prospect" from Bertie's new position makes little sense to her; she can distinguish only that which she can filter through her South African experience:

> A curious dull gray light came through the two windows at the other end of the room (it seemed hardly like daylight) and a far-off roaring sound, like a million sounds breaking into one. Bertie listened to it for a minute and then walked towards [? the windows]. Her little stockinged feet sank noiselessly into the soft pile of the carpet *as into moss by the rocks in the kloof.* She drew up both blinds and stood before a window looking out. A gray damp was everywhere. It seemed to ooze out of the walls of the buildings opposite, to ascend from the ground as much as come down from the sky. Opposite were the backs of houses in the next street, all built of the same dead yellow-gray brick, and all oozing. There were rows of windows all alike. Out of two windows on a top floor a line was stretched and a shirt was hanging out on it, but it was not drying; the water dripped from its sleeves as they hung down.

Up above, in what looked like a loft, a window was open and a boy's face looked out, then the window closed. Down below, between the tall houses, tiny back yards with high walls were crushed. . . . There was a pungent curious smell that seemed to burn in her nostrils, *something like when they burn harpuis bushes on the lands at home.* (*MM,* p. 332; emphasis added)

The unfamiliarity of the English cityscape — the gray light, the roaring sound, the never-drying shirt, the seemingly ascending wetness, the disembodied boy's face — denies Bertie a context for her experience.[43] The similarity of the houses resists the uniqueness and recognition implied by the idea of home. Confronted with a row of houses seemingly identical to the one she is in, and taunted by the somewhat ominous disappearing image of another human occupant, Bertie turns away from the alien reality of London to the room that is carpeted with the design of the desired English pink roses and decorated with five mirrors replacing the outward-looking windows (*MM,* pp. 332–33).

The home Bertie goes to London to achieve is at once the domestic and political home of colonial desire: "The velvet curtains at the window were lined with rich satin and had cords and ball-fringe, as heavy as the curtains in the picture of Queen Victoria that hung in the front room at the farm" (*MM,* p. 334). The curtains divert Bertie's attention from the wet streets of London and the homelessness that threatens her as a single woman and as an exile. Raised on this mythology conflating British opulence and Victorian domestic bliss, Bertie does not recognize the irony of either the South African source of the wealth she enjoys in London or the farce of her position as "mistress of the house." Bertie becomes an extreme example of what Schreiner calls in her economic treatise *Woman and Labour* (1911) a "sex parasite," a woman, either wife or prostitute (a distinction Schreiner refuses to make), who, because of the economic system that refuses all professions to women, supports herself by selling her sexual "function" to either husband or stranger. While surrounding Bertie with luxuries, "the Jew" keeps her a prisoner in the house, never allowing her money or the freedom to go out alone or to communicate with anyone outside.[44] Distressed by the destitute and ragged children she sees while on a drive with "the Jew" and horrified by the barely dressed women dancers she sees in a show "the Jew" takes her to, Bertie refuses to venture out again. In terror of these two fates, she spends her time daily rearranging the furniture, eating, and finally, in an ultimate fulfillment and perversion of domestic competence, neurotically mothering three kittens "the Jew" buys for her as companions.

Late one night not long after this, "the Jew," suspecting Bertie's relationship with his handsome Christian cousin, forces her from his house into the street. Isaac, the half-witted son of the housekeeper, and perhaps of "the Jew" himself, finds her standing in the street in the rain gazing in at the windows of brightly lit sitting rooms. Exiled from "the Jew's" house, she has nowhere to go until Isaac takes her to a lodging house run by a woman who once owed money to "the Jew." A picture of Queen Victoria hangs in Bertie's rented room, but this one is cracked and blistered by twenty-five years of hanging and is stained with marks that Bertie thinks might have been caused by tears (*MM,* p. 379). The same "horror of pain" comes on Bertie when she looks at the picture as when she turns to look out the window at "all the houses...so exactly alike" (*MM,* p. 382). In despair, and trying to make sense of her experience, Bertie turns back to the fantasy that unites home and empire and wonders if the warped picture is of Queen Victoria's wedding day. Through this image of the aged picture and through Bertie's predicament, Schreiner deflates the fantasy by exposing its sordid underside and suggesting its obsolescence. In *From Man to Man,* London represents not the glory of the imperial fantasy but rather the exploitation that fantasy encourages. In the fiction of the colonial writers Olive Schreiner, Jean Rhys, Katherine Mansfield, and, more recently, Buchi Emecheta, Michelle Cliff, and Zoë Wicomb, London is the site where the politics of women's economic freedom and of national independence come together. It is in London, therefore, that the women characters are disappointed in their desire for status as "wives" and national "subjects" and where they realize both the restrictions of those roles and the dangerous consequences of living outside them.

This metaphorical use of the colonial woman, however, is complicated in Schreiner's novel by the figure of "the Jew." For while "the Jew" economically exploits both Bertie and South Africa, as a Jew he, like Bertie, represents the eternal exile, denied political power and national status. By providing "the Jew" with a pitiful childhood and memories of his youth as a hard-working orphan starving in an East London garret, Schreiner also provides him with a sympathetic motivation for his behavior to Bertie. "The Jew's" extravagant consumerism is not for himself, but for her comfort. He continues as he has for years to live in a backroom, wear old clothes, and cook for himself on a burner while he provides Bertie with all that he had wished to give his younger sister in their days of poverty and exile. "The Jew" is not simply a villain bent on the corruption of all that is good and pure. He is often quite loving to Bertie, in some ways her double rather than her opposite.

Like Coleridge, Schreiner is both troubled and intrigued by the monstrous discrepancy "the Jew" seems to present.[45] On the one hand, he is the economic tyrant of *From Man to Man,* the prototypical "foreigner" whose accent after at least thirty-five years continues to corrupt the English language. On the other hand, he is also a loving and generous figure, a member of the race that, according to Rebekah's journal and Schreiner's own arguments in "A Letter on the Jew," created the best of European culture. In part, this is the dichotomy inherent in all stereotypes, infusing them with their emotional power and contributing to their survival over centuries.

The stereotypes that have staying power are those that encompass and seemingly explain behavior and relations that seem contradictory. The "barbaric savage" thus has his counterpart in the "noble savage"; the Jewish merchant who pollutes culture is matched by the gentle Jewish intellectual who invents culture. The dichotomous portrayals can therefore function simultaneously — surprisingly, the landless Jew can also be a landlord, and the miser can also be a philanthropist. This is not to say that all racial stereotypes fall only into contradictory patterns, but that among the many stereotypes of a particular group, there are those that *apparently* contradict others. Employed separately, however, these stereotypes can "cover" any behavior and categorize it as "natural" or "constitutional" to someone as a member of a particular group.[46]

In addition to this doubleness, stereotypes usually also have a "clause" that explains *all* behavior as "typical" or symptomatic. The black African is "unpredictable," the Asian is "inscrutable," and the Jew is "wily." Bertie's uncle can thus explain anything the Jew does as representative of his "race":

> You never can account for what a Jew will do. I've known a Jew give thirty pounds for a Sunday-school picnic for Christian children, when he would have wrung ten shillings out of a starving man who owed it him: a Jew has whims like a woman. (*MM*, p. 313)

This passage reveals two important elements of the Jewish stereotype: his inexplicable financial morality and his disconcerting, slightly disgusting femininity. The contradictions inherent in stereotypes allow Schreiner to lean on the traditional anti-Semitic portrayal of the Jew as *dangerous,* while simultaneously arguing for the rights of Jews as members of a dispossessed, *powerless* class. Although in other writing Schreiner repudiated the usual conception of Jesus as "gentle" and "mild," and saw him instead as "a dark little Jew, with flashing eyes and a hooked nose,"[47] in "A Letter on the Jew" she argues for the rights of Jews by, on the one hand, denying their difference (the Jew here is the quintessential Christian) and, on the other, emphasizing their martyrdom: "For eighteen hundred years, [the Jew] has been trampled, tortured, and despised beneath the feet of the more physically powerful and pugilistic" (WL, p. 212).

In her recurrent portrayal of Jews as weak or powerless, Schreiner is consciously countering the mythology of the international Jew while unconsciously creating a new mythology that negates Jewish strength. Comparing "the Jew" (generically male) with women, Schreiner argues that they, like women, are marginal to the military dominance she so abhors. In Woman and Labor she writes, "The human female [is] like the Jew, the male of that type farthest removed from the dominant male type of the past" (WL, p. 214). In From Man to Man she describes the Jew "mothering" Bertie: "He put down his face as if he were going to press [Bertie's] soles against it, as women press the feet of little children" (MM, p. 331). Comparing Jews to women allows Schreiner to argue for their rights as a dispossessed class, while also undercutting the threat they nevertheless present in her portrayal. The powerful Jewish figure of Woman and Labour, who controls "great questions of peace and war," is also a solitary "little asthmatic Jew" (WL, p. 213). In this description, Schreiner's association of Jews with women as powerless classes joins her personal identification with Jews. The disease with which she disempowers this Jew is not one of those communicable diseases more commonly associated with Jews in English journalism,[48] but is rather the condition she herself suffered from her entire life.

As a symbol of identification, then, the Jew works in Schreiner's writing as a metaphor for the political position of the colonial woman. The Jewish diamond merchant in From Man to Man is an exploiter of South African wealth, a representative of the figure of the "rich Jew" on whom even left-wing anticolonialists blamed the Anglo-Boer War.[49] At the same time, however, he is an outsider whose lack of citizenship exiles him from the centers of power. Like the white colonial woman, he enjoys some economic and racial privilege, but the sphere of his power is not of his own making and depends on the decisions of white male (gentile) politicians. Onto the image of the "bad" Jew (the financier) Schreiner can project the guilt inherent in colonial exploitation and acknowledge colonial abuses, while her identification with the "good" Jew (the feminized, exiled, cultured Jew) allows her to distance herself from responsibility for the privileges of her class.

Neither One nor the Other

The constellation of Jewish stereotypes is also seductive to Schreiner because it deconstructs central dichotomies of colonialist ideology. After the Jewish holocaust of World War II, intellectuals began to explore the powerful rhetoric of anti-Semitism and the similar self/other structure of racist and sexist ideologies. Using Jean-Paul Sartre's term "manichaeism," which describes the dichotomies inherent in anti-Semitism,[50] Frantz Fanon and, more recently, Abdul JanMohamed redefine the "manichean allegory" in terms of colonial race discourse: "a field of diverse yet interchangeable oppositions between white and black, good and evil, superiority and inferiority, civilization and savagery, intelligence and emotion, rationality and sensuality, self and Other, subject and object."[51] The Jew is a compelling figure for Schreiner because he represents what JanMohamed calls the "syncretic state," the merging or confounding of the two sides of the manichean allegory. In Schreiner's work the Jew can be seen to represent a third term in these dichotomies that underpin colonial ideology and social structure. What makes the Jew both fascinating and repulsive to the gentile consciousness is that he is "neither one nor the other." The Jew comes to represent the danger and pollution Mary Douglas finds attributed to all things that fall between cultural categories.[52] In the Anglo-European imagination, the Jew is not only between nations but between races, languages, and even sexes. Schreiner's interest in the Jew derives in part from this "in-between" status that not only challenges racial and sexual ideologies but also represents for Schreiner as a colonial woman a metaphor for her own "in-between" position.

The pseudoscientific classification of the Jew in the nineteenth century is highly ambivalent. For Knox and others, Jewishness is not primarily a culture, religion, or political entity but a distinct racial type that "breeds true." Writing about nineteenth-century German race studies, Sander Gilman finds that, conversely, Jews were often considered a mongrel people, "the least pure race, the inferior product of a 'crossing of absolutely different types.'"[53] Both points of view, valuing racial purity as they do, posit the Jew as other to the Anglo-Saxon or "Aryan" races. In terms of this racial discourse, "mongrelism" or "impurity" ultimately points to the "taint" of blackness in particular. In the mid–nineteenth century, the Jew stands for the "white Negro" in Europe at a time when colonial racial policy was solidifying in Africa.[54] The Jew, who had always occupied the role of other in European religious and literary discourse, is now conflated with Europe's new "problem," the black races. If we look back at Schreiner's first description of "the Jew" in *From Man to Man,* we can recognize the racial mixture inherent in her standard portrayal of the Jew: the Oriental "pallor," dark eyes, marked nose, and stiff upright hair. Gilman cites Adam Gurowski's 1857 description of Jews in which he equates these characteristics quite specifically with those of mulattoes:

> Number[s] of Jews have the greatest resemblance to the American mulattoes. Sallow carnation complexion, thick lips, crisped black hair . . . On my arrival to this country [the United States] I took every light-colored mulatto for a Jew.[55]

Although both these "third terms" of racial dichotomies, Jews and "mulattoes," eventually firmly occupy the space of "other" in Schreiner's work, their presence in South Africa disrupts the racial ideology of her society. The "half-caste," according to Schreiner's vocabulary, attests to the ultimate similarity of the white and black races and to the possibility of social and familial relations between them. The Jew, as a controversial racial "problem," neither black nor white and at the same time both black and white, undermines the colonial categories of difference. Built into the image of the Jew is the subversion his very presence implies. For Schreiner this is at the heart of her fascination and ambivalence; the Jew, by his very existence in the colonial society, deconstructs the ideology of that society, an ideology she both supports and critiques.

In Schreiner's South Africa, where, as we have seen, language differences elicit both political and social anxiety, the Jew's "obvious" accent presents a threat to the nationalist project. The Jew's language, like the Jew himself, is an anomaly, an outlaw of nineteenth-century classification. Like Afrikaans, Yiddish, the "hidden" language of the Jews, is a language with no name but that of its speakers.[56] But whereas Afrikaans is spoken nowhere but in South Africa and thereby underscores Afrikaner nationalism, Yiddish challenges the belief that languages are the property of nations and that they manifest political national identity.[57] Yiddish was not only spoken by most Jews in different countries across Europe until the Nazi decimation but is itself an amalgam of vastly different languages — German, Hebrew, Aramaic, French, Italian, Slavic.[58]

That this humble and vernacular language should be associated not only with the simplicity or nonlanguage status also attributed to Afrikaans, but also with secrecy, magic, and subversion,[59] speaks to the central role that language plays in the "national consciousness." Gilman's provocative study looks closely at the myths commonly projected onto Yiddish. He cites Martin Luther's claim that the language of thieves comes from Jews and discusses the general belief that Yiddish is a coded language used specif-ically for conspiracy and criminal activities.[60] This myth remains current in Schreiner's own time; Havelock Ellis in his study of thieves' slang in *The Criminal* (1910) cites Cesare Lombroso's observation that "Hebrew, or rather Yiddish, supplies the half of Dutch slang and nearly a fourth of Ger-man, in which I counted 156 out of 700, and in which all the terms for various crimes (except *band-spicler* for a cheater at dice) are Jewish."[61] Ellis explains this Jewish criminal slang as the same "psychic atavism" apparent in criminals:

> Even in its precise build criminal slang is paralleled by the slang found among savage races. Of the Cameroon tribes, C. H. Richardson remarks that, "in order to have a secret language that they may use in public for private pur-poses, they perform the wonderful feat of speaking their language backwards, and no one who has learned their language can understand them in the rapidity with which they reverse every word of a sentence."[62]

That Yiddish, too, is written "backwards," from right to left in Hebrew characters, encourages this remarkable connection between a "secret code," criminality, Africans, and Yiddish. In studying criminal "hieroglyphs" Lom-broso again compares them with the "savage totem," while Ellis adds that these symbols frequently "refer to the Jews." "It seems evident," Ellis goes on to say, "that the Jews, as an outcast class, were at an early period thrown in close connection with the criminal classes; this is also indicated by the frequency of Hebrew words in criminal slang. Like the latter, the secret hi-eroglyph is a method of social protection used by outcast classes as a weapon against society."[63] That Yiddish was the language of the immigrant Jewish working class in London and therefore of some of the widely read social-ist and anarchist newspapers contributed to the association of Yiddish with social unrest.

Yiddish is both the homeless language, the language of exile, and the domestic language, the language of the private sphere, of the home, of women. Unlike Hebrew, the language reserved for male scholarship and theology, Yiddish is the *mama loshen,* the language of the kitchen[64] and of the *Tsena-Urena,* the women's book of Bible stories and commentary. Through these associations, the Jewish language, like the Jew himself, is metaphorically feminine. In light of the androgynous characters so appealing to Schreiner in her writing, the enigmatic sexuality of the Jew in the popular mythology presents itself conveniently as another "problem," like those of race and language, confronting the dichotomies Schreiner critiques. Schreiner's tendency to feminize the male Jew occurs in the context of a powerful tradition suspicious of Jewish sexuality and sex-role definition. This is a tradition that includes the medieval belief in Jewish male menstruation (tied both to the Jews' refusal of the blood of Christ and to the resulting libel of blood guilt)[65] and the association of Jews with women in twentieth-century psychiatric and medical literature, such as Otto Weininger's *Sex and Character* (1903), which later profoundly influenced Nazi ideology and policy.[66] For Schreiner, however, the dissolution of sex roles and even of sexual difference is at the center of her utopian vision. In *Woman and Labour* the Jews' supposed lack of masculine aggression is the sign of their modernity, and, like women, their reliance on intellectual rather than physical power will benefit them in the new social order.

The Jew, as a feminine figure, provides an alternative to the rigid sex roles of British colonial society in South Africa. As a supposed corruption of the social traditions necessary to the idea of "a nation," especially one taking Victorian England for its model, the Jew appears in Schreiner's writing as a disruption that is not altogether undesired. Schreiner's ambivalence regarding both nationalism and her position as a national subject, her desire for a national identity and her fundamental objection to the colonialist project that would give her one, explains her interest in and use of the Jew as a literary and rhetorical trope. How the Jew functions in Schreiner's work as both subject and object, self and other, helps us understand not merely the ambivalence of Schreiner's individual political position, or even that of white creole women, but the contradictions inherent in cultural mythologies and the ways they both "explain" and undermine specific ideologies and social structures.

Tants and Ooms vs. the Mother Country

Similarly, Schreiner's portrayal of Afrikaners, the competing white colonial presence in South Africa, tells us much about her understanding of race relations, about her understanding of herself as an observer and interpreter of South African cultures, and about the way the Afrikaner presence in South Africa challenged British definitions of colonialism and of "home." Schreiner uses "the Boer" — the contemporaneous term meaning "farmer" — to critique English colonialism and, paradoxically, to claim the possibility of a white South African population. In the introduction to her collection of essays on Boer culture, *Thoughts on South Africa,* Schreiner acknowledges the specific English perspective she takes toward this familiar but still foreign culture. She claims not only that this is a "personal" record but also that it is to some extent more "disinterested" than it could be if she were of Afrikaner descent:

> It has been said I love the African Boer. That is true. But it has been given as a reason for my doing so that I share his blood, and that is not true. One could not belong to a more virile folk, but I have no drop of Dutch blood. (*TSA,* p. 15)

She is also aware, however, that behind this protestation and her identification with the English lurks a powerful ideology of racism and ethnocentrism. In Schreiner's vocabulary, "race" is a term that signifies ethnic group and nationality as well as color. With insight and courage Schreiner chronicles the systemic nature of racist ideology, both how it is taught and learned and how it expresses itself in daily relations. She recalls her own childhood knowledge of her so-called racial superiority as an example of early racial education, and her own psychological use of it:

> Neither do I owe it to my early training that I value my fellow South Africans of Dutch descent. I started in life with as much insular prejudice and racial pride as it is given to any citizen who has never left the little Northern Island to possess. I cannot remember ever being exactly instructed in these matters by any one, rather, I suppose, I imbibed my view as boys coming to a town where there are two rival schools imbibe a prejudice towards the boys of the other school without ever being definitely instructed on the matter. I cannot remember a time when I was not profoundly convinced of the superiority of the English. . . . I have only to return to the experiences of my early infancy to know what the most fully developed Jingoism means. (*TSA,* pp. 15–17)

She examines in detail specific encounters she had with Boer children and families and her simultaneous feelings of superiority and anxiety in relation to them. She remembers that as a child she was given a gift of sugar by a Boer girl, and although the sugar was a marvelously rare treat she let it drop to the ground because "to have eaten sugar that had been in the hand of a Boer child would have been absolutely impossible to me" (*TSA,* p. 16). She also remembers her refusal to sleep in her bed because it had been offered the night before to a minister of the Dutch Reformed Church — a man she was convinced must be Dutch, though in fact he was Scottish. In both cases, Schreiner learned the racist, or ethnocentric, lessons so well that they were experienced not merely as idea but as physical revulsion.

Like the other authors examined in this book, Olive Schreiner claims that, despite her early racist training, she also experienced in her childhood very close associations with members of the "races" she was taught to disdain. Similarly, all the writers occupied a minority status in relation to the despised groups, experiences that may have diminished the children's assumed superiority and left them in some ways desiring to "belong" among those very people they feared and were taught were inferior to themselves. Schreiner, for instance, attributes her later appreciation of Boer culture both to her study of South African history and to the years in which she served as a governess on Boer farms, where she claims that "sometimes for eighteen months I did not see an English face" (*TSA*, p. 19). This "other" white culture that so repulsed her as a child came to symbolize for Schreiner an instructive alternative to British culture, in both the public and the private spheres.

As one of the first feminists to argue that the ideal Victorian family facilitated English imperial policy, Schreiner depicted the Boer as a simultaneous challenge to both the constraints of the Victorian family and the English understandings of colonial settlement. To Schreiner the Boers, unlike the English settlers, are typically "South African" because they identify firmly with South Africa and acknowledge no connection with either Holland or France, their countries of ancestral origin. Typical of her attention to the influence of women on history, Schreiner offers a unique explanation for this national dissociation, attributing it to the absence of a familial home in the lives of the early women settlers. These women, according to Schreiner's history in her essay "The Boer" (1896), were sent for from orphan asylums in Holland to be wives of the Dutch settlers. Unlike the mothers of other colonial populations, these women taught their children no great love of or reverence for the "mother country" that had denied them an actual mother:

> Alone in the world, without relatives who had cared sufficiently for them to save them from the hard mercy of a public asylum, these women must have carried away few of the warm and tender memories happier women bear to plant in the hearts of their children. The bare boards and cold charity of a public institution are not the things of which to whisper stories to little children.... To such women it was almost inevitable that, from the moment they landed, South Africa should be "home," and Europe be blotted out. ("TB," p. 73)

Instead of re-creating Holland as the later English settlers tried to re-create England by naming their South African towns "East London," "Port Alfred," and "Queen's Town" ("TB," p. 77), and instead of imitating the political structures of England, these Dutch settlers and the later French Protestant refugees cut themselves off from Europe and attached themselves passionately to the South African land.

Schreiner's interpretation of this history disrupts the Victorian conception of "home" that fused family and empire. The nineteenth-century British colonial rhetorical use of the family metaphor not only masked national chauvinism and racism ("the Anglo-Saxon family") but justified women's subordination as patriotic duty.[67] As we shall see in her treatment of marriage in *From Man to Man,* Schreiner compares colonialism and marriage as two institutions that rationalize unsavory economic transactions by ideological mythmaking. Throughout *The Story of an African Farm,* Lyndall struggles with the hypocrisy of the romantic love myth that obscures the economic and sexual exploitation of women. She recognizes that the "chivalrous attention" upon which women are supposed to rely for safety and economic security is the social lie that keeps marriage a form of prostitution for women (*SAF,* pp. 190–91). Tant' Sannie's courtships and marriage are presented as an Afrikaner alternative to Lyndall's English finishing school training that seeks to produce charming but powerless wives for British officers and administrators of the empire. These schools for girls are called "finishing schools," Lyndall says, because "they finish everything but imbecility and weakness, and that they cultivate" by teaching girls to make cushions, silk flowers, and footstools (*SAF,* p. 185). The cult of domesticity that this school reinforces can be seen as part of the larger political project of creating the Victorian family, in which women from Queen Victoria down were encouraged to serve as wives and mothers not only to their immediate families but also symbolically (as well as economically) to the family of the British Empire and the Anglo-Saxon race.

Familial relations on Tant' Sannie's farm, where the two English girls Em and Lyndall are raised, are at once less majestic and more articulate about the economic purposes of marriage than this English model requires. As Otto, the German overseer, explains to Bonaparte, the English "stranger": "We are all a primitive people here — not very lofty. We deal not in titles. Everyone is Tanta and Oom — aunt and uncle" (*SAF,* p. 53). This extended family model, while it does serve to bind together all whites, and particularly Afrikaners, provides in this novel an equal status of adulthood for men and women alike, a status that, unlike the English model, is not based on marriage or parenthood. Unlike Lyndall, Tant' Sannie need not invest marriage with any symbolic relation to her self-identity. She is economically independent and through marriage seeks to increase her holdings of sheep and property and to have children.

Tant' Sannie's unromantic ideas of marriage serve as a foil to Lyndall's agonistic choice between love and freedom. As Tant' Sannie summarizes her beliefs to Em at the end of the novel:

> If a woman's got a baby and a husband she's got the best things the Lord can give her; if only the baby doesn't have convulsions. As for a husband, it's very much the same who one has. Some men are fat, and some men are thin; some men drink brandy, and some men drink gin; but it all comes to the same thing in the end; it's all one. A man's a man, you know. (*SAF,* p. 293)

This prosaic understanding of marriage is unavailable to Lyndall, who has been left no land and who, if she marries, will necessarily be economically dependent on her husband. Her search for both love and independence ends with her death in the Transvaal, unmarried and abandoned by the father of her dead baby. The differences between Tant' Sannie's comic and Lyndall's tragic attitudes toward marriage result, according to Schreiner, from the roles available to women in each of these different cultures.

In her essay "The Boer Woman and the Modern Women's Question,"[68] Schreiner describes sexual relations between Boer men and women as lacking both the philosophical complexity and the economic exploitation implicit in "modern" (that is, English) sexual relations. According to Schreiner, the Boer woman, unlike the European woman, still has a field of employment that is beyond her sexual function and that makes her valuable to her society. Because she is granted equal inheritance rights and education, she comes to marriage as an equal partner rather than as a "sex parasite."[69] She is, in fact, represented as a full citizen in a way English women are not. The "woman's movement," then, is fundamentally about the abridgement of women's rights under modern conceptions of nationality. For a Boer woman like Tant' Sannie, therefore, whose expectations within her own culture are more likely to be fulfilled than are Lyndall's, the "woman's movement" makes no sense:

> It is said of her that in the vast movement, which without leaders or instigators, is taking its rise from end to end of the civilized world, awakening...the heart of the young English girl on the solitary karoo plains... — it is said of her in this movement the Boer woman has no part. ("BW," p. 204)

In both the essay on Boer women and *The Story of an African Farm,* Schreiner contrasts the highly intellectual English woman with the more "primitive" but happier Boer woman. In contrast to Lyndall's bitterness and despair about women's position in relation to men, Tant' Sannie is a gleeful Wife of Bath whose choice of her third husband is boisterous yet shrewd:

> "Good Lord!" said Tant' Sannie; "it's the seventh [widower] I've had this month; but the men know where sheep and good looks and money in the bank are to be found," she added, winking knowingly. "How does he look?"
>   "Nineteen, weak eyes, white hair, little round nose," said the maid.
>   "Then it's he! then it's he!" said Tant' Sannie triumphantly: "Little Piet Vander Walt, whose wife died last month — two farms, twelve thousand sheep. I've not seen him, but my sister-in-law told me about him, and I dreamed about him last night." (*SAF,* p. 200)

Schreiner's condescending and comic representation of Tant' Sannie and Afrikaners in general disrupts her presentation of Afrikaner customs as serious alternatives for Britons or British Creoles. In Schreiner's fiction, Afrikaners are always the objects of admiration, pity, or amusement, but they are never given full subjectivity. Schreiner sets her novel on a Boer farm yet chooses for her protagonists characters of English and German backgrounds. The Boer scenes, such as Tant' Sannie's "upsitting," and the Boer characters involved in these scenes stand outside the narrative and generally serve as comic subplots to the tragedies of Lyndall, Waldo, and Em. Even as Schreiner introduces the Afrikaner presence into her descriptions of this rather "typical" upcountry farm to expand the British "imaginings" of South African identity, the impact of that portrayal is compromised by the form of nineteenth-century European ethnography.

The descriptions of "upsittings" and weddings in *The Story of an African Farm* have a generic quality and assume a readership that is ignorant about Boer customs. While the community turns out for an individual wedding, the chapter title "A Boer Wedding" marks its typicality as does the ethnographic stance of the descriptive voice: "To a Dutch country wedding guests start up in numbers astonishing to one who has merely ridden through the plains of sparsely-inhabited karroo" (*SAF,* p. 210). The description of the day, from the morning when the guests arrive, through the wedding ceremony and the evening revels, until the next morning when the festivities conclude, is impersonal and given in the historical present and passive tenses, underscoring that which is culturally repetitive rather than that which is specific to *this* particular wedding:[70]

> Bride and bridegroom, with their attendants, march solemnly to the marriage chamber, where bed and box are decked out in white, with ends of ribbon and artificial flowers.... Everything is removed from the great front room, and the mud floor, well rubbed with bullock's blood, glistens like polished

mahogany. . . . At twelve o'clock the bride is led to the marriage chamber and undressed; the lights are blown out, and the bridegroom is brought to the door by the best man, who gives him the key; then the door is shut and locked, and the revels rise higher than ever. (*SAF,* pp. 211–12)

Lyndall, the observing subject here, does not participate in the revelry but coolly watches and finally goes outside to wait with Waldo. She defines herself as outside this culture but enjoys the feeling of difference:

"It is so nice to lie here and hear that noise," she said. "I like to feel that strange life beating up against me. I like to realize forms of life utterly unlike mine." (*SAF,* p. 214)

The ethnographic conventions necessitate Lyndall's declaration of her separation from this other strange life form (this "white tribe") and make it clear that Schreiner is writing for an English audience. In fact, Karel Schoeman, an Afrikaner reader of this scene, finds it so generalized and irrelevant to the plot that he wonders whether it was inserted just before publication for the "delectation" of the English reading public. He points out that Tant' Sannie (whose wedding this is) is not even mentioned in this scene that, he argues, reads much like the "Colonial Scenes and Characters" published in *Eastern Province Magazine* in 1862.[71]

Although Schreiner's depiction of Boers as rough and primitive derives from a tradition of English travel writing,[72] Schreiner counters the English portrayal of Afrikaners before the Anglo-Boer War as "white savages" with her own critique of modern capitalism that has created the neurotic "brain worker" and the female "sexual parasite."[73] Because the Boer is in active confrontation with English imperialism and offers an alternative to English sexual politics — the two aspects of English culture Schreiner abhors — she romanticizes Boer culture in much the same way that nineteenth-century English novelists anxious about the growing industrial culture romanticize country or working-class characters. That romanticization presents a contradictory representation that, while working to vindicate the Boer, is also replete with both working-class and ethnic stereotypes.

Schreiner's Boers are simple and uneducated but have retained a moral purity lost to the more refined city people. The flip side of the imagined moral purity of the Boer or country character, however, is the imagined coarse, even loutish, simplicity of his/her mental life. The editor of the Afrikaans paper *Ons Land* found Schreiner's supposed "defense" of Boer culture in her 1896 essay "The Boer" (printed in the *Cape Times*) offensive in the extreme. The editor reminded his readers that Schreiner was responsible as well for the offensive caricature of Tant' Sannie and that *The Story of an African Farm* would never be acceptable to Afrikaners. The figure Schreiner chose to idealize, the paper charged, was "the most contemptible white frontiersman," and not typical of the Boer at all.[74]

Schreiner represents the juxtaposition of English and Boer culture with the metaphors of mind versus body also common to the city/country comparisons in Victorian literature. Tant' Sannie and all Boer women in Schreiner's work are heavy, "massive Tantes" (*SAF,* p. 211) whose lives are simple, while her English heroines are tiny, intellectually driven, and obsessed with questions of identity and sexual politics. Em, Lyndall's cousin who stays on at the farm with no desire to visit the English South African cities, is described as "a premature little old woman of sixteen, ridiculously fat." She is the robust, uncomplicated (and uneducated) foil to Lyndall. Just as the lifestyles of English country characters do not really offer possible alternatives to the corrupt or unfulfilled lives of the metropolitan characters, so the farm life of the Boer cannot save the English South African woman from her fate. In a modern world that is characterized by "brain work" in the city, the corporeal farm offers no solution to modern problems. Country life is a picturesque alternative not really possible any longer to the sensitive though troubled children of the more "developed" culture.

Schreiner's attraction to the "simple life" of the Boer was probably strengthened by Edward Carpenter's experiment in country living at Millthorpe. Schreiner had been reading Carpenter's writing since 1884 when Havelock Ellis suggested she read *Towards Democracy.* She became close friends with Carpenter a couple of years later when she was living a "simplified life" herself at a Dominican convent in the Harrow countryside.[75] In 1893, three years before she wrote "The Boer" and five before "The Boer Woman," Schreiner rented a cottage to be near Carpenter and the community at Millthorpe where London intellectuals, like herself, attempted to create idealized communal country life.

It is in the context of a late Victorian nostalgia for a lost agrarian economy that Schreiner describes the domestic and cultural life of the South African Boer.[76] But how can Schreiner idealize this economy for whites in South Africa and oppose colonialism? As J. M. Coetzee argues, the pastoral in white South African writing presents an embarrassing conflict because as it portrays the requisite white labor it must obscure black labor. The pastoral thus always threatens to reveal itself as a retreat stolen from blacks whose home it was a generation or two before.[77] To resolve this, Schreiner portrays the idealized rural life as not only inaccessible to a modern sensibility such as Lyndall's but doomed like the Boer himself to nostalgic memory. Although Schreiner claims that Boer culture is the "backbone" of South Africa ("Boer Woman," p. 220) — as opposed to the brain or nervous system that metaphorically represented modern society in contemporaneous medical discourse[78] — she also mourns its "necessary" passing. In "The Psychology of the Boer," Schreiner writes:

> The Boer will pass away. In fifty years the plains of South Africa will know him no more . . . He will have gone with the springbok and the koodoo and the eland and the lion, with all the charm and poetry of this South Africa of ours, that we loved so. . . . He will pass away, not supplanted by the stranger and the alien, but by his own cultured, complex, many-sided, twentieth-century descendants.[79]

Although Schreiner compares the "passing" of the Boer to the extinction of certain South African animals, noticeably "game" animals, there is no violence in this fantasy. Schreiner presents the Boers' "extinction" in evolutionary terms that pointedly deemphasize the racial competition she acknowledges when she discusses color relations. The disappearance is presented as a natural event for which the English South Africans can mourn. It is their loss, not their responsibility. By asserting the inevitable passing of Boer culture in this essay and of Afrikaans in "The Boer," Schreiner can introduce the Boer into English literature without really challenging English political dominance. The Boer is an artifact here, like native rock paintings, a fascinating South African relic.

In her passages regarding Boer assimilation, Schreiner projects a future in which the terrible conflict of national and ethnic loyalties in South Africa is already over. In the context of the English colonial readership, however, this literary fantasy of the cultural synthesis and absorption of the Boer does not reveal confidence in English cultural dominance but, rather, an anxiety about the outcome of the cultural conflict as the colony moves toward nationhood. It is the active presence of this "subnational" group that leads Schreiner to discount the Boers' political future. In the context of the British readership, on the other hand, South Africa itself is a "subnational" group that Schreiner attempts to differentiate from the "mother country" by describing its different geography, language, and population. By seeing Afrikaner culture as already fated to assimilation, Schreiner can support Afrikaners during the Anglo-Boer War as "South Africans" fighting against an unjust British hegemony.

Schreiner's vision of South Africa as an autonomous nation is really more anti-imperialistic than nationalistic. As she wrote to Edward Carpenter in 1899:

> It is a strange, strange thing Edward, to see a young nation waking up to the consciousness of its life and individuality. Chamberlain and the Capitalist may fight us and if All England joins solid behind them they may crush us. But it will be only for a time. We will rise again. . . . War means the ultimate severance of this country from England, but nothing can stop our ultimate freedom and growth.[80]

In the face of increasing British aggression, Schreiner's criticism of Afrikaner cultural isolation and her patronizing caricatures of Afrikaners in her fiction give way to her passionate identification with the Boer cause. In her story "Eighteen Ninety-Nine," the Boer women characters are not ludicrous Tant' Sannie figures but are dignified caretakers of their threatened culture.[81] The story is a history of the Afrikaner people told through the life of a Boer woman who as a child participated in the "great trek" out of the British occupied Cape Colony and who as an old woman dies during the Anglo-Boer War in a British concentration camp for women and children. The story uncritically adopts the Boer version of South African history, thereby implicitly shoring up the political mythologies and symbols of Afrikaner nationalism.

At the time of the Anglo-Boer War, Schreiner (herself under house arrest in Hanover) identified strongly with the Boer hostility to British rule and with the women imprisoned in British concentration camps. During this time she came to understand more fully the Afrikaner nationalism she sympathizes with in the story, although she ultimately rejected the racism at the center of the Afrikaner interpretation of South African history.[82] Her own interpretation of racial relations and her treatment of black Africans in her fiction and essays come out of a British racial discourse distinct from Afrikaner racist mythologies.

The Monster and the Martyr: Schreiner's Black South African

The recent attention to Olive Schreiner's writing is primarily the work of feminist scholars who focus on the strong liberal feminism of her novels and essays, on the role she played in the sex debates from the time of the Men and Women's Club in London in the late 1880s, and on her influence on Havelock Ellis, Karl Pearson, and the English male-dominated sexology movement.[83] For these scholars, who would like to claim Schreiner as a champion of women's rights, her writings about race relations are an embarrassment to be excused as a product of her time and of that "other" side of Schreiner's biography, her colonial roots.[84]

The critical tendency when reading Schreiner on race issues has been either to see her positions as failures of liberal ideology or to isolate these writings as separate from and inconsequential to her feminist writings.[85] But, in fact, the issues of racial and sexual oppression were not as separate in Schreiner's writing as some critics would have it. From *Undine,* a blatantly racist novel Schreiner never published, to her later essays arguing for suffrage and employment rights for Blacks, Schreiner struggled with the issues of race alongside the issues of gender. Often her struggles in one area influenced her thoughts on the other.[86]

Schreiner's interest in the connections between sexual and racial oppression and her representation of blacks and mixed-race Africans reflect a white creole sensitivity to definitions of citizenship, taxonomies of difference, and colonial privilege. Schreiner's arguments complicate Vron Ware's assessment that nineteenth-century feminism lacked a liberatory politics that connected the struggle against sexism with that of racist domination in the colonies.[87] Fluent as she is in the discourses of both British feminism and South African "nation-making," Schreiner makes exactly this connection. The result is at times startlingly radical and at others disappointingly limited. Indeed, Schreiner's works provide us with fascinating examples of how turn-of-the-century feminism, liberalism, science, and religion converge to reinforce English colonial paternalism and to create a powerful mythology of martyrdom. Schreiner's tendency to martyr her black characters allows her to maintain her position, however uncomfortable it may be, as both an oppressed and a privileged member of the colonial power structure. By identifying with the martyr, Schreiner can object to this structure without materially altering it.

Always at the center of Schreiner's political concerns is the social and economic position of women. Her analysis of racial issues is filtered both through her self-identification as a woman under male domination and through her guilt as a white colonial who benefits materially from the exploitation of black South Africans. Schreiner's writing about race and color in South Africa is at once an expression of nineteenth-century British colonial mentality, supported by the developing racism in British science, and a challenge to it from the perspective of a disenfranchised member of that society. In her fiction Schreiner expresses her plea for native rights in terms of a sympathetic identification with Blacks, which while providing a ground for objecting to colonial domination also leads Schreiner into a galling paternalism that protects colonial ideology. Seeking a bridge between Whites and Blacks in her writing, Schreiner aligns Blacks with women, permitting her to examine the similarities between racism and sexism; the conflation of the two in her work, however, ultimately supports a colonial rhetoric that devalues potential violent rebellion.

In most of her fiction and in *Woman and Labour,* Schreiner's black characters are women. Both Rebekah and Lyndall come to an early understanding of the problems of power relations by developing a sympathy for the black women servants of their households. Rebekah, who as an adult is grieved by her own husband's philandering, recalls her first sympathetic acknowledgment of the humanity of Blacks when as a child she learned simultaneously of polygamy and of the related suicide of a black woman servant and her two children. As she tells the story to her sons:

> When she couldn't bear it any more, she took her two little children and climbed the mountain to the very top where the precipice stands so high. And when she came to the place where it curves out, she tied her two children under her arms and jumped down. . . . Your grandfather and all the men went up, and there they found her . . . with the two children tied to her, quite dead. (*MM,* p. 416)

The adult Rebekah's identification with this woman is based on a shared position of female subjection and powerlessness in marriage. Significantly, this death is not the result of colonialism or of white exploitation but of indigenous marriage practices that, Rebekah realizes, are strikingly similar to her own culture's. Even more stunning, this death is a suicide, in fact a plunge from a precipice, which in American literature signals the "vanishing" of the aboriginal race.[88] Because the white colonialist is not responsible for this death, the white child can grieve the passing. Her one-sided childhood relationship with the servant is based on a sympathetic identification that she believes can somehow alter the situation:

> I sat down on one of the stones. I knew that was where she fell. I thought perhaps if she knew it she would have liked to think that, so many years after she was dead, a little white child came and sat there and felt sorry for her. (*MM,* p. 416)

In this example, Rebekah correlates the power of white men over white women with that of black men over black women. She tells this story, however, in the context of teaching her sons about white domination of black South Africa and extends her remarks about female oppression to explain racism. Rebekah tells her sons that "even if people aren't like us at all, deep down there is something that joins us together" (*MM*, p. 416), and that "something" for Rebekah is the shared oppression between women and Blacks in the South African colonial system.

As Lyndall in *The Story of an African Farm* struggles to articulate the power relations between men and women, she also ties her questions about sexual relations to those of race relations. Through her bitterness about the entrenched domination of women she confronts the subjugation of Blacks:

> There at the foot of the "kopje" goes a Kaffir; he has nothing on but a blanket; he is a splendid fellow — six feet high, with a magnificent pair of legs. In his leather bag he is going to fetch his rations, and I suppose to kick his wife with his beautiful legs when he gets home. He has a right to; he bought her for two oxen. . . . There is something of the master about him in spite of his blackness and his wool. . . . He is profoundly suggestive. Will his race melt away in the heat of a collision with a higher? Are the men of the future to see his bones only in museums — a vestige of one link that spanned between the dog and the white man? (*SAF*, pp. 227–28)

Because much of Schreiner's later writing on race continues these themes of human evolutionary progress and racial competition (with some modifications along the way), it is safe to read this passage and a similar one spoken by Waldo (*SAF*, 49–50) as examples of Schreiner's unexamined racism. It also expresses her early identification of the oppression of women with the oppression of black Africans as the basis of her argument for liberalized race relations.[89] As is clear from the above passage, however, Schreiner's conflation of racial and sexual domination does not challenge the Victorian hierarchies of race that inevitably placed white races above the black, conceiving in race relations a competition for survival. If for a moment Lyndall can picture the black African as a "master," that image is immediately negated by the language evolution and of social Darwinism. The "melting away" of the aboriginal race, like the "passing" of the Boer, renders their disappearance both natural and inevitable.

As a self-proclaimed freethinker, Schreiner turned from an intensely religious upbringing to what she supposed was the comparatively unprejudiced freedom of scientific thought.[90] Schreiner's novels reflect the Darwinian ideas of competition and natural selection, and her later essays incorporate her readings of Herbert Spencer and of social Darwinism. The complexity and contradictions of Schreiner's positions result in part from her simultaneous commitment to the "purity" of scientific thought, which became increasingly racist in her writing life, and to the moral positions of justice and equality, which found their support in South Africa not in scientific but in religious doctrine. Nevertheless, Schreiner, like many other Victorian thinkers, found in Darwinism the coherence and unity that religion no longer provided them.

Over the last half of the nineteenth century, British science, in which Schreiner and others put their faith, became increasingly racist. As Nancy Stepan argues in *The Idea of Race in Science,* race became a subject for scientific investigation at the end of the eighteenth century as scientists turned to nature to answer the moral questions raised by imperialism and slavery.[91] Prior to the emancipation of 1834, the British abolition movement had been bolstered both by pressures brought about by shifting economic needs and by three decades of racial study that emphasized the contiguities of the races.[92] But by the 1850s and 1860s the prevailing scientific community was shifting from a religiously based monogenist theory, which regarded racial differences as varieties within one human family that descended from one pair, to a polygenist theory, which held that racial varieties represented distinct species of humankind. While rejecting the seemingly dated creationism of the Judeo-Christian tradition, scientists found the Aristotelian chain-of-being model helpful in expressing the great mental and physical differences they increasingly found between the light and dark races. For many, this racial theory solved the uncomfortable question of the relation of Homo sapiens to the primates. While there were differences of scientific opinion as to whether "the African" was a separate species filling the gap between the ape and "the European," it was generally accepted that those of darker races ranked lower on a graded scale of the human races than did the European races.[93] Robert Knox's *Races of Men* (1850), which offered a theory of race explaining why the British were inevitably a conquering people, became increasingly influential over the years. Whatever one may think morally about colonialism, he argued, destruction is the destiny of the darker races.[94] This is the theoretical environment of Schreiner's contemporaries, many of whom maintained membership in both scientific and governmental organizations.[95]

The struggle for Schreiner and for other Victorian thinkers caught between religion, science, and politics was to determine the roles of society, ethics, and morality in a world that apparently was governed by natural selection and intense amoral competition.[96] Schreiner's essays regarding the relations between the races can be read through this debate about the responsibility of the socially powerful to those who are politically disfavored and in need of the help of liberal social policy in order to thrive. Whereas in *Woman and Labour* Schreiner challenges the ideology of difference between the sexes (*WL*, p. 182) and therefore demands political and economic equality for women, she vehemently asserts difference between the European and African races in *Thoughts on South Africa*. Her liberal plea for justice for the black races challenges colonial policy yet rests on the evolutionary science of her time and on the paternalism of English imperialism. In "The Problem of Slavery," written in 1892, Schreiner examines the racial varieties in South Africa, and, in light of the growing tensions between the English and the Afrikaners, she draws the disparate white society together with her racial concern about the dark "other" whom she presents in contradictory terms as both dangerous and powerless.

By portraying black Africans as culturally unsophisticated, as children compared with those of European descent, Schreiner can appeal to the English missionary zeal for "bettering" the indigenous peoples. In "The Problem of Slavery," the "Hottentot" are thus "our little Tottie[s]," "the eternal children of the human race," and the "[Bushmen] resemble, not so much a race of children as a race caught in the very act of evolving into human form" ("PS," pp. 115, 107). The phrase "caught in the very act" suggests something almost criminal or threatening in this assumed process of racial evolution. The political relationship Schreiner urges from this description is far from radical: "When we have dealt with the dark man for long years with justice and mercy and taught him all we know, we shall perhaps be able to look deep into each other's eyes and smile: as parent and child."[97]

Schreiner's attitude to the misnamed Bantus, on the other hand, is more respectful, if more cautious. In "The Problem of Slavery" she compares them to the Saxons before the introduction of Christianity ("PS," p. 112), and in *From Man to Man* she compares them to the Britons at the time of the Roman Conquest (*MM*, p. 411). Because the late nineteenth-century ideology of social evolution viewed the Roman, Saxon, and Norman conquests of Britain as historically and culturally beneficial, the conquest of South Africa is implicitly romanticized and justified by this comparison. The long allegory of the "White-Faced" people Rebekah tells her sons in *From Man to Man* does not challenge the idea of difference but rather maintains the power relations between the light and dark races. She creates an imaginary race from another planet whose skin is absolutely white as compared with the narrator's "tinted" white skin. This alien race is both lighter in color and more advanced culturally and scientifically, "They called us the Inferior races. Perhaps we were" (*MM,* p. 400). Schreiner's purpose here is to create an imaginary situation through which her white readers can sympathetically identify with Blacks. Schreiner does not ask her readers to challenge the terms upon which white domination of black Africans is based but to sympathize with and pity those who are dominated. In the allegory that Rebekah tells her sons, the earthlings who survive do not fight the invaders but work for them and begin to learn their skills. Schreiner's plea, then, is a fairly conventional missionary opposition to colonial barbarism. However, in her essay "The Englishman" the threat that lurks behind the missionary offer of protection and sympathy is striking:

> If it be suggested to us that the Natives of the land are ignorant, we have the reply to make that we are here to teach them all we know if they will learn — if they will not, they must fall.... We are here to endeavour to raise them as far as it is possible; we are determined to make them a seed-ground in which to sow all that is greatest and best in ourselves. ("TE," p. 361)

The black native is seen here as a *tabula rasa,* an as yet unploughed seed ground that, in their generosity, liberal colonials will cultivate. The added phrase "if they will not, they must fall" articulates both the determinism of current theories of social evolution and the violence implicit in colonial rule.

Conversely, implicit in Schreiner's call for black rights, and later for black suffrage,[98] is a threat to the British and Afrikaner colonial "master." The black South African in Schreiner's writing is a complex figure, at once piteously weak and dangerously powerful. As a woman Schreiner identifies with black Africans, but as a white creole whose life in South Africa depends on the system of white rule, she finds the black majority frightening. Seeking to reconcile this conflict, Schreiner creates the complex figure of the martyr, which recurs throughout her fiction and essays.

The Black Martyr

In *From Man to Man,* it is the story of yet another martyred black woman's suicide that allows seven-year-old Rebekah to pull down the wall she, imagining herself a little Queen Victoria, constructed between the Whites and Blacks:

> I always played that I was Queen Victoria and that all Africa belonged to me, and I could do whatever I liked. It always puzzled me ... what I should do with the black people; I did not like to kill them, because I could not hurt anything, and yet I could not have them near me. At last I made a plan. I made believe I built a high wall right across Africa and put all the black

people on the other side, and said, "Stay there, and, the day you put one foot over, you [*sic*] heads will be cut off."

I was very pleased when I made this plan. I used to walk up and down and make believe there were no black people in South Africa; I had it all to myself. (*MM*, pp. 414–15)

A short time after she creates this colonialist fantasy, the child Rebekah hears a story that remains with her into adulthood. The black woman martyr Schreiner creates in this story allows the little white girl growing up during the "Kaffir wars" to feel not only pity but safety as well:

The white men had their cannon and all their soldiers on the top of a hill, and the Kaffirs came out below from the bush; there were hundreds of them; they had hardly any clothes or guns, only assagais, and they came on naked up the slope; but before them walked a young Kaffir woman. Her arms were full of assagais. As the men threw their assagais she gave them new ones; she called on them to come on and not to be afraid to die. She walked up and down before the front row, and called on them to come on. The guns fired and the dead lay in heaps. When she got close up to the mouth of the cannon she was blown away too with the others. (*MM*, p. 415)

This story romanticizes the heroism of the black warrior while effectively rendering such rebellion hopeless and misguided. When Jane Marcus comments that Schreiner's writing, particularly her allegories, are "more evolutionary than revolutionary," she is noting Schreiner's perception of political change as visionary rather than imminent.[99] Both the Christian doctrine on which Schreiner was raised and Mahatma Gandhi's *satyagraha* movement of passive resistance in South Africa provided Schreiner with images of the hero who chooses martyrdom over violence.[100] In both cases, however, the revolution is a potentiality for the future, achieved without physical harm to those currently in power.[101]

As Schreiner wrote in a letter in 1912 concerning the militant suffragettes: "Personally I prefer the martyr to the warrior — but I admire the warrior too."[102] And yet, although she reluctantly came to accept suffragette militancy and to recognize the need for violence in some revolutionary movements, she never suggested support for black insurrection.[103] Schreiner's mixed feelings about the warrior bespeak both her investment in the colonial regime and her guilt as a liberal colonist regarding the use of force and the abuse of power that make her life in South Africa possible. By valorizing and identifying with the martyr, Schreiner can at once defuse the insurgent violence that threatens her as a colonist, disengage herself from the violence inherent in colonial rule, and align herself with the oppressed and marginalized. In this way she expresses her own frustration as a woman under patriarchy and relieves her guilt as a white colonist in South Africa.

Schreiner's complex political position allows her to reveal fundamental contradictions of colonial ideology, although her conclusions are often more tentative than her questions would suggest. As a Creole who defies colonialist national identity and claims a new classification of English South Africa, Schreiner repeatedly challenges colonialist binarisms of race and gender by creating androgynous and mixed-race figures and struggling with what they might mean. In her essay "The Problem of Slavery" Schreiner explores a merging of the light and dark races but imagines this merging as hypothetical rather than material. By setting this scene in the historical context of African slavery prior to the British outlawing of slavery in 1834, Schreiner can more easily explore her simultaneous identification with both the white master (the English) and the black slave (the African):

> There are times to-day, riding across the plains in the direction of Hottentots Holland, when the vision of these [slaves] creeping across the veld in search of freedom comes suddenly to one; and a curious feeling rises. We are not in that band that rides booted and spurred across the plain, looking out to right and left and talking loud. We are in the little group cowering behind the milk bushes; we are looking out with furtive, bloodshot eyes, to see how the masters ride! We — we — are there; — we are no more conscious of our identity with the dominant race. Over a million years of diverse evolution white man clasps dark again — and we are one, as we cower behind the bushes; the black and the white. ("PS," p. 120)

In this nonthreatening imaginative context Schreiner has been able to shift her identification from "we" the masters to "we" the slaves, a rare if not unique move in white colonial writing. Schreiner's identification with Blacks here, however, is primarily a dissociation from white rule, and she does not even hypothetically create a black figure beyond the terms of that domination. Neither does this merging of black with white improve the condition of the slave even in this scenario. So highly charged is this identification for Schreiner that this racial "merging" of her white colonial self with the black other is imagined only in a historical moment of her own creation rather than in her present time.

The "Half-Caste" Monster

While this figure of the impotent or finally martyred Black might comfort the white colonist into the *noblesse oblige* of the secure ruler, Schreiner recognizes that the real nightmare that haunts the white ruling class is not the Black who can be "contained" in this kind of imaginative sympathy but the physical merging of the so-called European and African races. This actuality is the open secret of white society and raises excruciatingly uncomfortable questions about claims of white superiority, sexual propriety, and moral virtue. While Schreiner's conflation of race and gender issues in her black female characters allows for her sympathetic identification and for her liberalism, it is important to note that this conflation of the female and the black African was already a powerful theme in Anglo-European art, science, and pornography. As Sander Gilman illustrates, throughout the nineteenth and into the twentieth century the black African was sexualized and feminized in art and medical science.[104] While this obsession about the sexuality of the black woman served to support the theories of African physical and rational primitivism and to justify the subordination of this metaphorically female race, it also revealed the white male sexual attraction for the black female, an attraction that threatened the colonial project. The possibility or likelihood of interracial sexuality was denied by the British scientific community, which explained and reiterated the "natural" antipathy between the races and the disastrous results of "dysgenesic" crosses.[105] But while in 1905 Schreiner's intellectual partner Havelock Ellis was reasserting that white men were repulsed by black women because of a natural hierarchy of racial beauty,[106] Olive Schreiner, living in the South African colony, could not ignore the presence of the offspring of such "impossible" unions. Schreiner's interest in the "half-caste" confronts such colonial hypocrisies and provides us with an excellent example of the relationship between Schreiner's feminism and her theories on race. It is enlightening, for instance, to compare Schreiner's creation of androgynous characters in her essays, stories, and novels that focus on "the woman question" with the characters of mixed race who appear when she addresses race issues.

Throughout her writing, Schreiner challenges the "separate-spheres" ideology that justified economic and political inequality between the sexes. Schreiner repeatedly creates figures who merge these spheres: the "virile woman" of *Woman and Labour* (*WL*, p. 67); the fetishized statue of Hercules cradling an infant in *From Man to Man* (*MM*, p. 455); Gregory Rose, who finds his "womanhood" and maturity when, cross-dressed as a "sister-of-mercy," he nurses Lyndall to her death (*SAF*, pp. 246, 264ff.); and Rebekah, who, accused of being "born with mannish ways" (*MM*, p. 131), becomes her own savior by dreaming herself both man and woman.[107] In Schreiner's socialist/spiritual allegory "The Sunlight Lay across My Bed," the narrator leaves the earthly hell where inequality and abuse of power reign and enters a multilevel heaven, where in the highest level resides Schreiner's androgynous ideal:

> Whether it were man or woman I could not tell; for partly it seemed the figure of a woman, but its limbs were the mighty limbs of a man. I asked God whether it was man or woman.
>
> God said, "In the least Heaven sex reigns supreme; in the higher it is not noticed; but in the highest it does not exist."[108]

This confounding of physical categories is similar to the challenge suggested by a growing mixed-race population to the foundations of the colonial, political, and social structures of South Africa. In the colonial context, the very existence of the "half-caste" is almost unspeakable for s/he represents a supposedly impossible contiguity between the races. Not only do sexual relations between the races challenge the imagined gulf between the white and black "species" that justified British and Afrikaner dominance, but the children of such relations immediately problematize the system of racial identity upon which the colonial society is based. Surprisingly, such figures are as repulsive to Schreiner as the androgynous characters are attractive. The "half-caste" is a frightening physical reality, not a utopian ideal of mediation and resolution. Her challenge to the colonial structure goes only so far as to admit but not to glorify the offspring of the two races, whom she sees as further evidence of white male aggression.[109]

Schreiner devotes the majority of her essay "The Problem of Slavery" to the growing issue of the "half-caste" population in South Africa. Her fascination with and aversion to those of mixed racial background focus on what she sees as their placelessness in society. In this view, the "half-caste" is rejected by both races and is not allowed a self-identity. Schreiner cites the aphorisms of both races that disinherit the "half-caste": "Who the white man is we know; and who we are we know, . . . but what are you? Half-monkey whom no one can believe!" ("PS," p. 124). Schreiner, whose national identity is at the center of her literary subjectivity, chooses to describe the "half-caste" as metaphorically without a "nationality" himself, and therefore as one "at war within his own individuality" ("PS," p. 127).

Although Schreiner's acknowledgment of the "half-caste" does challenge the colonial insistence on the vast gulf between the races, ultimately she does not see those of mixed racial background as representing a possible solution to the injustice of color prejudices and discrimination. Her fantasies of androgynous figures and her belief that the social merging of the sexes would be a solution to sex discrimination do not extend to a parallel fantasy for racial mixing, physical or social. Her argument for English and Boer responsibility for the "half-caste" ("He is here, our own; we have made him; . . . [he] is our own open self-inflicted wound" ["PS," p. 141]) becomes instead an emphatic denouncement of miscegenation. Whereas much of Schreiner's writing about black South Africans reveals a condescension and liberalism based on an underlying sense of English cultural and racial superiority, her presentation of the "half-caste" offers us a glimpse of the great fear and sense of imminent danger the black African inspires in the colonialist.

Despite Schreiner's scathing criticism of the British and white South African social structure, her investment in it as a white creole South African is clear from the close attention she gives to the supposed "antisociality" of "half-castes." Schreiner locates the etiology of this antisociality in the necessarily antisocial sexuality of their origins, in their social marginality, and in their genetic makeup. Although Schreiner uses these contradictory approaches in order to remove "blame" from these unfortunate outcasts, their plight as completely marginalized people intrigues her. An interesting parallel to Schreiner's inconsistent jockeying between psychosocial and biological determinants of "half-caste" behavior can be seen in the contemporaneous explanations of homosexuality in the works of Richard Krafft-Ebing, Havelock Ellis, and Edward Carpenter, works that Schreiner was sure to have read.[110] In the interest of what she believes is fair and disinterested scholarship Schreiner offers the then current biological arguments that attributed the "half-caste's" supposed predisposition to crime and prostitution to the disastrous results of interracial sexuality. She presents zoological data that shows that the crossing of two varieties of the same species can result in offspring that revert to characteristics of an original parent stock from which both varieties have descended. According to this argument, the supposed criminality of the "half-caste" is a trait of the parent stock from which both the Englishman and the Zulu descended, a less developed species predating the evolutionary divergence of black and white, which Schreiner believes existed long before the introduction of language ("PS," 133–34). Her considerations of the possible positive contributions of "primitive blood" — for instance, "less developed nervous system . . . and heavier animality, . . . an increase of hardihood and vitality, and greater staying power" — contribute little to a reevaluation of the self-serving European interpretation of racial difference ("PS," p. 144).

Although she is attracted by such essentially racist evolutionary theories, Schreiner ultimately finds psychosocial explanations more enlightening. Schreiner thus argues that science alone cannot explain that which most frightens white people about this renegade "race"; rather the explanation has more to do with the "half-caste" being ostracized from birth and growing up "raceless" and traditionless:

> The cowardice, inveracity, and absence of self-respect and self-restraint with which he is accredited, are exactly those qualities which ostracism, and lack of organic unity with the body social, must always tend to cultivate. ("PS," p. 132)

Schreiner's portrayal of the "half-caste" as tragic and violent is not unique. Vernon February traces this recurring image of the "half-caste" and later the "colored" throughout South African literature and attributes it to the emergent white South African nationalism (particularly, but not solely, to the development of Afrikanderdom).[111] If the "half-caste" is "nationless," like "the Jew," he is so in order that the white Creole might claim South African national identity. The issue of belonging and the threat of "homelessness" are present in all of Schreiner's writing. But whereas she has a great deal of sympathy for her homeless female characters Lyndall and Bertie, she projects the anxiety she herself experiences as a lifelong wanderer between countries onto the "half-caste" and "the Jew." It is in comparison with these created images of complete ostracism that Schreiner can center herself as a "belonging" member of the white settler society.

Schreiner's concern with "antisociality" reveals a measure of her acceptance of and investment in the standing social order she criticizes. Far from applauding antisocial behavior for its resistance to an unjust political hegemony, Schreiner views the "half-caste" as a "rogue elephant" who, "severed from our social herds,...does, and must, constitute an element of social danger" ("PS," p. 132). The threat of the dark "other" is again implicit, and yet rather than envisioning that danger fully, Schreiner chooses instead to check it with the specter of European military dominance. The analogy concludes once again, not with the havoc of a toppled regime, but with the martyred rebel: "Worn out with his own temper, he is killed by the creatures he attacks" ("PS," p. 132).

Schreiner concludes the essay with what she sees as a peculiarly South African social commandment: *"Keep your breeds pure!"* ("PS," p. 146). On the surface, this italicized edict appears to be no more than another articulation of Anglo-Saxon hysteria about "racial purity," which in the late nineteenth century was increasingly evident in the context of both developing colonial rule and expanding immigration of Eastern Europeans to England. Schreiner's feminism and her critique of colonial policy, however, inform this conclusion as much as her fear as a member of the white minority. Her prohibition of interracial sexual relations rests on a recognition that such unions in the colonial context were usually not mutual and free but were an enactment of white male dominance. Against the myth of the black seductress, Schreiner asserts that the "half-caste"

> has originated in almost all cases, not from the union of average individuals of the two races uniting under average conditions, but is the result of a sexual union between the most helpless and enslaved females of the dark race and the most recklessly dominant males of the white. ("PS," p. 126)

Schreiner's "commandment" finds its source partly in the English "radical chastity" movement that sought to "control" male sexuality. In fact, the fifth and final obligation on the pledge cards and pamphlets issued by the White Cross Army to men in the 1880s and 1890s was "Keep THYSELF pure."[112] Schreiner's edict, then, does not merely support the patriarchal colonial regime but challenges it as well.

In the novel *From Man to Man,* an exploration of the politics of sexuality and power, Rebekah's husband's liaison with the black woman servant is Schreiner's fictional acknowledgment of the mundane and domestic commonness of white male sexual power in colonial society.[113] Rebekah's husband, Frank, an Englishman who came to Cape Town for the business opportunities, thrives on adulterous relationships, including his short visits to the servants' quarters late at night. In the face of the servant's bravado, Rebekah realizes that, like herself, the black woman is pregnant by Frank. While Rebekah has some financial security outside of her marriage, the servant woman has none and is powerless in her relationship with Frank, whose sexual use of her is an expression of both white and male dominance. The "half-caste" child is an inconvenience to Frank, and he accepts no responsibility for her. Rebekah takes the child in when she is born and raises her with her own four boys, showing the girl tenderness but insisting that she call her "Mistress," not "Mother." How Rebekah comes to claim the child is unclear in the novel although that silence suggests the mother's own disregard for her.

Little Sartje is at once a sexualized figure — conceived illicitly and raised as the only girl with Rebekah's four sons — and a victimized one, an abandoned black child, a conspicuous curiosity in the white family. Like the famous African young woman of the same name, Saartjie Baartman, who was displayed in London as the "Hottentot Venus" from 1810 until her death in 1815 — and whose sexual parts are still on display in Paris[114] — little Sartje is a symbol of white men's obsession with black women and the sexual as well as the racial imbalance upon which colonial life is grounded.

Schreiner's interest in sexual relations is partly responsible for the differences in her portrayals of black women and black men. In her first novel, *Undine,* a black servant who dresses, talks, and carries himself like a wealthy white man is a particularly threatening figure to the white heroine (*U,* pp. 286–87, 350–51). As the servant of Albert Blair, the man Undine loves, this "swell" is the horrifying black alter-ego of the white gentleman. Whereas in this first novel the racial alterity represented by the "swell" is unsettling and frightening to Undine, in *From Man to Man* the black woman servant who serves as the racial foil to Rebekah is merely pitiful. The differences in the portrayals of these two black servants are functions of Schreiner's concerns with sexual power and the racist stereotypes of black men and black women working in Schreiner's time as well as in our own.[115] Consequently, the few black male characters in her fiction, like the man Lyndall watches walking home with his rations, are sexually threatening, while the black female characters, as counterparts to these men, are sexual victims of both white and black men. Schreiner's black characters are either dangerous, like Albert's servant or the hypothetical "half-caste," or completely powerless, like little Sartje. These gendered images of black Africans, as potentially violent or sexual, are the legacy of a racial discourse firmly ingrained in the English and colonial cultures of the late nineteenth century.

These last two chapters have examined the way a creole woman, suspicious of British imperialism yet strongly identified with English culture, defines nationhood and citizenship at the height of British colonialism in Africa. The contradictions of her arguments point up the constantly changing political terrain and her own changing strategies to have her opinions heard. If Schreiner indulges in offensive stereotypes of Afrikaners or Afrikaans in the 1880s, by the late 1890s her political commitment to a united South Africa makes such representations patently ethnocentric and nonstrategic. It is not clear if Schreiner herself ever recognized or regretted her more blatantly racist or anti-Semitic portrayals, and, indeed, these often serve her own political strategy of portraying competing national subgroups as nonthreatening and therefore deserving of governmental protection. These intriguing and disturbing portrayals of the South African people, languages, and landscape tell us much about the psychological and political position of the South African creole woman and her incentives to expand the vocabulary available to her. That vocabulary would change dramatically after World War II. The next part, then, examines the writings of Jean Rhys, another white creole woman for whom national identity, race, and English culture are also vexed questions.

Part II
White Creole Consciousness and
Decolonization

3 / "Great Mistake to Go by Looks"

Jean Rhys, the Caribbean Creole, and Cultural Colonialism

*So between you I often wonder who I am and where is my country and where do
I belong and why was I ever born at all.*   —Jean Rhys, Wide Sargasso Sea

*First it must be bleached, that is to say, its own colour must be taken out of it—
and then it must be dyed, that is to say, another colour must be imposed on it.
(Educated hair . . .)*   —Jean Rhys, Good Morning, Midnight

The Variously Positioned Native

In her biographies and in the criticism of her work, Jean Rhys is identified as a "white Creole," one who dates her family to the slaveholding
European plantocracy of the Caribbean. The need for the modifying racial
marker "white" reveals an important shift in colonial semantics between
Olive Schreiner's time and the present. While I will discuss that shift more
specifically in the chapter on Michelle Cliff, suffice it to note here that
during the half-century that Rhys wrote, the term "Creole," by which she
identified herself, came to connote less an attachment to Europe than an
active identification with indigenous cultural forms. First for her West Indian stories and then for what was to become the novel *Wide Sargasso Sea*,
Jean Rhys considered the title *Creole* and then finally discarded it because
it no longer signified merely the white, native West Indian. "Creole" had
also come to define the "colored" native of mixed racial origin and, more
generally, the West Indian culture itself, which was gaining a self-conscious
identification separate from the European culture of the colonials.[1]

While the changes in the meaning of "Creole" rendered the word too ambiguous to serve Rhys as a title (besides carrying fairly hackneyed, even pornographic, suggestions from its use in popular historical romances), this very shift in meaning can serve as a template for an analysis of Rhys's fiction. The changing vocabulary used to define colonial identities reflects changing relationships between races, classes, and nations. Rhys's fiction calls particular attention to the social and psychological disruptions wrought by colonialism and, more specifically, by its dismantling. Her focus on the experiences and conditions of white Caribbeans provides an early analysis of white racism and creole identification, an analysis that is only now being more fully explored and articulated. It is perhaps inevitable that in her attempt to understand gender relations through the lens of colonialist economics and to analyze the painful effects of colonialism and decolonization through the experience of white Caribbeans, Rhys at times elides those conditions and experiences particular to black Caribbeans. The difficulties or ambivalences in her work, like those in Schreiner's, reveal the complicated status of what Benita Parry calls the "variously positioned native."[2] By placing Rhys's work in the context of post–World War II colonial theory, I mean to underscore her theoretical contribution to contemporary postcolonial theory and culture.

A reading of Jean Rhys's work benefits from the recent attention of colonial discourse theorists to the complexity of the relationship between colonialists and indigenous peoples. Homi Bhabha and Gayatri Spivak resist the simple argument that there is a monolithic colonial discourse that is capable of creating "the native as a fixed, unified object of colonialist knowledge."[3] Both of these critics seek to reveal the contradictions inherent in imperialist representations of the "other." Like them, Rhys wants to emphasize the relationship between the colonizer and the colonized and the complexity of racial, cultural, and national identity. However, whereas Bhabha and Spivak primarily raise questions about the ambivalence of the black or Indian native in colonial and neocolonial society, Rhys explores what Parry calls the "variousness" of the creole position in its other racial varieties as well: the white native who lives in a cultural space between the European and black Caribbean societies and the native of mixed racial ancestry living in the islands and in England after World War II.

In the first chapters of this book I examined how Olive Schreiner's writing registers the conflicts inherent in her status as a South African colonial woman at the turn of the century. As we have seen, Schreiner struggled in her writing to define a space for the native colonial who, while culturally and politically tied to England, also revised the English colonial portrayals of Africa and Africans in important ways. There is no question in Schreiner's thinking, however, regarding this native colonial's *racial* location; while she might wonder about a possible Jewish ancestor, her perspective throughout is unambiguously that of a white, English-speaking South African. Jean Rhys, on the other hand, while racially identified throughout her autobiographical writing with Whites, indicates that that identification is, as we shall see, in a state of change and flux. Because Rhys is a fourth-generation West Indian on her mother's side, her identity as a white woman necessarily fraught with the tensions and doubts surrounding any such claims of "racial purity." White plantation owners' sexual abuses of black slave women, as well as more consensual sexual relations between Whites, Blacks, and "Coloreds" after emancipation, make the knowledge of race mixture an open secret among Whites. Rhys, therefore, had reason to wonder about her own slave-owner great-grandfather's wife who, family myth had it, was supposedly Spanish.[4] By claiming her position as a West Indian white woman, Rhys occupies a political space significantly different from that of both black West Indians and white Britishers. Whereas Schreiner's struggle is to present herself (especially in her political essays) as a coherent subject ready to engage with the male intelligentsia of London, Rhys consciously presents a more complicated subjectivity of the creole woman whose relationship with the "mother country" is decidedly more ambivalent.

Jean Rhys was born on the Caribbean island of Dominica in 1890 and was named Ella Gwendolen Rees Williams. Her pen name, made up of her middle name (which had been her father's first name), Rees (or Rhys), and her first husband's first name, Jean (Lenglet), is how she came to be known. Her mother's grandfather arrived in the West Indies from Scotland at the end of the eighteenth century. Rhys wrote of her own grandfather in her autobiography, "He died before the Emancipation Act was passed, and as he was a slave owner the Lockharts, even in my day, were never very popular. That's putting it mildly."[5] Comparing all available biographical studies on Rhys's family, Teresa O'Connor in her book on Rhys's life and work notes that Rhys's grandfather died in 1837, after the Emancipation Act, and that his estate was burned in 1844 by ex-slaves who feared a return to slavery.[6] Rhys's mother was born in Dominica, and Rhys's father, a less-favored second son of a clergyman, came from Wales as a young man. O'Connor's biography also integrates the unpublished journal exercise books Rhys kept in the 1930s.[7] In this journal Rhys wrote about her difficult relationship with Blacks as a white daughter of an erstwhile slave-owning family:

> I was curious about black people. They stimulated me and I felt akin to them. It added to my sadness that I couldn't help but realise that they didn't really like or trust white people. White cockroaches they called us behind our backs. (Cockroach again.) One could hardly blame them. I would feel sick with shame at some of the stories I heard of the slave days told casually even jocularly. The ferocious punishments the salt kept ready to rub into the wounds etc etc. I became an ardent socialist and champion of the down-trodden, argued, insisted of giving my opinion, was generally insufferable. Yet all the time knowing that there was another side to it. Sometimes being proud of my great grandfather, the estate, the good old days, etc. . . . Sometimes I'd look at his picture and think with pride, He was goodlooking anyway. Perhaps he wasn't entirely ignoble. Having absolute power over a people needn't make a man a brute. Might make him noble in a way. No — no use. My great Grandfather and his beautiful Spanish wife. Spanish? I wonder.
>
> I thought a lot about them. But the end of my thought was always revolt, a sick revolt and I longed to be identified once and for all with the others' side which of course was impossible. I couldn't change the colour of my skin.[8]

Her ambivalent assessment of her family's responsibility for the atrocities of slavery and of the potential glamour or corruption inherent in power deny her an easy identification with either Whites or Blacks. In most of her writing, she focuses less on the disadvantaged position of Blacks (as Schreiner did in her portrayals) than on her *own* exclusion, alienation, and envy as a white Creole living among Blacks.

That feeling of alienation was to stay with Rhys her entire life. She left home in 1907 for schooling and dramatic training in London. Likewise, all her siblings left the island: one brother went to India and Africa; a sister went to St. Lucia; her mother and another brother eventually went to England. David Plante attributes this migration to "the curious family situation of British colonials,"[9] a family situation, I will later argue, that allowed Rhys to turn her longing for family into a critique similar to Schreiner's of the ways the rhetoric of family serves political purposes. When Rhys's father died shortly after her arrival in England, she became an itinerant chorus girl and began her lifelong wandering throughout England and Europe. With her first husband she moved to Paris, where she met Ford Madox Ford, who, as the publisher of the *Transatlantic Review,* published Rhys's story "Vienne." As her editor, Ford wrote the preface and suggested the title of Rhys's first book of short stories, *The Left Bank,* and introduced her to the Paris circle of writers and artists.[10] However, these literary connections in Paris were not strong ones, and Rhys was always socially marginal, perhaps, as Coral Ann Howells suggests, as "a deliberately chosen position of resistance against what she saw as an Anglo-American fantasy about European cosmopolitan living."[11] Mary Lou Emery addresses the homelessness of Rhys's characters to underscore Rhys's own marginality and vulnerability in relation to even the other expatriate women writers of the Left Bank in the 1920s.[12]

Over the years Rhys continued to wander from city to city and to write. By 1939 she had published one book of short stories, *The Left Bank* (1927), and four novels: *Quartet* (1929), *After Leaving Mr. McKenzie* (1931), *Voyage in the Dark* (1934), and *Good Morning, Midnight* (1939). In 1936 she made her only return trip to Dominica, where she spent a short time and was, apparently, disappointed by it after her long absence. After World War II, Rhys began work on her last novel, *Wide Sargasso Sea.* During these years Rhys lived in a cottage in Cornwall with her second husband. For many years she drank heavily and published nothing. She remained removed from the literary world of London, and, until 1957 and the BBC adaptation of *Good Morning, Midnight,* many thought she was dead. Following the publication of *Wide Sargasso Sea* in 1966, Rhys published two more books of short stories, *Tigers Are Better Looking* (1968) and *Sleep It Off, Lady* (1974), and began her autobiography, *Smile Please.* The autobiography was not finished and was published posthumously in 1979, the year of her death.

Although Rhys occupies a similar position to Schreiner as a native-born, white, colonial woman, the differences between their individual biographical situations, geographical locations, and historical moments were considerable, and Rhys's particular situation made it possible, indeed necessary, for her to recognize and focus on the split subjectivity of the white, Caribbean, creole woman. Rhys's position as a colonial settler differs from Schreiner's in part because of the length of time her mother's family had been in the West Indies. Schreiner self-consciously calls herself a "South African" where others identify her politically as English; Rhys's self-identification as a West Indian seems less politically motivated, though no less ambivalent. And most importantly, Schreiner's representations of South Africa occur at the height of British imperialism in Africa while Rhys's representations of the Caribbean span the years of worldwide nationalist struggles for colonial independence.

It is also striking that the years of Rhys's publishing silence coincide with African and Caribbean nationalist movements and independence. While

Rhys did not write directly about these political changes, we can see a development in her own analysis of colonialism from her earlier to her later fiction. Whereas Rhys had earlier envisioned a collection of notes and anecdotes about Dominica that could be valuable for its unique perspective, by the 1960s her treatment was more ambitious, providing a political reading of colonialism and colonial culture. The unconscious ambivalences I will discuss in her earlier fiction become in *Wide Sargasso Sea* a focused and inspired analysis. Because her first four novels, published prior to World War II, take place in Europe and because her medium is fiction, critics have been slow to recognize Rhys as an important theorist of colonial relations.

Throughout her fiction Jean Rhys quite consciously complicates the dichotomy between the "colonizer" and the "colonized" by insisting on the fluidity of the categories and of the power relations inscribed in them. Many, particularly non-Caribbean, critics have focused on the individual psychological reasons for Rhys's ambivalence about issues of race and power and have given less attention to the historical and social forces that encouraged Rhys to explore the complexities of the colonial subject. In a summary of the critical responses to Rhys's work, Pierrette Frickey notes that European and American critics generally focus on Rhys's modernist style, her preoccupation with rootlessness, and her attention to feminist issues. Caribbean critics, on the other hand, are absorbed with questions of cultural identification and alienation.[13] Since this overview, however, several important works have succeeded in pulling these two strands of criticism together. Mary Lou Emery's excellent study, *Jean Rhys at "World's End,"* for instance, simultaneously provides colonial and feminist readings of Rhys's stylistic and thematic choices (such as exile, carnival, or possession). Similarly, Coral Ann Howells's book *Jean Rhys* and Judith Kegan Gardiner's close readings of Rhys's short stories in *Rhys, Stead, Lessing, and the Politics of Empathy* successfully complicate the psychoanalytic readings of Rhys and her women characters by attending to the specific historical and colonial context of Rhys's work.

The split in the critical treatment of Rhys's work is indicative of the cultural and political categories upon which literary canons rest. Two years after the novel's publication, Wally Look Lai, a Trinidadian lawyer, was the first West Indian critic to write about *Wide Sargasso Sea* or to claim it as a West Indian novel. His important piece "The Road to Thornfield Hall" laments the fact that while *Wide Sargasso Sea* had been hailed as an English masterpiece, "not a single review of the novel has ever appeared in any West Indian newspaper or periodical," despite the fact that, in his opinion, the novel is "one of the genuine masterpieces of West Indian fiction." With this article Look Lai opens up an important debate about the definition of West Indian fiction, fiction that even to this day must find its publisher and market in England, Europe, or North America. The difficulty for Look Lai is Rhys's early emigration to England and the European setting for her four previous novels. In order to claim her as a West Indian writer, Look Lai argues that the "whole artistic intention" underlying *Wide Sargasso Sea* is radically different from her earlier novels. That is, whereas the earlier novels used "rejected womanhood" as their central theme, *Wide Sargasso Sea* "utilized [it] symbolically to make an artistic statement about West Indian society."[14]

Kenneth Ramchand pursues the questions raised in this article in his book *An Introduction to West Indian Literature.*[15] In his earlier essay "Terrified Consciousness" (1969), Ramchand seems somewhat hesitant to read *Wide Sargasso Sea* as a novel *about* the Caribbean. Although he insists on the social relevance of the text, he maintains that in *Wide Sargasso Sea* "history and place, however accurately evoked, are being used only to lend initial credibility to a mood that establishes itself in the novel as a way of experiencing the world."[16] He does not make nationalistic claims for Rhys's work. On the one hand, he views her quite specifically as a *white* West Indian and compares *Wide Sargasso Sea* to novels by other white West Indian authors, Geoffrey Drayton and Phyllis Shand Allfrey. These novels, according to Ramchand, explore the "terrified consciousness" of the white minority of the Caribbean when the black population "is released into an awareness of its power." On the other hand, he argues for Rhys's "universal" concerns in her exploration of love, fear, and madness. His hesitancy to claim Rhys as a Caribbean writer thus appears to be not only because of her longtime residency in England and Europe but because of her racial status as a white writer.

In *Introduction to West Indian Literature* (1976), however, Ramchand locates himself more explicitly in this debate. As more Caribbean literature was published in the intervening years between Ramchand's two works, the criteria of inclusion and the definition of "West Indian" and of "creole" became more complex. In his book, Ramchand sets himself up in dialogue with the Barbadian poet Edward Brathwaite, who argues:

> White Creoles in the English and French West Indies have separated themselves by too wide a gulf, and have contributed too little culturally as a group, to give credence to the notion that they can, given the present structure,

meaningfully identify or be identified with the spiritual world on this side of the Sargasso Sea.[17]

Positioning himself between Look Lai, who argues that Rhys is a West Indian writer because the Caribbean is more than local color in her novel, and Brathwaite, who correlates indigenous culture with black creole culture and therefore reads Rhys's work as essentially European, Ramchand teases out additional criteria for the difficult category "West Indian literature." Most generally, he claims novels are West Indian "which describe a social world that is recognizably West Indian in a West Indian landscape; and which are written by people who were born or who grew up in the West Indies."[18]

Rhys interests Ramchand as a "test case" because of the ambivalence of her position. Ramchand is astute to note the importance of Rhys's position because she preceded a generation of Caribbean writers who emigrated and wrote fiction about both the countries in which they grew up and the countries in which they wrote and lived. Although he was more tentative in his earlier evaluation when he classified Rhys as a *white* creole writer, in his later study he praises her for her authentic reproduction of Caribbean dialect that "evokes, in a way no didactic account can, the whole system of the West Indies."[19] He now compares her not only to other white West Indian writers but to Wilson Harris and Derek Walcott, and he then goes on to compare the latter two writers' powerful treatments of the Caribbean landscape with Rhys's own work. For Ramchand, Rhys's exilic condition becomes not the proof of her European identity, but another way to claim her as almost prototypically West Indian.[20] He now places Rhys's earlier novel *Voyage in the Dark* with other Caribbean novels of exile and goes so far as to argue that "its critique of English life against the background of a West Indian existence full of warmth, colour and spontaneity brings it very close in temper to the literature of negritude."[21] How close? is a question that challenges the orthodoxies of many identity categories through which we read literature: cultural, racial, sexual, and national.

Although in much of her earlier fiction Rhys is interested in the complicated psychology of the stateless woman, she does not overtly tie the psychological to the historical and political until her later fiction. After *Good Morning, Midnight,* appeared in 1939, Rhys did not publish again until 1966 when she finished *Wide Sargasso Sea.* The war years and the subsequent movement toward the decolonization of Africa and the Caribbean gave rise to a discourse that questioned not only the politics but the *psychology* of colonization. Rhys's later fiction is part of this postwar rethinking of cultural and political relations and part of a new genre of psychohistory and politico-psycho autobiography.

Immediately after the war Jean-Paul Sartre published *Refléxions sur la question juive* (later translated and published as *Anti-Semite and Jew*), which both defined the psychological mechanism of anti-Semitism and described the fixity of assigned racial roles upon which Nazism depended. Sartre introduces the idea of cultural "manichaeism," which theorists of colonialism soon after find useful in their analyses. The anti-Semite, Sartre asserts, sees the world in terms of good and evil, attributing all that is evil to the Jew. The Jew, then, is *created* as an ideological construct by anti-Semitism and is not a fixed or stable reality. This is a crucial argument for the emerging colonial debate. In *Black Skin, White Masks* (1952), Frantz Fanon uses Sartre's work in his important debate with O. Dominique Mannoni's *Prospero and Caliban: The Psychology of Colonialism* (1950). Mannoni seeks to understand colonialism in terms of "two entirely different types of personality and their reactions to each other, in consequence of which the native becomes 'colonized' and the European becomes a colonial."[22]

Mannoni's perspective is an important one: that beyond the pressures of economic expansion, European colonization is also motivated by the European's infantile desire for unlimited power and for a world where there is no other authority. But although Mannoni defines personality as a social rather than a genetic construct, he views the colonial drama as taking place between two *already* constituted personalities: the independent personality of the European and the dependent personality of the Malagasy. According to Mannoni, not all peoples can be colonized—only those who experience the psychological need for dependence.[23] Mannoni's logic leads to the conclusion that "wherever Europeans have founded colonies, ... it can safely be said that their coming was unconsciously expected—even desired—by the future subject peoples."[24]

Frantz Fanon, a black psychoanalyst from Martinique, is also intrigued by the psychological aspects of colonialism, but in sharp contrast to Mannoni he sees the various colonial personalities as *results,* not causes, of the colonial experience. In his powerful response to Mannoni, Fanon argues that the inferiority complex Mannoni attributes to colonized people does not *antedate* colonization, nor is the dependency relationship between the colonized and the colonizer *constitutional.* Rather, that which Mannoni sees as fixed "personalities" are, in Fanon's view, the result of racist and economic exploitation. Following Sartre's argument, Fanon asserts that the feeling of inferiority of the colonized is the correlative to the European's feeling of superiority. Let us have the courage to say it outright: *It is the racist who creates his inferior....* What M. Mannoni has forgotten is that the Malagasy alone no longer exists; he has forgotten that the Malagasy exists *with the European.*[25]

Albert Memmi, a Jewish Tunisian, continues Fanon's arguments in his influential study of colonial roles, *The Colonizer and the Colonized* (1957). From his own position as a colonized Jew in a Muslim country, Memmi explores the process by which the roles of colonizer and colonized are created and maintained and adds the important analysis of *ambivalence* inherent in all colonial positions. Along with Fanon he concludes that the adherence of the colonized to colonialism "is the result of colonization and not its cause. It arises after and not before colonial occupation."[26] This debate about the locus of power in the construction of the colonial subject — a debate continued and currently being refined by critics such as Edward Said, Abdul JanMohamed, Gayatri Spivak, Trinh T. Minh-ha, and Homi Bhabha — calls into question the belief in a coherent and fixed colonial personality.

This analysis of the colonial subject that developed throughout the 1950s was greatly influenced by the Algerian struggle for independence from the French — the first successful armed struggle for independence in Africa in the twentieth century, a victory that led to the independence of colonies throughout Africa and, in part, to the West Indies Federation (1958–62). The Algerian War lasted from 1954 to 1962 and influenced Fanon, Sartre, and Memmi in their philosophical and political debate. Albert Camus's notorious silence between 1945 and 1954, the years just before rebellion, hint at how difficult it often is for writers of the "settler" class, like Camus and Rhys, to confront the problems of their native lands in their fiction — especially prior to a widespread nationalist movement and, more specifically, prior to the development of a nationalist vocabulary (a vocabulary that can, of course, also complicate writing by white creole writers).

Like Rhys, Camus was read as a white European rather than as a colonial writer. Conor Cruise O'Brien looks at Camus's silence in a way that pertains also to Rhys's own silence during these years of African, Asian, and Caribbean decolonization. In *Albert Camus of Europe and Africa,* O'Brien shows how colonial settlers, especially those whose families had lived several generations in the colony, are caught between the colonial myths propagated by their European educations and the realities of the colonial conditions in which they live:

Camus is a stranger on the African shore, and surrounded by people who are strangers in that France of which they are legally supposed to be a part. The splendidly rationalist system of education which molded Camus was propagating, in relation to his own social context, a myth: that of French Algeria.[27]

It was perhaps easier for Sartre, unambiguously a French citizen, and Fanon, a black West Indian, to position themselves politically at this time. Like Camus, however, Rhys was caught in the middle as a white Creole from a family that had lived in the colony for generations. As a first-generation Creole, Olive Schreiner helped contribute to the myth of an "English South Africa" in a way that Camus and Rhys can no longer do in their countries without negating their own mixed cultural experience or overtly proclaiming allegiance to antiliberation imperial policies and practices. There is also no vocabulary for such writers to consciously express their ambivalent loyalties and "terrified consciousness" as their class loses political power. In his Nobel Prize speech in 1957, Camus finally decides, "I believe in justice, but I will defend my mother before justice."[28] A generation later, Derek Walcott, the recipient of the Nobel Prize for literature in 1993, suggests a new way of thinking about conflicting loyalties and national identity that moves beyond Camus's choice based on racial and national identity,: "I have Dutch, nigger, and English in me, / and either I'm nobody, or I'm a nation."[29]

It is in the context of the analysis of the colonial subject during the 1950s and 1960s that Rhys finds her language and explodes out of a twenty-seven-year publishing silence with most of her "West Indian fiction" — the novel *Wide Sargasso Sea* (1966) and the short stories in *Tigers Are Better Looking* (1968) and *Sleep It Off, Lady* (1976). Although Rhys had read Sartre's plays and novels (*LJR,* 87, 98), there is no evidence that she read *Anti-Semite and Jew* or Fanon's essays. Nevertheless, during these years, nationalist movements, shifts in the economies of European nations, and the lingering effects of World War II began to change not only the political position of the settler classes but the language of the colonial debate itself. Set beside these theorists, Rhys can be read as an important theorist in her own right. Her medium was, indeed, fiction, but that is no reason to overlook the theoretical contribution her writing makes to a deconstruction of colonial binarisms (black/white, English/native, civilized/savage, pure/polluted). As we shall see in the chapter on Michelle Cliff, contemporary theorists of creolism turn to fiction and poetry for the most far-reaching analyses of history and social relations. By focusing on the complex positions of the white

Creole, Rhys adds to the language of racial and national definition; by focusing on women and sexuality, she asks new questions about the meaning
of gender in the economic systems of capitalism and slavery. My analysis of
Rhys's fiction highlights the connections and associations she made regarding race, culture, and gender, connections that anticipated central questions
being raised by current postcolonial theory.

Until Rhys's work, the theoretical debate couches itself in terms that
are strikingly male. Mannoni's colonizer, for instance, is a Prospero, a Crusoe, a male conqueror searching for a "world without men."[30] In Fanon's
writing about race and sexuality in *Black Skin, Whites Masks,* colonizers are
white men; white women appear in the drama of colonial power and sexuality not as Caribbeans but as Europeans encountered "over there." And
Memmi, too, mockingly imagines the colonizer as "a tall man, bronzed by
the sun, wearing Wellington boots, proudly leaning on a shovel," scanning
the distant horizon.[31] But what of the white creole woman? Is she a colonizer? Is she a colonized subject as well? Is she European or Caribbean?
These are the questions and complications Rhys raises in her fiction. Her
portrayal of racial relations and the place of the creole woman is directly
at odds with the belief in a fixed national/racial personality that Mannoni
so clearly defines:

> The colonial's personality is wholly unaffected by that of the native of the
> colony to which he goes; it does not adapt itself, but develops solely in
> accordance with its own inner structure.[32]

In sharp contrast to this view, Rhys examines in her fiction the influence
each culture exerts on the other and the fluidity of racial and cultural
roles. As we shall see, Rhys's explorations provide a groundwork for current writing (fiction and theory) that takes creolism and creole identity for
its theme.

How fluid those roles are in Rhys's fiction is an interesting point of crit-
ical debate. Benita Parry defends Rhys against Gayatri Spivak's charge that
Wide Sargasso Sea sacrifices the native female (Christophine) in the cause
of "the subject-constitution of the European female individualist," much as
Charlotte Brontë did by sacrificing Bertha in *Jane Eyre.* Parry argues that
Spivak's analysis does not recognize Rhys's specific representation of a creole culture "that is dependent on both [the English colonialist and the black
Jamaican] yet singular, or its enunciation of a specific *settler discourse, distinct
from the texts of imperialism.*"[33] This "settler discourse," then, can be seen in
contrast to that of explorers, travelers, or traders, all of whose "exposure"

to native cultures is more limited than that of the white Creole. Rhys's fiction offers a more complicated representation of the intersection of native cultures and the vicissitudes of race and power in the Caribbean.

At issue for all of Rhys's characters is their "social grounding," their struggle to find the camp in which they belong. *Wide Sargasso Sea* opens with the line, "They say when trouble comes close ranks, and so the white people did. But we were not in their ranks." From the start, Antoinette and her family exceed mythological racial categories of colonialism. They spill beyond the confines of white society and are certainly not part of the black society they so recently believed they "owned." Both the period when Rhys wrote *Wide Sargasso Sea* and the period in which she set it were times of great insecurity for white colonials, times when earlier forms of racial exploitation had been abolished and new forms had not yet been institutionalized in law.[34] Writing during the years of decolonization Rhys set her novel between 1834 and 1845 — the years just following the British Emancipation Act, which freed slaves throughout the empire. In both these periods, the social meaning of "white" was in great flux as power relations shifted in the islands. While in her earlier novels she explores the relationship between national identity and alienation more generally, after World War II Rhys is able to claim her "field" more specifically as an interrogation of colonialism and the complexities of the politics of cultural production and dissemination in the Caribbean. *Wide Sargasso Sea* is Rhys's most comprehensive analysis of the psychological and social dynamics of white creole identity and cultural status.

The brilliance of Rhys's novel lies in her claiming a subjectivity for a character denied a stable position in any cultural or social space. Antoinette's "various" social positions shift with every change of her name and put her in-between the symbolic orders of English culture and black Caribbean culture. The novel explores both the politics of shifting social locations and the confused psychology that results from it. Antoinette is excluded both from English culture because of her creole status and from the white (English) Jamaican society because of her mother's connection to French culture as a native of Martinique. Antoinette recognizes early her ambivalent status within both English culture and the culture of the island. Her friendship with the black girl Tia is cut short by both girls' acknowledgment of the difference between their races and the power and meanings associated with color. While Antoinette used to be part of the ruling white class, the Emancipation Act has stripped her family of its power. As Tia retorts after Antoinette calls her a "cheating nigger":

> Plenty white people in Jamaica. Real white people, they got gold money...
> Old time white people nothing but white nigger now, and black nigger better
> than white nigger.[35]

As this confrontation makes clear, racial categories are more complex than "blood" or color; the terms of racial differentiation reflect power relations as well. The term "white nigger" expresses both a likely truth about the mixed racial makeup of "old time" white Creoles and their recent loss of power on the island. By calling Antoinette a "white nigger," Tia is acknowledging the dramatic shift in power between the island Blacks and Whites following the emancipation. The only "real whites" now, according to Tia, are the non-Caribbean British, whose assets were not solely plantations or slaves.

From her perspective as a white Creole, Rhys challenges the geneticist concept of race by exploring the relationship of racial categories to power and culture. For Rhys, racial categories are not "natural"; they are not merely the classification of pigmentation or anatomy but are complex social and cultural constructions linking linguistic, cultural, geographical, and political locations. As a "white nigger" Antoinette not only faces Tia as a political opponent but also shares with her the status of "nigger." At the later confrontation between the Cosway/Mason family and the ex-slaves, Tia and Antoinette are (in Antoinette's perception at any rate) simultaneously opposites and mirror images of each other:

> Then, not so far off, I saw Tia and her mother and I ran to her, for she was all that was left of my life as it had been. We had eaten the same food, slept side by side, bathed in the same river. As I ran, I thought, I will live with Tia and I will be like her. Not to leave Coulibri. Not to go. Not. When I was close I saw the jagged stone in her hand but I did not see her throw it. I did not feel it either, only something wet, running down my face. I looked at her and I saw her face crumple up as she began to cry. We stared at each other, blood on my face, tears on hers. It was as if I saw myself. Like in a looking glass. (*WSS*, p. 45)

While many critics have discussed the mirror imagery of this passage and the shared powerlessness of Antoinette and Tia, it is important also to remember that this recognition of sisterhood is *Antoinette's* perception or desire, one that had already been challenged by Tia in the pool. This scene cannot tell us anything about Tia's tears or *her* understanding of her relationship to Antoinette; what it can tell us is something about the desires and identifications of white creole society.

H. Hoetink, in his important study of Caribbean race relations, argues that one of the great differences between the Caribbean colonial experience and that of Africa or Asia is the "creolization" of white society in the former.[36] As we have seen in the earlier chapters, the contrast in South Africa between the British and the Afrikaners highlights the different degrees to which white society identifies itself as either European or "native." Schreiner's desire to have it both ways, through her definition of the native "English South African," wrenches the comfortable categories of British imperialism in South Africa. The situation in the Caribbean, Hoetink argues, is significantly different from that in Africa. From the start, "white" society in the Caribbean is comprised of English, French, Dutch, Spanish, and Portuguese, each group maintaining different attitudes and policies regarding race relations in the different Caribbean colonies. These differences, according to Hoetink, result from the different religious perspectives of Catholicism and Protestantism, the different historical presences of "alien" people in each of the mother countries, the varying degrees of previous cultural contact with Africa, the different traditions of slavery in each country's history, and the varying economic structures on the different islands.[37] Because European and North American scholars have tended to identify with Caribbean Whites, Hoetink suggests, race studies up through the 1960s focused on "the Negro" and ignored the

> "creolization" of the whites — all the influences on culture, social behavior and thought which operated upon the native white group in a segmented society. The cultural variant (and the variant frame of reference) which originated within the native white group from certain social causes, has not been recognized as something in its own right.[38]

In her fiction and in her autobiography, *Smile Please,* Rhys is one step ahead of the sociologists Hoetink criticizes. Unlike Schreiner, who projects the experience of "in-betweenness" onto "half-castes" and Jews, Rhys explores what Hoetink calls the "social schizophrenia" of the Caribbean white creole society.[39] Annette's and Antoinette's madness can be read as the psychological conflict between their desires to belong to opposing communities and their recognition that they belong to neither. Even as a child Antoinette in *Wide Sargasso Sea* knows that her mother is "so without a doubt not English" (*WSS*, p. 36) and that social relations on the island are "not at all like English people think" (*WSS*, p. 34). One of the main truths of *Wide Sargasso Sea* is "Rochester's" horrified recognition that although Antoinette may be "Creole of pure English descent[,] ... they are not English or European either" (WSS, p. 67). In her fiction Rhys is beginning to identify creolization as a cultural, racial, and psychological phenomenon. In these terms, the concept of the "Creole" moves from a colonial claim of European presence in the colonies to an understanding of cultural influence, racial mixing, and "border crossing" that contemporary writers such as Michelle Cliff, Gloria Anzaldúa, Edouard Glissant, and Guillermo Gómez-Peña are exploring today.[40]

Race and Literary Culture

While contemporary writers are beginning to define what creole or hybrid culture is, Jean Rhys wrote without the benefit of this discussion and worked to carve out a new creole literary space from which she could suggest a critique of English cultural colonialism. *Wide Sargasso Sea* is her rewriting of history from the point of view of the white Creole, a perspective that the racial and cultural myths of colonialism obscured. Rhys first mentions working on what was to become *Wide Sargasso Sea* in October 1945. Her letters pertaining to the composition of the novel reveal her insistence that this book, while it can be read on its own, must also be seen as a fundamental challenge to a specific British cultural project, Charlotte Brontë's *Jane Eyre*. Rhys's book, which in 1949 she had begun to call *The First Mrs. Rochester,* was set in "about 1780 something" (LJR, pp. 39n., 50, 56). By 1957 the material was still "simmering" in her head and was now set around 1840. As she writes in a letter in 1957, "The book is there in my head like an egg in its shell, but it's fragile as an egg too, till safely on paper" (LJR, pp. 143, 146). Although she finished the first draft in 1959, she was anxious about the relationship between the mad creole woman in Brontë's *Jane Eyre* and her own Mrs. Rochester. Rhys writes that her desire is to take the madwoman who is *"off-stage"* in Brontë's novel and put her *"on-stage"* and to fill in the motivation missing in Brontë's novel; that is, she wants to reclaim Brontë's Bertha from the myth of the New World monster and give her a history: "She must be at least plausible with a past, the *reason* why Mr. Rochester treats her so abominably and feels justified, the *reason* why he thinks she is mad and why of course she goes mad, even the *reason* why she tries to set everything on fire, and eventually succeeds" (LJR, p. 156). Rhys wants to recall a specific political history in order to explain the English misrepresentation of the Antoinette/Bertha figure. Rhys is "fighting mad to write *her* story," and to do that she needs to foreground the political history that in *Jane Eyre* is assumed and depoliticized; in the earlier text neither colonialism nor Bertha's personal history is an issue open to question or judgment.

One of the many titles Rhys considered for the book was *False Legend* (*LJR*, p. 234) because the emphasis of Brontë's novel seemed so false to her. She believed that Brontë's story derived from a local legend of a mad creole woman locked in an English attic, a legend that she felt was probably based in fact. Telling the story from the mad woman's point of view in *Wide Sargasso Sea,* Rhys reinvents the English legend with the economic, political, and historical context necessary to a less "false" portrayal of the West Indian woman:

> The West Indies *had* a (melo?) dramatic quality. A lot that seemed incredible could have happened. And did. Girls *were* married for their dots at that time, taken to England and no more heard of. Houses were burnt down by ex slaves, some servants *did* stick — especially children's nurses. I don't know if "obeah" still goes on. But it did. And voodoo certainly does — Also anonymous letters — and still come tragedies. (*LJR*, p. 216)

The tragedies of days past and those that continue in the present in the West Indies take place, Rhys asserts, in these specific and real historical and cultural contexts.

The book is more than a Caribbean writer's treatment of her own country and its history (as her notes for the book *Creole* might have become); it is an incisive examination of the relationship between English *culture* and Caribbean existence. As she writes in 1958, "It might be possible to unhitch the whole thing from Charlotte Brontë's novel, but I don't want to do that. It is that particular mad Creole I want to write about, not any of the other mad Creoles" (*LJR,* p. 153). In other words, it is this particular Mrs. Rochester, the object of the English imagination, that interests Rhys.[41] She recalls reading *Jane Eyre* when she was sixteen or seventeen:

> Of course Charlotte Brontë makes her own world, of course she convinces you, and that makes the poor Creole lunatic all the more dreadful. I remember being quite shocked, and when I re-read it rather annoyed. "That's only one side — the English side" sort of thing. (*LJR*, p. 297)

In another letter Rhys struggles with the idea of reading Brontë's story through creole history and thereby giving Bertha the subjectivity that English history denies her:

> I believe and firmly too that there was more than one Antoinette. The West Indies was (were?) rich in those days *for* those days and there was no "married woman's property Act." The girls (very tiresome no doubt) would soon once

in kind England be *Address Unknown*. So gossip. So a legend. If Charlotte
Brontë took her horrible Bertha from this legend I have the right to take lost
Antoinette. (*LJR*, p. 271)

By making this figure the center of her text, Rhys raises for *her* subject the issues of economics, gender relations, and autonomy that Brontë
reserves for Jane Eyre alone. In giving Bertha (Antoinette) the subjectivity
denied her in *Jane Eyre*, Rhys examines these issues also in the context of
English colonialism, race relations, and international economics that are so
normalized in Brontë's text that they barely create a ripple in the story of
Jane Eyre's "progress."[42] In Rhys's work, the story is entirely different; in
fact, Jane does not appear at all in the novel, except perhaps as the unnamed
girl in white whom Antoinette sees in the halls at Thornfield.

Rhys's attempt to reclaim Bertha/Antoinette, and to do so by maintaining
the tie to the English novel *Jane Eyre*, opens up a field of questions about
the relationship between cultural and national identity. The white Creole
in *Wide Sargasso Sea*, neither English nor Caribbean, stands between these
cultures, and her political status is consequently of great complexity and
tension. Antoinette's cultural "education" reveals this ambiguity. The white
Jamaican culture is not English culture, and when Antoinette's mother marries the English Mr. Mason, Antoinette begins to recognize the differences.
Mr. Mason, like the unnamed "Mr. Rochester" character later, comes to
the island with no understanding of the social relations that have developed
between the Whites and the Blacks, the English and the Jamaicans, and the
French and English settlers. After several conversations with her new step-
father, Antoinette realizes to herself the great differences between English
and creole life that Mr. Mason does not recognize: " 'None of you understands about us,' I thought," and, "I wish I could tell him that out here is
not at all like English people think it is" (*WSS*, p. 34). Because so much
is repressed in this white colonial culture (both English and creole), Antoinette has no vocabulary for expressing what racial relations are "really" like
or even how she experiences them.

As Antoinette learns about power relations, Englishness and whiteness
become associated for her. Calling Mr. Mason "white pappy," Antoinette
intimates the ambiguity of her own racial status and her relationship to him.
As Orlando Patterson points out in his comparative study *Slavery and Social
Death*, Jamaican slaves often referred to their masters as "father"; this address
of "fictive kinship" was not so much a sign of respect as a mocking form of
aggression.[43] Mr. Mason is, in fact, Antoinette's "fictive" father, and her ac-

knowledgment, like that of the slaves to their masters and of Daniel Cosway (Antoinette's "illegitimate," colored half-brother) to his father, is rich in its recognition of the exploitation perpetuated by those with such status.

From Mr. Mason, Antoinette learns the traditional English colonial racism that ignores the reality of social and sexual relations between the races in Jamaica. Although as a child Antoinette played with her "colored" cousin (her father's grandson), Sandi Cosway, Mr. Mason's education cuts her off from her father's numerous "illegitimate" offspring. When the Coulibri Estate becomes Mr. Mason's, Antoinette learns to live "like an English girl," eating English food and longing to be like the girl depicted in the *Miller's Daughter,* a picture hanging above the dining room table; the picture shows "a lovely English girl with brown curls and blue eyes and a dress slipping off her shoulders" (*WSS,* p. 36). Although Mr. Mason is "so sure of himself, so without a doubt English," Antoinette is less sure of her mother's status and thus of her own: "My mother, so without a doubt not English, but no white nigger either. Not my mother. Never had been. Never could be" (*WSS,* p. 36). After the emancipation, Antoinette learns that to be white means to be English, that is, to possess fully what is culturally English. By allowing a space for the complexities of "subject constitution" in the colonies, Rhys grapples in her fiction with Spivak's crucial argument that the colonial absolute other is a myth, for "the project of imperialism has already historically refracted what might have been the absolute Other into a domesticated Other that consolidates the imperialist self."[44] The other, as Fanon also insisted, is thus enmeshed in, in dialogue with, and a product of European culture.

Rhys offers, perhaps, the clearest analysis of the ways the "other" is a domestic and domesticated product. In an early story, "Again the Antilles," published in *The Left Bank* (1927), Rhys investigates the complex relationship between race and culture and the business of the constitution of selfhood in colonial society.[45] As a British colonial subject, Rhys received an exclusively English and French literary education and was one of the earliest Caribbean writers to address the psychological and political effects of this curriculum. In the space of three pages Rhys reveals in this story that the stakes involved in cultural, particularly literary, knowledge are those of colonial and racial domination. The story rehearses a bitter debate that took place, apparently some years before, in the *Dominica Herald and Leeward Islands Gazette* between its editor, Papa Dom, and an English colonialist, Hugh Musgrave. The social positions of these two men are striking. Papa Dom, a native to the island, carries himself as a proper "gentleman":

"He wore gold-rimmed spectacles and dark clothes always — not for him the frivolity of white linen even on the hottest days." This is the solemn and proper exterior, however, of a "born rebel":

> He hated the white people, not being quite white, and he despised the black ones, not being quite black.... "Coloured" we West Indians called the intermediate shades, and I used to think that being coloured embittered him.
>   He was against the Government, against the English, against the Island's being a Crown Colony and the Town Board's new system of drainage. ("AA," p. 39)

Hugh Musgrave, on the other hand, is a white owner of a large estate and employs a great deal of labor for the production of sugar cane and limes. According to the narrator, Musgrave is harmless, in fact "a dear" though perhaps a bit "peppery" due to his "twenty years of the tropics and much indulgence in spices and cocktails" ("AA," p. 40).

The debate between the two men begins when, under a pseudonym in letters to the paper, Papa Dom accuses Musgrave of "some specifically atrocious act of tyranny" that the narrator cannot remember, but she quotes the letter at length:

> "It is a saddening and a dismal sight," it ended, "to contemplate the degeneracy of a stock. How far is such a man removed from the ideals of true gentility, from the beautiful description of a contemporary, possibly, though not certainly, the Marquis of Montrose, left us by Shakespeare, the divine poet and genius.
>   *"He was a very gentle, perfect knight."* ("AA," p. 40)

From this point the debate revolves ferociously around whether this is the line of Shakespeare or Chaucer and which of the two writers to the *Dominica Herald* has the greater casual knowledge of English poetry and culture. This is not merely a college quiz repartee but a struggle over the racial right to English culture and, by extension, the right to political power. Musgrave replies to the letter:

> The lines quoted were written, not by Shakespeare but by Chaucer, though you cannot of course be expected to know that, and run
>
>> He never yet no vilonye had sayde
>> In al his lyf, unto no manner of wight —
>> He was a verray parfit, gentil knyght.
>
> It is indeed a saddening and dismal thing that the names of great Englishmen should be thus taken in vain by the ignorant of another race and colour. ("AA," p. 41)

And the narrator adds, "Mr. Musgrave had really written 'damn niggers.'"

Papa Dom's next reply goes on to remind the newspaper's readers of the doubts of authorship in literary scholarship and his own writing from memory as opposed to Musgrave's obvious use of reference materials. The debate here is obviously about the ability, indeed the *right,* of nonwhite readers to understand and use English culture. The complexity and irony of the story go even further. Papa Dom, a "colored" man, questions Mr. Musgrave's "Englishness" and alludes to the "degeneracy of the stock." Papa Dom does not question English culture itself; from his own ambiguous position as a "colored" man he adopts not only the English valuation of English culture but the English racial hierarchy as well. In this story Rhys explores both the antiblack racism of the white English character and the resulting internalized self-hatred of a "colored" West Indian character.

Musgrave's sin, in Papa Dom's eyes, is his fall from "true gentility." Musgrave's reply, however, reveals the futility of Papa Dom's education and gentlemanly bearing, for no matter how scholarly or reserved Papa Dom may be in order to set himself off from the "easy morality of the negroes," he is nonetheless a "damn nigger" in English eyes, outrageously arrogant in his very attempt to use English poetry. Rhys's analysis of this hostility of the colonialist for the "not quite white" native anticipates by fifty-seven years Bhabha's analysis of the "almost the same but not quite . . . almost the same but not white" figure of colonial society.[46] Papa Dom is a good example of what Bhabha calls a "colonial mimic," a colonial subject who, while despising the English, has learned to play the role of the Englishman in many ways better than the Englishman himself. And yet, no matter how well he learns the rules, he will never entirely win because culture, Rhys acknowledges, is politically tied to race. In other words, only the white English-born can be English and hold those privileges associated with that status. Although Fanon argues that "the Negro in the West Indies becomes proportionately whiter — that is, he becomes closer to being a real human being — in direct ratio to his mastery of the language," Rhys seems to agree with Bhabha that this figure is, nonetheless, "the effect of a flawed colonial mimesis, in which to be Anglicized is *emphatically* not to be English."[47]

To push this short story one step further, we can interrogate the place of the *narrator,* the first reader of this war of letters. The last line of the story, indeed, demands the question. Papa Dom's final reply is followed by the narrator's enigmatic first-person conclusion, "I wonder if I shall ever again read the *Dominica Herald and Leeward Islands Gazette.*" This disruption of the narrative calls attention to the position of the narrator herself and ends on a question — Why is it likely she won't be reading this paper again? If, as is most probably the case, she might no longer have access to the paper, we can picture an Island native now living far removed from Dominica remembering this debate. "Again the Antilles" then becomes a bit of nostalgia, an ironic little snippet of the ridiculous and bizarre situations that are the legacy of British colonialism in the tropical islands.

The story as I first interpreted it reveals a subtle understanding of the relationship between culture, race, and power, an understanding possible chiefly to a native of the island. But an unconscious intelligence is embedded in this story as well that is perhaps somewhat less "removed" than the first reading would have it. The last line of the story displaces the newspaper debate and all its passion to a somewhat remote moment, at once undercutting its immediacy and making it serve as a *representative* rather than a specific or *real* conflict. This is a story remembered from the past, and the narrator's interpretations of the events are mediated by all she has since learned about nationality, race, and power. One must almost "read against" the narrative to see, or rather hear, the narrator at all.

In the first paragraph the narrator appears as the vehicle for seeing and describing Papa Dom:

> The editor of the *Dominica Herald and Leeward Islands Gazette* lived in a tall, white house with green Venetian blinds which overlooked our garden. I used often to see him looking solemnly out of his windows and would gaze solemnly back, for I thought him a very awe-inspiring person. ("AA," p. 39)

This narrator sets her younger self up as almost a mirror of Papa Dom's solemn image. That she once found him awe-inspiring, however, suggests that the narrator was either less well educated, less privileged racially, or quite a bit younger. The diction of the story and the appreciation of the literary debate place the narrator at a similar or higher educational level, and her description of Papa Dom's racial position is removed and condescending: she says he was "a stout little man of a beautiful shade of coffee-colour," and "I used to think that being coloured embittered him." She is clearly not English since she refers to "we West Indians," and her judgment of Mr. Musgrave as "a dear, but peppery," places her as a younger woman. In light of Rhys's other Caribbean stories (and her autobiography, *Smile Please*) in which the narrator or main character is usually a young girl, it is not surprising that she is young in this story as well. But the presence or consciousness of this specific narrator, a young, white, West Indian woman remembering her island girlhood, adds a more complex political reading of the story. Although the narrator was clearly awe-inspired by Papa Dom when she was a child, she has since learned to devalue his achievements and political beliefs and to view them with humor.

As a "mirror" to Papa Dom, then, the girl becomes an ironic reflection to his stately solemnity. The well-educated, well-dressed, serious man stares from his windows deep in thought to be confronted with a mimicking image of a young white girl staring back. Rather than a subject deep in thought, he becomes an object of her gaze and later of her amused memory of island life. Her position as mimic underscores not only his own mimicking of the English gentleman but the ways that they similarly mimic those figures they both revere and despise. Just as Papa Dom's admiration for English culture is undercut by his hatred of the English, the narrator's valuation of Papa Dom as "a very awe-inspiring person" is undercut by her ironic consciousness in the narration and by the heart of the story she tells — Papa Dom's literary mistake.

Far from being the "neutral" narrator her text implies, she remains a specific, though anonymous, narrator residing in a specific political space. From this perspective, she determines that Papa Dom is "a born rebel," "a firebrand," an "embittered" colored man. Similarly, Hugh Musgrave is "a dear, but peppery," and "certainly neither ferocious nor tyrannical." Papa Dom's political positions are rendered almost ridiculous by the way the narrator lists them:

> He was against the Government, against the English, against the Island's being a Crown Colony and the Town Board's new system of drainage. He was also against the Mob, against the gay and easy morality of the negroes and "the hordes of priests and nuns that overrun our unhappy Island," against the existence of the Anglican bishop and the Catholic bishop's new palace. ("AA," p. 39)

Each of Papa Dom's objections is given the same weight, and his political positions become mere personal characteristics, part of his crankiness. He is a "born rebel"; that is, his dissatisfactions are a product of his personality, not of specific political problems.

If Papa Dom exercises any control over the debate by his role as the paper's editor, the narrator, as "editor" of this text, takes that power back. If Papa Dom edits out Musgrave's insult of "damn niggers," the narrator puts it back into the text: "Mr. Musgrave had really written 'damn niggers.'" Presumably, since Papa Dom would like to silence this obscene racism, the narrator must have heard the original insult in the Musgrave camp where she also heard that Musgrave is a fair employer, against accusations to the contrary.

Whereas Papa Dom's political and cultural identification is the thematic center of the story, a submerged tension in the text is the narrator's "social grounding," her choice of community and identity. As a woman, she occupies a similar position to Papa Dom in relation to literary culture. Both the woman and the "colored" man are excluded from the cultural world of Shakespeare and Chaucer so carefully guarded by white Englishmen like Musgrave. The narrator's identification with Papa Dom, however, is obstructed by the promise of social power she gains by siding with the white English (male) colonialists. The story allows us to see Rhys simultaneously asking challenging questions about cultural identification and race, of the sort that Fanon asks later in *Black Skin, White Masks,* and disclosing through the unconscious of the text itself the racial and political ambivalence of the "settler discourse" and particularly of native white women.

The narrator of "Again the Antilles" stands between the European and Caribbean cultures. Like Papa Dom, she is a product of the two cultures, and, like him, she is a native West Indian writer who will never entirely be accepted by the guardians of English literature and political power. As a woman writer, Rhys creates a "colored" West Indian writer to represent her own exclusion, but as a member of the settler class, she nonetheless evaluates his literary endeavors with scorn. From her position as a white, West Indian, woman writer, Rhys portrays the tensions and ambivalences of creole culture that go unexamined in English texts of imperialism.

The question of this "ambivalence" is a vexed one in contemporary theory.[48] Some critics see in textual disparities and contradictions what Homi Bhabha calls "ambivalent indeterminacies," while others take a skeptical view of such claims of "ambivalence" in colonial texts and focus on the ideological function of what Abdul JanMohamed calls subconscious "imperialist duplicity."[49] Readings of Rhys's work benefit from both these approaches, the one that sees in textual ambivalences a challenge to the myth of the unified colonial subject and the other that reads such indeterminacies as central and necessary to colonialist ideology. Creole writing, like Rhys's and Schreiner's, allows us to entertain the two interpretations of ambivalence simultaneously, for, indeed, the creole position is both resistant to and complicitous with colonial definitions of status and place.

Rhys's short story "The Day They Burned the Books,"[50] published in the collection *Tigers Are Better Looking* (1968), provides us with another opportunity to engage in this kind of reading strategy. Building on her earlier work, in this story Rhys connects political and economic colonialism even more directly with what I will call cultural colonialism. In this story, once again, the main character is of mixed racial origin, and the narrator is a white creole girl. Eddie is the fair-skinned, delicate son of Mr. Sawyer, a white English businessman who lives in but hates the Caribbean, and his wife, a once beautiful, native, colored woman. Mr. Sawyer hates his wife as much as he hates the island and perpetrates public, racist humiliations of her:

> "Look at the nigger showing off," he would say; and she would smile as if she knew she ought to see the joke but couldn't. "You damned, long-eyed, gloomy half-caste, you don't smell right," he would say; and she never answered, not even to whisper, "You don't smell right to me either."
>
> The story went that once they had ventured to give a dinner party and that when the servant, Mildred, was bringing in coffee, he had pulled Mrs. Sawyer's hair. "Not a wig, you see," he bawled. Even then, if you can believe it, Mrs. Sawyer had laughed and tried to pretend that it was all part of the joke, this mysterious, obscure, sacred English joke. ("DTBB," p. 152)

Mrs. Sawyer's hatred for her husband expresses itself in her hatred for his library of English and French books at the back of the house. And Eddie, "the living image of his father, though often as silent as his mother," is caught between the two. Although he and the narrator spend hot Saturdays reading exotic English adventures like *The Arabian Nights,* Eddie matches his father's hatred of the Caribbean with his own distrust and rejection of English culture. This is a most unpopular, even shocking, position for a colonial boy to take, one that flies in the face of the entire colonial sense of inferiority to English culture. The narrator is at once shocked and thrilled by Eddie's rebellious distaste for such English staples as strawberries and daffodils:

> It was Eddie . . . who first infected me with doubts about "home," meaning England. He would be so quiet when others who had never seen it — none of us had ever seen it — were talking about its delights, gesticulating freely as we talked — London, the beautiful, rosy-cheeked ladies, the theatres, the shops, the fog, the blazing coal fires in winter, the exotic food (whitebait eaten to the sound of violins), strawberries and cream — the word "strawberries" always spoken with a guttural and throaty sound which we imagined to be the proper English pronunciation.
>
> "I don't like strawberries," Eddie said on one occasion.
>
> "You don't *like* strawberries?"
>
> "No, and I don't like daffodils either. Dad's always going on about them. He says they lick the flowers here into a cocked hat and I bet that's a lie." ("DTBB," p. 153)

Through Eddie's situation, the narrator comes to recognize her own in-between position as a colonial "product." Eddie is able to see the "lie" at the center of their cultural education because of his more obvious conflicting subject position as the son of a white father and a "colored" mother. To identify with either of his parents means to despise the culture of the other, and thus of himself. A witness to his father's feelings of racial and cultural superiority, Eddie can recognize that any admiration he might cherish toward English culture is necessarily a simultaneous degradation of his Caribbean culture and of himself. Eddie's position allows the narrator to recognize more consciously her own in-between status and her incipient resentment of the English education they had received:

> We were so shocked that nobody spoke to him for the rest of the day. But I for one admired him. I was also tired of learning and reciting poems in praise of daffodils, and my relations with the few "real" English boys and girls I had met were awkward. I had discovered that if I called myself English they would snub me haughtily: "You're not English; you're a horrid colonial." "Well, I don't much want to be English," I would say. "It's much more fun to be French or Spanish or something like that — and, as a matter of fact, I am a bit." Then I was too killingly funny, quite ridiculous. Not only a horrid colonial, but also ridiculous. Heads I win, tails you lose — that was the English. ("DTBB," p. 153)

At the heart of the story is the frustration that virtually every colonial writer faces upon realizing both the general absurdity and the more serious political implications of the traditional English educational curriculum reproduced in the English colonies. Rhys's choice of daffodils as the symbol of English cultural hegemony has become, since her story, a touchstone in contemporary postcolonial fiction. The Jamaican writer Michelle Cliff in her first novel, *Abeng,* describes two forms of Jamaican education — one for the poorer black and colored children and the other for wealthier, lighter colored girls learning to "pass." Mr. Powell has been teaching the poorer children for twenty-five years, and for all those years has been receiving identical manuals of instruction from the colonial office in London:

> Mr. Powell was told to have the younger children read poems by Tennyson, the older ones, poems by Keats — "supplied herewith." To see that all in the school memorized the "Daffodils" poem of William Wordsworth, "spoken with as little accent as possible; here as elsewhere, the use of pidgin is to be severely discouraged." The manual also contained a pullout drawing of a daffodil, which the pupils were "encouraged to examine" as they recited the verse.... No doubt the same manuals were shipped to villages in Nigeria, schools in Hong Kong, even settlements in the Northwest Territory —

anywhere that the "sun never set," with the only differences occurring in the pages which described the history of the colony in question as it pertained to England.

Probably there were a million children who could recite "Daffodils," and a million who had never actually seen the flower, only the drawing, and so did not know why the poet had been stunned.[51]

Lucy's hatred for daffodils in Jamaica Kincaid's novel *Lucy* surprises even herself. A Caribbean woman working as an au pair in New York, Lucy is taken by her employer to see the spring flowers, but instead of the beauty she is expected to appreciate, she sees "a scene of conquered and conquests; a scene of brutes masquerading as angels and angels portrayed as brutes.... I was glad to have at last seen what a wretched daffodil looked like."[52]

Any successful political resistance to colonial or neocolonial policies depends on a clear-sighted assessment of the self as valuable and capable. Having internalized the terms of British culture, colonial subjects like Eddie are stymied, unable to articulate an unambivalent disavowal of racist definitions or an alternative set of cultural terms. Both Papa Dom and Eddie Sawyer can be seen to represent Rhys's own ambivalences and frustrations as a writer. Their appreciation of English literature contrasts in confusing ways with their degraded positions in English social and cultural hierarchies. The solution, which neither of these characters can yet perceive, is to reframe the terrain of creative expression.

Rhys, therefore — much like Schreiner before her — wants to claim a literary space for the representation and symbolic use of her native culture and geography. While she was writing *Wide Sargasso Sea,* there developed a growing audience to appreciate such writing. After World War II a growing Caribbean readership was encouraged by local literary magazines such as *Bim,* a Barbadian journal, and *Focus,* a sporadically published Jamaican magazine. The weekly BBC *Caribbean Voices* radio "magazine" also broadcast readings by Caribbean writers and created a connection between the Caribbean and British audiences and between Caribbean writers and British publishing houses.[53] Rhys identified herself as one of these Caribbean writers working with Caribbean themes and expressed distrust of British writers working on this "material." In a letter in 1936 during her only trip back to Dominica she uses much the same criteria as Schreiner did to claim her authority as a national writer: "I'm awfully jealous of this place (as you gather no doubt). I can't imagine anybody writing about it, daring to, without loving it — or living here twenty years, or being born here" (*LJR,* p. 29).

A fourth-generation Caribbean Creole, however, Rhys is much more suspicious of British culture than is Schreiner. In "Again the Antilles" Rhys explores the ambiguous position of the "colored" Creole, educated under the British system, and, like Fanon, she connects the policies of race with culture. In "The Day They Burned the Books" Rhys complicates the issue by creating four (and I will later argue five) different positions with regard to Caribbean and English culture. Mr. Sawyer, a pointedly "uncultured" businessman "who hadn't an 'h' in his composition," hates the Caribbean and protects himself from it by slowly surrounding himself with books he orders from England and France. Mrs. Sawyer, a "nicely educated colored woman," takes her vengeance for years of her husband's racist abuse, not on the man himself, but on his books, which represent European domination. Eddie, though like his mother technically "colored," has a complexion as white as his father's and is caught between two cultures. Although Eddie claims his Caribbean identity by rejecting the daffodils and strawberries of his father's nostalgic memory, he also claims himself heir to his father's library and unsuccessfully tries to protect it from his mother's wrath. And the fourth position is that of the narrator who, though apparently white, has her own difficult relationship with English culture and her own identity as a "horrid colonial."

In the climax of "The Day They Burned the Books" Rhys ties her great hostility to English culture, apparent in her earlier novels *Voyage in the Dark* and *Good Morning, Midnight,* specifically to literary culture. After Mr. Sawyer's death, the children begin to spend their time in his library: "'My room,' Eddie called it. 'My books,' he would say, 'My books'" ("DTBB," p. 154). In this room are typical English books (many of the books Rhys remembers in her own family's library): *The Encyclopaedia Britannica; The Arabian Nights; British Flowers, Birds and Beasts;* Froude's *English in the West Indies;* and other histories and maps. In her autobiography Rhys makes special note of the family's novels, all of which, interestingly, are what might be called "novels of empire" or travel tales: *Robinson Crusoe, Treasure Island, Gulliver's Travels,* and *Pilgrim's Progress.*[54]

Into that cloistered English world of Mr. Sawyer's library, separated from the domestic space and from Caribbean nature — both of which are identified with the "colored" woman — bursts Mrs. Sawyer's fury. Mrs. Sawyer has decided to sell or burn all the books in the library. In Mrs. Sawyer the narrator sees not bad temper, or even rage, but absolute hate. Into the piles Mrs. Sawyer flings works by Byron and Milton. Her choice of the fate of each book is not haphazard or random; as a "nicely educated colored woman" she knows these works.

> But a book by Christina Rossetti, though also bound in leather, went into the heap that was to be burnt, and by a flicker in Mrs. Sawyer's eyes I knew that worse than men who wrote books were women who wrote books — infinitely worse. Men could be mercifully shot; women must be tortured. ("DTBB," p. 155)

Mrs. Sawyer's silence is not merely acquiescence but is, perhaps, a refusal to engage in a dialogue in which she is bound to lose. Women who write, particularly women like Christina Rossetti who, like Mrs. Sawyer and Rhys herself, are marginally English, betray the more deadly silence. By using the available vocabulary they, like Papa Dom, become parties to the cultural domination of English literature. Mrs. Sawyer's silence and her hatred of women writers throw Rhys's own literary endeavors into ironic relief. The ensuing battle between Mrs. Sawyer and Eddie is, therefore, not only over Eddie's patrimony of imperialist European thought but also over more ambivalent literary articulations, like Rhys's.

Eddie frantically but ineffectually tries to save "his" books from his mother's wrath. The confrontation between the two is weighted with complex symbolical significance, though the standard dichotomies are undermined. Centrally, it is a conflict between English and Caribbean culture, but that conflict can no longer break down racially. Both mother and son are "colored" Creoles, though Eddie is one generation "whiter" than his mother. Eddie's whiteness is both his power and his weakness. His paleness resists the sun's influence and refuses to darken at all, but it also reveals his consumptive state that makes him (and his class) "[not] long for this world." The confrontation between mother and son is also a conflict between Caribbean nature, as represented by Mrs. Sawyer through the narrator's eyes, and European culture, in the form of Eddie's library. With this act of revolutionary violence, Mrs. Sawyer regains the beauty she lost over the years while married to her husband:

> She looked beautiful, too — beautiful as the sky outside which was a very dark blue, or the mango tree, long sprays of brown and gold.
> When Eddie said "no," she did not even glance at him. ("DTBB," p. 155)

Here culture, typically represented as masculine to the feminine nature, is emasculated and made pitiful:

"No," he said again in a high voice. "Not that one. I was reading that one."

She laughed and he rushed at her, his eyes starting out of his head, shrieking, "Now I've got to hate you too. Now I hate you too."

He snatched the book out of her hand and gave her a violent push. She fell into the rocking-chair. ("DTBB," p. 155)

The book that his mother was about to destroy and the only book Eddie is able to save is, significantly, *Kim*. Kim is, interestingly, Abdul JanMohamed's example of a truly "syncretic" character in a classically colonialist novel.[55] While this text is Eddie's father's legacy to him, in the struggle the book is torn, and the first twenty pages are missing. What is torn away from the novel is, of course, Kim's true racial identity, which is given at the very beginning of the novel.[56] The *Kim* that is left to Eddie, then, can never resolve Kim's (or Eddie's) racial ambiguity because the "proof" of pedigree is missing. The liberal tag the narrator learned from her father, "Who's white? Damn few," merely irritates Eddie, for the uncertainty of racial location (despite his almost overdetermined whiteness) will be his cultural and psychological problem for life.

If Eddie's book *Kim* tells us something about the struggles that will be at the center of his life, the book the narrator saves from the flames and that she believes is "the most important thing that ever happened to me" also prophecies what the future holds for her. Alone in her room she is disappointed to find that it is in French and seems quite dull — *Fort comme la mort*. Guy de Maupassant's novel pairs an aging French artist with his dependent mistress, whom he abandons in favor of her young daughter. Where Rhys's character Eddie will have to confront racial bigotry, the narrator will struggle with the sexual exploitation and economic dependence Rhys's women characters inevitably face. Rhys herself had to contend with the struggles both these children are destined to find in their adulthoods.

Rhys's story focuses on the painful in-betweenness of Eddie primarily, and secondarily also of Mrs. Sawyer and of the narrator. But, as I hinted before, there is a significant, though less apparent, fifth presence in the story. If we ask the question, Who is the "they" in the title "The Day They Burned the Books"? then the figure of Mildred, the servant, steps from the background. In the narration of the story, Mildred fills in the stories told about Mrs. Sawyer and is generally present at the main "events" of the story. Mr. Sawyer's abuse of his wife at the dinner party occurs simultaneously with the introduction of Mildred bringing in the coffee. Within the dubious praise Mr. Sawyer lavishes on his wife's hair lies the racist comparison of her long hair with the "black hair" or "bad hair" of a woman like Mildred. As a witness to this scene, Mildred attributes to Mrs. Sawyer a powerful response:

> But Mildred told the other servants in the town that her eyes had gone wicked, like a soucriant's eyes, and that afterwards she had picked up some of the hair he pulled out and put it in an envelope, and that Mr. Sawyer ought to look out (hair is obeah as well as hands). ("DTBB," p. 152)

This, of course, is Mildred's interpretation, the response she feels is justified for the insult. And it is Mildred, not Mrs. Sawyer, who tells the children that the books are to be burnt: "Mildred's expression was extraordinary as she said that — half hugely delighted, half shocked, even frightened" ("DTBB," p. 154). Though behind the action of the story, Mildred represents a fifth position of racial/cultural relations — the black woman Caribbean, at once double and opposite of Mrs. Sawyer, depending on racial point of view.

Although she and Mrs. Sawyer are both "black" in relation to Mr. Sawyer's whiteness, Mrs. Sawyer is the mistress of a white household in which Mildred is the black servant. Mildred functions in the story as the articulation of what is hidden in Mrs. Sawyer's silence, but when we see Mildred as behind the scenes, it is provocative to ask whether she provides merely the articulation or, in fact, provides the *interpretation* and *instigation* of the action from her position as a black servant. Her emotional relation to Mr. Sawyer is much less compromised because she does not benefit from the "compensations" Mrs. Sawyer enjoys in the "very pleasant" house and garden. While the text focuses on the cultural struggle of the other four characters, Mildred represents a less divided potential threat to English culture that the others do not. She is not described as an "educated woman" as is Mrs. Sawyer, so her shock, delight, and fear have to do with the blatant affront to white power the burning suggests. Burning a pile of European books becomes a plantation firing in miniature, the destruction of European symbols of power and abuse.

As the children flee from the scene of struggle they "hear Mildred laughing, kyah, kyah, kyah, kyah." Rhys positions the black woman as simultaneously outside the struggle between the "colored" mother and son and part of its resolution. We can see Eddie and his mother at the center of the racial/cultural conflict, with the white narrator and black servant standing slightly outside. But whereas the narrator articulates her own identification with Eddie (through her awareness of them both as "horrid colonials" and through her imaginative marriage to him represented by the mixing of their tears under the mango tree), Mildred is not given the subjectivity to acknowledge what her racial relationship to Mrs. Sawyer is. Rhys sets up the four other characters as participants in an agonistic racial struggle, but by keeping Mildred in the background she attributes to her a consciousness uncomplicated by competing loyalties. Lucy Wilson argues that Rhys's black characters Christophine of *Wide Sargasso Sea* and Selina of "Let Them Call It Jazz" "possess a kind of resiliency that their white West Indian counterparts lack."[57] Although Wilson connects the creation of these characters with Rhys's envy of black Caribbean culture, she does not read that creation with suspicion. That is, to Wilson's view that these black women are Rhys's "unequivocal assertion of defiance" (which they are), I would add that they are also Rhys's projection of a mythical whole-ness and unity onto Blacks. By foregrounding the fragmented subjectivity of white Creoles, Rhys attributes an enviable and idealized wholeness to black Caribbeans.

And yet while Mildred's crowlike laughter undercuts the children's tragic response to the destruction of "the literature of empire," she does not provide the "articulate" critique of colonialism that Christophine manages before she exits *Wide Sargasso Sea*. That Rhys was herself ambivalent about Christophine's voice is evident from a letter she wrote to her editor at the completion of the novel:

> The most seriously wrong thing with Part II is that I've made the obeah woman, the nurse, too articulate. I thought of cutting it a bit, I will if you like, but after all no one will notice. Besides there's no reason why one par-ticular negro woman shouldn't be articulate enough, especially as she's spent most of her life in a white household. (*LJR*, 297)

"Articulate" is an adjective that is here and more generally coded as white (a perfect example of Fanon's understanding of language as a mark of race) and made especial note of when the speaker is black. Surprisingly, critics have not dealt with this important passage in Rhys's letters that points up quite clearly some of the problems inherent in her representation of black creole language. While Ramchand may praise her for her skill in represent-ing black Caribbean dialect and speech patterns, Rhys herself is uncertain about what kind of analysis is possible in that language. Her critique of colonial education is compromised by her belief that "articulate," intelli-gible analysis depends on it. Mildred's laughter is the inarticulate response Rhys meant for Christophine but which, over the long years of writing, developed and deepened into a cogent analysis that springs not from "reading and writing" but from Christophine's experience of slavery and her knowledge of African-Caribbean creole culture.

The black servant is thus both inside and outside "The Day They Burned the Books," the most subjected of the characters, but perhaps the most free and dangerous. Just as Christophine's knowledge and practice of Obeah in *Wide Sargasso Sea* stands against "Rochester's" Western empiricism,[58] so Mildred's knowledge of Obeah undercuts the power of Mr. Sawyer's racism, represented in the story by his European library. While she seems tangential to the story, she is given the fullest articulation of hate and retribution. Even Eddie's "Now I hate you too" is compromised by his own defense of his mother's racial status (and thus his own) a page later. The last we hear of Mildred is her laughter as she throws more books on the heap. She is at once an example of the colonial myth of the unified other and the catalyst to the fiery destruction of that myth. The story is thus deeply ambivalent. In it Rhys expresses her own discomfort with her position as a writer using English forms and vocabulary she recognizes as oppressive to her as a Caribbean writer and thinker. And yet for Rhys to turn to Caribbean symbols and forms that derive from African, not European, traditions is no less complex. Raised by Afro-Caribbean servants, Rhys was exposed to Obeah and the belief in zombis and soucriants, but she necessarily interprets such cultural forms in relation to her own position as a white Creole. In Rhys's hands, Caribbean traditions and beliefs about Obeah, magic, and zombiism become symbols of creole experience subverting, as Rhys's work so often does, our expectations about cultural inscriptions of power.

The Creole Zombi between Life and Death

The awakening of the self is paid for by the acknowledgment of power as the principle of all relations.

— Max Horkheimer and Theodor W. Adorno,
"The Concept of Enlightenment"

For a white Creole to appropriate the symbology of black Caribbean cosmology raises important questions about transculturation and the politics of cultural creolism. Rhys's is a significantly creole rendering of colonial relations in which individuals (and the classes they represent) can be both victim and victor, threatened and threatening. Like Schreiner, Rhys reveals the multifarious conditions of oppression and the ironies inherent in overlapping systems of privilege and power. The Afro-Caribbean creole religion of Vodou provides Rhys with a rich symbolic terrain to explore both colonial exploitation and the "terrified consciousness" of the white bourgeoisie;

her use of the pervasive symbol of the zombi underscores her ambivalent position as a white Caribbean Creole.[59]

While the figure of the zombi and the conjurer are grounded in Afro-Caribbean experience and belief,[60] Elaine Campbell argues that the belief in Obeah, a practice of magic related to the religion Vodou (Voodoo in North America), is deeply embedded in the white West Indian consciousness as well.[61] As a white Dominican, Rhys was introduced to the symbols and beliefs of Vodou very early in her life. As she recounts in *Smile Please,* "Our cook at Bona Vista was an obeah woman called Ann Tewitt. Obeah is a milder form of voodoo, and even in my time nobody was supposed to take it very seriously. Yet I was told about her in a respectful, almost awed tone" (*SP,* pp. 15–16). Jean Rhys's childhood was filled with rituals and stories about Obeah and zombis. Her description of her nurse Meta conveys the strong impression the black culture of Obeah had on her:

> It was Meta who talked so much about zombies, soucriants and loups-garous. She was the only person I've heard talk about loups-garous (werewolves) in the West Indies. Soucriants were always women, she said, who came at night and sucked your blood. During the day they looked like ordinary women but you could tell them by their red eyes. Zombies were black shapeless things. They could get through a locked door and you heard them walking up to your bed. You didn't see them, you felt their hairy hands round your throat. For a long time I never slept except right at the bottom of the bed with the sheet well over my head, listening for zombies. (*SP,* p. 23)

Through Meta's stories, and those of her black friend Francine, Rhys came to associate storytelling itself with the rituals of Obeah. In Rhys's memory the Obeah ceremonies were intimately connected with Caribbean as opposed to English fiction. Francine's stories, in fact, cannot begin without a symbolic reversal and degradation of European proprieties:

> But the start [of Francine's stories] was always a ceremony. Francine would say "Tim-tim." I had to answer "Boissêche," then she'd say, *"Tablier Madame est derrière dos"* (Madam's apron is back to front). She always insisted on this ceremony before starting a story and it wasn't until much later, when I was reading a book about obeah, that I discovered that Boissêche is one of the gods. (*SP,* pp. 23–24)

It is ultimately this potential for the reversal of power that attracts Rhys to the symbology of Obeah and zombiism. Inherent in these creole beliefs is the possible disruptions of what Patrick Taylor calls the manichean conflict of the zombi-sorcerer relationship.[62] The possibility of this disruption and reversal has powerful political significance. It is commonly noted in studies of Vodou, for instance, that the 1791 Haitian War of Independence, the only successful slave revolt in the Americas, began with a Vodou ceremony in which slaves pledged to fight to the death for their freedom.[63] Zora Neale Hurston found in her ethnographic studies of Haitian and Jamaican "Vodou" that the zombi also represents the possibility of disrupting and reversing class relations. The concept of the zombi threatens more than the freedom and autonomy of the individual; the potential loss of all material wealth, along with the influence and safety it affords, threatens the security and privilege of the entire upper class.[64]

This fear helps explain the irony in Rhys's fiction that, given the economic power of Whites in Dominica, she represents the conjure women as frightening but familiar symbols of black and female power[65] and the zombis as (for the most part) white figures who are "wandering souls" separated from their homes and families.[66] Wade Davis, in *Passage of Darkness: The Ethnobiology of the Haitian Zombi,* stresses the social alienation of the zombi; the zombi state, according to Davis, is "marked by confusion, disorientation, and subsequent amnesia."[67] After studying the two most thoroughly documented cases of modern zombis, Davis suggests that those who were made into zombis were probably *already* alienated from their communities at the time of their zombification. Their alienation made them susceptible to this particular kind of living death sentence.[68] His descriptions are suggestive for a reading of Rhys's work if we think of her heroines as social zombis.[69] In Rhys's fiction the zombi works as a metaphorical figure representing the psychological and physical experiences of slavery, colonialism, and the alienation of social "passing."

Many of Rhys's characters manifest all the characteristics ethnographers and anthropologists find in the legends about zombis. The zombi, as Rochester reads in the guide book *The Glittering Coronet of Isles,* is "a dead person who seems to be alive or a living person who is dead" (*WSS,* p. 107). Those who believe in zombis maintain that they are apparent casualties of either violent or unnatural deaths. After the living bodies are buried, their souls are stolen by Bokors, and the bodies are sold to plantation masters who force them to work in the fields. The zombis have no memory of their previous lives, and they have no way to plead for release. The Caribbean zombi is an embodiment of political meanings specific to the Caribbean social situation of slavery and the spiritual understandings of life and death that derive from West African religions and cosmologies. Alfred Métraux describes the mythical meaning of the zombi in the black Caribbean imagination:

> The zombi remains in that grey area separating life and death. He moves, eats, hears, even speaks, but has no memory and is not aware of his condition. The zombi is a beast of burden exploited mercilessly by his master who forces him to toil in his fields, crushes him with work, and whips him at the slightest pretext, while feeding him on the blandest of diets. The life of the zombi, on the mythical level, is similar to that of the old slaves of Santo Domingo.[70]

Metaphorically, the zombi can be seen to represent the condition of both the slave and the colony itself; like the colony, the zombi is a functioning economic body serving the demands of the master while its soul (or culture) has been stolen or forcibly put to sleep.

Rhys's sleepwalkers are slowly deadened by the economic exploitation and/or alienation they suffer. Like the zombi, they lack will and autonomy. For them, memory is often a painful struggle to find coherence and purpose in jumbled fragments. In that memory, a reclamation of history, lies the painful awakening and violence of the revenging zombi. For Rhys's characters, however, zombiism is also a self-inflicted condition serving as a form of protection against the intrusions and abuses of English and European culture. And whereas Davis specifies that traditionally people do not fear the zombi itself but only the threat of *becoming* one,[71] as a white child Rhys feared both becoming one and being harmed by one. Similarly, Anna Morgan in *Voyage in the Dark* both fears the female souciants and recognizes the souciant in herself:

> Obeah zombis souciants — lying in the dark frightened of the dark frightened of souciants that fly in through the window and suck your blood — they fan you to sleep with their wings and then they suck your blood — you know them in the day-time — they look like people but their eyes are red and staring and they're souciants at night — looking in the glass and thinking sometimes my eyes look like souciant's eyes.[72]

Antoinette at the end of *Wide Sargasso Sea* haunts the halls of Thornfield fearful of the ghost she has heard rumors about, not recognizing that the ghost is herself. As a white Creole, Antoinette occupies a cultural space as both self and other, as the haunted and as the ghost.

Obeah, as a specifically Caribbean experience, is, like maronage, a double-edged concept for the white Creole. The word "marooned," which Annette uses to describe her family's position after the emancipation and the poisoning of the horse, resonates not only with the white experience of abandonment but also with the black history of the "Maroons," the slaves who escaped into the hills and attacked the plantations with revolutionary fervor.[73] Similarly, Obeah is either a threat to Antoinette or her salvation, depending on her shifting power position in Jamaican society. Rhys's zombi women are always the victims of economic exploitation, regardless of their race or class.

Many of Rhys's heroines are reduced to types, to automatons, by the economy that demands their service. As mannequins or "marionettes,"[74] they, like the zombi, are manipulated to play the part expected of them by the "master." But these heroines also learn to collude in their own de-humanization. Fitting in, that is, hiding or killing off their individuality or differences, becomes a means of survival. As Anna Morgan puts it when describing her neighbor: "She looked just like most other people, which is a big advantage" (*VD*, p. 66). And Sasha claims that her life motto has become "faites comme les autres."[75] The denial of self that this demands is deadening. Anna, accused by her friend Laurie of always looking as if she is half-asleep (*VD*, p. 80), is thankful for that escape: "I do sleep. I sleep as if I were dead" (*VD*, p. 70). But awake, she feels like a "ghost" (*VD*, p. 71). Marya in *Quartet* is described as having eyes "oddly remote in expression" (*Q*, p. 119), and Mrs. Heidler's eyes, with their "deadened look," attest to her role as a well-behaved wife (*Q*, p. 123). Marya feels like a "sleep-walker" (*Q*, p. 212) when she begins her career of prostitution.[76] Selina Davis learns what to say and do to have everything go like "clockwork."

Like Papa Dom and Eddie Sawyer, these women learn to "pass" at the expense of their own culture and their own lived experience. What happens to that lived experience when confronted with a dominant culture that denies its existence? Without a language to articulate such experience and without validation from other cultural sources these characters kill or put to sleep their own experience, sometimes erasing even the memory of their differences. Threatened with starvation or incarceration, these women, like Laura in "I Spy a Stranger," learn the importance of "shamming dead,"[77] that is, acting like the others.

This strategy of survival can have drastic consequences, particularly when employed by those who have power. While critics have focused on Antoinette's strategies of self-protection and her further zombification by Rochester and Christophine, Rochester's own psychological zombilike condition and its disastrous consequences have not been as fully explored. Rochester, like Antoinette and the white creole class she represents, occupies both a privileged and an exploited position in the imperialist economy. Although Rochester is responsible for stealing or changing Antoinette's name when she becomes his wife and metaphorical slave, Rhys leaves *him* completely nameless in the text as well. His relation to his patrimony is as vexed as is that of Daniel Cosway (Boyd). As twin Esaus, both Daniel and "Rochester" are cheated out of their birthrights by larger systems they are born into, one by the racist customs of colonialist and patriarchal "legitimacy" and the other by nineteenth-century inheritance laws and customs. Both try to rectify their own victimization through Antoinette, whose inheritance is built on the victimization of still others. While Rochester pities himself as a victim of unfair family economics, the tragedy of *Wide Sargasso Sea* results from his inability to recognize what he shares with those he must see as "other" in the system that promises him superiority and power.

The zombi in Rhys's hands transcends racial or economic positions; Rhys is exploiting the deepest meanings of the Caribbean zombi, a condition from which the master is not immune. Significantly, the white men of *Wide Sargasso Sea* are simultaneously masters and zombi slaves in this system. Pierre, who is more dead than alive, and Mr. Mason, who Annette believes is less "alive" than the island Blacks (*WSS*, p. 32), are members of an ultimately doomed class of white rulers. Rochester, who accuses his father of having sold his soul (*WSS*, p. 70), is also deadened in a way that his foil, the "nameless" crying boy, is not. Rochester's narrative is framed by this boy, whose emotions infuriate "Rochester" both when he arrives and when he leaves the island. The boy's tears contrast with the terrible deadness of "Rochester's" own feelings of love and sadness. This crying boy is the one "Rochester" was forced to kill in himself years before:

> I thought these people are very vulnerable. How old was I when I learned to hide what I felt? A very small boy. Six, five, even earlier. It was necessary, I was told, and that view I have always accepted. (*WSS*, p. 103)

Rochester's zombilike state, like Antoinette's, began long before they met each other. When Rochester first meets Antoinette, he is already playing the part demanded of him; he already lacks the autonomy and self-knowledge that could save him:

> It was all very brightly coloured, very strange, but it meant nothing to me. Nor did she, the girl I was to marry. When at last I met her I bowed, smiled, kissed her hand, danced with her. I played the part I was expected to play. She never had anything to do with me at all. Every movement I made was an effort of will and sometimes I wondered that no one noticed this. I would listen to my own voice and marvel at it, calm, correct but toneless, surely. But I must have given a faultless performance. If I saw an expression of doubt or curiosity it was on a black face not a white one. (*WSS*, pp. 76–77)

The wedding takes place between two already dead people in a morgue of dead white slave owners:

I remember little of the actual ceremony. Marble memorial tablets on the walls commemorating the virtues of the last generation of planters. All benevolent. All slave-owners. All resting in peace. When we came out of the church I took her hand. It was cold as ice in the hot sun. (*WSS*, p. 77)

To the end, Rochester denies his own feelings of love and his longing for connection: "Who would have thought that any boy would cry like that. For nothing. Nothing..." (*WSS*, p. 173).[78] Rochester's denial of his own experience leaves him unable to negotiate a stable position in relation to the people and countryside around him.

It is therefore not an intrinsic part of the landscape itself that symbolically separates the Englishman from the colonized subject as it is, for example, at the end of E. M. Forster's *Passage to India*. As Antoinette tries to explain to Rochester, the landscape he experiences as a "green menace" is neither hostile nor secretive but is "indifferent" to them (*WSS*, pp. 129–30, 149). Rochester's projection of his fear and alienation onto the people and things around him ("The telescope drew away and said don't touch me" [*WSS*, p. 149]) has terrible consequences for all who find themselves with him. But this is not merely an individual story of psychological trauma and projection. Rhys presents Rochester's way of measuring himself against a projected "other" as metonymic of England's national and cultural need to create and control an "other," a process upon which the entire colonial process rests.

But here, as elsewhere, Rhys blurs the lines between victim and victimizer. Rochester's cruelty finds its source in his own victimization by a system that uses him as well as those whom he exploits. If Julia feels like a marionette in *Quartet,* she recognizes that Heidler and his wife are also being manipulated by strings none of them can see (*Q*, p. 182). Because of her own ambiguous position in colonial society, Rhys is able to present an analysis that deconstructs the dichotomies of colonized and colonizer, oppressed and oppressor, and indicts the larger system that exploits all of the participants, some more than others.

Antoinette's deadened existence, however, also began before this marriage. It is a state not just of her individually but of her family and the white creole society as a whole. This white creole class is caught in the limbo state of the zombi, fully alive in neither the English nor the black culture. Antoinette's mother and her brother Pierre, an imbecile who "staggers," are members of the living-dead. In the convent Antoinette remembers to pray for her mother "as though she were dead, though she is living;... her soul is wandering, for it has left her body" (*WSS*, pp. 55, 57). In Antoinette's understanding, both her brother and her mother died long before their bodies did: "There are always two deaths, the real one and the one people know about" (*WSS*, p. 128).

It is ironic that while Antoinette's zombilike stance highlights her utter isolation, particularly from other children after her break with Tia, the expression of that alienation that marks her (the mask of the zombi) also offers her a particularly Caribbean understanding of her misery and of her social status. It is two black children who first identify her condition and her refusal to socially engage: "[Your mother] have eyes like zombi and you have eyes like zombi too. Why you won't look at me" (*WSS*, p. 50). This scene is difficult because while Antoinette is repulsed by the "colored" boy and the black girl (the one too white, the other too black), *she* is the victim of their torments and *she* occupies the Afro-Caribbean position of the zombi. As scholars of Vodou point out, zombification in Haiti is a rare punishment meted out to individuals who have committed crimes against the larger community.[79] While this scene and Rhys's use of zombi symbology in general can certainly be read as an inappropriate focus on white victimization, it is also an important exploration of the affront of social (and racial) isolation and the dangers inherent in such a position. Antoinette's zombilike state can thus be read as both her painful alienation and the black community's punishment for the racist separation of her class. It is significant that after rejecting these children and Sandi Cosway, Antoinette can awaken from her zombi state at the end of the novel only by connecting emotionally and politically with Tia and Christophine. This transracial, transcultural connection — or even the claim of this connection — is itself a problem that demands examination. While Rhys expresses an ambivalent longing to identify with black Caribbeans — and Antoinette's burning of Thornfield Hall can be read as a political expression of that identification — her appropriation of Afro-Caribbean culture necessarily transforms it into a different symbol of white creole psychology. Unlike the traditional dynamics described above, in Rhys's fiction her characters both fear and embody the zombi, both the oppressor and the victim exhibit characteristics of the zombi, and both the Englishman and the black Caribbean woman act as conjurers in the zombification of the creole woman. Rhys's paradoxical use of the zombi material raises central questions about the orthodoxies of both identity politics and national culture that, as I will explore in the next chapters, authors such as Michelle Cliff and Zoë Wicomb are currently pursuing.

During the honeymoon Antoinette realizes both Rochester's power and his lack of understanding of Caribbean culture and customs. Through the first confrontations between Rochester and Christophine, Antoinette comes to recognize her deep connections to the island and its people. Cleaning up the "mess" Rochester has made of his crown of native flowers, Christophine warns him that such behavior is dangerous: "I send the girl to clear up the mess you make with the frangipani, it bring cockroach in the house. Take care not to slip on the flowers, young master" (*WSS*, p. 85). Perhaps only Antoinette can appreciate the subtlety of Christophine's warning, which is also directed at her should she become too much like the "English madams" or "white cockroaches." In this confrontation, and in Rochester's arrogant misunderstanding of the servants' respectful behavior, Antoinette recognizes his "otherness" to her Caribbean culture and her own closer identification with the black servants than with her husband. Like Christophine she somewhat mockingly warns Rochester of the dangers he does not understand:

> "I'll get up when I wish to. I'm very lazy you know. *Like Christophine.* I often stay in bed all day." She flourished her fan. "The bathing pool is quite near. Go before it gets hot, Baptiste will show you.... But be careful. Remember to put your clothes on a rock and before you dress again shake them very well. Look for the red ant, that is the worst. It is very small but bright red so you will be able to see it easily if you look. Be careful," she said and waved her little fan. (*WSS*, pp. 86–87; emphasis added)

For Rochester, Granbois represents a frightening secret he cannot understand. He senses danger behind the impassive masks of the servants. The blankness and servility of the servants are forms of resistance and denial to the inquisitive but insensitive master. For instance, when Baptiste finds Rochester lost in the woods, he denies him any knowledge of the island's colonial past or of the indigenous legends of zombis:

> I said, "There was a road here once, where did it lead to?"
> "No road," he said.
> "But I saw it. A *pavé* road like the French made in the islands."
> "No road..."
> "Is there something wrong about the house?" He shrugged his shoulders.
> "Is there a ghost, a zombi there?" I persisted.
> "Don't know nothing about all that foolishness."
> "There was a road here sometime."
> "No road," he repeated obstinately.... It was as if he'd put his service mask on the savage reproachful face I had seen. (*WSS*, pp. 105–6)

By denying the existence of a road Baptiste is denying the history of French rule and, by extension, Rochester's colonial privilege as well. His denial and the servants' general disinterest in discussing what happened "long ago" are subtle but effective resistances to European power.[80] Impassivity and silence keep the knowledge and understanding crucial to the existence of the black culture from the oppressor, who will use this knowledge to enhance his own power. Any aspect of community or cultural cohesiveness is threatening to the colonizer as a source of potential resistance, and the people of these islands have learned to hide that vitality behind the zombilike mask of indifference, ignorance, and servitude.

As Rochester becomes increasingly the English "master," especially in his sexual relations with the servant Amélie, Baptiste becomes increasingly inscrutable and "blank." Antoinette and the servants know more about Rochester as a white "master" than Rochester knows about himself. Early in the honeymoon when Rochester questions the affection Antoinette shows Christophine, he is oblivious to the ultimate hypocrisy of his racism that is so obviously typical to anyone who was raised on a slave plantation:

> "*I* wouldn't hug and kiss them," I'd say, "I couldn't."
> At this she'd laugh for a long time and never tell me why she laughed.
> (*WSS*, p. 91)

In the face of Rochester's ignorance or perhaps willful misunderstanding, Antoinette and the servants collude in denying him information. When he assumes the village called Massacre was named for the slaughter of slaves, Antoinette maintains a shocked silence at his revealed assumptions of colonial power. Similarly, none of the servants explains to Rochester the obvious answer to the riddle of the servant Emile's age. The explanation that Rochester accepts is based on his view of the inadequacy of Emile's intellectual capability and his "uncivilized" state of understanding, rather than the obvious explanation that Emile, having been born on a leap year, is both fourteen *and* fifty-six years old (*WSS*, p. 68).

By the end, Rochester is infuriated by Antoinette's blankness, which he first recognized as self-protection but later comes to fear as a sign of dangerous rebellion. He remembers Antoinette's objection to their marriage and his reassurance to which she had "given way, but coldly, unwillingly trying to protect herself with silence and a blank face. Poor weapons, and they had not served her well or lasted long" (*WSS*, p. 91). But when they first arrive at Granbois, Rochester notes Antoinette's blank eyes, which he finds disconcerting: "She never blinks at all it seems to me. Long, sad, dark alien eyes" (*WSS*, p. 67).

Who is responsible for Antoinette's zombilike existence? Certainly, Antoinette's passivity predates Rochester's arrival. By the time she enters the convent she appreciates the comfort of "know[ing] exactly what must be done" (*WSS*, p. 57) and finds safety, if not happiness, in the religion of the colonizer and the training in femininity. Unlike Christophine, Antoinette has been educated, trained, and bribed not only to serve but to identify with colonial and patriarchal interests. Her willing subservience and masochism (*WSS*, pp. 92–94) can be read as a metaphor for white creole complicity in Anglo-European colonialism. Rhys makes it clear that Antoinette's attempt to use Caribbean magic to attract Rochester and her choice of Rochester over Sandi Cosway are disastrous betrayals of herself, her black and colored extended family, and Caribbean culture. As Sandra Drake points out, had Antoinette married Sandi Cosway, casting her lot with the rising free black Caribbean middle class, she would not have lost either of her names.[81]

Even as Rhys depicts the willing acquiescence of the white Creole, she shows the violence of patriarchal, English, imperialist appropriation and renaming. While Antoinette has agreed through marriage to lose her last name, Rochester also repeatedly calls her Bertha, renaming her against her will as all masters rename their slaves or newly created zombis:[82] "Bertha is not my name. You are trying to make me into someone else, calling me by another name. I know, that's obeah too" (*WSS*, p. 147). Christophine recognizes the connection between the violence of patriarchy and the violence of colonialism with this ritual stealing of Antoinette's name and identity:

> She tell me in the middle of all this you start calling her names. Marionette. Some word so... That word mean doll, eh? Because she don't speak. You want to force her to cry and to speak.... But she won't. (*WSS*, p. 154)

When Christophine finally sees Antoinette's "face like dead woman" and understands that she, like a slave, is completely owned by Rochester, she agrees to use her magic to help Antoinette.[83] Whether the hex fails because Obeah is essentially a practice of the black community and is, as Christophine warned, not intended to be used by "békés" (*WSS*, 112), or whether Christophine meant to poison the white master to free Antoinette, the failure is disastrous for Antoinette, and Christophine provides the third force in making Antoinette a zombi, this time for her protection.[84]

Christophine sends her into a waking sleep (*WSS*, p. 155) and offers her rum, the drink Antoinette's mother was given to "forget" (*WSS*, p. 134).

But as Antoinette says, she "is not a forgetting person" (*WSS*, p. 133) and demands to return to Rochester and confront him with all her rage. She finally names him as her oppressor, as a slave master (*WSS*, p. 146), and threatens revenge: "Before I die I will show you how much I hate you" (*WSS*, p. 147). This is a scene that will certainly end in Antoinette's destruction, but Christophine intervenes and coaxes Antoinette back to the safe position behind the zombi mask that Rochester at once demands and finds so threatening: "I could see Antoinette stretched on the bed quite still. Like a doll" (*WSS*, p. 149).

The final confrontation between Rochester and Christophine, representing the conflict between Anglo-European and Afro-Caribbean epistemologies, is played out over the still body of Antoinette, the white Creole. Rochester is right to see in Christophine a dangerous enemy. Obeah healers like Christophine have traditionally represented a great source of resistance and rebellion for the oppressed lower classes of the Caribbean.[85] When Rochester finds himself confronted by this herb-woman who threatens his power and control, he attempts to reassert the European patriarchal hierarchy and deny the alternative power that Christophine represents. Following Mr. Fraser, the magistrate of Spanish Town, Rochester renames Christophine "Josephine" (*WSS*, p. 143), thereby denying her her symbolic association with the triumphant black revolutionary and ruler of Haiti, Henri Christophe. He aligns her instead with Joséphine deBeauharnais, the white Martinican wife of Napoleon Bonaparte, the French emperor who challenges Haitian independence and loses.[86] Ironically, either name points to the ultimate loss of European control of the Caribbean colonies.

This confrontation of European and native power ends with Rochester's reliance on "law" and Christophine's use of an Obeah curse ("Read and write I don't know. Other things I know"). The confrontation between European law and Obeah magic is a drama repeatedly enacted in Caribbean history. In the section of documents on "Obeah trials" in the collection of British travel journals *After Africa* there appears a journal entry from Matthew Gregory Lewis on the legal conviction of an Obeah worker in 1834, historically coincident with the emancipation and the moment of *Wide Sargasso Sea:* "The good old practice of burning has fallen into disrepute; so [the Obeah worker] was sentenced to be transported, and was shipped off the island, to the great satisfaction of persons of all colours."[87] Faced with this kind of legal power, Christophine walks out of the text at this point, but as Mary Lou Emery describes in a close reading of this dialogue (*WSS*, 153–54), Christophine has successfully implicated herself in Rochester's mind, and his own position becomes muddled and confused. With her magic Christophine has forced Rochester to mentally echo her own words and to hear Antoinette's despair.[88] Finally, she allows Rochester to devise his own curse so that his suffering derives from his own arrogant refusal to give credence to cultures and beliefs not his own:

> "I would give my eyes never to have seen this abominable place."
> She laughed. "And that's the first damn word of truth you speak. You choose what you give, eh? Then you choose. You meddle in something and perhaps you don't know what it is." She began to mutter to herself. Not in patois. I knew the sound of patois now. (*WSS*, p. 161)

He discounts Christophine's muttering as "madness," as he has discounted most of the important information Antoinette and Christophine have given him, but we know from Charlotte Brontë's *Jane Eyre* that indeed this curse is fulfilled when Rochester is blinded in the fire at Thornfield.

This confrontation with Christophine is the last active resistance he has to face until that fire. From this point he is mocked by impassive inscrutable faces: the "mask" on Christophine's face (*WSS*, p. 161); Antoinette's "blank hating moonstruck face" (*WSS*, p. 165); "her blank indifference" (*WSS*, p. 167); and her "silence" (*WSS*, p. 168). As they leave the island, Rochester claims that he has forced the last of Antoinette's expressed hatred from her eyes with the coolness of his own hate and has left her a "ghost in the grey daylight [with] blank lovely eyes" (*WSS*, p. 170). Her voice reveals nothing, no hatred, misery, or anger:

> I scarcely recognized her voice. No warmth, no sweetness. The doll had a doll's voice, a breathless but curiously indifferent voice. . . . I thought she would cry then. No, the doll's smile came back — nailed to her face. (*WSS*, p. 171)

She no longer tries to please him or communicate with him; she carries her secret of hatred deep within:

> Very soon she'll join all the others who know the secret and will not tell it. Or cannot. Or try and fail because they do not know enough. They can be recognized. White faces, dazed eyes, aimless gestures, high-pitched laughter. (*WSS*, p. 172)

But it is that secret that makes Antoinette far more dangerous to Rochester than a doll or a ghost. The domination Rochester has exerted over

Antoinette as he colonized her allowed only one form of resistance, a subservience behind which lies buried the vital spirit, the *essence*, of the individual that remains hidden from the colonizer's exploitative gaze. The zombi is not dead like the ghost nor inanimate like the doll, but a dormant spirit of outrage and revolt waiting to awaken to destroy the oppressor and to ravage his goods.[89]

By the end of her story Antoinette resembles a zombi, at once the most oppressed of all slaves and the most disquieting and threatening figure to her master and his entire class. Caught as Antoinette is between the European and Afro-Caribbean worldviews, it is not clear who finally has won Antoinette's soul, Rochester or Christophine. While Antoinette as a child had longed to see herself accepted by the black community, it has taken the white colonialist's racist evaluation of the meaning of her identity as a white Creole[90] and his economic and sexual use of her to force her to turn in her final moments to identify with Christophine and Tia. Lee Erwin points out that Antoinette's leap to Tia and Christophine is contingent on Rochester's belief that Antoinette is of mixed racial background (seen most clearly in his sudden fear that Antoinette and Amelie are related) and his projection of the sexual excesses of the white planters onto the women. It is finally his racism that causes Antoinette to claim a psychological and political connection with the Caribbean Blacks and to destroy the symbol of English power. Yet this revenge might also be the resolution incubating in Christophine's protective conjuring of Antoinette. This kind of doubling and mirroring present throughout the text reinforces the complexities of Rhys's rendering of power relations. From her perspective as a white Creole, Rhys has claimed some difficult connections across racial boundaries: the disenfranchisement of Daniel Cosway and Rochester; the commodification of Christophine and Antoinette; the zombilike affects and natures of Baptiste, Rochester, Pierre, Annette, and Antoinette; and the conjuring power of Rochester and Christophine. These complicated fluctuations of power and identifications, however, do not detract from Rhys's prediction about the final outcome of colonization and abuse. The figure of the zombi promises that history and memory will someday assert themselves to remind those who would forget of the price paid for Thornfield Hall and Coulibri Estate, as well as the price paid for their destruction.

Rhys most fully explores such fury, alienation, and misery in her portrayals of her West Indian characters cut off from the Caribbean and stranded in England or France. In these depictions, the Caribbean Creole comes to a recognition of her non-English cultural identification only by confronting the storybook version of England with the real thing. The Caribbean Creole, mesmerized by England's representations of itself, once there, wakens to a recognition of her alienation and exploitation and, furious, dreams of revenge.

4 / "This Cold Thief Place"

Rhys's West Indian Women in England and Europe

I come so far I lose myself on that journey.
—*Jean Rhys, "Let Them Call It Jazz"*

I am the little Colonial walking in the London garden patch — allowed to look perhaps, but not to linger.   — *Katherine Mansfield,* Journal

England: Dream and Nightmare

The displacement Jean Rhys's characters experience under British cultural and political domination on the islands is compounded when they "return" to their "mother country," the home of some or all of their ancestors. "The Day They Burned the Books" ends during Eddie Sawyer's childhood, but we can imagine him later making the journey to England for a British education he may distrust, but one that he nonetheless needs to maintain his social, economic, and even racial standing. Such is the journey made by many Caribbean fictional characters, such as Clare Savage in Michelle Cliff's *No Telephone to Heaven* and Tee in Merle Hodge's *Crick Crack, Monkey.* Others, like Samuel Selvon's characters in *Lonely Londoners,* journey to England after World War II hoping for work. For those whose parents or grandparents came from Great Britain, their trip is often considered a "return" to the "mother country" although they themselves may never have been there before. Rhys's stories such as "Let Them Call It Jazz" and "Temps Perdi," her novel *Voyage in the Dark,* and part 3 of *Wide Sargasso Sea* continue her exploration of West Indians' relationship to English culture,

144

but in these works the confrontation takes place on English soil. Christophine's assessment of England as a "cold thief place" captures the alienation and economic exploitation that Rhys's women experience in England and France. As Rhys makes clear in her depictions of "alien" women, selfhood depends not only on cultural reflections of one's experience and environment but also on economic agency. Rhys shows the ways in which cultural colonialism, operating through myths of home and family, is particularly implicated in the economic impoverishment and social exploitation of the colonized woman.[1]

We can recognize Rhys's fictional depictions of West Indians in England within a central theme in Caribbean literature (and even more generally in Anglophone postcolonial literature): the alienation of the colonial-born character in England after World War II. Typical of this genre are Samuel Selvon's and George Lamming's writings that focus on the adventures and difficulties of male West Indians in England trying to find work, love, and dignity in a racist society.[2] Rhys's work is specifically and adamantly about *female* West Indians from a variety of racial backgrounds. Because these characters are white or partially white Creoles, they make the journey to England a kind of "homecoming." While Rhys's analysis shares much with those of male Caribbean writers of her time, her work adds the crucial variable of gender to the relationship of colonialism, capitalism, race, and exile. In most of the critical surveys of West Indian literature of the 1960s and 1970s, when Rhys was writing her later work, she is the only woman represented.[3] Caribbean literature of the 1950s and 1960s was largely written by male writers depicting primarily male experience.

Following Phyllis Shand Allfrey, who wrote the novel *The Orchid House* (1953), Rhys was one of the first West Indian writers to focus on West Indian women. Her novels and short stories repeatedly articulate the complex social position of the "strange woman" for whom being "down-and-out," as are most of Rhys's characters, is an experience that differs significantly from that of her male counterparts in fiction and journalistic exposé.

Antoinette's ultimate disempowerment and impoverishment in *Wide Sargasso Sea* is facilitated by a fetishized representation of the British Empire grounded, as we have seen, in myths of family loyalty and safety. For Antoinette, who is passed from guardian to guardian — from mother to nurse to step-father to church to step-brother to husband — the stability of familial relations represented by the title of the dining room picture, the *Miller's Daughter,* is an attractive alternative to the confused girlhood she lives.

Rochester, who did not enjoy but rather suffered an English childhood, recognizes Antoinette's idealization for the colonial dream it is:

> She often questioned me about England and listened attentively to my an-
> swers, but I was certain that nothing I said made much difference. Her mind
> was already made up. Some romantic novel, a stray remark never forgotten,
> a sketch, a picture, a song, a waltz, some note of music, and her ideas were
> fixed. About England and about Europe. (*WSS,* p. 94)

Although, as we saw in the previous chapter, the English cultural domination of colonial education in many ways makes England more "real"
to the native Caribbean than his or her native land, there always remains
the intriguing mystery of the metropolis, the unsettling attraction of the
unfamiliar:

> England, rosy pink in the geography book map, but on the page opposite
> the words are closely crowded, heavy looking. Exports, coal, iron, wool.
> Then imports and character of inhabitants. Names, Essex, Chelmsford on
> the Chelmer. The Yorkshire and Lincolnshire wolds. Wolds? Does that mean
> hills? How high? Half the height of ours, or not even that? Cool green leaves
> in the short cool summer. Summer. There are fields of corn like sugar-cane
> fields, but gold colour and not so tall. After summer the trees are bare, then
> winter and snow. White feathers falling? Torn pieces of paper falling? They
> say frost makes flower patterns on the window panes. (*WSS,* p. 111)

A great part of Antoinette's education has very little to do with her actual
lived experience. The English place-names she learns are mythical sounds
to her, and she can only guess what cornfields or snow might look like
by comparing them with what she knows about her Caribbean world. In
contrast to Antoinette's confusion, the girl represented in the *Miller's Daughter* seems quite at home in this mythical world. Antoinette's identification
with that girl requires that Antoinette regard her own surroundings and
experiences as insignificant, less than real.

In her novel *Crick Crack, Monkey* (1970), Merle Hodge movingly expresses this feeling of inauthenticity and cultural doubleness experienced by
those inculcated with the imperial dream. Her heroine, Tee, growing up in
Trinidad, creates for herself an English double named Helen, who, like the
Miller's Daughter, is quite comfortable with her English surroundings:

> She was my age and height. She spent the summer holidays at the sea-side
> with her aunt and uncle who had a delightful orchard with apple trees and
> pear trees in which sang chaffinches and blue tits, and where one could wan-
> der on terms of the closest familiarity with cowslips and honeysuckle. Helen
> loved to visit her Granny for then they sat by the fireside and had tea with

delicious scones and home-made strawberry jam.... Helen wasn't even my double. No, she couldn't be called my double. She was the Proper Me. And me, I was her shadow hovering about in incompleteness.

For doubleness, or this particular kind of doubleness, was a thing to be taken for granted. Why, the whole of life was like a piece of cloth, with a rightside and a wrongside. Just as there was a way you spoke and a way you wrote, so there was the daily existence which you led, which of course amounted only to marking time and makeshift, for there was the Proper daily round, not necessarily more agreeable, simply the valid one, the course of which encompassed things like warming yourself before a fire and having tea at four o'clock; there were the human types who were your neighbors and guardians and playmates — but you were all marginal together, for there were the beings whose validity loomed at you out of every book, every picture (often there were Natives and Red Indians and things, but these were for chuckles and for beating back, to bring you once more the satisfaction that Right prevaileth always just before THE END), the beings whose exemplary aspect it was that shone forth to recommend at you every commodity proposed to your daily preference, from macaroni to the Kingdom of Heaven.[4]

It is not coincidental or accidental that for Hodge literature and advertising occupy the same position and have the same effect on Tee's consciousness. English literature *is* the advertisement for the benefits of English rule. Dionne Brand, who is from Trinidad, makes much the same point about American popular culture and U.S. imperialism when she compares the Dallas Cowboys with the U.S. Marines.[5]

Because much of their daily experience goes unreflected in the literature, art, and racial ideology that surrounds them, Rhys's characters suffer from an inability to articulate, let alone take control of, their political situations. The myth of England and of the colonials' spiritual and racial relationship to it contributes to their feelings of inauthenticity both at home and in England. The doubleness of their identities — as both Caribbean and English while also neither Caribbean nor English — forces them to shift between the two national "realities," much as one must focus on *either* the goblet *or* the women's profiles in the gestalt visual images. Seeing one image necessarily excludes the other; it takes a great deal of mental energy to retain the existence of both simultaneously. As the creole character Anna Morgan in Rhys's novel *Voyage in the Dark* puts it: "Sometimes it was as if I were back there and as if England were a dream. At other times England was the real thing and out there was the dream, but I could never fit them together" (*VD*, p. 3).

But it is not only the British Creoles like Anna and Antoinette who struggle to establish a stable lived reality in a place defined psychologically and culturally by myth. Rochester, too, has grown up with a cultural representation of a foreign land — that is, with the English literary creation of the abundant but menacing New World. Antoinette and Rochester represent for each other the seductive yet terrifying differences of the Old and New Worlds invented by European literature and art. The "dream" each of them seeks in the other embodies within it the nightmare of the strange:

> "Is it true," she said, "that England is like a dream? Because one of my friends who married an Englishman wrote and told me so. She said this place London is like a cold dark dream sometimes. I want to wake up."
>
> "Well," I answered annoyed, "that is precisely how your beautiful island seems to me, quite unreal and like a dream."
>
> "But how can rivers and mountains and the sea be unreal?"
>
> "And how can millions of people, their houses and their streets be unreal?"
>
> "More easily," she said, "much more easily. Yes a big city must be like a dream."
>
> "No, this is unreal and like a dream," I thought. (*WSS*, pp. 80–81)

For Antoinette, the colonial, England is a troubling double image — the exotic yet comforting England she learns about in school and identifies with as a white person and a place where her dream of violence, one she simultaneously struggles to suppress and to discover, will be enacted.

Like Schreiner's Bertie in *From Man to Man,* Antoinette finds that her place of escape is also her place of imprisonment; her dream of an England of snow, cornfields, and millers' daughters progressively becomes her dream of violence and destruction. Each time Antoinette has her dream, England becomes more menacing and she becomes more active. This "dream" is never referred to as her "nightmare," for by the end of *Wide Sargasso Sea* the violence visited upon the English institution (Thornfield Hall) and English literature (*Jane Eyre*) *is* the dream of the awakened and furious colonized figure.[6] The one thing Antoinette does not lose in the course of her journey of disintegration is this dream that progressively reveals England to be a strange, foreign place, *not* a home or refuge for the Jamaican Creole. This shifting dream of England and of her place in it is Antoinette's coherent psychological (and later her political) answer to her loss of agency as she is exchanged between English men. Although in the convent Antoinette does not yet recognize that the menacing place in her dream is England, we recognize the prophesy ("This must happen" [*WSS*, p. 60]) building in Antoinette's series of dreams about England and Thornfield Hall:

We are no longer in the forest but in an enclosed garden surrounded by a stone wall and the trees are different trees. I do not know them. There are steps leading upwards. It is too dark to see the wall or the steps, but I know they are there and I think, "It will be when I go up these steps. At the top." (*WSS*, p. 60)

These "different trees" that Antoinette does not recognize are English trees. Unconsciously she knows that England is not really the place she will find the beauty and comfort she longs for. Although on some level she knows the confrontation that awaits her "at the top" of Thornfield Hall, she cannot yet consciously connect this terror with England. In fact, Antoinette tells the nun in the convent that she had been dreaming about hell, not England.[7]

In "Temps Perdi" Rhys again describes England as hell, especially to the outsider. The narrator of this story continues Mrs. Sawyer's struggle against the "lies" of books and is relieved to find one book that she can use as a defense against the rest because "all saying the same thing they can shout you down and make you doubt, not only your memory, but your senses."[8] The book she finds validates her own experience of England as a cold, heartless place, and she quotes the passage triumphantly:

" . . . to conduct the transposition of the souls of the dead to the White Island, in the manner just described. The White Island is occasionally also called Brea, or Britannia. Does this perhaps refer to White Albion, to the chalky cliffs of the English coast? It would be a very humorous idea if England was designated as the land of the dead . . . as hell. In such a form, in truth, England has appeared to many a stranger." (To many a stranger . . .). ("TP," p. 257)

The association of England with hell is humorous to this unnamed author because it is in such obvious discord with England's own cultural self-understanding. But Antoinette's complex political and cultural status makes it difficult for her to separate the mythologized England from the harsh reality of the place. Nowhere is Benedict Anderson's definition of a nation as an "imagined community" more striking than in the power such imagination holds over the British Creole. Because their very identities are dependent on their connection with an imagined English mother country, Rhys's creole characters suffer greatly when, upon their journey "home," they confront an England that in its coldness and brutality proves the storybook England to have been a lie. Antoinette cannot reconcile her hatred of England and her final defiance against it (her dream) with the Creole's cultural love of England:

I must know more than I know already. For I know that house where I will be cold and not belonging, the bed I shall lie in has red curtains and I have slept there many times before, long ago. How long ago? In that bed I will dream the end of my dream. *But my dream had nothing to do with England and I must not think like this,* I must remember about chandeliers and dancing, about swans and roses and snow. And snow. (*WSS,* p. 111; emphasis added)

Antoinette remembers her hellish dream when she tells Christophine she wants to go to England, but she adamantly refuses to make the connection between her alienation and the mythical England of swans, roses, and snow. Even at the end, when she is imprisoned in the manor house she is about to destroy, Antoinette continues to split the idea of England in two, maintaining an idyllic England separate from the political reality of the England that has denied her freedom and civil rights. The "real" England in Antoinette's mind is the one in which she is more than an object of exchange and in which she can exercise her own economic transactions. In answer to Grace Poole's question about where she acquired the knife with which she attacked Richard Mason, Antoinette answers:

"When we went to England," I said.
"You fool," [Grace Poole] said, "this is England."
"I don't believe it," I said, "and I never will believe it."
(That afternoon we went to England. There was grass and olive-green water and tall trees looking into the water. This, I thought, is England. If I could be here I'd get well again and the sound in my head would stop. Let me stay a little longer, I said, and she sat down under a tree and went to sleep. A little way off there was a cart and horse — a woman was driving it. It was she who sold me the knife. I gave her the locket round my neck for it). (*WSS,* pp. 183–84)

England, the "home" and "mother" of the Creole, has betrayed Antoinette. Her response as a split subject — on the one hand, a loyal British subject and, on the other, a Caribbean nationalist of sorts — is a split conception of the England that has betrayed her. That which does not correlate with the myth of roses and bright snow — the manor house, her imprisonment, the damp cold — becomes not-England: "They tell me I am in England but I don't believe them. We lost our way to England. . . . This cardboard house where I walk at night is not England" (*WSS,* p. 181). Gayatri Spivak reads this "cardboard house" as the actual book *Jane Eyre* in which Antoinette finds herself trapped — the text that demands "a self-immolating colonial subject."[9] It is also, however, Antoinette's attempt to continue believing in a "real" England that matches the cultural mythology while she destroys the

England that entraps her. If she must see one England as "unreal" or "cardboard," she maintains the mythical England as real; the one she experiences as the theater prop can be struck at the end of the play.[10]

Antoinette's rebellion and destruction are therefore not directed against the "English" part of herself but against a brutal political reality that threatens her own identity as an English/Caribbean Creole. This reading attributes more ambivalence to Antoinette's act of violence and retribution than does Sandra Drake's or Mary Lou Emery's, both of which interpret the final act as a resolution of Antoinette's conflicted identifications and loyalties and as her commitment to indigenous as opposed to British culture. It is, however, Antoinette's inability to thoroughly dispose of her belief in a benign and motherly England that prohibits her from enacting a conscious and self-preserving resistance.

In contrast to Antoinette's persistent desire for and allegiance to this place, England, Christophine recognizes that England is as much a construct of "belief" as of "knowledge" or truth. Unlike the white Creole, she asserts her identity as separate from its existence:

> "England," said Christophine, who was watching me. "You think there is such a place?"
> "How can you ask that? You know there is."
> "I never see the damn place, how I know?"
> "You do not believe that there is a country called England?"
> She blinked and answered quickly, "I don't say I don't *believe*, I say I don't *know*, I know what I see with my eyes and I never see it.... Besides I ask myself is this place like they tell us? Some say one thing, some different, I hear it cold to freeze your bones and they thief your money, clever like the devil. You have money in your pocket, you look again and bam! No money. Why you want to go to this cold thief place? If there is this place at all, I never see it, that is one thing sure." (*WSS*, pp. 111–12)[11]

When Antoinette changes Christophine's more metaphorical "place"-England to the political "country"-England, Christophine recognizes the power of this vocabulary ("She blinked and quickly answered..."). As an Obeah woman whose knowledge exceeds the categories of English ontology, Christophine has been forced, at least in appearance, to acquiesce to the new "belief" system of legal incantations by which the new English order can imprison her as a practitioner of a competing code of power. When Christophine distances herself as a black Caribbean from the spiritual "place"-England, Antoinette switches the terminology to one of politics and fealty. Recognizing the threat implicit in the political terminology, Christophine retreats behind the double negative ("I didn't say I don't believe"), while countering the white creole myth of England with the black version of it as a "cold thief place." The magical word "country," Christophine discovers, only carries power in Prospero's mouth. She tries to use it as self-protection against Rochester's threats: "'No police here,' she said. 'No chain gang, no tread machine, no dark jail either. This is free country and I am free woman'" (*WSS*, p. 160). But apparently the political use of "country" is effective only for the white "children" of the "mother" country. For the black ex-slave, England is not a "mother" but a "thief," not a protector but an exploiter.

At the center of Rhys's writing is her extremely powerful deconstruction of this "family" — the mother country, England, and her children, the colonies. Just as Schreiner challenged the Victorian racist ideology of the "Anglo-Saxon family," Rhys takes on the later incarnation of the "family" of nonwhite nations under the parental Crown of England. The inclusion of non-Whites in this "family" does not offer them equal status with whites but gives them merely the status of children. Rhys's Caribbean characters returning to the mother country do not find themselves nurtured in the "home" they have been so persuasively educated to expect, but rather find themselves once again in exile, this time not on the frontier, but in the heart of the metropolis.

The metaphor of family for political relations is not haphazard but highlights the exploitation that Rhys sees at the heart of both the political and social family systems. Her characters' "homesickness" is the result of the unhealthy political and kinship relationships permitted by the sacred space of the "family." In her short story "Trio," an early story about West Indians in Paris, Rhys explores the similarities between the constructed relations of family and national identification.[12]

The two-page story is the description by a third-person narrator of three West Indians, a man, a woman, and a girl, eating in a Parisian restaurant. Like "Again the Antilles," also published in Rhys's first volume of stories, "Trio" is the study of racial location in which the three variously "colored" patrons and the narrator, who from her valuations of the others' pigmentation is presumably white, occupy different racial categories. Nevertheless, from the narrator's point of view, as West Indian compatriots and foreigners, these four characters occupy the same political space. The narrator describes the three dinner companions as follows:

> The man was very black — coal black, with a thick silver ring on a finger of one hand. He wore a smart grey lounge suit, cut in at the waist, and his woolly hair was carefully brushed back and brilliantined. The woman was

coffee-coloured and fat. She had on the native Martinique turban, making no pretension to fashion. Her bodice and skirt gaped apart and through the opening a coarse white cotton chemise peeped innocently forth.... From the Antilles...

Between them was a girl, apparently about fifteen, but probably much younger. She sat very close to the man and every now and then would lay her head on his shoulder for a second.... There was evidently much white blood in her veins: the face was charming.

She had exactly the movements of a very graceful kitten, and he, appreciative, would stop eating to kiss her... long, lingering kisses, and, after each one she would look round the room as if to gather up a tribute of glances of admiration and envy — a lovely, vicious little thing.... From the Antilles, too. You cannot think what home-sickness descended over me.... ("Trio," p. 34)

In an article on the use of physical place in Rhys's work, Kevin Magarey describes this story as "a loving description of a Martinique family in a Paris restaurant."[13] At first I dismissed this reading because it differed so radically from my own interpretation of the relationship between the members of this "trio." How could Magarey interpret the "long, lingering kisses" and the "huge delight" the girl provides the man by jumping up from the table and singing and dancing with feverish excitement as a loving description of family relations? While I do disagree with Magarey's reading of the story, it is provocative to consider what in the story *itself* could lead to such an interpretation. In other words, the gender and age configurations of the trio *can* be seen to constitute an ironic almost-family. It is significant that Rhys presents as a tableau a relationship between a young girl and her dubious guardians, an older man and woman. The relationship for all its apparent gaiety is not a happy one. Feverishly the girl sings a patois song, "F'en ai marre," roughly translated "I'm fed up with it," while the older woman, trying to keep her quiet, proudly attests to the girl's charm and teasing allure: "Mais... ce qu'elle est cocasse, quand même!" (She's still funny, after all!).

Far from reading this story as a loving description, I read it as a frightening and unsettling mystery, a story in which the subject (that is, both the issue and the consciousness in the story) is missing. While the story is primarily description, it is not a story of disclosure but of secrecy. The most obvious and unanswered question of the story is what the relationship among the three characters actually is. Is the older woman the girl's nurse? ("Doudou," she calls her, the comforting name Christophine gives Antoinette.) Is she in a position to protect this girl, and if so why is she not doing so? What is the economic relationship between the man with the "thick silver ring" and the frumpy woman, and are the girl's sexual favors to the man part of the "family" economics? What looks like a family is likely the bartering of the daughter; at the heart of the gaiety is weariness and a plea for help.

When "Trio" is set next to the family economics of *Wide Sargasso Sea,* the exploitation of the young girl is obvious. It is the myth and appearance of family that permits Mason (with the help of his son Richard) to barter his step-daughter to Rochester. In *Wide Sargasso Sea* Rhys reveals that family relationships are at root the legal terms, the excuse, that allow father, brother, and husband to define and use the daughter as exchange value between themselves and to transfer the wealth of the colonies once and for all to English banks. When Christophine (who herself became a commodity on the occasion of the Cosway wedding) advises Antoinette to take her money ("Pick up your skirt and walk out"), Antoinette must explain that English law denies her, now that she is Rochester's wife, her money and freedom:

> "...I am not rich now, I have no money of my own at all, everything I had belongs to him."
> "What you tell me there?" she said sharply.
> "That is English law."
> "Law! The Mason boy fix it, that boy worse than Satan and he burn in Hell one of these fine nights." (*WSS,* 110)

The much-noted repetition in Rhys's fiction of the relationship between a younger passive woman and an older seemingly caretaking man underscores what Rhys saw as the exploitation inherent in sexual and colonial relations when they are legitimized by the ideology of family-like relations. In their studies of the Black Exercise Books that Rhys kept, Teresa O'Connor and Mary Lou Emery point to the importance of Rhys's "psychosexual involvement" as a young girl in Dominica with the elderly Mr. Howard, an Englishman who took her for rides in his carriage and told her "serial stories" involving the two of them in violent and sado-masochistic sex, always concluding with "her own sexual submission and humiliation."[14] Mary Lou Emery sees Rhys's autobiographical story of this relationship, "Goodbye Marcus, Goodbye Rose," as being an analysis not only of an individual psychological experience but also of a more general sociological and political relationship as well. Emery recognizes that, in addition to the critique of colonial relations, Rhys's stories point to a connection between this particular kind of exploitation and the myth of "the family." The lovers who look something like fathers — Captain Cardew in "Goodbye Marcus, Goodbye Rose," Walter Jeffries in *Voyage in the Dark,* Hugh Heidler in *Quartet,* or the "coal black" man in "Trio" — all legitimate their sexual exploitation by their roles as advisers and financial caretakers. But the mother figures, like the woman in "Trio" or Hester in *Voyage in the Dark,* provide as little protection for the young women as did Rhys's own mother in the Mr. Howard episode. The parentless, particularly fatherless, young women in these stories long for the security of "belonging" that is promised but ultimately denied them by the social and political family.[15] They are neither daughters nor wives in their relationships; they are prostitutes or "kept" mistresses. Rhys asserts a striking similarity between sexual and racial positions and the threat of indeterminacy. The mistress, who Emery argues operates as a third term between wife and prostitute ("good" and "bad" woman),[16] occupies a similar position to that of Papa Dom, the "colored" man, neither black nor white, whose existence threatens the colonial dichotomies of racial and national difference.[17] Anna, Selina in "Let Them Call It Jazz," and Antoinette, among other Rhys heroines, are denied legitimate and equal membership in the so-called British family, not only because they are mistresses or rejected wives but because they are Creoles, "horrid colonials," manifesting the inferiority of their birthplaces.

Although the ambiguity of Rhys's social place as a white creole woman allows her to observe the instabilities inherent in such colonial binarisms, the uncomfortable ambivalence of her own position can be seen in "Trio." The two centers, or rather gaps, in the story provide an intriguing connection and antithesis. The first, as we have seen, is the unknown position of the young girl in the triangle of the almost-family. The second is the unknown identity and relation of the white creole "watcher," the narrator. What we know by the last line is that the narrator feels related to the trio and that this relationship would probably be unrecognized (for racial reasons) by the rest of the patrons in the restaurant: "It was because these were my compatriots that in that Montparnasse restaurant I remembered the Antilles" ("Trio," p. 35). These two crucial gaps in the story connect the narrator's political relationship with the trio with the "familial" relationship of the three diners. While we are never sure how the three belong together, we are told that the narrator belongs with them as a "compatriot" in a way she does not with other Parisians. By claiming this more intimate relationship with these three strangers, the white creole narrator creates another almost-family. While it allows her a place of "belonging" in her European alienation, it also underemphasizes the important racial differences between the trio and herself and thereby masks the economic exploitation embedded in *their* relationship. In fact, the narrator's "homesickness" depends on a memory of island culture that undoubtedly privileged her economically at the expense of black West Indians. The narrator's claim of egalitarian fraternity evoked by her use of "compatriot" is one-sided; whether or not any of the trio would experience this bond with the narrator as anything more than a romantic myth is questionable.

At the moment that Rhys reveals an ugliness at the heart of an accepted structure of power, the family, she nevertheless re-creates a mythic family of Caribbeans. As a white Creole she can see the exploitative use of the ideology of the family by British men such as Rochester, Mr. Sawyer in "The Day They Burned the Books," or Captain Cardew in "Goodbye Marcus, Goodbye Rose." But her very longing for a fulfillment of the empty myth of the British family leads her to adopt a romantic myth of a multiracial Caribbean family that, not unlike the British version, claims loyalty and safety where none exists.

In this way, we can read "Trio" with the same strategy we used when reading "Again the Antilles" and "The Day They Burned the Books." On one level, we can appreciate the subtle connections Rhys makes regarding the racial, cultural, and sexual relationships she perceives. On another level, we can ask where these perceptions are coming from and what additional story is being told. By naming what goes unnamed in the text, in this case the racial and political location of the narrator, we can recognize a possible strain or discomfort that determines the shape and scope of the story. In other words, the story that is told can be seen as a defensive gesture masking the "real" story the author has to tell. In this case, the story of the man and woman's use of the young girl is told instead of the story of the narrator's (or Rhys's) use of black Caribbeans. Similarly, the power struggle between Eddie Sawyer and his mother stands in for the unspoken relationship between the narrator and the black servant, Mildred. Just as Rhys focused her attention on Brontë's off-stage Bertha and discovered a story that had not yet been told, so we can find rich and important stories embedded in Rhys's own texts, particularly her earlier ones. If the story Rhys tells critiques the metaphors that sustain colonialist politics (metaphors linking race to culture or family to empire), the story embedded within it reveals the collusion and participation in this politics of even such an astute critic. The nostalgia of the narrators in both "Again the Antilles" and "Trio" becomes the point of entry into the not-told story. That nostalgia, and the contradictions it reveals, is the mark of the white creole woman writer, who occupies a position of both privilege and estrangement. Reading for the silence of the stories tells us much about the seductive power of colonialist metaphors and myths even for those who, like Rhys, recognize their disastrous effects.

Rhys's conflict between her envy and fear of Blacks and her shame and pride of being white manifests itself in these stories through her critique of colonial definitions and uses of "race" and the incompleteness of that analysis vis-à-vis the white creole narrator. This is not to say, however, that Rhys's characters are simply autobiographical representations or that Rhys was incapable of consciously exploring the desires, fears, and blindnesses of her white creole characters. In *Wide Sargasso Sea,* for instance, Rhys makes it clear that Antoinette *imagines* a sisterhood with Tia that, to Antoinette's bewilderment, Tia rejects. The connection with Christophine and Tia that Antoinette finally attains at the end of the novel is unquestionably Antoinette's fantasy, her final desire of her final dream. That Rhys chose to render this profound connection as a dream suggests that after so many years working on this representation of white creole identification, Rhys fully recognized the psychological, economic, and cultural impediments to positive interracial relationships in colonial societies.

"Let Them Call It Jazz"

In one of her later short stories, "Let Them Call It Jazz,"[18] Rhys attempts to portray such interracial relationships from the point of view of a black, or more precisely, a "colored," West Indian immigrant woman, Selina Davis, who is uneducated and struggling for subsistence within a bigoted and sexist English society. The story is told in Selina's voice, a Caribbean English distinct from the voice of Rhys's white creole narrators. Selina's poverty, her impending homelessness, and her isolation are an indictment of the false promises of the colonial rhetoric in which all British subjects — English and colonial, white and black, male and female — are valued and cared for. This story, appearing in *Tigers Are Better Looking* (1968), was written during the period of increasing publication of Caribbean emigrant literature by writers such as George Lamming and Samuel Selvon, almost all of which centered on the West Indian male experience. The characters in this story and some of Rhys's later characters are fictional representations of the wave of immigrants who came to London looking for work after World War II, taking the "mother country" up on her promise of imperial protection, now in the form of promised jobs. The Jamaican poet Louise Bennett perfectly catches the irony of this mass movement in her poem "Colonization in Reverse." Here are several stanzas:

Wat a joyful news, Miss Mattie,
I feel like me heart gwine burs
Jamaica people colonizin
Englan in reverse.

By de hundred, by de tousan
From country and from town,
By de ship-load, by de plane-load
Jamaica is Englan boun.

Dem a pour out a Jamaica,
Everybody future plan
Is fe get a big-time job
An settle in de mother lan.

What a islan! What a people!
Man an woman, old an young
Jus a pack dem bag and baggage
An tun history upside dung! . . .

Wat a devilment a Englan!
Dem face war an brave de worse,
But me wonderin how dem gwine stan
Colonizin in reverse.[19]

In the 1950s and 1960s almost all of this important literature by African, Indian, and Caribbean immigrants is by and about men. Rhys's focus on women immigrants' experience raises crucial questions about the intersections of racism, sexism, and xenophobia pursued by contemporary writers such as Buchi Emecheta, Ama Ata Aidoo, and Michelle Cliff. "Let Them Call It Jazz" depicts the life of one such immigrant, a woman whose "placelessness" is both her own personal struggle for survival and a symbolic threat to the English state. Homelessness is more than a metaphorical condition in this story of exilic alienation; the story opens with Selina losing her apartment in London when the English landlord, changing the terms of her tenancy, demands a month's rent in advance. Selina knows from previous experience that as a "colored" foreigner in England she can call on no authority to rectify this injustice. When it is her word against anyone else's, she will lose: "Don't talk to me about London. Plenty people there have heart like stone. Any complaint — the answer is 'prove it.' But if nobody bear witness for me, how to prove anything? So I pack up and leave" ("LT," p. 158). Having no job and no place to go, she considers herself lucky when she meets a man who offers her an empty flat he owns that until recently was occupied by another woman. Selina finds herself trapped in the flat by her own psychological passivity, her lack of alternative lodging and money, and the danger of being a woman "on the road" in England.

She lives in the damp flat all summer meaning to leave — "I think I go but I don't go" — drinking and singing songs loud enough to disturb the propriety of the suburban neighborhood. The neighbors stare at her "as if I'm wild animal let loose" and complain to the police to have her removed. The police, Selina knows, are not there to protect her rights; when her savings were stolen from her last lodging, the police treated her like a suspect instead of a victim and refused to pursue the case. The pressure the police exert represents a complex catch for the dispossessed person. Her legitimacy depends on her stability, as their questions imply: "What is my name? Am I a tenant of a flat in No. 17? How long have I lived there? Last address and so on" ("LT," p. 165). It is her wandering and joblessness that make her suspect and give the neighbors the right to hound her and later the police the right to remove her from her lodgings, further eroding her ability to demand protection from the state.[20] After a neighbor woman calls the police, maliciously accuses her of being a prostitute, and further ridicules her for not even being a white one, Selina breaks her window with a stone. Unable to defend herself articulately in court, she is sentenced to a prison term in Holloway. Selina's primary crime is not breaking the window but being an outsider with no place of her own. As Rosalind Miles puts it in *The Fiction of Sex,* the "crime" most of Rhys's heroines commit is not fitting in: "The 'punishment,' deprivation of cash, food, and a place to live, is, with nightmarish circularity, a further continuation of the 'crime.'"[21] Selina's neighbors determine that everything about her — her color, her accent, her "obscene" dancing and singing — has no place in this "proper" English suburb. Significantly, Selina's response is an attack not on the neighbors themselves but on one of their houses, the representation of stability and the authority of the propertied class.

At the same time that Selina is pressured to "move along," the state also punishes her vagrancy. While England will not provide her a safe and permanent home, her mobility and rootlessness are unsettling reminders of the human costs of empire and capitalism. Selina's transience undermines the myth of England as "home," and ironically the homeless woman is perceived to be a thief and vandal, rather than those who benefit from her underpaid migratory labor.[22] Holloway, the London prison, represents the ultimate power of the state over the stateless woman.

Ostensibly arrested for her attack on the neighbor's house, Selina believes she was really jailed for her singing. For her, music offers a kind of freedom that escapes the immobility of the body. Imprisoned, ill, and despairing behind the thick walls, Selina finds hope in a song she hears coming from one of the punishment cells. Although she had refused to read in jail because books are cultural products that perpetuate society's myths — "I don't think it's at all like those books tell you" — she hears in the bluesy song the power to bring the prison walls down: "One day I hear that song on trumpets and these walls will fall and rest" ("LT," p. 173). For her own singing she was fined with "drunk and disorderly," but even the prison walls cannot curtail the song that she believes "can jump the gates of the jail and travel far" ("LT," p. 173). The song of resistance, "Tell the girls cheerio and never say die" ("LT," p. 173), disrupts Selina's isolation and despair. Here is a voice that not only understands her position but stands defiantly against unjust authority.

The value of the song is its anonymous nature, owned by no one and sung by an unseen woman prisoner. For Selina it serves as a metaphor for what in culture and human life stands outside the economic relations by which she always loses. But Selina is disappointed in her gratification of even this one transgressive possibility. Overhearing the tune she whistles at a party after her release from prison, someone at the party plays it on the piano, jazzes it up, and ultimately sells it under his own name. Because she "helped" him with it, he sends her five pounds. The song, a woman's prison song, is now owned, copyrighted, and sold by a man who does not understand its origin or its value as a common good. It is now a fixed, unchanging commodity, a legitimate part of the economic market. Selina, too, has learned how to be a "legitimate" part of that market and lies her way into several jobs. She has learned how to talk and act and lie in this foreign world: "I know what to say and everything go like clockwork" ("LT," p. 175). With the money from the song she buys a new dress. Although the song, like herself, has become a functioning part of the larger economy, Selina holds as a precious memory the song as it was sung in the prison by the invisible woman.

Like "The Day They Burned the Books," this story pursues the question of economics and culture. Not only does English culture impose itself on the people of its colonies, but it *uses* the culture of the colonial subjects to revitalize itself. The irony is that despite the ideology of white cultural superiority, white artists use and claim as their own (often for handsome profits) the music and art of the cultures they supposedly disdain. It is interesting to pair Alice Walker's story "Nineteen Fifty-Five" with "Let Them Call It Jazz."[23] It too treats the "theft" of culture, specifically that of the black woman blues artist Gracie Mae Still (Big Mama Thornton) by a young, white, male singer, Traynor (Elvis Presley), who cannot really understand the song he becomes famous for. The title of Rhys's story, "Let Them Call It Jazz," evokes both a resignation to this kind of theft and an implication that no matter what is done to the song, what style is imposed upon it, how it is marketed, the culture of the dispossessed will always provide a transgressive, elusive space beyond the economics of colonial possession:

> After all, that song was all I had. I don't belong nowhere really, and I haven't money to buy my way to belonging. I don't want to either.
>
> But when that girl sing, she sing to me and she sing for me. I was there because I was *meant* to be there. It was *meant* I should hear it — this *I know.*
>
> Now I've let them play it wrong, and it will go from me like all the other songs — like everything. Nothing left for me at all.
>
> But then I tell myself all this is foolishness. Even if they played it on trumpets, even if they played it just right, like I wanted — no walls would fall so soon. "So let them call it jazz," I think, and let them play it wrong. That won't make no difference to the song I heard.
>
> I buy myself a dusty pink dress with the money. ("LT," p. 175)

If at the end of the story Selina has been "tamed," coerced by the law and by poverty, this is not to say that Rhys romanticizes the "free" life of the transient woman. She does, however, recognize the threat such a woman poses to the constructions of gender, family, and the state, all of which make up the fragile but emotionally charged promise of "home." Unlike Schreiner, who, more strongly identified with English culture, fears the anti-sociality of the "half-caste," Rhys applauds such antisocial behavior of an in-between character (in-between cultures and races) like Selina Davis. Even though her behavior does not "pay" in economic terms, Selina's drinking and singing, her passivity and sexuality, her color and her language, are all an affront to the state that would like her to disappear entirely or to remain abroad in the colonies, providing goods, markets, and vacation getaways for the English.

In Darkest London and Paris

The poverty Rhys's women suffer is both the cause and the result of what Wally Look Lai calls their "spiritual displacement." Rhys consistently makes that displacement geographical and national as well, underscoring the psychological and economic effects of colonialism and of women's shaky claims to citizenship and national identity. Whereas Look Lai identifies *Wide Sargasso Sea* as a distinctly Caribbean book in relation to Rhys's other novels, other critics, such as Helen Tiffin, Erika Smilowitz, Mary Lou Emery, and Coral Ann Howells, identify colonial themes and identities in *all* of Rhys's work. The connection between Rhys's West Indian women and her English women is most clearly seen in the character of the Martinican mulatto woman who appears briefly in a story told in *Good Morning, Midnight*. Sasha sees in the story of the almost monstrous West Indian woman who is "no longer quite human, no longer quite alive," an image of herself trapped in this foreign place, " 'Exactly like me,' I say" (*GMM,* p. 95). Like Selina, all of Rhys's women have "lost themselves" and become impoverished by their displacement. Just as Rhys's later fiction is a feminist addition to the male West Indian fiction of the 1960s and 1970s, her earlier fiction presents the female experience and analysis of poverty missing in the celebrated urban modernist writing and the journalistic accounts of the "homeless" in the first third of this century.

These accounts, from General William Booth's *In Darkest England and the Way Out* (1890) to Mrs. Cecil Chesterton's *In Darkest London* (1926), leaning as they do on the titles of H. M. Stanley's African expeditions, metaphorically compare the poor neighborhoods and poor people of London with the savagery and danger these writers project onto the African jungle. As a writer from one of the "savage" places of the empire (Heidler calls Marya "savage" in *Quartet*), Rhys does not compare but contrasts the brutality of urban life with the tranquility of her remembered tropical origins. Her outsider status permits her to make disinterested observations and to offer unique criticisms of the class relations peculiar to English and French society. But she is also more of an insider to the life of destitution than are those middle- and upper-middle-class writers who make poverty their professional interest or disguise themselves as poor people in order to wander through the slums undetected.

George Orwell is perhaps the most celebrated writer of this genre. Orwell wrote *Down and Out in Paris and London* after his adventures vagabonding in both cities between 1928 and 1931. Changing his clothes for those of a tramp, Orwell lives the life (for short periods of time) of the homeless wanderer. The world of poverty he depicts in his "reportage" is a world peopled almost entirely by men. Near the end of the book he explains the relative absence of women vagabonds with the generalization that "there are very few women at [the tramps'] level of society." Citing figures from charity houses, Orwell concludes, "It will be seen from these figures that at the charity level men outnumber women by something like ten to one. The cause is presumably that unemployment affects women less than men; also that any presentable woman can, in the last resort, attach herself to some man."[24] Daphne Patai addresses this lack of a female presence in Orwell's study of poverty and his narrowness of vision.[25] Citing statistics and studies of women's lower pay and the separate institution of women's rooming houses for female indigents, she shows that the problem was, indeed, a real one even if Orwell chose not to document it. Because he focuses on male experience and the more adventuresome subject of tramping and group lodging-house life, Orwell ignores the world of female poverty and rooming-house life that does not share the romantic aura of adventure or survival. Patai argues that Orwell's attraction to the "free man" on the road derives from a masculine cultural image: "One cannot say a 'free woman' and evoke any comparable resonance."[26] The poor, single, unemployed, familyless woman is in no sense romantically "free" in the masculinist terms governing the public and private spheres. When a woman moves from the private sphere of the home to the public sphere of the road, or even of those housing situations steps closer to the road, she becomes "free" primarily in terms of the price she can demand in the sexual market.

As the collection of articles in the volume *Women Writers and the City* makes clear, women's experience of the city in literature is significantly different from that of men in both "classic" and modern city novels. Whereas the city offers both male characters and their male authors a place to gain experience, knowledge, and power, female characters and authors almost inevitably find that they are trespassers in a space owned and governed by men. Some women writers, like Virginia Woolf and Vita Sackville-West, revel in this transgression and in the freedom the city offers them from the constrictions of the middle- and upper-class domestic sphere. Others, like Katherine Mansfield, find that the city (i.e., London) can be a hostile place to them as women and as colonials. A wanderer like Rhys, Mansfield discovered that the knowledge the city streets offer men — particularly sexual knowledge — has devastatingly different results for women.[27] Both Coral Ann Howells and Mary Lou Emery note that Rhys's characters, because of their conditioning as women and their weakened sense of selfhood as non-Europeans, are repeatedly unable to enjoy the epiphanic moments of self-revelation offered by the city in urban modernist texts by men.[28]

It is perhaps not coincidental that Schreiner, Rhys, and Mansfield, all colonial women disappointed in their dreams of an English home, were for most of their lives itinerant. Teresa O'Connor records that

> as soon as Rhys arrived in London she began what was to be a mode of living that persisted almost her entire life — the taking of lodging in temporary, and often inhospitable, quarters. In England her life was spent living in constantly changing boarding houses and bed-sitting rooms. Later, on the Continent, she lived the same life in small hotels.[29]

Even before Orwell became the spokesman for the male world of transience and poverty, Rhys had taken up the subject of the female experience of urban poverty in such stories as "Discourse of a Lady Standing Dinner to a Down-and-Out Friend" (1927) and "Mannequin" (1927) and in the four prewar novels.[30] For the Caribbean creole characters, the journey from the Caribbean and the collapse of the mythological, dreamlike England leave them stunned, fragmented, and poor. Even when the exiled woman is not West Indian, she is of foreign nationality, and her alienation is cultural, linguistic, and economic. In *Good Morning, Midnight,* for instance, Sasha is an English woman wandering alone in Paris. Because she is legally married to a man who is not English, her political nationality differs from her obvious Englishness, which makes her suspicious to hotel managers, concierges, and so on (*GMM*, p. 14). Her hatred of England, her own country, though never really explained, adds to her national alienation and homelessness. Although Sasha's movements from rooming house to rooming house in *Good Morning, Midnight,* are generally for financial reasons, she also takes up a compulsive daily wandering throughout the city in an attempt to claim certain territories for her own and avoid others where she is likely to be rejected. The physical places of cafés, restaurants, and hotels embody for Sasha and Rhys's other wandering characters the possibility of psychological stability (what Marya calls a "solid background") or at least of safety. Sasha "maps out" her day in *Good Morning, Midnight,* setting herself a routine and placing herself in an otherwise anonymous city: "I have been here five days. I have decided on a place to eat in at midday, a place to eat in at night, a place to have my drink in after dinner. I have arranged my little life" (*GMM*, p. 9). Her psychological state, feeling she belongs or does not, is projected onto physical places:

> My life, which seems so simple and monotonous, is really a complicated affair of cafés where they like me and cafés where they don't, streets that are friendly, streets that aren't, rooms where I might be happy, rooms where I never shall be. (*GMM*, p. 46)

Paris is thus marked out as a series of "waiting rooms" to be tested and then either returned to or avoided: "Not too much drinking, avoidance of certain cafés, of certain streets, of certain spots, and everything will go off beautifully" (*GMM,* p. 15). In every café Sasha judges her reception, sensitive to voiced suspicions about her, a foreigner, and unvoiced or imagined ridicule.

The work Rhys's heroines can get in this modern economy adds to both the alienation and the anonymity of their situations. Most of Rhys's heroines find work as "dolls" — as models, mannequins, or prostitutes. After having been a live "mannequin" herself, Sasha becomes a salesgirl in a high-class French dress shop and ironically notes the perfection of the artificial mannequins, which are as competent at their "jobs" as are living women:

> I would feel as if I were drugged, sitting there, watching those damned dolls, thinking what a success they would have made of their lives if they had been women. Satin skin, silk hair, velvet eyes, sawdust heart — all complete. (*GMM,* p. 18)

In her earlier story "Mannequin" (1927), Rhys elaborates on the ironies of working as a constructed woman. Hired and trained to represent genres of womanhood, these women are completely interchangeable within their types:

> There were twelve mannequins at Jeanne Veron's.... Each of the twelve was a distinct and separate type: each of the twelve knew her type and kept to it, practising rigidly in clothing, manner, voice and conversation.
> Round the austere table were now seated Babette, the *gamine,* the traditional blonde *enfant;* Mona, tall and darkly beautiful, the *femme fatale,* the wearer of sumptuous evening gowns. Georgette was the *garçonne;* Simone with green eyes Anna knew instantly for a cat whom men would and did adore.... Eliane was the star of the collection. ("M," pp. 22–23)

In sharp contrast to her very adult responsibilities and her fear of losing this underpaid job, Anna is required to "learn the way to wear the innocent and springlike air and garb of the *jeune fille*" ("M," p. 21). Anna, occupying one of the lowest positions in this international clothing industry, is paraded before American, English, and European buyers. A man's comment in *Voyage in the Dark* that "a girl's clothes cost more than the girl inside them" underscores Rhys's understanding of the "value" of women in this economy (*VD,* p. 28). In Sasha's life, too, the modeling profession (as in Anna Morgan's life the acting profession) is the training ground for prostitution in which women are paid to represent male ideas of womanhood itself. For so many of Rhys's characters, the way to economic survival involves the suppression of their individual personalities and the presentation of themselves as types, fitting the expectations or desires of those with money. The ultimate irony appears in the story "Discourse of a Lady Standing Dinner to a Down-and-Out Friend," in which the wealthier woman demands from her dinner guest an "appropriate" representation of destitution.

Anna Morgan in *Voyage in the Dark* starts her career in England as a traveling chorus girl. She is frightened by the cold and grim reality of English urban life and alienated from the other girls who call her "Hottentot," identifying her difference as racial and national. Cut off from Hester, her English step-mother, and her Caribbean relatives, Anna falls in love with a man who helps her financially. When he drops her, she drifts from rooming house to rooming house looking for "a situation." The market most available to her is prostitution in one form or another, and by the end of the novel, Anna is homeless, moneyless, and almost dead from a botched abortion.[31] Anna has become a "public woman"; she has found her way into the social downward spiral potentially awaiting unattached women. In an excellent discussion of the shifting perceptions and restrictions of single women in late nineteenth-century England, Mary Lou Emery suggests that the modern period saw traditional kinship systems of exchange breaking down, thereby leaving unattached women vulnerable to increasing legal and medical scrutiny and control. And yet it is such rituals of kinship exchange that transfer Antoinette from the Cosway to the Rochester family and deprive her of her economic independence. The daughters do not therefore necessarily do better under the so-called protection of the patriarchal kinship system; the difference Emery addresses is that the modern woman (or girl) must negotiate the terms of her economic exchange on her own and that the negotiation takes place in the street, not in the home. With her father dead and her step-mother and uncle withholding their financial and emotional support, Anna is cast out of the private world of home and family and learns to make her way in public restaurants, cafés, and streets. Her last stop before the end of the novel is working as an "in-house" manicure and massage girl. Anna's private world of "home" and the public market of anonymity and prostitution become one. As Anna and her women acquaintances dream of marriage and economic security, Rhys exposes the myth of such security for working-class women (or women in general if we think of Antoinette's fate) and shows what home and family really are for these characters.

There are important similarities between Schreiner's and Rhys's portrayals of the relationship for working-class women among sexuality, economic security, and the putative privacy and protection of the home. Rhys's Anna and Schreiner's Bertie are confused by a middle-class ideology of marriage in which the economic and sexual transactions of the exchange are obscured by the girls' ignorance and their dreams of romance. With no money of their own with which to negotiate, both young women come to see embedded in family and home nothing more than female prostitution. In both Rhys's novel and the proposed conclusion to Schreiner's *From Man to Man,* the women seem to resign themselves to the physically dangerous and psychologically exhausting life of prostitution they did not freely choose.

This acquiescence has infuriated many of Rhys's critics. Nancy Casey, for instance, attributes Anna's apparent passivity to the "lethargy" and "lassitude" of her Dominican upbringing:

> Because her Dominican life has taught her to do nothing, she believes that being attractive, well-dressed, and appealing to men is sufficient. In England, however, she discovers that a woman is expected to do something with her life.[32]

But Rhys's critique is of a much larger scope than Casey admits. Anna's passivity is not due so much to her early years in what Casey calls "an unsophisticated, unchanging world" but to her recognition that the economic exploitation of women by men, of the poor by the rich, of the colonized by the colonizer, is bigger than her own individual situation. Whereas Casey believes that Anna's summation that "the poor do this and the rich do that, the world is so-and-so and nothing can change it" is an articulation of the security she felt in the "unchanging" Caribbean world, I read this as Anna's political understanding of her own entrapment as a colonial woman in an economic system that includes both countries.

Peter Wolfe's discussion of the employment of Rhys's heroines similarly overlooks Rhys's analysis of the place of women in the international economy and, as with much criticism of Rhys's work, limits the analysis to a psychological study, even judgment, of Rhys's heroines and sometimes of "women" in general. "Few women can resist the temptation of trading on their looks," Wolfe states. He then offers the judgment that in Rhys's works the heroines'

> casual attitude toward sex and their readiness to lean on men also limit their private domains. The neo-romantic urge to connect found in E. M. Forster and Virginia Woolf invites attention in Jean Rhys because of its absence. She does not connect the female principle with serenity, comfort, and healing-power. The most basic ties — the parental and the sexual — barely exist.

> Marriage never lasts, ... neither does motherhood or its fulfillments. ... Their free participation in these empty relationships uncovers a self-destructive streak in the women.[33]

The expectation here of what a "healthy" woman is, what a "tragic hero-ine" should be, limits an understanding of Rhys's larger indictment, that, in fact, the women's participation, as Wolfe calls it, is far from "free." Wolfe's baffling statement that Rhys's "understanding of women is more novelis-tic than political"[34] misses the strikingly political analysis Rhys provides in her portrayal of women who, denied a private world of home, find them-selves dispensable and interchangeable in the public sphere. As a woman, Anna is the unspoken, unclaimed casualty of a masculinist economy; as a Caribbean, she is the unacknowledged by-product of an imperialist econ-omy. Just as Schreiner connects exploitation of women with the Victorian imperialist project, Rhys connects the economic and psychological disen-franchisement of her heroines with their national status and the power relations between England and the colonies. The foreign woman is a ca-sualty on the two separate but connected economic fronts — the sexual and the colonial.

Whereas Orwell's presentation of the male vagabond life in *Down and Out in Paris and London* concentrates on the *individual* stories of degradation and the subsequent adventures of survival, Rhys's novels focus on a kind of poverty and destitution that does not result from specific financial calamities of her women characters. Rhys's fiction indicts the larger English economic and political system that uses but refuses to acknowledge the "free" woman, the unattached, unprotected woman. Anna and Selina, as Caribbean women stranded in England, find themselves implicated in an economy through which they will invariably suffer.

In their exhausting wanderings Rhys's heroines are simultaneously seek-ing and avoiding the security of what Sasha in *Good Morning, Midnight,* calls being "taken care of," the gangster vocabulary of a violent silencing tied to the benevolent promise of economic security. Some critics have criticized what they see as Rhys's heroines' self-destructive attacks on their own would-be caretakers.[35] We can understand these otherwise inexplicable rejections as expressions of the women's frustration with the exploitation inherent in this "caretaking" and of their fear of being shut away in silent acquiescence. Sasha's wanderings, for instance, are a desperate avoidance of the stagnation of a metaphoric Sargasso Sea in which the self is lost and trapped:

I have no pride — no pride, no name, no face, no country. I don't belong anywhere. Too sad, too sad.... It doesn't matter, there I am, like one of those straws which floats round the edge of a whirlpool and is gradually sucked into the center, the dead center, where everything is stagnant, everything is calm. Two-pound-ten a week and a room just off Gray's Inn Road.... (*GMM*, p. 44)

Although Sasha attributes immense importance to the difference between this restaurant and that, this café and that, she is also haunted by the belief that these physical places to which she anchors herself are really indistinguishable:

Walking in the night. Back to the hotel. Always the same hotel. You press the button. The door opens. You go up the stairs, always the same room.... (*GMM*, p. 32)

Her world threatens to become a jumble of fragments, one experience indistinguishable from another. This is the bleak side of modernism, the sordid fragmentation of urban existence. Perhaps because of Rhys's own ambiguous position in colonial racial classification systems — her complex national identity, her unstable class position, and her occupation of several sexual categories (mistress, wife, divorcée, widow) — her heroines recognize that the distinctions available in this world are ultimately fictitious. Rhys's modernism not only questions Victorian cultural structures but also challenges the developing twentieth-century ideologies of capitalism that posit an economy based on free agents who both freely sell their labor and freely choose and purchase goods and services. Sasha's recognition of the randomness and the lack of true differentiation in her environment is a denial of the false comforts modern capitalist society seems to offer. In a panic, Sasha attempts to "escape her fate" by moving to a better hotel. She realizes, however, that this supposed difference in hotel rooms will not make a significant difference in her life:

A beautiful room with a bath? A room with a bath? A nice room? A room?...But never tell the truth about this business of rooms, because it would bust the roof off everything and undermine the whole social system. All rooms are the same. All rooms have four walls, a door, a window or two, a bed, a chair and perhaps a bidet. A room is a place where you hide yourself from the wolves outside and that's all any room is. Why should I worry about changing my room? (*GMM*, p. 38)

In her desperation to locate herself physically and socially, Sasha comes to recognize that beyond the apparent "choices" of accommodation and lifestyle that use up her attention and energy lies the ultimately undisguisable struggle for survival in a hostile world. The variety of rooms, restaurants, dresses, even lovers does not provide escape but implicates her in the economy that exploits her.

As Bruce Robbins puts it in his critique of modernist advertising, "Consumerism sells itself over and above any particular content. . . . The shocking novelty of an infinite proliferation of images both conceals an underlying sameness and, more importantly, precludes any glimpse of the controlling machinery outside."[36] Sasha's agony, perhaps more than any of Rhys's other characters, is her perception of that machinery, a perception that, obscured by both nineteenth-century systems of classifying difference and twentieth-century myths of free choice, is almost impossible to "think." Sasha's internal response to "Mr. Blank," her employer, is a devastating critique of power relations between owners and workers, men and women:

> Well, let's argue this out, Mr. Blank. You, who represent Society, have the right to pay me four hundred francs a month. That's my market value, for I am an inefficient member of Society, slow in the uptake, uncertain, slightly damaged in the fray, there's no denying it. So you have the right to pay me four hundred francs a month, to lodge me in a small, dark room, to clothe me shabbily, to harass me with worry and monotony and unsatisfied longings till you get me to the point when I blush at a look, cry at a word. We can't all be happy, we can't all be rich, we can't all be lucky — and it would be so much less fun if we were. Isn't it so, Mr. Blank? . . . Let's say that you have this mystical right to cut my legs off. But the right to ridicule me afterwards because I am a cripple — no, that I think you haven't got. And that's the right you hold most dearly, isn't it? You must be able to despise the people you exploit. But I wish you a lot of trouble, Mr. Blank, and just to start off with, your damned shop's going bust. Alleluia! Did I say all this? Of course I didn't. I didn't even think it. (*GMM,* p. 29)

The crucial distinctions between white and black, European and Creole, rich and poor, wife and prostitute are nineteenth-century oppositions that become more difficult to maintain after World War I. Whereas the psychological fragmentation of T. S. Eliot's or William Faulkner's characters results from the loss of stable signs of class distinctions, those signs (as well as those of race, nationality, and sexuality) were *always* arbitrary to Rhys's female characters. These distinctions, like the differences of hotel rooms, are meaningful not in their own right, but because of cultural agreements that benefit some to the detriment of others. In *Voyage in the Dark,* Anna realizes that the value of her virginity is her only power, arbitrary and limited. While Walter sentimentalizes her virginity, arguing that "it's the only thing that matters" (*VD*, p. 22), Anna understands its value as a commodity in the marketplace, not significantly different from chocolate: "I kept on wondering whether she would ask me what I was living on. 'What is Purity? For Thirty-Five Years the Answer has been Bourne's Cocoa'" (*VD*, p. 36).

Robbins argues that this kind of advertising shares much with modernist fiction itself, in that both collapse history into "a perpetual present of mythic repetition." And yet, as recent Rhys critics have argued, Rhys's novels challenge the disembodied angst of male high modernism that mourns the "end of history."[37] If Rhys exhibits, like Eliot, a modernist nostalgia for the lost distinctions of class and culture, as one might argue she does in "Trio" or "Again the Antilles," it is a highly ambivalent longing, complicated by the contradictions of her creole status in the Caribbean and in Europe. Rhys's perspective is valuable. The supposedly lost "golden age" before World War I for which some male modernists mourn created the classifications of race and culture that leave Rhys and her characters stranded between the Old and the New Worlds right through the twentieth century. In contrast to the visions of the modernist elites, Rhys shows that nothing has "fallen apart" or even changed much. The system, be it capitalism, colonialism, or sexism, remains intact. The center is holding fast. Rhys's critique of modern urban life, therefore, does not look *back* to a time of wholeness when the system worked more smoothly (for better or for worse), but to the *ongoing* insanity inherent in the system that has always used women in specifically cruel ways: "'What is Purity? For Thirty-Five Thousand Years the Answer has been...'" (*VD*, p. 36).

While it is true that Rhys's heroines do not achieve the goals of traditional romantic novels — successful marriages and happy families — the cause is largely economic. The result of this exploitative economy is the displaced woman who does not fit the sexist determination by society (and obviously by some of Rhys's critics) of what a woman *is* essentially, either wife or mother. It is perhaps frustrating to current feminist expectations that neither Schreiner nor Rhys provides us with triumphant conclusions of independent womanhood. Yet Rhys herself vehemently objected in her letters to the critics' call for such "positive" representations:

> I do read a lot and have a very definite impression that "thought control" is on the way and ought to be resisted. But will it be resisted?
> Why say as Mr. Green does "I demand a positive and creative view of life?" What is that? And why *demand* a view of life. Not his business surely. (*LJR*, 99–100)

Just as Lyndall's death in *The Story of an African Farm* and Bertie's prostitution, insanity, and death in the proposed conclusion of *From Man to
Man* indict not the women themselves but the society that forced them into
their self-destructive choices, so the Rhys heroines' destitution and despair
reveal not merely an intolerable psychological condition but the political
and sexual economics that form it.

The passivity of Rhys's heroines stands in contrast to their cool and dis-
tanced understanding of the political reasons for their powerlessness. Only
Antoinette actively retaliates by reburning the big house, making Thornfield what Coulibri was for the ex-slaves (and this only in a dream in Rhys's
novel, the fulfillment known from *Jane Eyre*). And yet, in their insistence
on survival and their sharp analysis of their positions, Rhys's other heroines
also resist the ideologies that cause their suffering.

Their tenacious survival itself becomes a statement of political resistance. In *Voyage in the Dark,* Anna begins the cycle that Sasha continues
in *Good Morning, Midnight*. Because Sasha is older, and therefore even more
delinquent in not fulfilling one of the "respectable" roles for women, her
presence becomes for those who "belong" an irritating defiance of the acceptable "self" in society. Who is the woman sitting silently in the corner
of the café? What is she thinking? What does she want? Where does she
fit in? Sasha interprets the insensitive but probably innocuous question the
English girl asks in the café, "Et qu'est-ce qu'elle fout ici?" as "Qu'est-ce
qu'elle fout ici, la vielle? What the devil (translating it politely) is she doing here, that old woman? What is she doing here, the stranger, the alien,
the old one?" (*GMM,* p. 54). Unlike the other women who eat with their
husbands, lovers, and friends, Sasha is alone and longs for connection at
the same time that she fears attention; her own paranoia and hostility isolate her from any possible relationship with this other English woman, and
she instead attributes to her the rejection and exploitation she has experienced as a woman on her own. Sasha's defensive refrain, "I'm here because
I'm here because I'm here," is both a rejection of any imagined individual
reasons for her destitution and a declaration of political presence. She refuses to be invisible, to disappear, or to become an object of ridicule for
the comfort of those whose place is more secure. The antiracist poster that
Michelle Cliff describes tacked to a London bulletin board in *No Telephone
to Heaven,* "We are here because you were there," would have pleased Rhys
very much. Both statements and Sasha's later one, "Here I am, and here
I'm going to stay," defy the xenophobia of the smug middle class that uses
cheap foreign labor but refuses to acknowledge the historic origin of that

labor force, the social presence of the workers, or their right to the benefits of the economy they serve.

Rhys's insight into the psychic and economic impoverishment wrought by cultural colonialism and modern capitalism makes her a central figure for contemporary Caribbean writers, teachers, and theorists. In the last decade, many women writers from countries that were once European colonies have taken up the issues of cultural and racial identification, colonial education, and neocolonial economic exploitation that Rhys raised in her fiction a generation and more ago. As women of color, these new writers acknowledge Rhys's contribution and challenge some of the assumptions of white creole writing. Both Michelle Cliff and Zoë Wicomb, for instance, reveal the deep connections between the ideologies and practices of colonialism and those of the so-called postcolonial societies in which they were raised. Identified as "colored" they also critique the portrayals of mixed-race characters in white colonial fiction and demand a more thorough assessment of colonial history and its legacies.

Part III
"Colored" Perspectives and
Neocolonialism

5 / "With the Logic of a Creole"

Michelle Cliff

Our history (or our histories) is not totally accessible to historians. Their methodology restricts them to the sole colonial chronicle. Our chronicle is behind the dates, behind the known facts: we are Words behind writing. Only poetic knowledge, fictional knowledge, literary knowledge, in short, artistic knowledge can discover us, understand us and bring us, evanescent, back to the resuscitation of consciousness.

> —*Jean Bernabé, Patrick Chamoiseau, and Raphaël Confiant,*
> "In Praise of Creoleness"

The Antiguan-born author Jamaica Kincaid describes the European version of colonial history as a fairy tale of "how we met you, your right to do the things you did, how beautiful you were, are, and always will be."[1] A central task, then, for contemporary Caribbean authors is both to deconstruct these Eurocentric versions of history and to reconstruct the past by invoking indigenous, African, and immigrant perspectives. As we have seen, Jean Rhys contributes to this literary historiography by insisting on the historical divergence of European and white creole interest. Nevertheless, just as *Wide Sargasso Sea* is bound in crucial ways by *Jane Eyre,* so is Rhys's frame of reference bound by the European historical narrative.

The contemporary Jamaican-born writer Michelle Cliff, of African, Carib, and English heritage,[2] also calls herself "creole," invoking both African and European roots and meanings of Caribbean and postcolonial culture. Aware that the European narrative has dominated Caribbean education, that, as one of her characters puts it, "We have taken the master's past as our own," Cliff examines the social and political legacy of both the violence of colonial history and the master's benign rendering of it. From her critical perspective, colonialism did not end with the emancipation or with independence but persists through neocolonial economic plundering, massive cultural exploitation and misappropriation, and the psychological bondage of all Caribbeans (white, black, or "colored") by colonial theories of racial and sexual difference and identity that survive.

Confronting European and white creole renderings of racial identity, Cliff offers a trenchant analysis of the relationship among categories of race, sexuality, and class as historically (not biologically) derived. By exposing the complexities and paradoxes of colonial mythologies, Cliff shows the way these systems can bind us to damaging beliefs and relationships at the same time that they provide occasions for more radical conceptions of identity and political resistance. The slippages and exaggerations of the colonial racial categories that Cliff describes lead us to more incisive theoretical understandings of "creolism" or "creole identity" that do not rest on outmoded conceptions of purity or authenticity. In this way, Cliff shifts us from Rhys's insistence on the cultural and racial category "white Creole" (though itself a challenge to colonial national definitions) to a broader and perhaps more challenging recognition that such distinctions, while experienced as real, are elaborate and costly fictions. By developing sympathetic characters that fall between dichotomous racial and sexual markers, Cliff calls for new epistemologies to supersede those that supported and were produced by colonialism. Yet even as she values the liberatory visions of a generation that has benefitted from the work of black Caribbean historians and cultural critics, Cliff nevertheless remains skeptical about any utopian claims of postcolonial freedom. The social, economic, and psychological damage of colonialism she examines in her writing renders the beautiful dreams of a "creole" future, where race is an insignificant marker and where "peasant" and bourgeois cultures are equally articulate, a long way off.

Cliff has written three novels, *Abeng* (1984), *No Telephone to Heaven* (1987), and *Free Enterprise* (1993); a book of essays and prose pieces, *The Land of Look Behind* (1985); and a collection of short stories, *Bodies of Water* (1990).[3] *Abeng* and *No Telephone to Heaven* both follow the life of a light-skinned creole girl, Clare Savage. *Abeng* describes Clare's early life and the effect of colonial history on her family, her schooling, and her social relations. By the end of *Abeng,* Clare has begun to learn the difference her light coloring will make in her life, the "privilege" she will enjoy, and the complex meanings of race and sexuality in the Caribbean. *No Telephone to*

Heaven begins years later with Clare traveling in the back of a truck as part of an armed guerrilla group. The novel moves back and forth through her life to determine how Clare, named for an English college and taught to "pass" as white, would end up a revolutionary. In the course of the novel, Clare immigrates with her family to New York City, then moves to England for her university education, travels around Europe, and returns to Jamaica and her grandmother's land.

Almost twenty years after Jamaican independence, Cliff begins to examine in fiction, poetry, and prose the political and cultural implications of neocolonial relations between Jamaica, Britain, and the United States. Cliff examines how the Caribbean has become a tourist playground for North Americans, the economic devastation of Jamaica (assisted by tourist ads Cliff quotes, such as "Make It Your Own"), and the consequent migration of Caribbeans to England, Canada, and the United States. Cliff is particularly interested in the effect of historical colonial ideologies on current social relations between Caribbeans, the way those ideologies are deconstructed by racially and sexually indeterminate individuals, the possibility and significance of individual choice within social paradigms, and the cultural and political benefits and limitations of the concepts "creole" or "creolism."

"The Creole": A Study of Definitions

The history of the concept "creole" is a rich one and is important because while it originally attempted to delineate a racial hierarchy, it necessarily reveals the uncontrollable mixture of races and cultures and the possible manipulations of the categories. The changing meaning of the word "creole" and its variations (see introduction) give us insight into the cultural construction of racial categories and the ways in which these categories shift and change over time and place. These categories are a crucial link between the political and social formations of Europe and those of the so-called New World. The obsession with racial classification and identity in the Americas from the late sixteenth century on extends the trials of the Spanish Inquisition into the present. At the turn of the fifteenth century, the trials for citizenship in Spain required the proof of *pureza de sangre* (purity of blood), which involved trials of faith, race, and national origin. José Piedra finds in his studies of these trials that it was possible to litigate one's standing and gain a fictional genealogy and, in certain cases, a certificate of whiteness. Furthermore, the Spanish concept of "imperial apprenticeship," in which newcomers (including black slaves) theoretically could progress in rank of citizenship based on linguistic mastery, reveals the ways classifications of race are cultural constructs at once restrictive and fluid.[4] In the Spanish colonies, Piedra argues, the subdivisions of racial categories proliferated, and the terms of racial difference became even more ambiguous.

The contemporary meaning of "creole," emphasizing the mixture of races and cultures, appears ambiguous and vague, but it remains attached to the history of an elaborately descriptive hierarchy of racial distinctions. In the United States the system was mathematical, based on the erroneous belief that "always half a person's 'racial traits' are transmitted to his children in the blood."[5] This is the "one drop rule" that informed U.S. laws regarding racial identity until the 1980s.[6] While not as rigorously determined in the Caribbean, the idea of race as traits passed down in the blood and always "there," even if not visible, remains in constructions of racial identity.

In *Wide Sargasso Sea* those characters who define themselves as "creole," like Aunt Cora or Antoinette, do so both to acknowledge their cultural separation from England *and* to assert their biological (that is, racial) connection with white England. It is a difficult and uncomfortable position to maintain. On the one hand, the settler class with each generation looked less to the mother country for its identity, and English culture became less expressive of the experience and thought of white Caribbeans. On the other hand, it is only through European descent that these "Creoles" could claim racial superiority, justifying their exploitation of black slaves and, after emancipation, of black servants. The truth that Tia voices about the construction of racial categories, both by economic position ("Real white people, they got gold money") and by fictitious bloodlines, threatens to undermine the very identity of the creole society. The creole society that Jean Rhys describes and that Antoinette so fiercely defends as "white" may see itself as creating a new culture, but that new culture, even though influenced by African slaves and their descendants, is conceived of as a new *white* culture.

In his essay "Caliban,"[7] Roberto Fernández Retamar recalls José Martí's 1891 distinction between the "exotic Creole" and the "authentic mestizo." This distinction is between the so-called white and the mixed-race person born in the colony. For the most part, Jean Rhys's subject is the white Creole who, while sometimes acknowledging the mythical nature of concepts of racial purity (as the narrator's father in "The Day They Burned the Books" remarks, "Who's white? Damned few"), nevertheless maintains the fictions of pure bloodlines and ancestry for his or her own family. Thus

Antoinette has no problem acknowledging the existence of Daniel Cosway but vigorously defends the purity of her own inheritance ("Not my mother. Never could be") and chooses Rochester over Sandi. Jean Rhys has given subjectivity to Antoinette/Bertha, the exotic white Creole, but, with the exception of Selina Davis in "Let Them Call It Jazz," has left the "colored" Creole to be defined by others, usually, as in "Again the Antilles" and "The Day They Burned the Books," by the white creole character, whose portrayal is worth questioning.

Like Schreiner's depictions of "half-castes," Rhys's depictions of mixed-race characters can in part be understood as a response to European conceptions of the white Creole as degenerate, untrustworthy, and weak. The source of this unwholesomeness was imagined as an acquired trait, a result of environmental influences, what race scientists in the mid–nineteenth century called "tropicalization."[8] As we have seen with British images of Afrikaners, supposed creole degeneracy is the result of "going native." Even Rhys's own portrayal of the effects of "twenty years in the tropics" on Hugh Musgrave hints at the degenerative influences of the colonies on white men. "Going native," in the European imagination, is, of course, closely linked to miscegenation.[9] In Rhys's short story "Pioneers, Oh, Pioneers," the white society's denouncement of the Englishman, Ramage, as mad and indecent stems from his sexual relations with a "colored" woman.[10] At the same time that the white Creole contends with these suspicions of supposed environmental contamination, the related threat of racial "degeneration" contributes to his or her anxiety about European identification. It is not surprising, then, to find these pseudoscientific definitions of both pure and degenerate races projected by the white Creoles themselves onto the "colored" or mixed-race progeny of white and black inhabitants of the colonies. In the white creole imagination, the "colored" individual represents the real degeneration that results from improper racial mixture. In *Wide Sargasso Sea,* Jean Rhys creates a number of frightening or pathetic mixed-race characters. Daniel Cosway is one of these figures who, while invoking the myths of white creole degeneracy, "the madness that is in . . . all these white Creoles," describes himself as a "little yellow rat" (*WSS,* pp. 96, 125). Rochester, while frightened by Antoinette, is more thoroughly disgusted by Daniel. Antoinette, too, recalls with horror a mixed-race boy:

> He had a white skin, a dull ugly white covered with freckles, his mouth was a negro's mouth and he had small eyes, like bits of green glass. He had the eyes

of a dead fish. Worst, most horrible of all, his hair was crinkled, a negro's hair, but bright red, and his eyebrows and eyelashes were red. (*WSS*, 48–49)

Amélie, whom Rochester calls "a little half-caste" and who is proud of her "white girl hair," embodies the sexuality attributed to mixed-race women. Rhys's nightmarish figure of the mulatto woman in *Good Morning, Midnight,* is used as a symbol of the white narrator's isolation, passivity, and powerlessness.

Whereas the white Creole defined him/herself in colonialist terms — either connected to or independent from Europe, ambivalently attracted to or repulsed by the non-European other — a new generation of writers seeks to redefine "creole consciousness" in ways that no longer invoke the purities of racial or cultural identity. Such contemporary rethinking of creoleness as a positive and challenging psychological and cultural identity informs much recent Caribbean fiction, particularly the work of Michelle Cliff. The challenging question Cliff and others are posing for themselves is how creole writers, particularly those defined as mixed-race and mixed-culture, can redefine identity beyond colonial categories of race and nation and thereby not only correct the historical record but offer a new vision of the future.[11] By what philosophical move can the injurious images we have seen of mixed-race or "hybrid" Creoles be dispelled?

As Jean Bernabé, Patrick Chamoiseau, and Raphaël Confiant suggest in their manifesto "In Praise of Creoleness," *la créolité* must be redefined as incorporating but not being reduced to language, personal and collective history, race, and culture. They describe creoleness as a consciousness that is rooted in colonial history but that is also created through more recent immigration, emigration, and intranational migration. Proclaiming oneself to be "creole" in these terms is claiming an identity that transcends the colonial experience of defining the self solely through European values. Creoleness for these writers is a new understanding of the self, an "interior attitude" that looks neither to the external definitions of Europe (colonial education) nor to those of Africa (negritude) for terms of self-definition. While it is through negritude, according to these writers, that "Caribbeanness" has been able to develop beyond colonial mimicry, creoleness "is an annihilation of false universality, of monolingualism, and of purity." Creoleness, then, is a mixed culture connecting all Caribbeans with each other and with the multiple countries of their ancestral origins.[12]

Is there a way of writing literature that would incorporate the history, language, and politics of this "creoleness"? These writers believe that a new literature is coming into being, a creole literature that expresses contemporary creole experience in all its richness by incorporating "the traditional configurations of . . . orality" and "adopt[ing] the language of our towns, of our cities," thus touching languages and cultures throughout the world.[13] Michelle Cliff is inspired by these challenges and offers in her work a rich exploration of creole consciousness through her incisive analysis of creole identity and the politics of race, color, and class and through her incorporation of creole language, mixed literary forms, and orality. Far from utopian, however, Cliff's depiction of "creole consciousness" emphasizes both the liberatory power of resistant self-definition and the seductions of painful self-betrayal.

Creolism and Color

As a light-skinned woman, born in Jamaica and educated there and in England and the United States, Michelle Cliff explores in her writing how racial identity is constructed, how race "means," and the differences and connections of those meanings in the three countries she has called home. In *Abeng* and *No Telephone to Heaven,* Cliff explores not only these complex systems of difference but also the subjectivities such systems create. Cliff's central character in these novels is Clare Savage, who comes from a family whose racial ancestry is clearly mixed. Her father, "Boy" Savage, claims his English origins through his great-grandfather, Judge Savage, an owner of large plantations and of one hundred slaves, whom he murders on the eve of emancipation. Judge Savage came to Jamaica in 1829, leaving his wife in England. His unwilling mistress, a woman who was half Miskito Indian and half African, is converted in the family mythology to Indian and Spanish, a personification of the New World that avoids the "taint of the tar-brush." Even though the judge's son marries a "high yellow" woman who passes for white, Boy Savage and his family cling to their mythical whiteness:

> The definition of what a Savage was like was fixed by color, class, and religion, and over the years a carefully contrived mythology was constructed, which they used to protect their identities. When they were poor, and not all of them white, the mythology persisted. (*A,* 29)

Clare's mother, Kitty, is also of mixed background, but her family, the Freemans, do not maintain a family mythology claiming hereditary whiteness:

> Kitty's mother was both Black and white, and her father's origins were unknown — but both had brown skin and a wave to their hair. Her people were called "red" and they knew that this was what they were. No one had suggested to them that they try to hide it — were they able to. They were as old

a family as the Savage family. All Jamaican families were old families. There had been no waves of immigration. No new settlers seeking a frontier. Only a settling of blood as some lighter skins crossed over one or another of the darker ones — keeping guard, though, over a base of darkness. (*A*, 54)

Nevertheless, Boy teaches Clare that regardless of her mother's more obviously colored background, as his daughter she is white. "You're white because you're a Savage," he tells her, ignoring not only the lack of logic in his claim but the way his own name betrays him by occupying the wrong side of the equation of colonial semantics that juxtaposes the white colonialist with the black savage.

In the Caribbean context, Cliff identifies Clare as neither white nor black but as "creole" and mulatto. In Cliff's terminology, "creole" is a shorthand expression covering a much more complex system of racial difference within the three-color system (white, creole, black). At his Jesuit boarding school, Boy is taught the mathematical, and therefore natural, regularities of racial identity:

> A lesson from the third form on the history of Jamaica sprang to mind: mulatto, offspring of African and white; sambo, offspring of African and mulatto; quadroon, offspring of mulatto and white; mestee, offspring of quadroon and white; mestefeena, offspring of mestee and white.... These Aristotelian categories taught by a Jesuit determined they should know where they were — and fortunate at that. In the Spanish colonies there were 128 categories to be memorized. The class of multicolored boys rose and recited in unison. (*NTH*, p. 56)

While the mathematical metaphor belies the fantastic nature of such a system, the New World racial categories to which the priests refer are vivid in their definitions of difference. In a study of the New World caste system of the late eighteenth century, Iris M. Zavala maps out what she calls "the authoritative carnivalesque" of the racial structure that the Savages inherit and must negotiate. Here is a sample of that taxonomy:

1. Spaniard and Indian woman = mestizo
2. Mestizo and Spanish woman = *castizo*
3. *Castizo* woman and Spaniard = Spaniard
4. Spanish woman and Negro (*sic*) = mulatto
5. Spaniard and mulatto woman = Moorish
6. Morisco woman and Spaniard = albino
7. Spaniard and albino woman = a "throwback" (*torna atrás* or *salta atrás*)

8. Indian and *torna atrás* woman = wolf (*lobo*)
9. Wolf and Indian woman = *zambayo, zambaigo, zambo*...
13. *Barcino* and mulatto woman = coyote (*coyote*)
16. *Coyote* mestizo and mulatto woman = "There you are" (*Allí te estás*)
20. *Calpamulato* and *cambujo* woman = "suspended in the air" (*tente en el aire*)
21. *Tente en el aire* and mulatto woman = "I don't understand you" (*No te entiendo*)
22. *No te entiendo* and Indian woman = a "throwback" (*torna atrás*).[14]

That the different "races" were imagined as different species is clear from the animal names given to children of mixed parentage. The mixture of human races results in a degeneration from the human genus altogether — the product is animal (coyote or wolf) or something else that defies even naming ("There you are," "I don't understand you," or "suspended in the air").[15] While it is possible after three generations for the Spanish "purity of blood" to be redeemed after a cross with the Indian, African blood is conceived of as a stain of degeneration that can never be removed.

This strange system, simultaneously emphasizing order and disorder, the natural classification of the unnatural, underlies both Boy's desperation to pass as white and Clare's confusion about her place. While the English colonial imaginings of mixed-race people are less lurid or fantastic than the Spanish categories (or at least produce fewer iconographic images), they represent the same dread of "the taint of the tar-brush." Clare has internalized the images and meanings of both systems when she describes herself as an "albino gorilla," exotic and highly valued prey for poachers, but prey nonetheless (*NTH,* p. 91).

A central tension in *No Telephone to Heaven* is found in the shifting between sameness and difference in all relationships, a shifting that moves between defining and deconstructing identity. Just as Antoinette must recognize her difference and separation from Tia in the mirror scene, Cliff creates for several of the characters child companions through whom they play out the myths of both similarity and difference. In *Abeng,* Clare spends her summers in the country at her grandmother's house and is "given" a playmate, Zoe, the daughter of a woman who lives on Clare's grandmother's land and works for her. At this stage of her development, Clare does not understand the privilege she possesses in relation to her friend, nor does she examine the way their different positions in race and class hierarchies are played out in the friendship. It takes Zoe to put an end to their hunting game (a game Clare made up to prove she was "smaddy," somebody) and explain to Clare their different social positions and their inevitably different futures:

> Wunna is town gal, and wunna papa is buckra. Wunna talk buckra. Wunna leave here when wunna people come fe wunna. Smaddy? Wunna no is smaddy already? Gal smaddy. Kingston smaddy. White smaddy. Dis place no matter a wunna a-tall, a-tall. Dis here is fe me territory. Kingston is fe wunna. Me will be here so all me life — me will be marketwoman like fe me mama. Me will have fe beg land fe me and fe me pickney to live pon. Wunna will go a England, den maybe America, to university, and when we meet later we will be different smaddy. But we is different smaddy now. (*A*, p. 118)

The night after acknowledging her own racial mixture to a white woman whose "coon" baby was taken from her at birth, Clare dreams of fighting with Zoe, a fight that clearly plays on Antoinette's fight with Tia in *Wide Sargasso Sea* when the children acknowledge their different social positions based on color:

> That night Clare dreamed that she and Zoe were fist-fighting by the river in St. Elizabeth. That she picked up a stone and hit Zoe underneath the eye and a trickle of blood ran down her friend's face and onto the rock where she sat. The blood formed into a pool where the rock folded over on itself. And she went over to Zoe and told her she was sorry — making a compress of moss drenched in water to soothe the cut. Then squeezing an aloe leaf to close the wound. (*A*, p. 165)

In this dream, as opposed to Rhys's scene, the black child is hurt at the hands of the lighter child. Whereas Rhys focuses solely on the alienation of the white creole child, Cliff examines the harm done not only to but by light-skinned Creoles. Her focus is on the social system that determines the relationships between those who are lighter and darker and richer and poorer.[16] In the dream Clare is able to express her regret and to heal the wound she has made. In their adult futures, Clare is unable to help Zoe in her poverty, and the accuracy of Zoe's childhood analysis of their difference is made painfully clear. Clare's dream is her own acknowledgment of not only her difference from Zoe but her desire to close the gap or wound between them. In *No Telephone to Heaven* the adult Clare "applies herself" to a decade-old wound on the ankle of her lover, a black Vietnam veteran, and though she again uses aloe vera, this time she cannot heal him. What she is up against is U.S. imperialism, warfare, racism, and destruction in the form of Agent Orange, which keeps the wound festering year after year. While she is drawn to this man, the wound is the gap between them, the different experiences each has had in the racist societies in which they have lived.

In Cliff's novels, the relationships between children eventually become those between employers and servants. Clare's mother, Kitty, and the darker woman, Dorothy, who works for her were raised together by Kitty's mother, Miss Mattie. In contrast to the "citified," light-colored Boy, Kitty and Dorothy share country beliefs and memories of Miss Mattie. Dorothy, however, becomes servant to the Savage family, just as Zoe's family served Clare's. When Miss Mattie dies, both Kitty and Dorothy recognize the omen of the howling dogs, an omen the teachers tried to dispel as "bunga [African] nonsense." But Kitty has learned that as mistress it is her experience that matters, and she does not think of Dorothy's grief:

> "Dorothy, I don't know what I would do if Miss Mattie dead. What if it she?" She spoke to her maid exclusively, as if this would be her own loss entirely, not giving room at all to the fact that Dorothy had been one of Miss Mattie's adoptions, and that Kitty and Dorothy had wet the same bed when they were small.
> "Nuh mus' go on." Dorothy rose in a sudden cool from the edge of the bed and walked out of the room. Out of the mistress's earshot she sucked her teeth. Dem never change. (*NTH,* p. 70)

Both of these women are "colored," but their relationship to each other further delineates the complex hierarchies constituting mixed-race creole identity. Even Christopher, the dark-black garden-boy from the slum, plays with the son of the "cuffy-pretend-backra" family when they are children. This is the family that Christopher eventually murders one night, sending other colored creole families fleeing with Whites from black violence. Through these relationships Cliff shows the ways in which racial identity is not fixed but is determined by class advantages and loyalties, family mythologies, and color.

In the United States, Kitty experiences the most blatant racism of her life but is still set up against the darker skinned African-American women with whom she works. Her color and the privileges she receives preclude any solidarity between them. Kitty does not turn to them for support or comfort because she recognizes the differences between them; as she sees it, she is a "house-slave inconvenienced by massa whim, while dem worked the cane" (*NTH,* p. 77). What is revolutionary about the brigade Clare joins in *No Telephone to Heaven* is the attempt of these guerrillas to forge their alliance on their similarities and work against the ways they have been forced apart. The novel opens with this movement between sameness and difference, a central theme throughout:

> These people — men and women — were dressed in similar clothes, which became them as uniforms, signifying some agreement, some purpose — that they were in something together — in these clothes, at least, they seemed to blend together. This alikeness was something they needed, which could be important, even vital, to them — for the shades of their skin, places traveled to and from, events experienced, things understood, food taken into their bodies, acts of violence committed, books read, music heard, languages recognized, ones they loved, living family, varied widely, came between them. That was all to be expected, of course — that on this island, as part of this small nation, many of them would have been separated at birth. Automatically. Slipped into places where to escape would mean taking your life into your own hands. Not more, not less. Where to get out would mean crashing through barriers positioned by people not so unlike yourself. People you knew should call you brother, sister. (*NTH*, pp. 4–5)

Although the wide range of racial categories of the Caribbean can accommodate more detailed family and national histories than the binary black/white dichotomy of the northern United States, that very precision and complexity of the system allow it to prevail. By creating a "place" for everyone, this system suppresses friction between ideological divisions and the experience that might refute them. It is not until Clare goes to the United States, where she falls out of the racial system that has defined her, that she is able to scrutinize the mythologies of the system itself. The drama for Cliff's characters who question the contours of the places they have been "slipped into" represents what Virginia Domínguez identifies as a central issue for those who study "race": "to interpret the struggle between individuals actively trying to exercise choice over who and what they are and epistemological and institutional systems that seem to stand in their ways."[17]

Hybrids and Inverts

The lack of choice in racial identity and the privileging of "whiteness" have ensured white power in the colonial and postcolonial Americas. One of the most charged threats to this "pigmentocracy" has been miscegenation, which reveals the proximity of the separate "races" and contributes to the proliferation of ever-more similar categories of difference. The ideologies of race are therefore imbricated with those of sexuality, as contemporary scholars of both fields are finding.[18] Colonial discourse is rich with theories attributing sexual difference to the indigenous people of new

territories or to the "exotic" environment itself. From H. M. Stanley's portrayal of a monstrous African fecundity to the belief that the tropics render
white colonists sterile[19] or degenerate, colonial imaginings of racial difference are conflated with anxieties about sexuality. In her own fiction,
Michelle Cliff highlights this conflation, and, critical of the implicit racism,
sexism, and homophobia she finds there, she reworks the theories to suggest
new ways of thinking about identity and political alliance.

In envisioning herself an albino gorilla, a not-quite-human, not-quite-
animal "freak," Clare succumbs to the white imagination of the nightmarish
results of miscegenation.[20] In her fiction Cliff allows subjectivity to these
exotic "freaks" and describes the human suffering that the racial and sexual
taxonomies of colonialism and nineteenth-century science perpetrate into
the present. In several short stories from *Bodies of Water* and in *No Telephone
to Heaven,* Cliff explores the ways the colonial horror about miscegenation
is rooted in anxieties about sexuality as well as about race. A black woman in
Cliff's short story "Burning Bush" exploits the white imagination by representing herself in a traveling freak show as "the girl from Martinique," a
"parti-colored . . . checkerboard of a woman," white and black. The towns-
people flock to see the woman who displays so visibly on her body the
secret "practices of her native land," as her caption reads. She has painted
herself with white shoe polish, playing on the popularity of such displays
of "exotic" women: "The poor man's Josephine Baker. Without the ba-
nanas and with an added panache. Or the poor man's Hottentot Venus —
without the butt."[21] The small town's public fascination with the imagined
sexual practices of Martinique, specifically with miscegenation, is paired in
the story with the secret sexual abuse of a young white girl by her father, who, while gazing at the woman on display, fondles his daughter's
breast and comments, "There but for the grace of God . . . " (p. 78). This
hysterical rejection of racial exogamy masks an incestuous use of the girl
by both her father and brother. This family, cut off from social and sexual interaction with the rest of the town, is a symbolic representation of
the hypocrisy of ideologies of racial purity and the dangers of cultural
insularity.

The daughter of the fraudulent freak is, in fact, of mixed race, and the
next story in the volume, "Screen Memory," recounts her own memories of growing up "bright-skinned," a "white nigger," an affront to her
grandmother, a "race woman" for whom all that is best is black. The light-
skinned daughter, now an alcoholic film actress, remembers a scene from
her girlhood when dressed like a "lady" she watched a darker girl ("who

could not pass the paper bag test"), a tomboy, jump rope to the taunts of the other girls: *"Bulldagger! Bulldagger!..."* The woman remembering the scene asks herself, "Where does she begin and the tomboy end?" echoing Booker T. Washington's comment, "How difficult it sometimes is to know where the black begins and the white ends."[22] In this story, both racial and sexual positions — light-skinned "lady" — rely on the existence of the opposing category. Just as the meaning of "white" depends on a category "black," so "heterosexual" (ladylike) requires "homosexual" (tomboy) for its significance. It is worth remembering that the term "homosexual" predates the term "heterosexual" and can be seen as necessary for the creation of the latter category.[23]

Historians of science and cultural critics have shown the ways in which the categories and hierarchies of presumed racial difference not only justified colonial exploitation but also were intricately related to ideas of class difference and sexual difference.[24] Growing out of the feminist analysis of the construction of sexual difference, the recent scholarship on the construction of sexual identity[25] allows us to see the ways in which the classification systems of race and sexuality influence each other and, in particular, how people of color and homosexuals are conflated through the late nineteenth-century ideas of evolution and degeneracy.[26] The proliferation of sexual categories produced by the new science of "sexology" resembles the racial categories not only in their dizzying number but in the slippage between racial "degeneration" and sexual "degeneracy." In *No Telephone to Heaven,* Cliff reworks this conflation by creating Clare and Harry/Harriet as racial and sexual "doubles" for one another.

As a child immigrant to the United States, Clare abruptly learns about race in a two-color system where "creole" (a term from a ternary system of racial classifications) no longer defines her. Both the fictive nature of racial systems and their very real effects become clear to Clare when she confronts the boundaries of racial identity and learns who has the power to assign racial position. When Clare enrolls for school in New York, Boy is quizzed on the racial status of his light-skinned daughter, and the principal sternly admonishes him, "I do not want to be cruel, Mr. Savage, but we have no room for lies in our system. No place for in-betweens" (*NTH,* p. 99).

Clare's in-between position is paralleled throughout the novel by the character Harry/Harriet, a gay, mixed-race hermaphrodite who, rather than representing fragmentation or split consciousness, is the most whole and clear-sighted character in the book. In an interview Cliff describes this representation of Harry/Harriet as particularly important: "I was determined in *No Telephone to Heaven* to make the most whole and sane character in the novel somebody who was homosexual, which is what Harry is. People may want to think of him as a transvestite, but he's not." Harry/Harriet is both the traditional Anansi trickster character and the revolutionary guerrilla fighting neocolonialist exploitation.[27] When Clare articulates the connection between them, "We are neither one thing nor the other," Harry/Harriet redefines the New York principal's words and gives Clare back the power of self-definition: "At the moment, darling, only at the moment. . . . The time will come for both of us to choose. For we will have to make the choice. Cast our lot. Cyaan live split. Not in this world" (*NTH*, p. 131).

At the end of the novel, both Clare and Harriet have made their choices: identifying with her darker roots, Clare has returned to her grandmother's land with a guerrilla group committed to fight against the white exploitation of Jamaica. Harry/Harriet has become a woman and goes among her people as a nurse, as both healer and warrior: "The choice is mine, man, is made. Harriet live and Harry be no more." Cliff complicates the mirroring of the racial and sexual still further. Just as Harry/Harriet is both sexually and racially indeterminate, Clare is, according to Cliff, meant to become a lesbian had she lived and matured fully. In fact, Harry/Harriet is her *lesbian* model, be he male or female: "Harry/Harriet is the novel's lesbian in a sense; he's a man who wants to be a woman and he loves women."[28]

It is significant that neither Clare nor Harriet makes a physical change at the end: Clare is still light-skinned, and Harriet has not had a sex-change operation. By their own choices each has challenged the boundaries of racial and sexual classifications and stepped beyond the biological determinism of these positions. Clare and Harry/Harriet are provocative figures because they simultaneously challenge both the system of representation based on the visible and the idea of a true, if hidden, nature upon which a politics of resistance can be based. Despite her exploration of positions that fall between the racial, sexual, and national categories, Cliff sidesteps the danger of merely fine-tuning the system with additional "identities." Clare and Harry/Harriet are characters whose choices challenge the essentialist ideologies of both the right and the left, the colonialist legacies and the revolutionary postures of identity politics. Cliff's is not so much an argument that seeks recognition for another racial or sexual category misrepresented by a dominant discourse; rather, she allows her characters to reveal the fantasies of the dominant discourse itself, fantasies that locate subversion in biology rather than in culture.

Cliff ensures that Clare's challenge to the racial system is not biological. Her sexual relation with Bobby, a black American Vietnam vet, results in a miscarriage that renders Clare sterile. At this point, before her political awakening, Clare imagines herself not only as an "albino gorilla" but as a sterile mule, the colonial representation of the "mulatto": "All that effort for naught. Lightening up. Eyes for naught. Skin for naught. Fine nose for naught. Mule — most likely. Circling the cane-crusher" (*NTH,* p. 169). It is significant that she is only able to educate herself about and oppose neocolonial power once her own sexuality has been cut loose from the reproductive drama of racial "progress" or "degeneration."

Clare and Harry/Harriet not only challenge the hierarchies of race science and sexology but also complicate the meaning of "identity politics," a powerful concept for feminists, gay men and lesbians, and people of color. Resisting the positions to which they have been assigned, Clare and Harriet do not take on new "truer" positions, but they choose roles that permit them to perform the political actions they believe in. This view of identity, at once shifting and strategic *and* psychically "real," approximates Judith Butler's theoretical articulation of postmodern identity as "performative."[29] Stuart Hall similarly works to articulate a more fluid theory of identity that he believes is crucial to an understanding of colonization and resistance. Cultural identity, according to Hall, is not fixed in an essentialized past, waiting to be recovered or rediscovered, but is constantly "becoming" in response to the "play" of history, culture, and power.[30]

Even as Clare and Harry/Harriet challenge the coercive apparatuses that seek to assign them to static racial and sexual positions, there is nothing utopian in Cliff's vision of in-between racial or sexual positions; the choices Clare and Harriet make are not freely chosen, nor do they guarantee freedom. Deconstructing the boundaries of modern identity or recognizing cultural contradictions does not automatically offer an effective politics.[31] While the guerrilla group is international and interracial, Cliff makes no claims for global "sisterhood" or "brotherhood." Because even the "revolutionary" stances Clare and Harry/Harriet claim occur within the framework of colonial discourse, the possibility of their success is already compromised. Postcolonial society, or neocolonial society, as Cliff would more likely call it, has inherited and not yet cast off the colonial social structure that thrives on conflicted loyalties, promises privileges to those who can "pass" as white, and rewards betrayal. The psychology that is created by such a system is of intense interest to Cliff; by asking how we come to experience discourses as real, she explains not only their psychological power but the weaknesses or vulnerabilities that continuously disrupt political movements of resistance.

"Passing": Survival, Betrayal, and Metaphors of Race

Like Schreiner and Rhys, Cliff seeks to understand how myths of difference (in this case those of race, class, and sexuality) are internalized in early childhood. In the face of this education, Cliff's racially and sexually indeterminate characters develop strategies of survival that they either cling to their entire lives (as Boy Savage does) or amend in response to new knowledge or new identifications (as Harry/Harriet and Clare do).

The weight of the history of "racial" classifications determines, at least in her early life, Clare's highly specific placement, a placement different from that of her darker mother and sister. Cliff describes the politics of "colorism" in her essay "If I Could Write This in Fire, I Would Write This in Fire":

> None of this is as simple as it may sound. We were colonists and we aspired to oppressor status. . . . Color was the symbol of our potential: color taking in hair "quality," skin tone, freckles, nose-width, eyes. We did not see that color symbolism was a method of keeping us apart: in the society, in the family, between friends. Those of us who were light-skinned, straight-haired, etc., were given to believe that we could actually attain whiteness — or at least those qualities of the colonizer which made him superior. We were convinced of white supremacy. If we failed, we were not really responsible for our failures: we had all the advantages — but it was that one persistent drop of blood, that single rogue gene that made us unable to conceptualize abstract ideas, made us love darkness rather than despise it, which was to be blamed for our failure. Our dark part had taken over: an inherited imbalance in which the doom of the creole was sealed.
>
> I am trying to write this as clearly as possible, but as I write I realize that what I say may sound fabulous, or even mythic. It is. It is insane.[32]

Cliff is leery of the pseudoscientific language of heredity and genetics that through its materiality ("one rogue gene") allows her to internalize a mythic tale of her own superiority/inferiority and the superiority/inferiority of others. On one level, the fine distinctions of complexion and hair texture are a tribute to the success of colonialist imaginings of racial difference. But the wide spectrum of variation conceived of *within* the black-white dichotomy blurs the edges of that dichotomy to the point of confusion and distrust. The fear of racial fraud, of passing, is also an admission of the possibility of crossing boundaries that are conceived of as "natural." Cliff stresses not only the historic weight of racial myth but the insanity of such a system where family "bloodlines" (if they are known) define one's racial place, and yet color divides parents from children and siblings from one another.

Racial identification in Cliff's work is always relational, the constant evaluating of sameness and difference. In Cliff's writing, colonialism has created of the light-skinned creole a compromised figure whose self-identity is shifting, at times opportunistic and self-betraying. In Jamaica, the "colored" creole family defining itself as "not black" hires black domestic and garden workers. Threatened with the revolutionary violence of the darker people they exploit, however, they revert to a consanguineous self-definition of racial identity:

> One night, the man who serves the table, who attends meetings on his evenings off, unable to hold his tongue any longer, turns to the people at the table, and says, "You know, Mas' William, when we get de power, de power fe de people, t'ings not gwan be easy fe de white smaddy of Jamaica dem. Per'haps wunna and wunna family should t'ink 'bout de hemigration. Wit' all respect, sah."
>
> "I never did hear such rudeness, Faith." The master speaks across the server to the mistress.
>
> "We are not white, Joshua, so we are not worried." The mistress taking pity on the houseboy and deciding that his words came from benign concern. Flattered nonetheless that even this hignorant countrybwai did t'ink she white. Not understanding his use of metaphor. (*NTH,* p. 20)

The "houseboy's" metaphor acknowledges the way race is not an essential biological category but one intricately connected to class and political choice.

This is the difficult terrain Clare travels in the novel as she negotiates between assigned place and political choice. The ambivalence expressed by Schreiner and Rhys about their undefined and at times conflictual positions is heightened in Cliff's writing by her attention to the issue of "passing." Cliff's examination of the pressures on and privileges of light-skinned Creoles reveals the contradictions inherent in the concept and the experience of passing. Like Olive Schreiner, but more deliberately, Cliff analogizes her own political and racial position with that of Jews in history. Her different, at times contrasting, use of Jewish historical experience as metaphor reveals the contradictions she theorizes are inherent in passing itself. In an earlier essay Cliff invokes the experience of the Marranos, either passing in Spain as Christians or escaping to the New World, to describe the experience of racial passing in the English colonies. This analogy allows her to recognize in the act of passing some resistance, rather than complete capitulation, to colonial ideologies:

> Sometimes I used to think we were like the Marranos — the Sephardic Jews forced to pretend they were Christians. The name was given them by the Christians, and meant "pigs." But once out of Spain and Portugal, they became Jews openly again. Some settled in Jamaica. They knew who the enemy was and acted for their own survival. But they remained Jews always. ("IICW," pp. 71–72)[33]

Like those of mixed race, the "impure" Jew is imagined as an animal. Marc Shell in his study of the treatment of Jews in Christian Spain notes the increasing loss of a human intermediate term between "national kin and national non-kin" after the Christian reconquest. The non-Christian becomes an animal, a pig, bull, or monster, which must be ritualistically killed.[34] In *Abeng,* Cliff makes a connection between colonialist and anti-Jewish policies, recalling 1492 as the year of both the Spanish claim of the Caribbean and the expulsion of the Jews. As Shell notes: "Spain at the time of the Reconquest plays a central role in the European history of the idea of caste or race. . . . The Christian Reconquest culminating in the expulsion of the Jews in 1492 and the Muslims in 1502, was *the* nationalist event in Spanish history. (On the very day in 1492 that Christopher Columbus set sail from Palos for what turned out to be the New World, he noted in the log the shiploads of Jews and *conversos* leaving under threat of death their Old World home of a millennium.")[35] Imagining Columbus himself as a Marrano (who changed his name from Cohen to Colón), Cliff complicates the impulse for the exploration that led to colonialism (*A,* p. 67). Cliff's invocation of the history of Jewish oppression is more than merely metaphoric, as it is in Schreiner's writing; both colonial racism and anti-Semitism share the history of the Inquisition that not only invented "purity of blood" but set up the tension between assigned racial position and the possibilities of movement between these positions. In Cliff's Marrano example, passing is seen as a kind of camouflage, a necessary strategy of survival, a role that can be cast off when no longer needed.

Trained not to recognize racism in Jamaica, the twelve-year-old Clare of *Abeng* becomes obsessed with Anne Frank and through contemplating the history of anti-Semitism begins to recognize the workings of racism in her own country. This time the Jew serves as a symbol not of resistance but of victimization, the ultimate result of racist ideology and policy:

> This twelve-year-old Christian mulatto girl [Clare], up to this point walk-
> ing through her life according to what she had been told — not knowing
> very much about herself or her past — for example, that her great-great-
> grandfather had once set fire to a hundred Africans; that her grandmother
> Miss Mattie was once a cane-cutter with a cloth bag of salt in her shirt
> pocket — this child became compelled by the life and death of Anne Frank.
> She was reaching, without knowing it, for an explanation of her own life.
> (A, pp. 71–72)

In *No Telephone to Heaven* a slightly older Clare, now living in New York,
becomes similarly obsessed with the girls killed in the bombing of the
Birmingham church in 1963. In both cases, Clare learns about racism in
her own country by first recognizing it elsewhere. Her identification with
Anne Frank or the African-American girls is complicated by her training
and education to identify with those who have power. She has been educated to disavow any identification with African Americans or dark-skinned
Jamaicans, including her mother, who leaves Clare with her father in New
York to accrue the "advantages" of her light skin.

Survival, then, can be uncomfortably close to betrayal in Cliff's analysis.
What happens after generations of playing the role? Is it so clear who the
"enemy" is when one has internalized and identified oneself by the values
of the oppressor? Part of the legacy of the colored Creole as Cliff sees it
is the "quashee," the betrayer. The distrust of Jamaican "Coloreds" by both
"Whites" and "Blacks" is part of the historical legacy of colonialism and
slavery.[36]

Although Clare is not the informer who ultimately betrays the guerrilla
group, she has identified with and served colonial interests before she reed-
ucates herself about Jamaican history. It is "with the logic of a creole" that
she chooses to study in London (*NTH*, p. 109) and, deprived of an education about her African roots, Clare is described by Cliff as having "once
witnessed for Babylon." The use of the Rastafari metaphor highlights the
complexity of Clare's national allegiance. If Babylon is the land of servitude and exile and Zion the homeland, Jamaica is both. "Babylon" is not so
much a place (for Clare finds herself in exile in Jamaica, England, and the
United States) as a state of mind, an affiliation with the master, the colonialist. This is the state of mind promised and fulfilled by her education,
an education that promises her "advancement" while requiring her self-
betrayal. Like Jean Rhys, Cliff is keenly aware of the imperialistic power
of education and culture, what Ngũgĩ wa Thiong'o has called "the colonization of the mind."[37] Built into this cultural domination, however, is

an irrepressible cultural and linguistic resistance: creolism. Creolism, for Cliff, is more than a recognition of ambiguous racial status; it also refers to the conflicts of clashing cultures and the possibility of new perspectives resulting from such conflict.

Snow on the Cane Fields

As I have suggested in earlier chapters, the colonizing power of European culture, articulated through language, literature, and religion, has as much influence, ultimately, as the military and economic subjugation of a people. Cultures, however, do not die as definitive deaths as do people. Different languages, religions, symbols, and forms may exist at the same time, sometimes obviously competing, sometimes merging and being used with no sense of conflict. In their struggle to find a literary language, many postcolonial writers express frustration with the education that teaches them alien forms. Cliff describes this education as an active suppression of Caribbean creole culture: "The Anglican ideal — Milton, Wordsworth, Keats — was held before us with an assurance that we were unable, and would never be enabled, to compose a work of similar correctness. No reggae spoken here."[38]

Yet there is something of interest and beauty to be salvaged from what Brathwaite has called a "disaster area." Out of the double consciousness revealed by the schoolchildren of Brathwaite's example (see introduction, p. 8), Caribbean writers produce creolized cultural products combining the British literary tropes with Caribbean symbols and metaphors of a rich oral tradition. Regarding her use of language in *No Telephone to Heaven,* Cliff writes that she had to both reclaim the *"patois* forbidden us" and rework the language and form of standard English, "mixing in the forms taught us by the oppressor, undermining his language and co-opting his style, and turning it to our purpose. In [*No Telephone to Heaven*], I alternate the King's English with *patois,* not only to show the class background of characters, but to show how Jamaicans operate within a split consciousness. It would be as dishonest to write the novel entirely in *patois* as to write entirely in the King's English."[39]

The authors of "In Praise of Creoleness" call on writers to "inseminate Creole in the new writing." The oral as opposed to the literary nature of Creole is seen as a way of reclaiming Caribbean history beyond the obfuscations of colonial history. Creoleness and a resistance to colonial identifications are to be found, perhaps, in creole languages of the Caribbean:

> Our Creole culture was created in the plantation system through question-
> ing dynamics made of acceptances and denials, resignations and assertions.
> A real galaxy with the Creole language as its core, Creoleness has, still to-
> day, its privileged mode: orality. Provider of tales, proverbs, "titim," nursery
> rhymes, songs, etc., orality is our intelligence; it is our reading of this world,
> the experimentation, still blind, of our complexity. Creole orality, even re-
> pressed in its aesthetic expression, contains a whole system of countervalues,
> a counterculture; it witnesses ordinary genius applied to resistance, devoted to
> survival.[40]

Central to Cliff's novel *No Telephone to Heaven* is an incisive analysis of
competing discourses: colonial and creole. Beyond the outrageous ubiquity
of English cultural symbols in Caribbean primers and textbooks is the relationship of colonized subjects to the English language itself and the racist
assumptions built into that language. The text of the novel moves between
the literary "King's English" and the oral "Jamaican English," sometimes
smoothly in dialogue and sometimes jarringly in the middle of a narrative
passage. At the moments when the text shifts to Jamaican English it is as if
the character wrests the language from the realm of British literature and
substitutes an English that has been reshaped by African languages and Caribbean experience. Sometimes this new English shifts the narrative from the
voice of the formally educated narrator to that of the illiterate character:

> When he was eight, Christopher's grandmother died. What she thought was
> a touch of dropsy was in fact something else, and her belly swell up and she
> gone. Him grandmother dead when him eight but him stay on in de shack.
> De government men tek her body away fe bury dem say and leave him dere,
> never once asking if him have smaddy fe care fe him. (*NTH*, p. 40)

The shift in midsentence is a violent wrenching away of the text by Christopher's voice, a voice of great anguish and bewilderment, a voice that
expresses the experience of Jamaican poverty in the language of the slum.
The movement into Jamaican English is made to seem almost unconscious,
not a deliberate move of the novelist. Cliff deftly moves into Christopher's
world where there can be no other language for his grief. Through this
linguistic conflict, here within the sentence itself, Cliff has found a way to
express a character's psychological experience that is so powerful that the
controlling voice of the British-educated narrator collapses into that of the
uneducated Jamaican character.

But Cliff is not claiming a "real" or "authentic" Jamaican voice that
stands outside the politics of cultural conflict. Language and accent are
highly politicized in her work and become conscious strategies of passing,

masquerade, or political solidarity for most of the characters. Edouard Glissant offers us the standard colonialist understanding of Creole as language: "According to traditional textbooks, Creole is a patois that is incapable of abstract thought and therefore unable to convey 'knowledge.' "[41] Contrary to this attitude, Glissant sees creole language as a kind of camouflage, a protective language of the people.[42] For Cliff *all* language can be used for protection and for resistance, even the King's English. After her education in London in *No Telephone to Heaven,* for instance, Clare learns to turn on "Oxbridge" accents or to use the Jamaican accents and vocabulary of her youth depending on the needs of the moment. For her, neither mode is "natural," and neither is merely parodic.

Clare's mother, Kitty, also suffers from the "split consciousness" of her linguistic position. In America she finds her "strange" accent keeps her both from jobs (*NTH,* p. 74) and from connection with the African-American women with whom she works. In her isolation she turns her fury on the language itself, attempting to dismantle the racism ingrained in the language she speaks. Her job at White's Sanitary Laundry is to insert a helpful cleaning hint from a mythical American homemaker, "Mrs. White," into the newly laundered shirts and sheets. Silenced in America, Kitty finds her voice by writing new messages on the inserts, new messages bubbling from Mrs. White's mythical image: "EVER TRY CLEANSING YOUR MIND OF HATRED? THINK OF IT"; "WHITE PEOPLE CAN BE BLACK HEARTED"; "MARCUS GARVEY WAS RIGHT"; and finally, "HELLO. MRS. WHITE IS DEAD. MY NAME IS MRS. BLACK. I KILLED HER" (*NTH,* 78–83). Coloring in Mrs. White's face with her pencil Kitty sends this "furious Aunt Jemima" out into the world as her only resistance to the racism she experiences in the United States. That her resistance should be through language is as significant as is her inability to entirely deconstruct the English language metaphors of whiteness and blackness, tied as they are to ideas of goodness and evil, cleanliness and dirt. While she can identify the racism implicit in the image of Mrs. White (an image reflecting no woman in the neighborhood of the laundry), Kitty has no other language but English to use and so still relies on a metaphor such as "black hearted" to express her evaluation of white culture.[43] As Jamaica Kincaid puts it, "For isn't it odd that the only language I have in which to speak of this crime is the language of the criminal who committed the crime?"[44]

Out of such resistance to racist cultural teachings can emerge new forms that incorporate black Caribbean interpretation into colonial traditions. In

No Telephone to Heaven, this kind of resistance is found in the poorest of the Kingston slums. While most of this novel explores Clare's world, another side of Jamaica is represented by Christopher, a black boy starving in the Kingston slum. He represents both Clare's doppelgänger, providing a counternarrative of resistance,[45] and the nightmarish underside of the colonialist's religious, economic, and cultural dream of the New World.

Christopher is discovered by Brother Josephus, a black pastor who trudges up and down the Dungle, the stinking lots of the slum, challenging the colonialist image of a white Jesus that he recognizes as the religious underpinnings of racism in the once-English colony. The portrait of Jesus he carries with him through the alleys is of "a small dark man with wooly hair, beardless face, and a hump between his shoulder blades" (*NTH,* p. 36). Unlike Kitty, Brother Josephus is able to redefine the semantics of color while redefining the image of God: "Dis, children . . . dis, children is Lickle Jesus, Black as his mother was Black. As the world came from the darkness of his Father." Due to their religious educations, sent certainly like the school curriculum from a European home office, most inhabitants of the slum think Brother Josephus has lost his mind. As one woman puts it before walking out on the brother's revolutionary preaching: "Me have seen Jesus. Me know is who Him favor. . . . Teacher nuh show me when we lickle children? Him is backra man fe true. White-white wid blue yeye. . . . Dat picture dere favor slave, not Savior" (*NTH,* pp. 36–37). It is Brother Josephus who sees in Christopher a symbolic connection between the native fruit of Jamaica, the Christophine; the so-called discoverer of the New World, Christopher Columbus; the Haitian revolutionary, Henri Christophe; and Christ the savior. That Brother Josephus sees all this in the weak and malnourished Christopher is his resistance to the education that would have Blacks accept for their own savior an image of the European conqueror. And yet at this moment, his own gloriously syncretic offering of a black Christ is rejected by his people. The savior he sees in the black boy from the slum is too damaged and confused to claim his power. Having murdered the light-skinned family that employed him as a yardboy, Christopher wanders the streets, mad, prophetic, a "Neger Christ," who calls for the fiery destruction of white Jamaica yet is used to suppress any such resistance.

National resistance depends on the wide acceptance of a non-European reinterpretation of history such as that offered by the new teachers of this generation, Brother Josephus and Harry/Harriet. Sitting with Clare in a tourist restaurant gotten up to suggest a galleon on the Spanish Main, complete with Spanish doubloons and pieces of eight set into upturned rum barrels, Harry/Harriet imagines parodic names for these places, such as "Triangle Trade" or "Middle Passage," insisting on an acknowledgment of the real history of Jamaica. Warning that "our homeland is turned to stage set too much," Harry/Harriet insists on the danger that Jamaicans "have taken the master's past as our own" (*NTH,* pp. 121, 127).[46]

Despite the determination of these teacher/warriors, however, Cliff recognizes that colonialism, immigration to the Caribbean, and emigration from the Caribbean to England, Canada, and the United States, while creating a rich cultural mix, make any resistant nationalist claim or movement difficult to maintain. Unlike the claims of national character and authenticity made by writers at the turn of the century (including both Theodore Watts and Olive Schreiner), contemporary claims are strikingly insufficient for *any* country today. Paul Gilroy's and Kobena Mercer's work on contemporary British culture, for instance, shows that while England has long prided itself on a distinct identity and culture, the postcolonial era has opened that culture to important influences that have changed it forever.[47] Claims, then, of a coherent national culture, of British culture, American culture, or even Jamaican or Caribbean culture, can be both defensive and reactionary.

Cliff argues that claims of cultural nationalism are particularly difficult in Caribbean nations, which, she agrees with Antonio Benítez Rojo, lack both a center and a boundary.[48] William Luis similarly addresses the inappropriateness of the European modernist idea of a "nation" to the Caribbean islands, which changed hands so many times and whose people have moved and continue to move among the island nations and back and forth between the islands and Europe and North America. When Luis speaks of a developing "national literature," therefore, he describes a "West Indian narrative" that crosses not only political boundaries but language boundaries as well.[49] The kind of "national" identity Cliff addresses is distinctly postmodern in its rejections of authenticating origins (the indigenous people of the region, the Arawaks and then the Caribs, having been eradicated) and its acknowledgment of the mixture of peoples and cultures within and across the many Caribbean nations and territories. Any successful nationalist movement, then, will have to acknowledge the oppressive economic and cultural influences from more powerful countries and multinational corporations as well as the internationalism of anticolonial resistance movements.

The guerrilla band Clare joins in *No Telephone to Heaven* is pointedly an international group, some members being politically and militarily active in South Africa as well. Recalling Harry/Harriet's critique that Jamaica has become a stage set, it is not coincidental that their target is an American movie set on location in Jamaica making a B movie exploiting all the stereotypes of an exoticized foreign terrain. The script being filmed is an offensive distortion and corruption of the Jamaican history of Maroon resistance. While the film is created with an ignorant American audience in mind, Cliff shows in *Abeng* and *No Telephone to Heaven* the way American films become part of Jamaicans' historical and cultural knowledge as well.[50] The producers of the films, availing themselves of the floundering economy dependent on U.S. dollars, have taken the tourist ad "Make It Your Own" at its word and have purchased the Jamaican military to protect the set and crew from the local people.

A similar connection between cultural and military imperialism is made in the short story "I Used to Like the Dallas Cowboys" by Dionne Brand, a Trinidadian writer, now living in Toronto, Canada ("IUL," pp. 115–29). The story is narrated by a woman who has returned from Canada to a Caribbean island to which she is not native (presumably Grenada), a nation under attack by U.S. bomber planes and soldiers scouring the streets. As she awaits death in an apartment hallway with several of her friends, she recalls learning to admire U.S. football games on television. She remembers as a child absorbing American culture in seemingly harmless teen magazines: "To be honest, if I really look back, it was the clandestine *True Confession* magazines from America which I read at thirteen that led to my love for the Dallas Cowboys. There was always a guy named Bif or Ted or Lance who was on the college football team and every girl wanted to wear his sweater. Never mind we didn't have sweaters or need them in the tropics, this only made them romantic items" ("IUL," p. 119). The story examines the connection between sports, race, and class (including the narrator's description of cricket as a slave owner's game) and ultimately the connection between U.S. sports and war. The team she loved to watch was the most "American" to her:

> Another thing about the Cowboys, all my football buddies used to say that they were the most fascist team. Well I agreed, you know, because football, or most any American sport, has that quality to it. I said that was exactly why I liked Dallas because in this gladiatorial game called football they were the most scientific, the most emotionless, and therefore exactly what this game was about. ("IUL," pp. 124–25)

Having joined the revolution, the narrator comes to see that it is this cold and brutal aspect of American culture that she has been taught to admire, both in Trinidad where she grew up and in Canada where she worked, that is also at the heart of U.S. military aggression. She has been taught to admire and identify with a culture that will most likely destroy her. Her revolutionary position is as much a disavowal of U.S./American culture as it is a military battle for the island:

> Four days ago the island was invaded by America. The Americans don't like cricket. But deep inside of those of us hiding from them in this little corridor, and those in the hills and cemeteries, we know they've come to play ball. . . . When they're not playing, the Cowboys can be deadly. . . . The day I finally creep to the door, the day I look outside to see who is trying to kill me, to tell them that I surrender, I see the Dallas Cowboys coming down my hot tropical street, among the bougainvillea and the mimosa, crouching, pointing their M16 weapons, laden with grenade-launchers. The hibiscus and I dangle high and red in defeat; everything is silent and gone. Better dead. Their faces are painted and there's that smell, like fresh blood and human grease, on them. And I hate them. ("IUL," pp. 127, 129)

The defeat that ends this story is much like that which ends *No Telephone to Heaven*. Clare's guerrilla band, waiting to attack the movie set, is intercepted by the military and wiped out. Clare's body is burned into the land by machine-gun fire, and as she loses consciousness, she slips from language into the preverbal, preliterary sounds of a land before meaning, language, or symbolic use: "She remembered language. Then it was gone."[51] This is "place" prior or subsequent to the uses made of it by a logic of difference that assigns each of us a place — national, cultural, racial, sexual — determining our rights and the way we come to know ourselves and to define our battles. As tempting as it might be, however, Cliff does not offer a utopian conclusion in which the diverse creole community — united across races, classes, and sexes — gloriously overcomes the neocolonial exploitation and reestablishes Jamaica, the homeland of the people. Although Clare has made her own choice to claim Jamaica and not England as her "motherland," Cliff uses the ending to dramatize the way individual choices occur within historical paradigms. Clare's and Harry/Harriet's choices, while they are important symbolic challenges to the hierarchical classification systems of race and sex, are no match for the force of these systems once set into motion. The betrayer of the band, identified by the slavery-era term *quashee,* exposes Clare's and Harry/Harriet's ambitions to create a new Jamaica overnight as a romantic dream, impossible at this time.

The peace at the end of the novel exists out of time, beyond history, beyond culture. But Cliff does not even leave us in the meaningless ahistoric world of nature, for the final two words of the novel jolt us back into history where Clare and Christopher, the "Neger Christ," and perhaps Harry/ Harriet lie riddled with bullets — "Day broke." *No Telephone to Heaven,* as its title implies, is not a novel of salvation. While it shares with Schreiner's and Rhys's novels the longing for home, it discards the idea of a coherent national identity as imagined by modernist literature. Participating in the postmodern deconstructions of race, sex, and nation, Cliff values and searches for the buried histories, perspectives, and knowledges that, when unearthed, will complicate the fictions we have been taught to live as truths.

6 / "Miskien of Gold Gemake"

Zoë Wicomb

Calling South African writer Zoë Wicomb "another 'coloured,' from another end of the Empire," Michelle Cliff describes a transnational connection between those still defined by colonial categories.[1] Cliff's identification with Wicomb is based on their shared racial status as "Coloured," their shared acknowledgment of the ironies of their English literary educations, and their skepticism about English as the language of their own writing. Cliff's comparison of her own position with Wicomb's underscores the similar effects of European colonialism on an international group of people who can roughly be identified by their experiences as colonized subjects; an examination of Wicomb's powerful novel *You Can't Get Lost in Cape Town* (1987),[2] however, also highlights the specificities of colonial and postcolonial history in different parts of the erstwhile empire. Like Cliff's work, Wicomb's novel examines the racial and cultural categories promoted by European colonialism, particularly the category "Coloured," but the specificity of the South African context underscores the important differences of meaning implicit in and perhaps obscured by the terminology of postcolonial discourse. Whereas Cliff describes a society in which color and class are intricately related, the minute gradations of color in Jamaica are a social rather than statutory hierarchy. Unlike Rhys and Cliff, who refer to the Caribbean everyday acknowledgment of racial and cultural creolism, Wicomb describes a system that, while officially recognizing a "mixed-race" category called "Coloured," attempts to reify and legislate discrete categories of racial — and cultural — difference.

From 1948 until 1994 (and in 1987 when Wicomb published her novel) the Nationalist government of South Africa promoted these supposedly natural differences as "national" differences. And yet to be recognized as a member of a nation within South Africa did not guarantee one the rights of South African citizenship reserved for white South Africans, only some 13 percent of the population. Members of the so-called nations of black and colored South Africa were denied those rights granted by traditional concepts of citizenship: voting, housing, employment, and freedom of movement.

In South Africa, culture, color, and race have a peculiar relationship to one another. On the one hand, English and Afrikaner communities are "white" and share the minority position of economic dominance. On the other hand, historical antagonisms between these two colonizing groups have led to emphasized differences of culture in language, religion, and political mythologies. Many Afrikaners and "Coloureds" share Afrikaans as a language, share a rural history, and share branches and roots of their family trees. While "Coloureds" were accorded some rights and privileges denied black South Africans, since the 1970s "Coloureds" have for the most part preferred to be called "Blacks" and have aligned themselves with black South Africans. Wicomb's decision to write in English is somewhat more complex than Cliff's. Although Wicomb shares Cliff's recognition of English as a language representing historical and contemporary repression, in South Africa English also represents a political disavowal of Afrikaans, the language of the Nationalist government. And yet, despite this political position, most "Coloureds" speak Afrikaans, especially in rural areas, and some are working to develop a counterhegemonic literary use of the language.[3] Since 1948, with the introduction of the Christian National Education policy, Afrikaans, the *moedertaal-onderwys,* or mother tongue, became the required language of instruction for most "coloured" students. Like the black students who revolted in 1976 against the exclusive use of Afrikaans in schools, most "Coloureds" believed that the purpose of this policy was to keep them from learning English, a language that would allow for more universal political and economic connections. With Afrikaans as the language associated with Afrikanerdom and apartheid, English becomes not merely another colonial language but a language representing antiparochialism and defiance of the government's definition of the South African nation and the "nations" it contains.[4]

Literature has been an important part of constructing the so-called nation of so-called Coloureds, and Wicomb's work is a profound response to the damning portrayal of "Coloureds" throughout South African literary history. The influence of literary representations of "Coloureds" on politics and policy in South Africa is apparent by the fact that in 1949 the works of both Olive Schreiner and Sarah Gertrude Millin were used to support proposed legislation against interracial sexual relations and interracial marriage.[5] V. A. February traces the derogatory images of "coloured" characters to the earlier portrayals of the Khoikhoi in literature by Schreiner, Millin, and others. The stereotype of the Khoikhoi, or "Hottentot," that February points to in the literature is recognizable in Schreiner's portrayal of both the "Hottentot" maid in *Story of an African Farm* and the "half-caste" in her essays: comic, drunken, irascible, morally loose.[6]

Perhaps the most renowned of such portrayals of "Coloureds" are found in Sarah Gertrude Millin's novels, particularly *God's Step-Children,* published in 1924.[7] This novel, popular through several editions in South Africa, England, and the United States, chronicles four generations of "Coloureds" who trace their white ancestry to an English missionary in the 1820s who made the "fatal mistake" of marrying a "Hottentot" woman and spawning generations of misery, frustration, and shame. In each generation, no matter how light their skin or how English their upbringing and education, these mixed-race men and women are nonetheless always undone by the trace of "black blood" bequeathed them by their ancestor's foolish attempt to prove to the village that the Christian God makes no distinction between Whites and Blacks. With the birth of the missionary's first child (named Isaac in recognition of the sacrifice his father made of his son's "pure white" blood) the terrible drama of miscegenation begins, a drama that is later played out particularly in the lighter branches of the family. As the narrator reminds the reader, once "black blood" enters a white family tree, "there can be no more white children" (*GSG,* p. 274).[8] While the "white blood" of the missionary raises his offspring from the baboonlike nature Millin ascribes to the native people, the "degenerate" blood of the "Hottentot" at some point always reveals itself in the form of sexual infidelity (in women), arrested intellectual development (in both sexes), or cowardice (in men).

For anyone who has read Millin's novel, Zoë Wicomb's 1990 short story "Another Story" presents a sly and satisfying attack on this novel in particular and raises important questions about the rights and responsibilities of authors in general.[9] "Another Story" is exactly that — a contemporary rewriting of Millin's "coloured" characters by a "coloured" author. In the story, an older "coloured" woman, Deborah Kleinhans, visits her well-educated great-niece Sarah Lindse, whom she has never met. Sarah teaches in a university in Cape Town and has invited her great-aunt to visit in order, we come to understand, to track down some family history she believes has been misrepresented by a white woman writer she does not name. The characters' names in this story, however, are the names of Millin's characters in *God's Step-Children* (Deborah Kleinhans, Elmira), and the author intending to set the record straight shares the name Sarah with the original author. Wicomb's Deborah Kleinhans is presumably a younger cousin of Millin's Barry Lindsell, who belongs to the last generation chronicled in *God's Step-Children,* and Sarah Lindse would be of the generation of Barry's disavowed child.

Quoting directly from Millin's unnamed novel, Sarah describes what she knows of her aunt's rural home: "...nothing but an untidiness on God's earth — a mixture of degenerate brown peoples, rotten with sickness, an affront against Nature" ("AS," p. 10; *GSC,* p. 303). Deborah is appalled by this description of her childhood home and family and angrily defends its cleanliness until Sarah reassures her that she is only remembering this description from a story she has read. With all the excitement of an academic with a new project, Sarah tries to interest Deborah in both the white woman's story and the possibility of its revision:

> "It's an interesting story that needs to be told by..."
>
> "And what would you know about it?" Deborah interrupted. "It's never been interesting. Dreary as dung it was, sitting day after day waiting for something to happen; listening for hooves or the roll of cartwheels." But she checked herself. Hearing only the wind howl through the bushes and the ewes bleat, she had made up stories....But she said, "You know I have my books — *Rooi Rose* every fortnight, I haven't missed a book since I started working for the de Villiers and when I retired I kept it up. Every fortnight. Good stories that seem to be about real life, but well, when you think about it, you won't recognise anyone you know. They'll give you no useful tips. They're no better than the nonsense I used to make up in my own head to kill the time. My advice child is to stick to your business and forget about stories of old times."
>
> "It depends surely on who tells the story. Auntie Deborah, that's what I must ask you about. Do you know if someone has written the story of our family, from the beginning, right from the European missionary? Do you by any chance remember a woman, a white woman speaking to your mother or brothers or yourself about those days? A woman who then wrote a book? Have you ever heard of the book, of..."

"No, I don't believe it. What nonsense, of course there was no such woman. A book for all to read with our dirty washing spread out on snow white pages! Ag, man, don't worry; it wouldn't be our story; it's everyone's story. All Coloured people have the same old story." ("AS," p. 12)

Although clearly anxious to counter the racist representation of "Coloureds," Wicomb is suspicious of the recuperative possibilities of new stories and the rights of writers to produce them. Sarah's inspiration to retell Millin's story and her belief that *who* tells the story makes all the difference are undercut by Deborah's lack of interest and her general distrust of written accounts. It is Sarah's education that has introduced her to such books as *God's Step-Children* and has taught her to take them seriously. Deborah's disdain for this book and for *any* book that publicly explores the family life casts Sarah's project and Millin's project (which both date the "beginning" of the family with the white missionary) as more similar than different. That Wicomb names this would-be revisionist with the same name as the original author undermines Sarah's assertion that a "coloured" writer could correct the story by virtue of her identity. Perhaps writing itself produced in the colonial/postcolonial context is too compromised an activity to serve anticolonial projects. Deborah's objection lies less with the identity of the author than with the relationship between the object of the writing and the audience. For whom are stories written down? Who validates their telling? What guidance and what psychological value do they offer? Deborah, who reads romances and remembers the daydreams of her youth, is not sure of the answers to the questions her lack of enthusiasm suggests.

The storyteller in "Another Story" turns out in the end not to be Sarah but Deborah, who, after Sarah is arrested in the middle of the night by the police, returns to her home and carefully chooses the audience for the story of her own surprising act of resistance against the police. Having served white men all her life, Deborah offers the police coffee, prepares it to their tastes, and before their eyes, calmly tips the mugs and pours the coffee down the drain. Wicomb's story ends with Deborah's oral storytelling, translated by the narrator from Afrikaans, the language Deborah speaks most comfortably. While Sarah's story is not told (we do not know what happens to her after her arrest, nor do we know if she ever revises *God's Step-Children*), Wicomb's story does revise Millin's novel and does offer Deborah's private oral Afrikaans story in a public written English. Wicomb's ambivalence about the meaning and efficacy of writing is expressed by the title of the story itself, a title that, like Deborah's actions, simultaneously makes revolutionary claims for itself (much like the current term "Another

South Africa") and makes no claims at all. While, indeed, this is another story altogether, portraying Millin's characters in a radically different light, it is also *merely* another story among innumerable stories about South Africa and South Africans.

Political Grounding

As offensive as the term "Coloured" is for most South Africans so described, Wicomb and other writers resort to it lacking any other word that would demarcate the particular racial identity created and then reified by recent apartheid legislation. Although these laws have now been repealed, the discourse of apartheid is still central to South African culture, politics, and consciousness. In "Another Story," Zoë Wicomb describes the frustrating tenaciousness of the racist language when racial identity determines one's life. Waiting at the airport for her great-aunt, Sarah looks for an elderly "coloured" woman and then corrects herself:

> So-called Coloured, for she did not think that the qualifier should be reserved for speech. It grieved her that she so often had to haul up the "so-called" from some distant recess where it slunk around with foul terms like half-caste and half-breed and she stamped her foot . . . as if to shake down the unsummoned words. Lexical vigilance was a matter of mental hygiene: a regular rethinking of words in common use, like cleaning out rotten food from the back of a refrigerator where no one expects food to rot and poison the rest. ("AS," p. 7)

While Sarah's great-aunt, who has worked as a servant in white people's homes most of her life, uses the term unself-consciously, Sarah, like most of her generation since the 1976 student uprisings and the Black Consciousness movement, would probably choose the term "black" to describe herself and her political solidarity with all non-Whites in a society that privileges British and Afrikaner white South Africans. This political use of "black" (employed similarly in the United Kingdom) reclaims and reworks the nineteenth-century meaning of "coloured" in South Africa that designated all non-Europeans, be they black Africans, Asian immigrants and their descendants, or "mixed-race" people.

The nineteenth-century census reports of colonial South Africa identified only two broad groups, "European" and "Coloured."[10] In the 1904 census, however, the term "Coloured" was used for the first time to designate a third group of people differentiated from "Whites" and "Bantus" (this last label is often used by the white government but rejected by black

South Africans on both political and linguistic grounds).[11] While the creation of this new class provided those now designated as "Coloured" some protection from the housing, employment, and health ordinances that increasingly impoverished black South Africans, it also restricted the "passing" of "non-Bantu-speaking non-Europeans" into the white population.[12] The disastrous effect on black South Africans of some of these protections or "preference policies" for "Coloureds" is vividly described by the life story *Poppie Nongena* as told to the writer Elsa Joubert.[13] Until 1950 the system of racial classification was not rigid; people could "pass" from one group to another based on their physical features. The Population Registration Act of 1950 was designed to put an end to this by registering the entire population, issuing identity cards, and restricting movement, residence, and employment based on racial identity. This act provided the cornerstone of apartheid policy.

V. A. February, in his study of the image of "Coloureds" in literature, traces through governmental acts the vague and tautological criteria of the so-called racial designations. For instance, the 1950 act depended to a great extent on community recognition. A "white person," according to this act, is defined as "a person who in appearance obviously is, or who is generally accepted as a white person, but does not include a person, who, although in appearance obviously a white person, is generally accepted as a coloured person."[14] To complicate matters further, the definition of a "coloured person" in subsequent acts is "a person who is not a white person or a native." This definition of negation and exclusion does nothing to clarify the confused reliance on descent, community definitions, appearance, and "general acceptance." In 1959 the "coloured" category was subdivided into seven further categories including "Cape Coloured" (persons of mixed ancestry) and "Asiatics."[15]

Making it even more obvious that these were fictional and political designations were the "exceptional cases," those individuals who every year succeeded in "changing" color. *Time* reported that in 1986 1,600 people successfully petitioned for a change in their racial identity:

> Nine whites became colored, 506 coloreds became white, two whites became Malay, 14 Malays became white, nine Indians became white, seven Chinese became white, one Griqua became white, 40 coloreds became black, 666 blacks became colored, 87 coloreds became Indian, 67 Indians became coloreds, 26 coloreds became Malay, 50 Malays became Indian, 61 Indians became Malay, four coloreds became Griqua, four Griquas became colored, two Griquas became black, 18 blacks became Griquas, twelve coloreds be-

came Chinese, ten blacks became Indian, two blacks became other Asian, two other coloreds became Indian, and one other colored became black.[16]

The article also quoted a government minister's pointed remark that no Blacks applied to become Whites and no Whites became Blacks. The terms of the vast category "Coloured," mediating in this way between "Black" and "White," did not threaten those poles of difference in South African political mythologies but, in fact, protected and reified them. In 1989 Françoise Lionnet described these intermediate classifications as

> so many protective barriers — a kind of cordon sanitaire — aimed at prevent-
> ing transgressive boundary crossings between the "white" and "black" areas.
> However absurd and unreal this juridical codification may seem, it serves
> in effect to legitimate the status quo — the mere fact that one can change
> one's label undermines the very possibility of according the label any kind of
> strictly *biological* validity: it simply reinforces the *ideological* presuppositions of
> apartheid.

Despite (or perhaps because of) the obvious overlap of physical character-istics between the categories "White" and "Coloured," and the cultural and linguistic ties between these two groups, the fiction of biological and cul-tural difference was rigidly maintained by laws and the physical force of apartheid that was anything but fictitious.

The ambiguity of the "Coloureds'" position vis-à-vis Afrikaner cul-ture led the Nationalist Party into an increasing insistence on "coloured" uniqueness. Then minister of "coloured" affairs, M. Viljoen, addressing the first session of the Coloured Persons' Representative Council in 1969, argued:

> To take part in politics in South Africa and not to see that there are dif-
> ferent nations living here — yes, to refuse to see and admit the differences
> between nations — is surely not common sense. . . . The country's pattern
> for the development and progress of our diversity of peoples is parallel
> development.[17]

In 1972 Dr. S. W. van der Merwe, minister of coloured relations and rehoboth affairs, answered the question "Who are the Coloureds?":

> The fact that Coloureds have had Coloured forbears for many generations . . .
> indicate[s] that they may be a nation in the making — and they are, in fact,
> regarded as such by the Government. . . . This process of becoming a nation
> will be assisted by the present policy in the political and social spheres and by
> geographical distribution.[18]

These statements accompany the government's removal of "Coloureds" from the common roll between 1951 and 1957 and from representation in Parliament in 1969 (at this point only Whites could serve as representatives for "Coloureds," but "Coloureds" lost even that representation with the creation of the controversial government-appointed Coloured Persons' Representative Council). In response, "coloured" political leaders were forced to argue against this concept of a unified and unique identity. For example, in 1972, H. J. Hendrickse, the national chairman of the Labor Party, argued: "I cannot ascribe any biological differences to any people. In terms of Government classification we are termed a Coloured group but genetically we can never be regarded as a biological group.... We have no peculiar colour, we have no peculiar language."[19] Zoë Wicomb's work elaborates on this rejection of biological interpretations of difference and focuses instead on the psychological (and therefore political) effects of such racial beliefs and laws.

You Can't Get Lost in Cape Town

You Can't Get Lost in Cape Town can be read as "another story" representing apartheid from the point of view of a "coloured" young woman; like "Another Story," however, each story that makes up the collection is troubled by questions about the meanings and purposes of storytelling and the rights and responsibilities of storytellers. Like the other colonial and postcolonial writers examined in this book, Wicomb struggles with the language and modality of her expression and the relationship between those she writes about and her reading audience. *You Can't Get Lost in Cape Town* is a novel made up of ten stories that follow the main character, Frieda Shenton, a "coloured" girl, from the veld to the "coloured location" to Cape Town to England and back home again. Because the stories do not focus exclusively on Frieda and do not always employ the same narrative voice, the meaning of racial, cultural, and national identities in South Africa is explored from a variety of perspectives. All the characters of the novel are defined by a racial mythology that has become law.

South African law assigned individuals to the racial categories upon which privileges and restrictions relating to all aspects of life (residence, employment, franchise, marriage and sexuality, recreation) were based. While South African legislation furnished perhaps the most codified and politicized categories of "racial" difference in the world, the novel does not describe these laws overtly but rather reveals their effects through the bodily experiences and perceptions of the characters. By recognizing Frieda's frame of reference — who she knows, where she stands, what language she speaks — we come to understand that she is "coloured" and to evaluate her status in relation to other "Coloureds" of her family and village. *You Can't Get Lost in Cape Town* explores the thematics of racial and cultural identity under apartheid at the same time that it questions the possibility of a meaningful and representative literary culture.

Writing about a country where cultural symbols signify identity, territory, and citizenship, or lack thereof, Wicomb examines those symbols and their collisions. In this context, where language and literature themselves are far from neutral markers, each of Wicomb's stories and the novel they comprise vacillate between describing the social and psychological meanings and effects of being "coloured" in South Africa and destabilizing those descriptions and explanations. Each chapter reveals the way nature (be it landscape, skin color, or flowers) is understood through the lens of apartheid culture. Only when cultural definitions conflict is it possible to imagine nature as neutral and unencumbered by human projections.

The brilliance of Wicomb's novel is her ability both to tell the stories created by colonialism and apartheid and to critique them. To the extent that the narrator-protagonist, Frieda Shenton, is a product of the interpretive systems and stories of apartheid culture, she reproduces those stories herself. The clichéd images we saw in Schreiner's writing of the "half-caste" as lost, doomed to failure or death, get resurrected in Frieda's own stories of her day-to-day life. Yet the contradictions implicit in her always contested identity as "coloured" and her rural familial and community attachments allow her access to a variety of interpretations that in the last half of the novel provide her with incisive critiques of English-language education and Afrikaner nationalism. Through this intense conflict, Frieda becomes an astute reader and critic of apartheid culture; her attempt to be a writer of new stories is the subject of the novel.

Zoë Wicomb was born in 1948, the year the Afrikaner Nationalist Party came to power in South Africa and defined apartheid, or "separate development," as the central task of the government. Roughly autobiographical, the connected stories in *You Can't Get Lost in Cape Town* mark the growing intensity of apartheid legislation between 1948 and the mid-1980s. The laws that define Frieda's life are not so much named and identified by Frieda as they are enacted through her choices, desires, and understanding of her own body and place in the world. Six of the ten stories take place before Frieda goes to England, and they record the creation of a multicultural subject for whom "home" is a suspect term derived from either a colonial nostalgia she cannot fully share or a nationalist mythology (complete with "homelands") she knows enough to distrust. The first half of the book explores the fictions she learns to live, and the second half unravels not only the stories she learns but the ones she writes, the ones we read. Her ten-year stay in England is a gap in the center of the text because no story deals with that time directly. England is a place she looks to as an escape from South Africa and later recalls as a place of loneliness and alienation: "The telly will give you a better idea [of England] than I can. Mine will always be the view of a Martian" (*YCGL,* p. 123).

The stories that take place after her return do not celebrate her comfort upon coming home but question her authority as someone who can explain her native country, speak for or even about her displaced people. This book is unsettling because while it undermines the traditional genres of novel, short story, and autobiography, it also does not fit comfortably with the body of overtly political fiction and poetry called "resistance literature" by Barbara Harlow and others.[20] Even as this book examines the political forces that create Frieda as a multiple subject, it also describes how and why this subject is incapable psychologically and politically of speaking on behalf of an originary "pre-colonial" culture or of a "people."

The rhetoric of anticolonial struggles in much of the world is impossible for Wicomb to use unself-consciously. The "coloured" population in South Africa, with its cultural ties and shared history with the white Afrikaner population, cannot claim to predate colonialism. In the context of South African apartheid ideology, to argue for cultural distinction or "traditional way of life" among "Coloureds" is to use the government's language of "separate development." Karen Press describes an important difference between South African and other national liberation movements:

> Any attempt to retrieve a typically African set of cultural practices in South Africa would be highly problematic, given the fact that the ruling National Party has built the entire structure of the apartheid system with the help of precisely such a retrieval. The National Party's insistence on ethnic "own cultures" for sections of the population has been the basis for a fostering of "traditional" cultural activities which is intended to maintain the present, racial form of political oppression.[21]

The concept of separate "nations" allowed the white South African minority both to claim cultural and racial purity and to promote "separate development" of the supposedly different political nations of South Africa, sovereign in their own "homelands." Although Wicomb does attempt to provide a portrayal of rural "coloured" culture in *You Can't Get Lost in Cape Town* (as Alex La Guma did for the urban "coloured" world of District Six), she cannot argue with passion for the liberation of a national culture or the acquisition of national territory. And while she offers important representations of "coloured" characters and the specific and particular meanings of apartheid for "Coloureds," particularly for women, the confidence and entitlement of those descriptions are checked at each turn by her recognition of how totalizing and restrictive portrayals of communities are in South Africa. *You Can't Get Lost in Cape Town* provides a rich and nuanced examination of the way experience is shaped by such discourse and its legal enactment.

The first story of the collection, "Bowl like Hole," opens Wicomb's exploration of the relationship among language, politics, and social position. It is significant that this first chapter, which raises questions about "coloured" identity, focuses specifically on language and the meaning of English for Frieda's family. For Wicomb's own parents, who spoke Afrikaans as their native tongue, English was the language of culture and opportunity, and so they learned and taught their children English despite the fact that, as Wicomb describes it, "it was an English they weren't very sure of themselves — no one within 200 miles spoke it."[22]

You Can't Get Lost in Cape Town, like *Wide Sargasso Sea,* opens with a sentence expressing racial exclusion and identification: "At first Mr. Weedon came like any white man in a motor car, enquiring about sheep or goats or servants." Although to Frieda and the other children "all white men looked exactly same," this visit of the Englishman is painfully confusing for the young girl. Because Mr. Weedon does not speak any Afrikaans, the language of the "coloured" residents and of the white employers of the area, Frieda's father, the schoolmaster, interprets between the English owner of the gypsum mines and the black African miners. Frieda's mother, who insists that Frieda speak English, is as enamored of the Englishman, "a true gentleman," as she is disdainful of the neighboring "boers" and suspicious of Mr. Weedon's chauffeur, whom she suspects is a "play-white" or a "registered Coloured" from urban Cape Town. Curled up under the table, Frieda watches her mother and describes the mother's cultural positioning in crudely physical terms by interpreting "in her two great buttocks the opposing worlds she occupied." Frieda's story, too, will be one of bilingual, bicultural negotiation as she leaves the veld to be educated in English in a white high school and a "coloured" university.

The narrator does not share the Shenton family's idealization of either

English employers or the English language. The description of Mr. Weedon's awkward interactions with the miners does not romanticize English culture but highlights the colonial relations between Weedon and those who labor for him. After passing out packets of cigarettes to the half-naked men, Weedon congratulates himself on his relations with the miners, which he imagines are superior to (and more enlightened than) those of Afrikaner employers:

> After a particularly united blow at the rock the men laid down their picks and waited in semaphoric obedience. Mr. Weedon smiled. Then they stepped forward holding out their hands to receive the green and white packet of Cavalla cigarettes that the smiling man dealt out. Descants of "Dankie Meneer" and he flushed with pleasure for he had asked many times before not to be called Baas as the Boers insisted on being called. This time not one of the men made a mistake or even stuttered over the words. A day to be remembered... (*YCGL,* pp. 7–8)

The miners' use of the term "meneer" (sir) as opposed to "baas" (boss) is not inspired by any material difference in their relationship with the English employer or the conditions of their work, but by his insistence.

Weedon's discomfort with the reality of his position is matched by his discomfort and alienation from the land that provides his wealth. Both Mrs. Weedon and Mrs. Shenton suffer from asthma, but Mr. Weedon sends his wife to the Bahamas in the winter, a remedy Mr. Shenton is not impressed by: "He would hate to spend several days away from home, let alone months." Indeed, this land is home for Shenton and his wife (if not for his daughter, as we shall see) in a way it is not for Weedon. The sardonic humor of the narrator focuses on Weedon's romantic misunderstanding of the land, his perceptions relying on the English poetic appropriations of Africa so ridiculed by Olive Schreiner.

Excited by this foreign landscape and the sweating torsos of the miners, Weedon engages in the most maudlin poetic descriptions of the mine, the miners, and "nature's bounty." The narrator's dry response undercuts Weedon's romanticization: "And so midst all that making of poetry, two prosaic mounds rose on either side of the deepening pit" (*YCGL,* pp. 6–7). Weedon's understanding of the land is that of an outsider, an ignorant exploiter of its wealth:

> "These man-made mountains and the bowls they once fitted into, beautiful and very useful for catching the rain, don't you think?"

So he had no idea that it never rained more than the surface of the earth could hold, enough to keep the dust at rest for a day or so. Father decided not to translate. (*YCGL*, p. 7)

What Frieda's parents take from their encounter, however, is not primarily a recognition of the Englishman's ignorance but a lesson in English pronunciation. When Mr. Shenton gets home he muses, "Mr. Weedon said that the mine was like a bowl in the earth. Bowl like hole, not bowl like howl." The Shentons' aspirations to English are racial as well as cultural, as is clear from the form Mrs. Shenton's anxiety takes when she learns her pronunciation has been mistaken. She turns on Frieda with the same racial insult, "a tame Griqua,"[23] she endures from her race-conscious in-laws before she methodically repeats, "Fowl, howl, scowl and not bowl." This potential mortifying mistake will not happen again; Frieda knows that "unlike the rest of us it would take her no time at all to say bowl like hole, smoothly, without stuttering," having learned, like the miners, to describe her world in the words of the economically powerful.

In Wicomb's novel, language is the central metaphor for the tangled histories and relationships among the different groups in South Africa and the complex negotiations of power and assertions of identity. For Wicomb the language of private expression is intensely political. Frieda's sense of her body, her racial identity, and her social place in the world are transacted through her use of language, particularly in the story "Waiting for the Train." When Frieda and her father are forced to move to a "coloured" location by the Group Areas Act,[24] Mr. Shenton turns his aspirations to his daughter's education and sends her to an all-white girls' boarding school that has agreed to accept several "coloured" girls. Waiting at the platform for the train that will take her away, Frieda encounters the hostility of several black or darker "coloured" boys listening to the radio blaring "Boeremusiek." Her color, her education, and her use of English separate her from them and rouse their hostility. Like them, she is subject to the Reservation of Separate Amenities Act and is not permitted on the "actual platform," the paved platform for whites, but stands in the dust of the "unpaved strip for which I have no word other than the inaccurate platform." And yet the difference between them is asserted by her father's use of English, which represents his ambitions for his daughter. One boy expresses his anger at Frieda by speaking to her in a mockingly exaggerated English and hinting at terrorist sabotage of the trains. Her response is a calculated linguistic *bricolage* that embodies the complexity of her position racially, culturally, and sexually under apartheid:

> Why you look and kyk gelyk,
> Am I miskien of gold gemake? (*YCGL*, p. 35)

The bilingual pairing of synonyms "look" and "kyk" argues for her own mastery of and rightful place in both white English and "coloured" South African cultures and for the boy's similar bicultural status, though he ridicules her for her more intentional pursuit of white, English, middle-class privilege. The second line of her rhyme (translated "Am I perhaps made of gold?") ironically measures their relative value, acknowledging that that value is determined by color. Indeed, it is Frieda's "gold" color that allows her to begin with this train ride her journey into white, English South African society.

What Frieda keeps to herself is her understanding of the relative value of her "golden" status. Though she fears the gaze of this boy, she is much more terrified of the attention she desires from white boys she might meet at St. Mary's: "I saw the eyes of Anglican boys, remote princes leaning from their carriages, penetrate the pumpkin-yellow of my flesh" (*YCGL*, 33). Her consciousness of the male and/or white gaze around which she builds her defiant rhyme is central to every chapter of the novel. While apartheid is, like all law, an idea made physical, it is most specifically about the body, its classification and placement. *You Can't Get Lost in Cape Town* is about how apartheid is experienced and understood as a physical phenomenon. Despite the opening chapter, which describes the complexity of Frieda's linguistic environment, it is possible to begin this novel and not know until Frieda wipes her shoes while waiting for the train that she is "coloured." While she has no language for the unpaved platform for non-Whites, her racial status under apartheid is clear from the physical act of wiping dust from her polished shoes.

Identifying with the teenage "coloured" girls on the platform who hide their hair beneath scarves (much to the disdain of Frieda's tormentor, who "runs his hand through an exuberant bush of fuzzy hair"), Frieda has internalized a racist aesthetics. Her very body becomes the site of apartheid's physical enactment. Through adolescence and into young adulthood, her attention is almost completely consumed by controlling her hair, her skin, her body:

> I check my preparations: the wet hair wrapped over large rollers to separate the stands, dried then swirled around my head, secured overnight with a nylon stocking, dressed with vaseline to keep the strands smooth and straight and then pulled back tightly to stem any remaining tendency to curl. (*YCGL*, p. 26)

Her reward is a college education in the new "coloured" university, a white boyfriend in Cape Town, and a growing feeling of inauthenticity and alienation.

As Wicomb suggests in the chapter "A Clearing in the Bush," set in the new "coloured" university Frieda attends after St. Mary's, systems of racial and sexual oppression are related, particularly for women. Frieda's obsessive attention to her hair, her complexion, her weight and dress, while clearly a response to racist valuations of beauty, is a particularly gendered response. More critical and traditionally political responses to racism are reserved for the young men. These light-skinned women learning to align themselves with white interests do not claim for themselves the models of black female resistance available to them.[25] While the young men plan a boycott of the school's ceremony honoring the just-assassinated prime minister Hendrik Verwoerd, Frieda is preoccupied with her cosmetic ministrations and her unfinished essay on Thomas Hardy's *Tess of the d'Urbervilles.*

Frieda's struggle with the English novel is, in fact, a political struggle in which she is not equipped to prevail. Her instructor's lectures, sent from a correspondence university, represent at once a colonial and sexual education that diffuses political resistance. Frieda's confusion about the novel is linguistic, cultural, and sexual. The English of the novel is difficult for her, the descriptions of Wessex are far removed from her knowledge both of the veld and of the bush surrounding the university; and most confusing of all to her is the sexual story of the novel and the interpretation provided by her instructor:

> The novel, he says, is about Fate. Alarmingly simple, but not quite how it strikes me, although I cannot offer an alternative. The truth is that I do not always understand the complicated language, though of course I got the gist of the story, the interesting bits where things happen. But even then, I cannot be sure of what actually happens in The Chase. . . . Seduced, my notes say. Can you be seduced by someone you hate? (*YCGL,* p. 41)

The lesson that power relations, in this case those of sex, gender, and class, are a function of fate and not culture provides no reason for resistance nor promise of its success. Defining rape as "seduction" similarly disempowers an argument for legal restitution; Tess's violence, like the political assassination of Verwoerd, apartheid's chief architect, is termed "murder" and "madness."[26]

Wicomb's description of the reaction on this small campus in the bush to Verwoerd's assassination underscores her critique of apartheid conceptions of racial identity, particularly of "coloured" identity, and, like the rest of the novel, it portrays highly charged political moments through the psychological experience of those moments. Dr. Verwoerd is credited with constructing the "coloured" university in an attempt to foster a "coloured" identity that would promote a racial and cultural nation of "Coloureds" separate from the nations of Whites.[27] It is ironic that the memorial service for Verwoerd, set on the "coloured" university campus he created as a cornerstone of apartheid ideology, serves as a reminder that there is no homogeneous "coloured" identity to cultivate.

The call for the commemoration of the prime minister evokes a variety of responses from the supposedly culturally unified "Coloureds." While everyone but the Afrikaner administrators and eleven "coloured" seminary students boycott the ceremony, Frieda uses the extra time to hurriedly compose her late essay on Tess, "branded guilty and betrayed once more on this page" (*YCGL,* p. 56), in accordance with the instructor's lecture. It is significant that this is one of only two stories of the collection in which the narrator's frame of reference shifts from Frieda's first-person narration. This story is told from both the first-person perspective of the student Frieda and the third-person perspective of the canteen cook, Tamieta Snewe, who provides us with the only outside view of Frieda in the book. At least a generation older than Frieda, Tamieta is also from rural Namaqualand, knows "the Shenton girl," and has worked in domestic service her entire adult life. Frieda's fear of such employment has propelled her onto the train to St. Mary's and then to this college, advancing her class status and thus allowing her to be served by this older and presumably darker woman. Charlie, a young man who works in the kitchen with Tamieta, represents an aspect of "coloured" urban culture quite foreign to both Tamieta's and Frieda's rural background. Charlie is from District Six, the predominantly "coloured" neighborhood in Cape Town that the Nationalist government expropriated from the "Coloureds" and designated a white-only residential area in 1966, the year in which this story is set. While Tamieta is a devout Christian, Charlie is Muslim, speaks Afrikaans with some English, and delights in irreverently ridiculing white proprieties. Neither he nor Tamieta has the class advantages of the students they serve, who do not include them as participants in the political boycott. While Charlie needs no encouragement to take the afternoon off and would not have stayed for the ceremony, boycott or not, Tamieta is never told by the students of the action and obediently shows up as the only "coloured" person (other than the eleven future Mission Church ministers who ignore the boycott), sitting in shame at the back of a sea of empty chairs. She has no special regard for the dead prime minister, whom she thinks of as "a man with a large head," but she is pious, and, as the guardian of her young cousin, she cannot afford to lose her job.

At this particularly intense moment following the assassination, Wicomb derails expectations derived from the genre of resistance literature, which Barbara Harlow describes as writing in which the emphasis is on the "political as the power to change the world" as opposed to the "personal and social."[28] Rather than focusing on the public confrontation, violent or not, of conflicting political stances, the story instead attends to the mundane and utterly banal concerns of three people intimately affected by the ideology promoted by the state. This story is less about a heroic resistance to apartheid than about the effects of apartheid on daily life and consciousness. Charlie, Tamieta, and Frieda, having been formed by the racial laws governing them, are, at least at this moment in each of their lives, bound to the scripts they have known. Frieda is living her father's story of social advancement, a story in which student protest has no place. Her attention is riveted by her self-conscious knowledge of herself as an object of racial, sexual, and class significance. Tamieta, who prides herself on her Christian piety, suffers through the ceremony in an agony of shame, uncertain about the appropriateness of her presence. She is not at all interested in the politics of honoring the state, but, rather, as the only "coloured" person in the audience facing the platform of "Boers," she is terrified that she misunderstood and attended a service meant only for whites. When the few "coloured" students take their seats, she longs for the starched cap of her domestic service days and the role she knew how to play. For Charlie, too, the service and the protest are inconsequential as he spends the afternoon preparing himself for the New Year's carnival parade, in which at midnight Blacks traditionally accost Whites on the sidewalk and smear their faces with black shoe polish. Even Charlie recognizes the saturnalian ritual as a script, played out perhaps for the perverse pleasure of Whites.

Concentrating on these three characters for whom the assassination of the prime minister does not register as particularly significant, Wicomb refocuses the concept of the "political" to include the psychological experiences of living in this society. Wicomb does not overtly judge the lack of political resistance or even the complicity of the characters with the rituals of apartheid; rather she explores the ways these rituals and scripts become internalized and reenacted in daily life. As feminism has taught us so effectively, this focus on the "private" is not in conflict with the "political." Njabulo Ndebele's theoretical treatment of resistance literature, or "protest literature" in South African terms, is ultimately more relevant to a reading of Wicomb's work than is Harlow's. Ndebele entreats South African writers to turn from the "spectacular" to a "rediscovery of the ordinary" in order to recognize "the unproclaimed heroism of the ordinary person."[29] The fiction he honors may offer no direct political insight or program but instead focuses on the day-to-day lives of people in order to understand the consciousness and negotiations of the oppressed. This understanding, he contends, is necessary "to free the entire social imagination of the oppressed from the laws of perception that have characterized apartheid society."[30]

Frieda's perception is precisely what Wicomb's novel is about. The irony of Frieda's position as a "reader" of the stories she has been taught becomes increasingly obvious to her as an adult when she confronts the legal restrictions of apartheid. In the title chapter of the book, "You Can't Get Lost in Cape Town," Frieda's two-year relationship with Michael, a white young man, culminates with her pregnancy. On the bus through Cape Town on her way to an illegal abortion, Frieda overhears a black woman telling her friend a story about the daughter of the white family she works for and the precariousness of the young woman's wedding plans and the irony of her white wedding dress now that she has already slept with her fiancé. Sitting in the back of the bus with these women whose work and lives she has assiduously sought to avoid, Frieda is surely in an ambiguous position as the audience to the bawdy story. While as a non-White she is seated with these domestic workers behind the white passengers, the story elicits her identification not with the black servant storyteller but with the white would-be bride. And yet her identification with the white heroine is uncomfortable, and she imagines her own white lace gown covered in ash, devoured by moths (*YCGL*, pp. 74–75).

When Michael offers to escape with her to England, where they could legally marry, Frieda rejects this plan as the naive product of English literary romance:

> Gripped by the idyll of an English landscape of painted greens, he saw my head once more held high, my lettuce-luscious skirts crisp on a camomile lawn and the willow drooping over the red mouth of a suckling infant.
>   "Come on," he urged. "Don't do it. We'll get to England and marry. It will work out all right," and betraying the source of his vision, "and we'll be happy for ever, thousands of miles from all this mess." (*YCGL*, p. 74)

These two stories, the English romantic tale and the African story exposing the hypocrisies of white institutions, represent the conflict central to Frieda's difficulty in claiming the role of storyteller herself and to Wicomb's understanding of the peculiar difficulties of the educated "coloured" writer in claiming an interpretive literary voice.

Michael Vaughan identifies as a recurring theme in South African literature an emphasis on "storytelling" that functions in the fiction as a way of recontextualizing the origin and shape of political thought.[31] For example, the nonintellectual African storyteller figure who appears in Njabulo Ndebele's stories, according to Vaughan, provides space for the vernacular voice, stimulates the growth of the protagonist's inner life, and calls into question the ability of the narrative voice to "translate" township culture.[32] These three separate perspectives (storyteller, protagonist, and narrator) create space for conflict and evaluation. Wicomb uses the storyteller characters in similar ways, and by making the protagonist the narrator of most of the stories and a potential storyteller herself, she additionally raises important questions about the complex and compromised position of the literary South African storyteller. The tension between the writer, educated in English-language schools, and the traditional oral culture from which she came is present in most of the stories that make up *You Can't Get Lost in Cape Town*. As Frieda learns what Vaughan calls the "sophisticated skepticism" taught by English-language education toward the non-English oral culture of the wider population, she becomes unable to "read" the stories of her family and chooses, instead, those of Thomas Hardy.

The story "Home Sweet Home," which takes place just before Frieda's "escape" to England, opens with a letter from Uncle Hermanus, who has emigrated to Canada. Unlike the other "Coloureds" the family knows, Frieda, a product of her education, has chosen to go to England and, before she leaves, has come home to spend time with her father and the extended family with which she no longer identifies. Her relationship with them is identical to the one Vaughan describes of the protagonist trained as an intellectual who has learned to view her or his original culture with skepticism and disdain. Hoping that she would serve their interests as one of the few "coloured" intellectuals, Frieda's family is clearly disappointed with her decision to live in England, and her aunt describes her as a stubborn mule who "always pulls the other way" (*YCGL*, p. 86), a description that becomes relevant later in the story. While she remembers a time she felt "young and genderless, . . . belonging without question to this country, this world," on this trip home Frieda is alienated from the landscape that has changed in her absence and from the family stories that commemorate and articulate a South African history in which "coloured" South Africans are central, not coincidental by-products of the collisions between white and black South African histories. Frieda rejects both the "whole-ness" of the stories the family spins on the "stoep" in the afternoon heat (*YCGL*, pp. 87–88) and the political myths her uncle offers her of "the old days" when the "coloured" people trekked from Griqualand. Confronted with her older uncle, who appears to her a caricature of rural "coloured" life, "Oom Dawid in his ankle-hugging veldskoen and faded khaki shirt, flourishing his whip" (*YCGL*, p. 94), Frieda refuses his seemingly naive and obsolete request that while in England she see the queen about "these Boers and how they treat us." Her uncle challenges her to "put her heart with someone," be it Vorster, the queen, or "our Griqua chief," and take a position of political leadership for her people (*YCGL*, p. 95).

Frieda's unwillingness or inability to take an active political role has everything to do with her relationship with the family and community she has been educated away from. At this point in the book, the stories and storytellers of Frieda's youth are objects of her disdain. They are not full subjects, and the narrator does not even accord the stories narrative space. While dismissing the stories of her youth, Frieda contrasts them with her own stories.

Within the narrative of "Home Sweet Home," Frieda presents two stories of her own, stories she says she will not tell, believing her family would have no way of understanding them and would reject them as offensive. The first accounts her train trip home, in which she is terrified by both the blue-eyed Afrikaner guard and the drunken man ("coloured" or black) the guard allows to share her sleeping compartment. The second story concludes the narrative, and, as one of the most ambiguous endings in the collection, it demands an interpretation by the reader. The inset story highlights both the active role of the protagonist as storyteller and the cynical nature of Frieda's stories at this point of her life. Running away from the family storytelling on the "stoep," Frieda discovers a mule sinking in the quicksand of the riverbed:

> Before me, between two trickles of water, a mule brays. It struggles in what must be a stretch of quicksand. Transformed by fear its ears alert into quivering conductors of energy. With a lashing movement of the ears, the bray stretches into an eerie whistle. It balances on its hind legs like an ill-trained circus animal, the front raised, the belly flashing white as it staggers in a grotesque dance. When the hind legs plummet deep into the sand, the front drops in search of equilibrium. Then, holding its head high, the animal remains quite still as it sinks.
>
> Birds dart and swoop through the pliant Jan Twakkie branches, and a donkey stirs from its sleep, braying.

[Father] did not say "Beware of the quicksand." Not that I would ever tell what I have seen in the river today. (*YCGL*, p. 103)

Frieda's feelings of claustrophobia and suffocation that climax in this chapter find their symbolic representation in this image of the mule — the colonial symbol of the "cross-breed" mulatto — slowly drowning in mud. Wicomb, herself, left South Africa for England "because of this sense of claustrophobia that living in South Africa brought."[33] Aunt Cissie's description of Frieda as a "mule" always resisting has also set up the symbolic reading of this grim ending. The story Frieda constructs is one of useless and tragic resistance. Taught to identify with English culture, she cannot at this point find any positive identification with her community and therefore is unwilling and unable to imagine any successful gesture of political resistance. Her stories (and indeed Wicomb's) up to this point of the novel are based on an authority and on a set of cultural "readings" of South Africa provided by an English-language education. The grim story of the doomed mule (as opposed to the waking donkey) is the pessimistic assessment of "coloured" South African life by an arrogant young writer who believes she fully understands the meanings and possibilities of South African culture and politics.

The story Clare Savage tells, too, before her political involvement in *No Telephone to Heaven,* is of a mule shackled to a cane crusher with no choice but to walk in endless circles. Both Frieda and Clare, steeped in colonial education, imagine themselves by racist colonial symbols and imagine resistance in terms of failure and death. Like Clare, Frieda returns from England to her homeland to learn an alternative history. Neither Wicomb nor Cliff imagines in her fiction successful political actions against exploitative governments. Since both writers examine the psychological experience of repression and privilege, they accord great political significance to the process whereby their characters come to reconceptualize colonial history and their own positions within that history.

The last half of *You Can't Get Lost in Cape Town* unravels the cultural meanings and interpretations Frieda has learned before she leaves for England and interrogates Frieda's (and Wicomb's) position and authority as a South African storyteller. The story following "Home Sweet Home," "Behind the Bougainvillea," takes place after Frieda returns from England; the ten years there remain undocumented save for Frieda's memory of loneliness and her bitter disappointment that in England, too, she felt like an object of scrutiny. She returns to conflicting assessments of the decade she missed in South Africa. While in his eternal optimism, her father claims that she will "find the Boers quite civilised now" (*YCGL*, p. 105), her childhood black friend, Henry Hendrikse, has prepared himself for the unreported war "being fought in the bush." If this were a novel celebrating political resistance, Henry might serve as the heroic protagonist. The protagonist of this novel, however, when juxtaposed with Henry, appears conspicuously nonheroic and disconnected from South African political life. This trip home reveals to Frieda herself the narrowness of her understanding of South Africa and of the majority of its people. While Henry has gone to Namibia to learn Xhosa (as either a revolutionary or a spy, she never knows), Frieda cannot tell the difference between Zulu and Xhosa and is only newly aware that she does not understand much of the language and interactions around her. Even as an aspiring writer, until now she has not been interested in the stories that surround her. Waiting in the doctor's courtyard with the other non-Whites, she now finds herself unable to immerse herself in the English book she has brought for the long wait:

> I read, "The right side was browner than a European's would be, yet not so distinctly brown as to type him as a Hindu or Pakistani and certainly he was no Negro, for his features were quite as Caucasian as Edward's own." (*YCGL*, p. 111)

She is newly self-conscious of her literacy and of her chosen reading material. As a "willing slave" of literature (*YCGL*, p. 111), Frieda has ignored the "eloquent world" around her, specifically the rich oral traditions of South African culture.

A sample of the oral tradition appears in "A Fair Exchange," a chapter that provides a dramatic and jarring shift in the novel. Frieda is no longer the narrator or protagonist for the majority of the chapter, nor is the story about her. It is about Skitterboud and Magriet (called "Meid"), characters the reader has not met in the novel. It is only halfway through the chapter that Frieda reappears as the audience and the self-conscious narrator who has actually transformed and translated Skitterboud's story from an oral Afrikaans to a literary English. Frieda, who never listened to the stories around her before, has come in search of this story about Skitterboud and Meid's life as workers for white landowners, about their marital and family life, and about their cultural conflicts over the years with white bosses, magistrates, and doctors. This is the only story in the novel from the point of view of rural characters who have never left the country nor been encouraged to be anything other than servants and fieldhands for white Afrikaners. Unlike Frieda's family, which values Frieda's education as the way to political and economic advancement, Skitterboud provides a critique of the values Frieda has been taught to admire.

Both Frieda and Skitterboud are aware of the potentially exploitative use of the uneducated "informant" by the educated would-be writer who has come in search of this old man's story. Skitterboud makes Frieda pay for the story by giving him her glasses, much to her reluctance.[34] Their argument over the glasses provides the thesis of Skitterboud's story as well. Although Skitterboud is impressed by what he can see when he wears Frieda's glasses, she claims that he needs glasses especially prescribed for him. Her assumptions are born of her belief in the opinions and measurements of the "experts" and of her privilege. In response, Skitterboud describes his trip to the doctor when he asked for glasses:

> Well, [Dr. van Zyl] said to me, "Skittie you need a nose to wear glasses. Next time you'll be asking me to replace your baboon's nose." (*YCGL,* p. 139)

Furthermore, Skitterboud has no papers certifying his age, and by examining his teeth the young white "baas" has determined he is too young to qualify for old-age medical benefits. Skitterboud's impatient dismissal of the magistrates' logic and disrespect provides Frieda with an alternative set of values to the ones she has been trained to regard as "civilized."

The main story Skitterboud tells Frieda is about the intervention of white Christian law into his family life and the immoral and shameful values he finds implicit in the patriarchal law. When Meid leaves Skitterboud for another man, the magistrate awards Skitterboud the children and everything of Meid's "to the last scrap of underclothing she is wearing." Rather than experiencing Meid's humiliation as a triumph, Skitterboud is personally shamed by "the filthy words of the magistrate" (*YCGL,* p. 142). Through Skitterboud's stories, Frieda begins to explore the oral tradition and perspective denied her by her colonial education and gains a critical perspective on that education and on her relationship to both Anglo-European and African value systems.

As she comes to recognize her ignorance of African languages, traditions, and experiences under apartheid, Frieda's authority as a writer and as a narrator of this book becomes increasingly problematic. The novel unravels both Frieda's and Wicomb's attempts to represent South African culture. By underscoring Frieda's presence in the rendering of Skitterboud's story, Wicomb attempts to represent a new South African voice while at the same time acknowledging the translation and potential for distortion implicit in such attempts. She makes explicit and problematizes what Elsa Joubert leaves implied in her rendering of "Poppie Nongena's" story. Both books engage issues of authenticity, but Wicomb's also questions the ability of writers to produce valuable and truthful literary contributions to South African culture.

The final chapter of the book is an ironic and self-conscious unwriting of the novel that precedes it.[35] In "A Trip to the Gifberge," Frieda makes the journey to Namaqualand to visit her mother, a character who has been dead in every story after the first. In this story, however, Frieda's father is dead, and her mother has separated herself from his family, the Shentons, a family of self-professed "respectable Coloureds" who value light skin and the Scottish ancestor responsible for it. The last voice of this novel is Frieda's mother's calling into question the perspective of the novel that has demanded her erasure. While she, too, has taught Frieda English and the cosmetics of self-hatred, she now criticizes Frieda for her disrespectful use of that language, her misuse of her education, and her ignorance and disavowal of South Africa. She accuses Frieda of not having the courage or the knowledge to tell the "whole truth":

> "Ask me for stories with neat endings and you won't have to invent my death. What do you know about things, about people, this place where you were born? About your ancestors who roamed these hills? You left. Remember?" She drops her head and her voice is barely audible.
> "To write from under you mother's skirts, to shout at the world that it's all right to kill God's unborn child! You've killed me over and over so it was quite unnecessary to invent my death. Do people ever do anything decent with their education?" (*YCGL*, p. 172)

Indeed, Frieda's position as a "coloured" girl who has been able to pass for white has made her highly sensitive to the signs and symbols of South African apartheid culture while her formal English-language education has provided her with an escape from an emotional or political identification with South Africa. This last story undermines Frieda's belief that her rejection of South Africa expresses a liberatory political perspective.

Mrs. Shenton demands that Frieda take her for a drive up into the mountains, and in the course of the trip Frieda comes to recognize her mother's attachment to and knowledge about the land, an attachment and knowledge that exceed the cultural meanings given to nature that Frieda has come to believe. Mrs. Shenton's search for protea blossoms in the mountains, for instance, sickens Frieda since proteas serve as the national bloom of Afrikaner South Africa:

"You must take up a little white protea bush for my garden," she says as we walk back to the bakkie.

"If you must," I retort. "And then you can hoist the South African flag and sing 'Die Stem.'"

"Don't be silly; it's not the same thing at all. You who're so clever ought to know that proteas belong to the veld. Only fools and cowards would hand them over to the Boers. Those who put their stamp on things may see in it their own histories and hopes. But a bush is a bush; it doesn't become what people think they inject into it. We know who lived in these mountains when the Europeans were still shivering in their own country. What they think of the veld and its flowers is of no interest to me." (*YCGL*, p. 181)

Mrs. Shenton's resistance offers Frieda a new model. While she has not shed her training of reading the physical properties of hair, skin, and facial features through the lens of apartheid culture, Mrs. Shenton is able to refuse to read nonhuman nature through that lens. Unlike Frieda's mad cousin, Jan Klinkies, who refuses to eat or drink anything associated with or advertised with the symbols of Afrikaner culture (*YCGL*, p. 17), Mrs. Shenton does not willingly give up South African attributes in her resistance to nationalistic uses of them. Both her mother and Skitterboud offer Frieda new forms of resistance; while they acknowledge the power of the dominant culture to name and define, these older people have learned to claim that power for themselves. Skitterboud's story, like Mrs. Shenton's, offers strategies for self-definition.

Named after a foreign flower, the marguerite, Skitterboud's wife was always called "Meid," first by her employer and ultimately by her husband. For her daughter, she searches for the name of a local flower, so local it will not get lost, so vague it will not be changed. Imagining the numerous Namaqua daisy, she names her daughter "Blom, plain flower, a name that no one could take away from her. She would never take her to the big white house" (*YCGL*, p. 133).

This modest resistance is more than Frieda — as the product of her education and of her disappointed identification with English culture — has been able to imagine. At the top of the mountain, Frieda and her mother are confronted with a fence that keeps them from the view for which they have journeyed. Too old to climb the fence herself, Mrs. Shenton is surprised that Frieda is so easily dissuaded from their goal. But Frieda has learned in both England and South Africa to question her own presence:

In England I have learnt to cringe at the thought of wandering about, hanging about idly. Loitering even on this side of the fence makes me feel like a trespasser. If someone were to question my right to be here, . . . I shudder. (*YCGL,* pp. 179–80)

This is far from the consciousness one might imagine from a hero at the end of a piece of resistance literature. Instead, Wicomb describes a particularly ineffectual psychological response to oppression and questions the meaning and value of the writing (including her own) emanating from such a per- spective. Her mother identifies Frieda's cynicism as that of an outsider, not as that of one who considers South Africa her home and concerns herself with its future. In a self-reflexive moment, the last line of the novel un- ravels the preceding stories and leaves as a question other possibilities for the antiapartheid intellectual. In response to Frieda's statement that she will probably return to South Africa to live, her mother has the last line of the book: "With something to do here at home perhaps you won't need to make up those terrible stories hey?" (*YCGL,* p. 182).

This last sentence suggests that this novel is ultimately the product of Frieda's and Wicomb's alienation from the people and political struggles of South Africa. This ending suggests a longing to *not* write, to engage with life in a way that even prohibits a literary response. Meid's story about a young woman who looked at the midday sun and was not blinded but struck dumb (*YCGL,* p. 125) suggests a host of questions troubling many South African writers today about the effect of the monumental changes in South Africa on literary production. As South African writers have in- creased opportunity to engage in political and pedagogical work toward a postapartheid society, will their literary work suffer? As South African writers like Wicomb return from exile, will they have time and eco- nomic support to write? Will the political changes in South Africa demand aesthetic changes, and what might those be?

Preparing to return to South Africa from Scotland in 1990 after the release of Nelson Mandela, Wicomb defined her new priorities:

We have to rethink notions of literature and art; the Western notions of "elevated" writing will have to be put aside. I think more in terms of writing as empowerment, and in terms of literacy. The question of literacy is far more important. When I think of my own process of writing, the fact that I didn't write for years and years, though I wanted to, it has to do with a sense of confidence. Unless your daily transaction with words is successful, unless words work for you, unless when you speak there are results, you're not going to have the confidence to use language. And where there is no question of using words in that everyday way, how can you possibly use them in the alternative way — which is to transform those words into what people would call literature.

> What I'm suggesting is that we must stop thinking in terms of literary language and we must think in terms of ways in which we can recover the ability to use language.... What is going to be our national language? I want to be involved in that kind of work.[36]

Calling for a rethinking of the idea of "nation" itself as South Africa reforms itself, Wicomb is particularly concerned about the role of the writer in this process because "the question of a national language has always been at the heart of the notion of nation."[37] The questions she asks after returning home and teaching at the University of the Western Cape underscore her earlier fears about being "struck dumb":

> As for writing, the question is not simply how to transform our racially inflected chants: the fixed syntagms of we-the-oppressed-black-majority or we-who-fight-Apartheid.... The question is surely what to do about those real voices that intrude upon us as we sit down to write: how to continue the activity of writing that is disturbed by the beggars beating at our doors for food: how not to think of writing in this context as a shameful activity that does little or nothing about redistributing cultural and linguistic capital.... I have no grand statements to make about the writer and her writing; all I have arrived at is a set of questions:
>
> How do liberal humanist assumptions about the function of art, of writing, relate to those who cannot read? What place could the dispossessed decently occupy in our schemes of representation?... Is there really a case for privileging representational art? Is there a case at all for giving writing a central position in our culture?[38]

And how, Wicomb asks, can the new cultural agenda become interracial when, on the one hand, the needs are so clearly racial (developing and sustaining black writing) and, on the other, literary culture still "conducts its business in a minority language and its minority dialect of standard English that few have access to"?[39] An important voice in this debate, Wicomb suggests that a radical pedagogy would create "an awareness not only of power, but of the equivocal, the ambiguous, and the ironic which is always embedded in power."[40] Wicomb's own fiction does just this, both articulating the rich cultural possibilities available to the "coloured" individual who partakes of English, Afrikaner, and black South African traditions and the limitations that result from her or his encouraged collusions with the public racism of apartheid ideology and the private racism of social interaction. What Frieda's role will be as a "returned South African" (Schreiner's name for herself) is left as a crucial question at the end of the novel for all South African writers. It is clear, however, that as apartheid is dismantled Frieda will have to construct an increasingly conscious political identity that can effectively use the ironies and ambiguities inherent in her interracial, multicultural position.

From their perspectives as creole women, each of the writers examined in this book has sought to correct the colonial record, to expose the myths that constitute their identities as white or "colored," English, South African, or Caribbean. Implicit in much of this writing is an imagined English and North American audience whose historical and cultural knowledge excludes the effects of colonial and neocolonial myths and practices on South Africans and Caribbeans. Frantz Fanon has argued that until the writer addresses his or her own people, that writing will not constitute a "national literature."[41] While it might be possible to trace an increasing acknowledgment of a "national" readership in contemporary Caribbean or South African literature, each of these writers, and almost any so-called postcolonial writer today, addresses at least two audiences (for instance, English and South African). In fact, most writers are now aware as they write of a wider "postcolonial" readership as well; Michelle Cliff, for example, responds in her writing to postcolonial writers and theorists from around the world. The call, then, for a "national literature" is complicated by these creole women writers who, given their own complicated national statuses, their knowledge of the relationship between national and racial mythologies, and the androcentric and heterosexist constructions of nationalism, are suspicious of any exclusionary categories of culture or definitions of a "people." Perhaps more flexible is Brathwaite's term "national language," which he defines as "sometimes...English and African at the same time."[42] Each of the writers examined in this book might define herself and her writing in similar, and even more complex, terms. The multiplicities of their positions and of their perspectives, while at times leading to difficult ambivalences and self-doubt, also allow for some of the richest and most incisive explorations of the effects of colonial history and neocolonial economics on contemporary culture.

List of Abbreviations of Key Texts

A	*Abeng,* by Michelle Cliff. Trumansburg, N.Y.: Crossing Press, 1984.
"AA"	"Again the Antilles," by Jean Rhys. In *The Collected Short Stories.* New York: W. W. Norton, 1987.
"AS"	"Another Story," by Zoë Wicomb. In *Colors of a New Day: Writing for South Africa.* Ed. Sarah Lefanu and Stephen Hayward. New York: Pantheon, 1990.
"BW"	"The Boer Woman and the Modern Women's Question," by Olive Schreiner. In *TSA.*
"DTBB"	"The Day They Burned the Books," by Jean Rhys. In *The Collected Short Stories.*
ESAV	*An English South African's View of the Situation: Words in Season,* by Olive Schreiner. London: Hodder and Stoughton, 1899.
GMM	*Good Morning, Midnight,* by Jean Rhys. 1939. Reprint, London: André Deutsch, 1967.
GSC	*God's Step-Children,* by Sarah Gertrude Millin. London: Constable, 1924.
"IICW"	"If I Could Write This in Fire, I Would Write This in Fire . . . ," by Michelle Cliff. In *The Land of Look Behind.* Ithaca, N.Y.: Firebrand Books, 1985.

"IUL"   "I Used to Like the Dallas Cowboys," by Dionne Brand. In *Sans Souci and Other Stories*. Ithaca, N.Y.: Firebrand Books, 1989.

LJR   *The Letters of Jean Rhys*. Ed. Francis Wyndham and Diana Melly. New York: Viking, 1984.

LOS   *The Letters of Olive Schreiner 1876–1920*. Ed. S. C. Cronwright-Schreiner. London: T. Fisher Unwin, 1924.

"LT"   "Let Them Call It Jazz," by Jean Rhys. In *The Collected Short Stories*.

"M"   "Mannequin," by Jean Rhys. In *The Collected Short Stories*.

MM   *From Man to Man or Perhaps Only . . .* , by Olive Schreiner. New York: Harper and Brothers, 1927.

NTH   *No Telephone to Heaven*, by Michelle Cliff. New York: Dutton, 1987.

OSL   *Olive Schreiner Letters, Volume 1: 1871–1899*. Ed. Richard Rive. Oxford: Oxford University Press, 1988.

"PS"   "The Problem of Slavery," by Olive Schreiner. In *TSA*.

Q   *Quartet,* by Jean Rhys. In *The Complete Novels*. New York: W. W. Norton, 1985.

"SA"   "South Africa: Its Natural Features, Its Diverse Peoples, Its Political Status: The Problem," by Olive Schreiner. In *TSA*.

SAF   *The Story of an African Farm,* by Olive Schreiner. 1883. Reprint, Harmondsworth, England: Penguin Books, 1971.

SP   *Smile Please: An Unfinished Autobiography,* by Jean Rhys. New York: Harper and Row, 1979.

"TB"   "The Boer," by Olive Schreiner. In *TSA*.

"TE"   "The Englishman," by Olive Schreiner. In *TSA*.

"TP"   "Temps Perdi," by Jean Rhys. In *The Collected Short Stories*.

TSA   *Thoughts on South Africa,* by Olive Schreiner. 1923. Reprint, Johannesburg: Africana Book Society, 1976.

U   *Undine,* by Olive Schreiner. 1928. Reprint, New York: Johnson Reprint, 1972.

WL   *Woman and Labour,* by Olive Schreiner. 1911. Reprint, London: Virago, 1978.

WSS   *Wide Sargasso Sea,* by Jean Rhys. New York: W. W. Norton, 1966.

YCGL   *You Can't Get Lost in Cape Town,* by Zoë Wicomb. New York: Pantheon, 1987.

Notes

Introduction

1. For two excellent critiques of the term "postcolonial," see Anne McClintock, "The Angel of Progress: Pitfalls of the Term 'Post-Colonialism,'" *Social Text* 10, nos. 2 and 3 (1992), pp. 84–98; and Ella Shohat, "Notes on the 'Post-Colonial,'" in the same volume, pp. 99–113.

2. For a critique of the idea of "progress" embedded in postcolonial theory, see McClintock, "Angel of Progress."

3. José Piedra, "Literary Whiteness and the Afro-Hispanic Difference," *New Literary History* 18 no. 2 (winter 1987), p. 317.

4. Thomas M. Stephens, "Creole, Créole, Criollo, Crioulo: The Shadings of a Term," *SECOL Review* 7, no. 3 (fall 1983), p. 30.

5. Ibid., pp. 28–39.

6. Ibid., p. 33.

7. Virginia R. Domínguez, *White by Definition: Social Classification in Creole Louisiana* (New Brunswick, N.J.: Rutgers University Press, 1986), pp. 149–51. For Domínguez's summary of the changing meaning of "creole" over time and across languages, see pp. 12–16.

8. Mark Broyard and Roger Guenveur Smith, *Inside the Creole Mafia,* performed at University of California, February 1994. The editorial cited is by Louis Metoyer, *Bayou Talk,* April–May 1991, pp. 6–8.

9. Ulf Hannerz, "The World in Creolisation," *Africa* 57, no. 4 (1987), pp. 546–59.

10. Françoise Lionnet, *Autobiographical Voices: Race, Gender, Self-Portraiture* (Ithaca, N.Y.: Cornell University Press, 1989), p. 9.

11. Jean Bernabé, Patrick Chamoiseau, and Raphaël Confiant, "In Praise of Creoleness," trans. Mohamed B. Taleb Khyar, *Callalloo* 13 (1990), pp. 886, 902, 903.

12. As Wicomb writes, "Race has for some time been dressed in quotation marks and we must now ask the question, in what sense can the concept of nation be refurbished?" (Zoë Wicomb, "Nation, Race and Ethnicity: Beyond the Legacy of Victims," *Current Writing* 4 [1992], p. 15).

13. "South Africa forms naturally one national and distinct entity, widely dissevered from any other national entity, European or otherwise" (Olive Schreiner, "The South African Nation," in *Thoughts on South Africa* [1923; reprint, Johannesburg: Africana Book Society, 1976], p. 367; hereafter the book is referred to in text citations as *TSA*).

14. Benedict Anderson describes what he calls the "formal universality of nationality as a socio-cultural concept": "In the modern world, everyone can, should, will 'have' a nationality, as he or she 'has' a gender" (Benedict Anderson, *Imagined Communities: Reflections on the Origin and Spread of Nationalism* [London: Verso, 1983], p. 14).

15. As Elleke Boehmer puts it: "If women are portrayed as the objects and men the subjects of national aspiration, this would seem to have two main implications for nationalism: one, that the structures of nations or nation-states are soldered onto the struts of gender hierarchies; and two, that imagining nations may be a process profoundly informed by those structures, that it may be extremely difficult to conceive of nationalism outside of gender. Rising out of this, my claim then is that gender as iconic language of nationalism is both reflective of and reproduces concentrations of power within nationalist movements and in nation-states.... Gender, I would argue, thus operates at a primary level of structuration in nationalism — its symbology is both constituted by and is constitutive of patriarchy in nationalism" (Elleke Boehmer, "Motherlands, Mothers and Nationalist Sons: Representations of Nationalism and Women in African Literature," in *From Commonwealth to Post-Colonial,* ed. Anna Rutherford [Sydney: Dangaroo Press, 1992], p. 234).

16. Jean Rhys, *Voyage in the Dark* in *The Complete Novels* (New York: W. W. Norton, 1985), p. 9.

17. Edward Kamau Brathwaite, "English in the Caribbean: Notes on Nation Language and Poetry — An Electronic Lecture," in *English Literature: Opening Up the Canon,* selected papers from the English Institute, 1979, ed. Leslie Fiedler and Houston A. Baker Jr. (Baltimore: Johns Hopkins University Press, 1981), pp. 18–19.

18. Merle Hodge, *Crick Crack, Monkey* (London: Heinemann, 1970), p. 67.

19. Brathwaite, "English in the Caribbean," p. 19.

20. Michelle Cliff, "Claiming an Identity They Taught Me to Despise," in *The Land of Look Behind* (Ithaca, N.Y.: Firebrand Books, 1985), p. 41.

21. Frantz Fanon, *Black Skin, White Masks,* trans. Charles L. Markmann (New York: Grove, 1967), p. 18.

22. Houston A. Baker Jr., "Caliban's Triple Play," *Critical Inquiry* 13 (autumn 1986), p. 195.

23. As Michael Omi and Howard Winant describe the importance of race in Western culture: "Without a racial identity, one is in danger of having no identity" (*Racial Formation in the United States from the 1960s to the 1980s* [New York: Routledge, 1986], p. 62).

24. Just prior to the Anglo-Boer War, Schreiner described her position as an African-born British subject as one of privileged knowledge: "Our standpoint is at once *broader* and more *impartial* in dealing with South African questions in that we are bound by twofold sympathies," and she presented herself as a mediator and an interpreter "between those our position compels us to sympathize with and to understand, as they may not, perhaps, understand one another" (*An English South African's View of the Situation: Words in Season* [London: Hodder and Stoughton, 1899], pp. 34, 74).

25. For more on this line of thinking, see Joan Wallach Scott, "The Evidence of Experience," *Critical Inquiry* 17 (summer 1991), pp. 773–97.

26. For excellent discussions of Caribbean and Latin American "modernism," see Simon Gikandi, *Writing in Limbo: Modernism and Caribbean Literature* (Ithaca, N.Y.: Cornell University Press, 1992); and Iris M. Zavala, *Colonialism and Culture: Hispanic Modernisms and the Social Imaginary* (Bloomington: Indiana University Press, 1992).

27. Even this phrase, "creative subject," offers provocative possibilities since the Creole *is* both a subject under British rule and a speaking subject in her/his own right. For a discussion of the difference between colonial and creole political identity, see Edward Brathwaite, *The Development of Creole Society in Jamaica, 1770–1820* (Oxford: Clarendon Press, 1971), pp. 100–101.

1 / "An English South African"

1. Doris Lessing, introduction to *The Story of an African Farm,* by Olive Schreiner (New York: Schocken Books, 1976), p. 2.

2. J. M. Coetzee, *White Writing: On the Culture of Letters in South Africa* (New Haven: Yale University Press, 1988).

3. In the past few years feminist publication has found a center in the themes of exile and colonization. Employing these terms both literally and metaphorically, writers have sought to describe women as less committed to or privileged by patriarchal definitions of national culture than are men. These essays often cite Virginia Woolf's statement in *Three Guineas:* "As a woman I have no country. As a woman I want no country. As a woman my country is the whole world." It is certainly appropriate to view Virginia Woolf as a critic of English jingoism and chauvinistic interpretations of culture, but to take her own description of herself as "alien" too literally or to speak of women writers as necessarily "in exile" reveals a desire in much Western feminist literary criticism to view *all* women as constituted less by political place than by gender. The similar metaphorical use of European colonialism to describe European and Euroamerican women's exclusion from literary culture and their second-class status economically also dilutes an understanding of the ways colonialism and European imperialism specifically affect women or the ways women confront specific pressures and relationships wrought by European or U.S./American economic, political, and cultural colonial and neocolonial projects. This position, which views all women as "colonized," privileges women's alienation from political power by claiming that marginality invests women with a valuable disinterested perspective on the activities of the dominant male culture. In this argument women are, themselves, a "world apart," removed from the material and psychological influences of national ideologies.

In her article "Toward a New Yiddish," Cynthia Ozick examines this idea of exile and objects to the argument of a privileged perspective derived from marginality. This essay is in part a reply to George Steiner, who, according to Ozick, characterized "exile as an area for humankind's finest perceptions, free of 'lunatic parochialism,'" and argued "that to be most exiled is to be most exalted, . . . [that] far from being cultural disaster, outsideness becomes cultural opportunity." Although she recognizes that Steiner's position is a reaction against the image of Jew as victim, Ozick warns that to celebrate diaspora and exile may be inadvertently to celebrate the history that led to that exile, and that marginality is *silence,* not liberation (see Cynthia Ozick, "Toward a New Yiddish," in *Art and Ardor: Essays* [New York: Alfred A. Knopf, 1983], pp. 154–60).

The following are several recent publications that focus on the themes of women, exile, and colonialism: Mary Lynn Broe and Angela Ingram, eds., *Women Writing in Exile* (Chapel Hill: University of North Carolina Press, 1989); the fall 1987 issue of *Tulsa Studies in Women's Literature,* ed. Nina Auerbach, focuses on women and nationality and borrows Woolf's words for its epigram; Laura E. Donaldson (see *Decolonizing Feminisms: Race, Gender, and Empire-Building,* ed. Donaldson [Chapel Hill: University of North Carolina Press, 1992]) also borrows the quotation to discuss Zora Neale Hurston's *Moses, Man of the Mountain* (1939; reprint, Urbana: University of Illinois Press, 1984). For anthologies that address the themes of colonization and women, see Sidonie Smith and Julia Watson, eds., *De/colonizing the Subject: The Politics of Gender in Women's Autobiography* (Minneapolis: University of Minnesota Press, 1992); Karen R. Lawrence, ed., *Decolonizing Tradition* (Urbana: University of Illinois Press, 1992); Nupur Chaudhuri and Margaret Strobel, eds., *Western Women and Imperialism* (Bloomington: Indiana University Press, 1992); and Donaldson, ed., *Decolonizing Feminisms.*

4. Benedict Anderson, *Imagined Communities: Reflections on the Origin and Spread of Nationalism* (London: Verso, 1983), p. 14.

5. For a discussion of the history of the inequality of British nationality and citizenship laws for men and women, see Jacqueline Bhabha et al., eds., *Worlds Apart: Women under Immigration and Nationality Law* (London: Pluto Press, 1985).

6. Sheila Jeffreys, *The Spinster and Her Enemies: Feminism and Sexuality, 1880–1930* (London: Pandora Press, 1985), p. 7.

7. Anne Wiltsher, *Most Dangerous Women: Feminist Peace Campaigners of the Great War* (London: Pandora Press, 1985), pp. xi–xii.

8. Ibid., p. 83.

9. Ibid., p. 92.

10. Ibid., p. xiii.

11. Vron Ware, *Beyond the Pale: White Women, Racism and History* (London: Verso Press, 1992), pp. 100, 163.

12. Ibid. p. 163.

13. Anderson, *Imagined Communities,* p. 15.

14. For more on the Men and Women's Club, see Judith Walkowitz, "Science, Feminism and Romance: The Men and Women's Club, 1885–1889," *History Workshop* 21 (spring 1986), pp. 37–59.

15. Cited in Jane Marcus, "Olive Schreiner: Cartographer of the Spirit/A Review Article," *Minnesota Review* 12 (spring 1979), p. 59. Marcus also cites Mrs. Scott's reference to *Dreams* in Margaret Llewelyn Davies, ed., *Life as We Have Known It* (1931; reprint, New York: W. W. Norton, 1975), p. 101.

16. Schreiner's letters to her brother and to W. T. Stead in England just after the Jameson raid and in the next two years as Will Schreiner gained political power attest to her self-perception as an influential, if marginal, political voice. This was an accurate assessment according to Joyce Avrech Berkman, who refers to the effectiveness of Schreiner's political activity and her political writing. See Joyce Avrech Berkman, *The Healing Imagination of Olive Schreiner: Beyond South African Colonialism* (Amherst: University of Massachusetts Press, 1989), p. 101. For particularly interesting letters Schreiner wrote concerning the Jameson raid, see *Olive Schreiner Letters, Volume 1: 1871–1899,* ed. Richard Rive (Oxford: Oxford University Press, 1988), pp. 260–69, 299–300, 306; hereafter referred to in text citations and notes as *OSL.*

17. Perhaps Schreiner was aware of Catherine Impey's magazine *Anti-Caste,* which began in 1888 and was "devoted to the interests of the colored race." On the front page of the magazine in January 1893, Impey published a picture of a lynching, perhaps inspiring Schreiner's controversial frontispiece of *Trooper Peter Halket* of the lynching of three black Africans by a group of white men. See Ware, *Beyond the Pale,* p. 174.

18. Berkman, *Healing Imagination,* pp. 108–11.

19. Ruth First and Ann Scott, *Olive Schreiner: A Biography* (New York: Schocken Books, 1980), p. 265.

20. As Patricia Morris has shown in her review of the major biographies of Olive Schreiner ("Biographical Accounts of Olive Schreiner," in *Olive Schreiner and After: Essays on Southern African Literature,* ed. Malvern van Wyk Smith and Don Maclennan [Cape Town:

David Philip, 1983], pp. 3–13), each of Schreiner's biographers has created her or his own "Olive Schreiner," ranging from Uys Krige's prescient prophet to Marion Friedmann's sexual neurotic. More recent studies have focused less on Schreiner's psychological peculiarities (an interest heightened perhaps by Schreiner's own self-presentation as a "case study" for Havelock Ellis's work on the psychology of sexuality) than on her political and social position. Some critics, like Nadine Gordimer, focus on Schreiner's fictional work and mourn the loss of her creativity, which they believe disappeared "into the sands of liberal pamphleteering." Indeed, Schreiner's publications do become increasingly tied to specific political events. But her three novels — *Undine, The Story of an African Farm,* and *From Man to Man* — also concern themselves with the political position of women in a society that denies them education, economic independence, and emotionally satisfying relationships with the men who control their lives. Ann Scott and Ruth First's biography of Olive Schreiner addresses the psychological effects of these frustrations on Schreiner's political positions, and Joyce Avrech Berkman provides an excellent intellectual history to contextualize her metaphorical reading of Schreiner as a would-be "healer" of the wounds wrought by racism and sexism. Karel Schoeman's biography, the first major treatment of Schreiner in Afrikaans (translated in 1991 into English), provides an important literary history of South Africa at the time Schreiner began her three novels. This biography focuses on Schreiner's life up until the point she leaves for England at twenty-six and grounds her in the particularity of the rural South African society and culture of her youth. Schoeman's second study of Schreiner provides valuable information about Schreiner and her environment during the Anglo-Boer War (see *Only an Anguish to Live Here: Olive Schreiner and the Anglo-Boer War, 1899–1902* [Cape Town: Hamm and Roussca, 1992]). Richard Rive provides a copiously edited collection of Schreiner's letters that are of invaluable use to those studying Schreiner's work or life (see *OSL*).

21. Mary Louise Pratt gives as an example of creole self-fashioning the way Alexander von Humboldt's descriptions of South America "become essential raw material for American and Americanist ideologies forged by creole intellectuals in the 1820s, 1830s, and 1840s." These Euroamerican writers used Humboldt's European invention of America to reinvent for themselves (and for Europe) an America politically separate from Europe and inhabited by the newly fashioned white American. See Mary Louise Pratt, *Imperial Eyes: Travel Writing and Transculturation* (New York: Routledge, 1992), p. 175.

22. Olive Schreiner, *The Story of an African Farm,* (1883; reprint, Harmondsworth, England: Penguin Books, 1982), pp. 27–28; hereafter referred to in text citations and notes as *SAF*.

23. Ralph Waldo Emerson, "The American Scholar" (1837), in *Selected Essays, Lectures, and Poems of Ralph Waldo Emerson,* ed. R. E. Spiller (New York: Simon and Schuster, 1965), p. 78.

24. Erich Auerbach, *Mimesis: The Representation of Reality in Western Literature,* trans. Willard R. Trask (Princeton, N.J.: Princeton University Press, 1971), p. 491 (cited in István Csicsery-Rónay Jr., "The Realistic Historical Novel and the Mythology of Liberal Nationalism: Scott, Manzoni, Eötrös, Kemény, Tolstoy," Ph.D. diss., Princeton University 1982, p. 26).

25. In 1897, when Virginia Woolf was sixteen, Leslie Stephen supplied her with the histories he thought essential for her education as a biographer and literary essayist. Of fifteen histories and biographies, he recommended five by or about Carlyle, who, as Leonard Woolf noted, "shifted the study of history to 'how men lived and had their being' — that is, to knowledge of the ordinary lives of ordinary people." See Katherine C. Hill, "Virginia Woolf and Leslie Stephen: History and Literary Revolution," *PMLA* 96, no. 3 (May 1981), pp. 351–62. For Woolf's focus on the history of how *women* lived and had their being, see

her essays "Women and Fiction" (in *Collected Essays,* ed. Leonard Woolf, vol. 2 [London: Hogarth Press, 1966]) and "Lives of the Obscure" (in *The Common Reader* [London: Hogarth Press, 1951], pp. 146–67), her introduction to Margaret Llewelyn Davies's *Life as We Have Known It* (London: Leonard and Virginia Woolf, 1931), and *Three Guineas* (London: Hogarth Press, 1938).

26. For the rich etymology of many of the words Schreiner uses, see Jean Branford, *A Dictionary of South African English* (Cape Town: Oxford University Press, 1978). For explanations of other specifically South African references, see David Adey et al., *Companion to South African English Literature* (Craighall, South Africa: A. D. Donker, 1986).

27. Dan Jacobson, introduction to *The Story of an African Farm* (London: Penguin Books, 1971), pp. 18–19. Stephen Gray also notes this passage in *Southern African Literature: An Introduction* (Cape Town: David Philip, 1979), p. 152.

28. Nadine Gordimer, personal conversation, Stanford University, November 12, 1987.

29. Emerson, "American Scholar," p. 63. Stephen Gray also compares Schreiner's literary enterprise to Emerson's call for an American literary independence (see *Southern African Literature,* p. 133).

30. Theodore Watts[-Dunton], "The Future of American Literature," *Fortnightly Review,* June 1891, p. 917.

31. Homi K. Bhabha, "DissemiNation: Time, Narrative, and the Margins of the Modern Nation," in *Nation and Narration,* ed. Homi K. Bhabha (New York: Routledge, 1990), p. 315.

32. Lord Meath, "Anglo-Saxon Unity," *Fortnightly Review,* May 1891, p. 622.

33. Anderson, *Imagined Communities,* p. 59.

34. Olive Schreiner, *An English South African's View of the Situation* (London: Hodder & Stoughton, 1899), p. 31; hereafter referred to in text citations as *ESAV.*

35. While it is not clear what role Schreiner's publishers played in marking these words as "foreign," Stephen Gray, a South African critic, finds the punctuation notable and holds Schreiner responsible (see *South African Literature,* p. 5).

36. According to her niece, Olive Schreiner was not allowed to use Dutch words or phrases growing up and was punished harshly when she did. As a native South African, however, she learned many phrases and, unlike her parents, considered them part of her national heritage. Her niece credits her with an "astonishing facility in Cape Dutch, which she spoke with pride and an uncompromising English accent." Karel Schoeman believes Schreiner spoke Afrikaans fluently although she could not write it well (Schoeman, *Olive Schreiner: A Woman in South Africa, 1855–1881* [Johannesburg: Jonathan Ball, 1991], p. 334). Other sources do not credit her with such knowledge. See Lyndall Gregg's reminiscences in *Until the Heart Changes: A Garland for Olive Schreiner,* ed. Zelda Friedlander (Cape Town: Tafelberg-Uitgewers, 1967), p. 21.

37. Olive Schreiner, "The Boer," in *TSA;* the essay is hereafter cited in text citations as "TB."

38. Richard Rive, foreword to Schreiner's *TSA,* pp. xiii–xiv. Karel Schoeman, however, argues that the first Afrikaans text that can be called a novel is S. J. du Toit's *Die Koningin fan Skeba,* which was not published until 1898, and that a mature novelistic tradition in Afrikaans would take another half-century (Schoeman, *Olive Schreiner,* p. 415).

39. Whether Afrikaans is truly a "creole" language or a "contact" language is still a matter of linguistic as well as political debate. The white-supremacist position is that Afrikaans developed from the Dutch maintaining its dialectal features and grammatical structures and resisting influence from African and Malayo-Portuguese-speaking slaves. See Thomas L. Markey, "Afrikaans: Creole or Non-Creole?" *Zeitschrift für Dialecktologie und Linguistik* 49, no. 2 (1982).

40. Bruce King in his overview of "New English" literature notes in Schreiner's work the tension and strength of her nationalist interest in local subject matter and dialect and her internationalist impulse: "If local realism was usually associated with nationalism, and aestheticism with an English or European bias, Schreiner's work shows that such distinctions are not watertight and that the best writing usually combines both local and international cultural movements of the time" (*The New English Literatures: Cultural Nationalism in a Changing World* [London: Macmillan, 1980], pp. 11–12).

41. Stephen Greenblatt, "Learning to Curse: Aspects of Colonialism in the Sixteenth Century," in *First Images: The Impact of the New World on the Old,* ed. Fredi Chiappelli (Berkeley: University of California Press, 1976), p. 562.

42. José Piedra, "Literary Whiteness and the Afro-Hispanic Difference," *New Literary History* 18, no. 2 (winter 1987), pp. 303–32; and Kirpatrick Sale, *The Conquest of Paradise: Christopher Columbus and the Columbian Legacy* (New York: Plume, 1991).

43. Hyde Clark (excerpted by W. T. Stead), "The Neglect of the English Language," *Review of Reviews* 2, no. 8 (August 1890), p. 163.

44. Olive Schreiner, "The Problem of Slavery," in *TSA,* p. 108; hereafter the essay is referred to as "PS."

45. Greenblatt, "Learning to Curse," p. 586.

46. Olivia Smith, *The Politics of Language: 1791–1819* (Oxford: Clarendon Press, 1984).

47. Ibid., p. 9.

48. *Cape Times,* May 10, 1905.

49. Olive Schreiner, "South Africa: Its Natural Features, Its Diverse Peoples, Its Political Status: The Problem," in *TSA,* p. 29; hereafter referred to in text citations as "SA."

50. Schreiner criticism suffers from the naive and often sexist tendency to read the heroines of texts by women as autobiographical representations of the authors themselves, an approach that denies the literary quality of their work. While feminist critics such as Michèle Barrett, Cora Kaplan, and Judith Newton encourage us to examine the historical and theoretical contexts of literary images, they also warn us not to forget the *literarity* of the text or to "construe the novelist as a sociologist manqué" (see Michèle Barrett, *Women's Oppression Today: Problems in Marxist Feminist Analysis* [London: Verso, 1980], pp. 100, 107). I do not, therefore, look to Schreiner's work in order to learn "what women were like" in South Africa or any other such "reality," but to explore the possibilities of representation available to Schreiner as a white South African woman in her historical moment.

51. Doris Y. Kadish, *The Literature of Images: Narrative Landscape from "Julie" to "Jane Eyre"* (New Brunswick, N.J.: Rutgers University Press, 1986), pp. 5–7.

52. Olive Schreiner, *Undine* (1928; reprint, New York: Johnson Reprint, 1972), pp. 1–2; emphasis added; hereafter referred to in text citations as *U.*

53. See Dorothy Hammond and Alta Jablow, *The Africa That Never Was: Four Centuries of British Writing about Africa* (New York: Twayne, 1970), pp. 124–26. For an analysis of travel narratives in particular, see Pratt, *Imperial Eyes.*

54. This is not to say that Schreiner does not at times use the British tropes of African archaism. In her essay "South Africa" she does use the cliché "prehistoric" to describe Africa in contrast to Europe (see "SA," p. 64).

55. M. van Wyk Smith gives examples of this "mandatory description of the terrors of the African night" in both juvenile novels and exploration narratives (see "The Origins of Some Victorian Images of Africa," *English in Africa,* March 1979, p. 19).

56. Kadish, *Literature of Images,* p. 7. J. M. Coetzee argues that landscape art is "by and large a traveler's art intended for the consumption of vicarious travelers; it is closely

connected with the imperial eye." This is one of the explanations, he argues, for the proliferation of South African landscape description in English and the rarity of those in Afrikaans, for Afrikaners were neither stranger-travelers nor did they write for an audience unfamiliar with the terrain. See Coetzee, *White Writing,* pp. 174–76.

57. Karel Schoeman cites the repetitive quality of travelers' depictions of South Africa until the 1870s, these depictions emphasizing the desolation and barrenness of the landscape. He argues that by the 1870s, when Schreiner wrote, the descriptions had become more positive, granting a recognition of beauty. For instance, the traveler known only as M. E. wrote about his trip to the diamond fields and employed the same contradictory vocabulary as Schreiner: "A dreary, desert-like tract of land, seeming to roll itself out in front of us, day after day, exactly the same. The constant mirage on the horizon was the only beauty, unless the strangeness and weirdness of such a scene might be termed its beauty" (Schoeman, *Olive Schreiner,* p. 428).

58. Anderson, *Imagined Communities,* p. 61.

59. Olive Schreiner, *Woman and Labour* (1911; reprint, London: Virago, 1978), p. 165; hereafter referred to in text citations and notes as *WL*. Schreiner's example might also be in response to the "Anglo-Saxonism" argument by some journalists and scientists of the time who pointed to the poverty of the Irish in the United States as evidence of the hereditary inferiority of the Irish and the Celtic "race" as compared with the "Saxons," who flourished and set their stamp upon the nation. See Paul B. Rich, *Race and Empire in British Politics* (Cambridge: Cambridge University Press, 1986), p. 15.

60. See Sarah Grand, *The Beth Book* (1897; reprint, New York: Dial Press, 1980); May Sinclair, *Mary Olivier: A Life* (1919; reprint, New York: Dial Press, 1980); Virginia Woolf, *The Waves* (1931; reprint, Harmondsworth, England: Penguin Books, 1972); James Joyce, *A Portrait of an Artist as a Young Man* (1916; reprint, New York: Viking Press, 1975).

61. Anderson, *Imagined Communities,* p. 3.

62. Emerson, "American Scholar," p. 66.

63. Mary Louise Pratt calls this European representation of Africa the "monarch-of-all-I-survey" mode that articulates an ideology of conquest. See Pratt's "Conventions of Representation: Where Discourse and Ideology Meet," in *Contemporary Perceptions of Language,* ed. Heidi Byrnes (Washington, D.C.: Georgetown University Roundtable in Languages and Linguistics, 1982), p. 147, and her later development of this idea in *Imperial Eyes,* pp. 201–8.

64. Coetzee, *White Writing,* p. 167.

65. As John Povey relates, Roy Campbell was similarly disgusted with the overblown metaphors and meanings projected onto the African landscape by travelers and early colonialist settlers. Lampooning these literary excesses, Campbell wrote:

> But "nameless somethings" and "unbounded spaces"
> Are still the heritage of "younger races" —
> At least our novelists will have it so,
> And, reader, who are we to tell them, "No!"
> We, who have never heard the "call" or felt
> The witching whatdyecallum of the veld?

See John Povey, "Landscape in Early South African Poetry," in *Olive Schreiner and After,* p. 121.

66. Sigmund Freud, "The 'Uncanny,'" in *On Creativity and the Unconscious* (New York: Harper and Row, 1958), pp. 122–61. See also "The Antithetical Sense of Primal Words," in the same volume, pp. 55–62.

67. For example, the essay "South Africa" was published in the *Fortnightly Review* in July 1891 and in the *Cape Times* in August 1891. *An English South African's View of the Situation: Words in Season* was published as a book in London and as a series of letters in the *South African News* and the *Standard and Digger's News* in 1899. Joyce Berkman suggests that Schreiner's dreams and allegories were the most popular of her writings precisely because they were removed from the specificity of terrain of her other works and therefore could be equally enjoyed by her incompatible audiences (Berkman, *Healing Imagination,* pp. 212–13).

68. Henry Stanley, *Through the Dark Continent* (New York: Harper and Brothers, 1878), vol. 2, p. 78. Mary Louise Pratt has pointed out that descriptive terms in explorers' texts often rely on the home culture, that is, "pearly mist" or "steel-colored" ("Conventions of Representation," p. 146). This is not to say that the landscapes are explicitly compared to England but that the descriptions rely on a particular economic and cultural discourse.

69. For a range of what Africa symbolizes in British literature, see Hammond and Jablow, *The Africa That Never Was,* and Patrick Brantlinger, "Victorians and Africans: The Genealogy of the Myth of the Dark Continent," *Critical Inquiry* 12, no. 1 (autumn 1985), pp. 166–203. Brantlinger traces the ways the myth of Africa as dark and savage developed in response to political changes in Europe and the United States during the nineteenth century. Most notably, Brantlinger remarks, "The more Europeans dominated Africans, the more 'savage' Africans came to seem" (p. 184).

70. Gray, *South African Literature,* p. 156.

71. Eric H. Gombrich, *Art and Illusion: A Study in the Psychology of Pictorial Representation* (New York: Pantheon Books, 1960), p. 269.

72. H. Rider Haggard, *She: A History of Adventure* (1886; reprint, New York: Airmont Books, 1967), pp. 64–65.

73. In this essay and in her novel *From Man to Man,* Schreiner provides an early example of the creole critical evaluation of the "mother country" that became a touchstone in postcolonial texts from the 1950s until the present.

74. Patrick Brantlinger points out the male "adolescent quality that pervades most imperialist literature," a quality obvious in the current revamping of this genre with the *Indiana Jones* movies and the television series *Young Indiana Jones.* See Brantlinger, "Victorians and Africans," pp. 188–90.

75. Hammond and Jablow, *The Africa That Never Was,* pp. 71–72 and 148–56.

76. For a discussion of male and female narrative space, see Teresa de Lauretis, *Alice Doesn't: Feminism, Semiotics, Cinema* (Bloomington: Indiana University Press, 1984), pp. 118–19. "Male narratives," of course, are not only those written by male writers or those that focus on male characters. As we shall see in the chapters on Jean Rhys, Charlotte Brontë sets her Bertha up as the dangerous female "other" to both Jane and Rochester, with Bertha standing in the way of domestic harmony, legitimacy, and legality.

77. Mary Louise Pratt has found a similar tendency among American creole women writers of rewriting the feminized landscapes of male European writers. See *Imperial Eyes,* pp. 193–94.

78. Ibid., p. 61.

79. Olive Schreiner, *From Man to Man or Perhaps Only...* (New York: Harper and Brothers, 1927), p. 400; emphasis added; hereafter referred to in text citations as *MM.*

2 / Seeking a Third Term

1. Olive Schreiner, introduction to *TSA,* p. 16.

2. See Lillian Smith, *Killers of the Dream,* rev. and enlarged ed. (New York: W. W.

Norton, 1978); Minnie Bruce Pratt, "Identity: Skin Blood Heart," in *Yours in Struggle: Three Feminist Perceptions on Anti-Semitism and Racism,* by Elly Bulkin, Minnie Bruce Pratt, and Barbara Smith (Brooklyn: Long Haul Press, 1984); Barbara Deming, *We Are All Part of One Another: A Barbara Deming Reader,* ed. Jane Meyerding (Philadelphia: New Society, 1984).

3. Margaret Lenta, "Racism, Sexism, and Olive Schreiner's Fiction," *Theoria* 70 (October 1987), p. 24.

4. Joyce Avrech Berkman, *The Healing Imagination of Olive Schreiner: Beyond South African Colonialism* (Amherst: University of Massachusetts Press, 1989), pp. 83–90.

5. Ridley Beeton, "In Search of Olive Schreiner in Texas," *Texas Quarterly,* 17, no. 3 (autumn 1974), p. 108.

6. For an analysis of the effect of Schreiner's health on her intellectual and emotional life, see Berkman, *Healing Imagination.*

7. Ruth First and Ann Scott, *Olive Schreiner: A Biography* (New York: Schocken Books, 1980), pp. 261–62, 301–5.

8. Bryan Cheyette, "Jewish Stereotyping and English Literature, 1875–1920: Towards a Political Analysis," in *Traditions of Intolerance: Historical Perspectives on Fascism and Race Discourse in Britain,* ed. Tony Kushner and Kenneth Lunn (Manchester: Manchester University Press, 1989).

9. Cited in S. C. Cronwright-Schreiner's biography of his wife, *The Life of Olive Schreiner* (London: T. Fisher Unwin, 1924), p. 6.

10. Ibid., p. 7.

11. Jane Marcus, "Olive Schreiner: Cartographer of the Spirit/A Review Article," *Minnesota Review,* 12 (spring 1979), pp. 62–63. Vera Buchanan-Gould also cites Frank Harris's description of Schreiner as a Jewish woman in his *Contemporary Portraits:* "She was at that time a girl of about nineteen [twenty-eight in reality], distinctly pretty, with dark eyes, black hair, and a little, square, strong figure; the figure betraying the Jew in her more strongly than her face. Yet the race characteristics were marked in a slightly beaked nose and the dark southern complexion" (see Vera Buchanan-Gould, *Not without Honour: The Life and Writings of Olive Schreiner* [London: Hutchinson, 1948], p. 21).

12. Cronwright-Schreiner, *Life of Olive Schreiner,* p. 7n.

13. George Eliot, *Daniel Deronda* (1876; reprint, Harmondsworth, England: Penguin Books, 1967), p. 417.

14. Ibid., p. 437.

15. Throughout this chapter I use the male pronoun in reference to "the Jew" in accordance with the works by gentile authors in which the literary and political generic Jew is a male figure. The "Jewess" in literature is endowed with a markedly different set of stereotypes, most often dealing with her exotic sexuality, allure, and inaccessibility. The figure of "the Jewess" is as self-contradictory as that of "the Jew," as evidenced by the current circulation of "JAP (Jewish-American princess) jokes," which assert not Jewish woman's sexual exoticism or promiscuity but rather her sexual frigidity and avid consumerism. For a critique of the "JAP" stereotype and of its use in the legal arena, see Elisa New, "Killing the Princess: The Offense of a Bad Defense," *Tikkun* 4, no. 2 (March/April 1989), pp. 17ff. On the sexual stereotypes of the "Jewess," see also Jean-Paul Sartre, *Anti-Semite and Jew,* trans. George J. Becker (1946; reprint, New York: Schocken Books, 1965).

16. Stephen Gray, *Southern African Literature: An Introduction* (Cape Town: David Philip, 1979), p. 140.

17. It appears that Schreiner herself as a girl of sixteen or seventeen had been seduced by an older and more sophisticated German man, Julius Gau, who was in South Africa as a representative of a Swiss insurance company. First and Scott attribute Schreiner's first asthmatic episode to this aborted affair (First and Scott, *Olive Schreiner,* pp. 61–63).

18. Robert Knox, *Races of Men* (Philadelphia: Lea and Blanchard, 1850), p. 144.

19. Ibid., p. 144; emphasis added.

20. Eliot, *Daniel Deronda,* p. 875.

21. Gillian Beer, *Darwin's Plots: Evolutionary Narrative in Darwin, George Eliot and Nineteenth Century Fiction* (London: Routledge and Kegan Paul, 1983), p. 218. See also Cheyette, "Jewish Stereotyping," pp. 16–17.

22. Published in the *Times* on July 23, 1887 (cited in William J. Fishman, *East End Jewish Radicals 1875–1914* [London: Gerald Duckworth, 1975], p. 71). That this metaphor of colonization was still pervasive a decade later can be seen in Labouchére's sarcastic use of it in his article "The Colonisation and Exploitation of England" in the journal *Truth,* reproduced in the *Jewish Chronicle,* December 31, 1897 (cited in Fishman, *East End,* p. 89). Israel Zangwill also speaks of "Jewish colonies" in the East End of London in *Children of the Ghetto: A Study of a Peculiar People* (1892; reprint, Philadelphia: Jewish Publication Society of America, 1938), p. xvii.

23. Charles Booth's group study *Conditions and Occupations of the People of Tower Hamlets, 1886–1887* attributes "nihilism and the bitterest kind of socialistic theories" to Jewish immigrants in the East End of London (see Fishman, *East End,* pp. 71–72). Schreiner's own involvement in socialist circles was informal. Although she joined few organizations, "she knew and valued the friendship of several working-class militants and became a determined advocate of the rights of organized labour" (First and Scott, p. 110). In 1889 Schreiner went to live in the East End of London close to the area where crowds gathered to hear speakers from the Social Democratic Federation. The next year when the Anglo-Boer War broke out, Schreiner found her anti-war position supported in England by the Social Democratic Federation and other close socialist friends (First and Scott, *Olive Schreiner,* pp. 187, 239).

24. Olive Schreiner, "A Letter on the Jew," in *Letters of Olive Schreiner,* ed. S. C. Cronwright-Schreiner (London: T. Fisher Unwin, 1924), appendix F; hereafter the volume is referred to in text citations and notes as *LOS.*

25. In a letter to Havelock Ellis, Schreiner writes of her personal identification with Heinrich Heine: "I love in that same personal way, Heinrich Heine. I personify myself with him" (*LOS,* April 12, 1884, p. 16).

26. Cronwright-Schreiner, *Life of Olive Schreiner,* p. 7n. The concluding passage of "A Letter on the Jew" is not given with the rest of the letter in appendix F of *LOS* but appears in a footnote in the Cronwright-Schreiner biography.

27. The figure of the Jewish character is of particular interest in later "postcolonial" fiction as well. In Alan Paton's *Too Late the Phalarope* (1953), a novel concerned with the barriers legislated by apartheid, the Jew stands somewhat on the edge of the social world of Venterspan, a grayness in a world of black and white. The only person to whom Pieter van Vlaanderen can imagine confessing his violation of the Immorality Act is the Jew, Matthew Kaplan. As the unmarried narrator, Sophie, puts it: "Kappie, who being like myself set apart in the world, would notice this and that." In Doris Lessing's *Martha Quest,* the Cohen boys challenge the anti-Semitism of Martha's South African society and offer her an intellectual and material way out of the backcountry. See chapter 5, in this book, for Michelle Cliff's use of Jewish identity.

28. For an excellent discussion of the language used in antialienist agitation, see John A. Garrard, *The English and Immigration 1880–1910* (London: Oxford University Press, 1971), esp. pp. 4, 18, 61, and chaps. 4 and 5. For instance, an article in the *Pall Mall Gazette* (1901) blamed disease on foreign immigrants: "The small-pox now creeping through London...is caused (make no mistake about it) by the scum washed to our shores in the dirty waters flowing from foreign drainpipes" (cited in Garrard, *The English and Immigration,* p. 18).

29. Henry James, *The American Scene* (1907; reprint, New York: Horizon Press, 1967), p. 117.

30. Ibid., pp. 85–86.

31. Bryan Cheyette also notes this scene in relation to James's own sense of national displacement. See Cheyette, *Constructions of "the Jew" in English Literature and Society: Racial Representations, 1875–1945* (Cambridge: Cambridge University Press, 1993), p. 6.

32. Ibid., p. 206.

33. Arguing for Jewish emancipation in 1831 in the *Edinburgh Review*, Thomas B. Macaulay pointedly rejected the widespread accusation that Jews' "lack of patriotism" was shown by their "living morally and politically in communion with their brethren who are scattered all over the world" (see Fishman, *East End*, p. 63). Also see Colin Holmes, *Anti-Semitism in British Society 1876–1939* (London: Edward Arnold, 1979), p. 12, on the 1878 English debates between the chief rabbi Hermann Adler and the Oxford history professor Goldwin Smith (an enemy of Disraeli) over the possibility of Jewish patriotism.

The prominence of the Rothschild banking family and the huge publicity surrounding the Dreyfus Affair contributed to the myth of Jews' disregard for the interests of their nations. The Rothschild banks, operating from five European countries, were taken as proof of an international conspiracy of Jews secretly directing the course of European politics to their own financial benefit.

The international interest in the 1894 trial, the conviction, and the public degradation of Alfred Dreyfus heightened the debate surrounding Jewish patriotism. Dreyfus, a Jewish officer in the French army, although later proven innocent, was tried for treason (for allegedly sending secret military documents to the German embassy) and sentenced to life imprisonment on Devil's Island. The question of Jewish patriotism and the meaning of Jewish emancipation in a supposedly liberal country such as France is at the heart of the tremendous emotionalism surrounding this case, which divided French politics through World War II. On these subjects, see entries for "Dreyfus Affair," "Rothschild," and "The Elders of Zion" in *Encyclopedia Judaica* (Jerusalem: Macmillan, 1971).

34. Cheyette, *Constructions,* pp. 206–7.

35. T. S. Eliot, *The Complete Poems and Plays 1909–1950* (New York: Harcourt, Brace and Company, 1952).

36. For more on T. S. Eliot's use of the anti-Semitic stereotypes and on the literary and cultural traditions of such usages, see Melvin Wilk's excellent *Jewish Presence in T. S. Eliot and Franz Kafka,* Brown Judaic Studies 52 (Atlanta: Scholars Press, 1986); Leslie Fiedler, "What Can We Do about Fagin?: The Jew Villain in Western Tradition," *Commentary* 7 (May, 1949), pp. 411–18; Robert Alter, "Eliot, Lawrence and the Jews," *Commentary* 85 (Oct. 1970), pp. 81–86; Edgar Rosenberg, *From Shylock to Svengali: Jewish Stereotypes in English Fiction* (Stanford, Calif.: Stanford University Press, 1960).

37. Rosenberg, *From Shylock to Svengali,* pp. 187–205.

38. The *Protocols of the Learned Elders of Zion* is perhaps the most anti-Semitic piece of propaganda ever circulated. Written in the last decade of the nineteenth century, it outlined the supposed international Jewish conspiracy to control the governments of the world. The forgery was immensely popular, especially after World War I, and was used as Nazi propaganda as a justification for the genocide of the Jews. In 1920, when Eliot and Pound were writing, Henry Ford published excerpts from this forgery in his newspaper the *Dearborn Independent.* He distributed in the United States half a million copies of an English translation of the *Protocols* retitled *The International Jew: The World's Foremost Problem.* This version was translated into sixteen languages. See Wilk, *Jewish Presence,* pp. 42–45.

39. Hannah Arendt, "The Pariah as Rebel," in *The Jew as Pariah,* ed. Ron H. Feldman (New York: Grove Press, 1978), pp. 67–90, esp. 79–81. Although Arendt notes that Chaplin

claims Irish and Gypsy descent, she believes "he has epitomized in an artistic form a character born of the Jewish pariah mentality" (p. 69). The others she chooses for discussion are Heinrich Heine, Bernard Lazare, and Franz Kafka.

40. Coleridge, *Table Talk*, 14 August 1833. Cited in Rosenberg, *From Shylock to Svengali*, p. 55n., and Fishman, *East End*, p. 62. See also Israel Zangwill's description of the Christian caricature of the Jewish clothes peddler and the physical consequences of it for Jews living in England in *Children of the Ghetto*, p. 66.

41. See Doris Kadish's discussion of the political meaning of the incorporation of the pastoral tradition and the narrative garden description in nineteenth-century fiction in *The Literature of Images: Narrative Landscape from "Julie" to "Jane Eyre"* (New Brunswick, N.J.: Rutgers University Press, 1986).

42. In a letter to Edward Carpenter that sounds much like Antoinette in Jean Rhys's *Wide Sargasso Sea*, Schreiner articulates the "dream" that England is to the colonial Creole who writes from "a wild place in the Karroo 200 miles from Cape Town": "Fancy there really is a London! It's all such a dream to me" (*OSL*, April 19, 1890, p. 169).

43. Robert Ross points out that Schreiner is the first Commonwealth writer to describe the difficulty of coming to England (see "A New Time for the Fiction of Sarah Gertrude Millin and Olive Schreiner," *World Literature Written in English*, 24, no. 2 [1984], pp. 242–43).

44. Vineta Colby notes the contradiction of "the Jew's" "kindness," but she does not examine his metaphorical meaning *as a Jew:* "The Jew who takes her to London treats her with kindness and generosity, but isolates her from other people" (Vineta Colby, *The Singular Anomaly: Women Novelists of the Nineteenth Century* [New York: New York University Press, 1970], p. 99).

45. This ambivalence is seen in a letter from Schreiner: "The people at this boarding house seem nice and pleasant, especially a little Jew man and his young Jew wife. It's funny I always like Jews! I seem always to see their best side, under an often repulsive surface" (*OSL*, Oct. 1898, p. 336).

46. Bryan Cheyette similarly argues that "'the Jew,' like all 'doubles,' is inherently ambivalent and can represent both the 'best' and the 'worst' of selves.... Jews were, simultaneously, at the centre of European metropolitan society and, at the same time, banished from its privileged sphere by a semitic discourse" (Cheyette, *Constructions*, p. 12). See also Homi Bhabha, "The Other Question: Stereotype and Colonial Discourse," *Screen* 24, no. 6 (Nov.–Dec. 1983), pp. 18–36.

47. Cronwright-Schreiner, *Life of Olive Schreiner*, p. 7n.

48. See Garrard (*The English and Immigration*) for examples ranging from smallpox to tuberculosis.

49. See Holmes *Anti-Semitism*, pp. 12–13. See also Garrard, *The English and Immigration*, p. 191: "In *Justice* [the publication of the Social Democratic Federation] Hyndman editorialized at length about 'The Jews' War in the Transvaal,' and, thirteen years later, reminisced about 'the abominable war on behalf of German-Jew mineowners and other international interlopers.' Similarly, in 1900 the *Clarion* referred sarcastically to 'the suffering Uitlanders of Jewhannesburg.'"

50. Sartre, *Anti-Semite and Jew*, pp. 40ff.

51. Abdul R. JanMohamed, "The Economy of the Manichean Allegory: The Function of Racial Difference in Colonialist Literature," *Critical Inquiry* 12, no. 1 (autumn 1985), p. 63.

52. Mary Douglas, *Purity and Danger: An Analysis of the Concepts of Pollution and Taboo* (1966; reprint, London: Routledge and Kegan Paul, 1985).

53. Sander Gilman, *Jewish Self-Hatred: Anti-Semitism and the Hidden Language of the*

Jews (Baltimore: Johns Hopkins University Press, 1986), pp. 6–8. Gilman is quoting from Houston Stewart Chamberlain, *Foundations of the Nineteenth Century,* trans. John Lees, 2 vols. (1899; reprint, London: John Lane, 1910), vol. 1, pp. 388–89.

54. Gilman, *Jewish Self-Hatred,* p. 6.

55. Ibid., pp. 7–8 (citing Adam G. de Gurowski, *America and Europe* [New York: Appleton, 1857], p. 177).

56. Cynthia Ozick, "Sholem Aleichem's Revolution," *The New Yorker,* March 28, 1988, p. 99.

57. It is telling that as Jews were fleeing from Nazi Germany, the "Purified Nationalist Party" of South Africa demanded an amendment to the Aliens Bill in 1937 asking for a ban on the immigration of "'persons or classes of persons or races, who, such as among others the Jewish, cannot be readily assimilated,' together with the abolition of Yiddish as a specially recognized European language" (see T. R. H. Davenport, *South Africa: A Modern History* [Toronto: University of Toronto Press, 1987], p. 322).

58. Ozick, "Sholem Aleichem's Revolution," p. 99. See also Gilles Deleuze and Félix Guattari, *Kafka: Toward a Minor Literature,* trans. Dana Polan (Minneapolis: University of Minnesota Press, 1986). Deleuze and Guattari interpret Kafka's understanding of Yiddish "less as a sort of linguistic territoriality for the Jews than as a nomadic movement of deterritorialization that reworks German language" (p. 25). They also quote Kafka on the general fear of Yiddish, which he describes as "dread mingled with a certain fundamental distaste" (p. 25).

59. Gilman, *Jewish Self-Hatred,* p. 16.

60. Ibid., pp. 68–86.

61. Havelock Ellis, *The Criminal* (London: Walter Scott, 1910), pp. 208–11.

62. Ibid., p. 209.

63. Ibid., pp. 210–11.

64. Gilman, *Jewish Self-Hatred,* p. 75.

65. Ibid.

66. George Mosse, *Nationalism and Sexuality: Respectability and Abnormal Sexuality in Modern Europe* (New York: Howard Fertig, 1985), pp. 143–46.

67. See Anna Davin, "Imperialism and Motherhood," *History Workshop: A Journal of Socialist Historians* 5 (spring 1978), pp. 9–65.

68. Olive Schreiner, "The Boer Woman and the Modern Women's Question" (1899 according to First and Scott), reprinted in *TSA,* pp. 191–220; hereafter referred to in text citations as "BW."

69. This is Schreiner's term from *WL.*

70. Describing ethnographic conventions, shaped to a great extent by nineteenth-century descriptions of South African peoples, Mary Louise Pratt points to the use of the timeless present tense and the collective or representative subject, in this case the Boer bride, bridegroom, and wedding guest. "These descriptive practices," notes Pratt, "work to normalize another society, to codify its differences from one's own...[The homogenized object] is a *sui generis* configuration, often only a list of features, situated in a different temporal order from that of the perceiving and speaking subject" (Pratt, *Imperial Eyes,* p. 64).

71. Schoeman, *Olive Schreiner,* pp. 332–33.

72. Pratt, *Imperial Eyes,* pp. 53–56, 61–63.

73. In the late nineteenth century, scientists found it convenient to describe domestic class differences in the same terms as colonial race differences. This conflation helps to underscore the image of the Afrikaner farmer as a "white savage," both economically and racially inferior. See Douglas Lorimer, "Theoretical Racism in Late Victorian Anthropology, 1870–1900," *Victorian Studies* 13, no. 3 (spring 1988), p. 430.

74. See First and Scott, *Olive Schreiner,* p. 225.

75. Ibid., p. 158.

76. William Morris, a most important influence on the English socialist movement and specifically on Carpenter, published *News From Nowhere* in 1890. As the title implies, the ideal of a simple and healthy social existence, as Morris imagines it, is both "new" in the pattern of other challenges to Victorian culture (the new woman, the new fiction, the new fellowship, new unionism) and literally utopian in the most disappointing sense, that is, "nowhere" in actual existence. This utopia is specifically a reversion to a preindustrial economy. The nostalgia for a lost agrarian past seen in Schreiner's depiction of Boer farm life is part of the Victorian literary and artistic attempt to escape from the present social upheavals of the riots, disease, and slums of the industrial city. As Morris wrote in the prologue to his escapist poems *The Earthly Paradise* (1868–1870):

> Forget the six counties overhung with smoke,
> Forget the snorting steam and piston stroke,
> Forget the spreading of the hideous town;
> Think rather of the packhorse on the down,
> And dream of London, small and white, and clean,
> The dear Thames bordered by its garden green.

William Morris, "The Earthly Paradise," in *News from Nowhere and Selected Writings and Designs,* ed. Asa Briggs (Harmondsworth, England: Penguin Books, 1980), p. 68.

77. Coetzee, *White Writing,* p. 5.

78. See John S. Haller and Robin M. Haller, *The Physician and Sexuality in Victorian America* (Urbana: University of Illinois Press, 1974); Carol Smith-Rosenberg, "The Hysterical Woman: Sex Roles and Role Conflict in Nineteenth Century America," in *Disorderly Conduct: Visions of Gender in Victorian America* (New York: Oxford University Press, 1985); Elaine Showalter, *The Female Malady: Women, Madness and Culture in England, 1830–1980* (New York: Pantheon Books, 1985).

79. Olive Schreiner, "The Psychology of the Boer," in *TSA,* p. 320.

80. *OSL,* pp. 362–63 (quoted in Chushichi Tsuzuki, *Edward Carpenter 1844–1929: Prophet of Human Fellowship* [Cambridge: Cambridge University Press, 1980], p. 152).

81. Olive Schreiner, "Eighteen Ninety-Nine," in *An Olive Schreiner Reader: Writings on Women and South Africa,* ed. Carol Barash (London: Pandora Press, 1987), pp. 155–85.

82. For an excellent discussion of Afrikaner racist mythology, see Leonard Thompson, *The Political Mythology of Apartheid* (New Haven: Yale University Press, 1985).

83. On the subject of Schreiner's role in the English women's movement at the end of the nineteenth century, see Judith R. Walkowitz, "Science, Feminism and Romance: The Men and Women's Club, 1885–1889," *History Workshop* 21 (spring 1986), pp. 37–59; and Betty M. Fradkin, "Olive Schreiner—An Opposite Picture," *Contrast* 12, no. 3 (1979), pp. 75–88. On Schreiner's relationship to Havelock Ellis and her contribution to his research on female sexuality (including Ellis's "case study" of her), see Ridley Beeton, "In Search of Olive Schreiner in Texas," *Texas Quarterly* 17, no. 3 (autumn 1974), pp. 105–54. Betty M. Fradkin also examines the relationship between Schreiner and Ellis in "Havelock Ellis and Olive Schreiner's 'Gregory Rose,' " *Texas Quarterly* 21, no. 3 (autumn 1978), pp. 145–53.

Jane Marcus puts Schreiner's work in the context of the contemporaneous search for female power in literature, history, and anthropology (see "Olive Schreiner: Cartographer of the Spirit," pp. 58–66). On Schreiner's feminism in her fiction and her influence on later feminists, see Laurence Lerner, "Olive Schreiner and the Feminists," in *Olive Schreiner and After: Essays on Southern African Literature,* ed. Malvern van Wyk Smith and Don Maclennan

(Cape Town: David Philip, 1983), pp. 67–79; Alan Bishop, "Olive Schreiner and Vera Brittain," in the same volume, pp. 80–82; Robin Visel, "'We Bear the World and We Make It': Bessie Head and Olive Schreiner," *Research in African Literatures* 21, no. 3 (fall 1990), pp. 115–24; and Kathleen Blake, "Olive Schreiner: A Note on Sexist Language and the Feminist Writer," *Women and Literature*, n.s. 1 (1980), pp. 81–86.

84. Vera Buchanan-Gould's early critical biography, *Not without Honour,* talks hardly at all about Schreiner's literary treatment of Blacks. She dismisses Schreiner's pseudoscientific racial discussion in *Thoughts on South Africa* as typical of her "characteristic simplicity" but does not go on to analyze the complexity of Schreiner's language or metaphors. In fact, Buchanan-Gould *admires* Schreiner's superficial descriptions of her Afrikaner and black characters: "Olive is at her best in some ways when describing the coloured and Afrikaans people whom she puts into her three novels, for she does not attempt to get into their skins and to give us sight of their naked souls" (*Not without Honour,* p. 75). But Patricia Morris finds that Schreiner's "apparent racism is at the least embarrassing, and at the most, crucial to any biographical assessment of her" ("Biographical Accounts of Olive Schreiner," in *Olive Schreiner and After,* p. 12). Ruth First and Ann Scott attempt to explain this racism in terms of contemporaneous anthropological work: "Such references as there are to South Africa's indigenous people are firmly rooted in the racist stereotypes of contemporary ethnology which she was clearly unable to transcend" (First and Scott, *Olive Schreiner,* p. 195 [cited in Morris, "Biographical Accounts," p. 13]). Rodney Davenport concurs when he remarks that "[Schreiner's] thinking about race marked her as a child of her own generation — not a remarkable thing in itself, but a limiting factor in the outlook of a prophet." Davenport does go on to examine the ways Schreiner at times escaped the Darwinian conclusions popular in her time ("Olive Schreiner and South African Politics," in *Olive Schreiner and After,* p. 103). Joyce Berkman describes Schreiner as "swathed in Victorian biases" even as she attempts to argue against racist colonial policies (*Healing Imagination,* pp. 84–87).

85. For examples of articles that do not deal with Schreiner's feminism, see Alan Paton, "Trooper Peter Halket of Mashonaland," in *Olive Schreiner and After,* pp. 30–34; and Rodney Davenport, "Olive Schreiner and South African Politics," pp. 93–107.

86. By bringing together Schreiner's writings on women and on South African politics in a carefully selected volume, Carol Barash hopes readers will recognize feminism at the root of both Schreiner's anticolonialism and her racism (see Carol Barash, ed., *An Olive Schreiner Reader: Writings on Women and South Africa* [London: Pandora Press, 1987]).

87. Ware, *Beyond the Pale,* p. 163.

88. Along with other cultural historians, Lora Romero examines the "cult of the vanishing American" in antebellum American literature, focusing particularly on James Fenimore Cooper's *The Last of the Mohicans.* See Romero's "Vanishing Americans: Gender, Empire, and New Historicism," *American Literature* 63, no. 3 (Sept. 1991), pp. 385–404.

89. In a letter to Edward Carpenter a decade later (October 8, 1894), Schreiner again draws a parallel between sexual and racial relations, arguing that just as women need economic independence from men, so Blacks need economic equality in South Africa (see *OSL,* pp. 241–42).

90. As Schreiner wrote to Ellis about her love of scientific literature: "You don't know what a gap would be left in my life if all the good I have had from scientific books were to be taken out of it (making the word 'scientific' cover everything from Darwin and Carl Vogt to little primers on Heat and Light). I think that even the mere reading helps one to the feeling that truth is before all things, and to have a kind of love for things in their naked simplicity" (*OSL,* p. 40).

91. Nancy Stepan, *The Idea of Race in Science: Great Britain, 1800–1960* (London: Macmillan, 1982), p. xiii.

92. It is also true, of course, that the scientific discourse of the early nineteenth century was greatly influenced by the abolition movement of the times. Stepan notes about the relationship between science and political moments: "Factors traditionally thought of as lying somehow 'outside' science in fact entered decisively into the making of racial science, as constituent elements of that science...Ideas about the nature of blackness, the social order, natural and social hierarchies, change, progress and purpose unconsciously shaped the way scientists defined scientific problems and the scientific theories they put forward to explain them. Ideological issues...were embedded in scientific argument" (Stepan, *Idea of Race,* pp. xiv−xv).

93. Ibid., pp. 6, 14−18.

94. Brantlinger, *Rule of Darkness,* p. 21.

95. Examination of membership in the British Anthropological Institute, where much of this debate continued during the 1870s and 1880s, shows a high number of members of Parliament, colonial army officers, and clergymen (at least one-third of the membership were employed by the government) who were influential in determining colonial policy and rhetoric at the height of British expansion in Africa. See Douglas Lorimer, "Theoretical Racism in Late-Victorian Anthropology, 1870−1900," *Victorian Studies* 31, no. 3 (spring 1988), pp. 405−30.

96. T. H. Huxley in his famous 1893 lecture "Evolution and Ethics" articulates the ethical reservations of applying Darwin's "survival of the fittest" doctrine to social struggles: "The influence of the cosmic process on the evolution of society is the greater the more rudimentary its civilization. Social progress means a checking of the cosmic process at every step and the substitution for it of another, which may be called the ethical process." The cosmic struggle for existence "is directed, not so much to the survival of the fittest, as to the fitting of as many as possible to survive." But even Huxley, who has been seen as one of the strongest opponents to "social Darwinism," assumes in his arguments a notion of the "ethical man" who is by definition neither working-class nor "savage" (see T. H. Huxley, *Evolution and Ethics* [London: Macmillan, 1893]). The phrase "survival of the fittest" was actually coined by Spencer. For a discussion of the politics behind Huxley's argument against both the individualism of Spencer and the socialism of Alfred Wallace and Henry George, see Michael S. Helfand, "T. H. Huxley's 'Evolution and Ethics': The Politics of Evolution and the Evolution of Politics," *Victorian Studies* 20, no. 2 (winter 1977), pp. 159−77.

97. Olive Schreiner, "The Englishman," in *TSA,* p. 361; hereafter referred to in text citations and notes as "TE."

98. Olive Schreiner, "The Native Question," (1908), reprinted in *An Olive Schreiner Reader,* pp. 186−97.

99. Jane Marcus, "Olive Schreiner: Cartographer of the Spirit," p. 65. Rodney Davenport explains Schreiner's nonrevolutionary stance as a characteristic of traditional South African liberalism: "Cape liberals did not recommend revolution, and this has led their modern Marxist critics to charge them with false consciousness linked with overriding class loyalties, for advocating change only in a manner unlikely to make it happen...The South African liberal [was] an anti-revolutionary. His strategy was not so much to engineer change as to promote thinking about change in the hope that thereby change would come about" (see Davenport, "Olive Schreiner and South African Politics," p. 100). Joyce Berkman also notes that because Schreiner could not tolerate her virtuous characters using violence, "the unjustly oppressed never organize to rebel or even seek individual revenge" (Berkman, *Healing Imagination,* p. 192).

100. While Schreiner supported Gandhi in South Africa and he was flattered by her interest, she opposed his early support of the empire and his taking the side of England during the Anglo-Boer War and World War I. For more on Schreiner's relationship with

Gandhi and her pacifism, see First and Scott, *Olive Schreiner,* pp. 304–5; Berkman, *Healing Imagination,* pp. 64, 101, 188–89. Berkman argues that Schreiner's pacifism was inspired by Buddhism and not by her Christian training; I believe her attraction to the figure of the martyr, however, has everything to do with her early Christian education.

101. Carol Barash remarks that the idealism in Schreiner's visionary prose in *Woman and Labour* "was often a way to avoid confronting the complexities and ambiguities of political change" (see Barash, introduction to *An Olive Schreiner Reader,* p. 5).

102. *LOS,* August 27, 1912, p. 317. Both Virginia Woolf and Rebecca West wrote about Schreiner's attraction to martyrdom, or as West calls it in *The Freewoman* (October 3, 1912) "female masochism"; see Marcus, "Olive Schreiner: Cartographer of the Spirit," p. 65.

103. Berkman, *Healing Imagination,* p. 123.

104. Sander Gilman, "Black Bodies, White Bodies: Toward an Iconography of Female Sexuality in Late Nineteenth-Century Art, Medicine, and Literature," *Critical Inquiry* 20, no. 1 (autumn 1986), pp. 204–42.

105. See Nancy Stepan on Robert Knox's *The Races of Man* (1850) and on Spencer's discussion of hybridization between widely separated races (Stepan, *Idea of Race,* pp. 41–42, 105). Francis Galton, Charles Darwin's cousin, agreed with this position of hybridization and in 1883 introduced the word "eugenics" into the vocabulary, establishing racial "improvement" as a viable science and social program through the 1930s, with its culmination in Nazism (Stepan, *Idea of Race,* p. 111).

106. Gilman, "Black Bodies," pp. 218–19.

107. Schreiner's desire to meet her intellectual companions on their own turf expresses itself in her notes to Ellis on her relationship to her own sex and gender. She often signed her letters to him, "Your man friend." In a letter Schreiner comments: "I sometimes think my great love for women and girls [is] *not* because they are myself but because they are *not* myself." See Blake, "Olive Schreiner," pp. 81–86. In the light of this conflict for Schreiner, Rebekah's transsexual dream is fascinating. Rebekah dreams herself to be a "primitive" man lying on a mat on the floor of his hut with a small pregnant woman in his arms (*MM,* pp. 202–3).

In the character of Gregory Rose, Schreiner, like Ellis in his own studies, explores transvestism and sex roles. Ellis in his long chapter "Eonism" in *Studies in the Psychology of Sex* (New York: Random House, 1936) understands "cross-dressing" (Edward Carpenter's coinage) in the psychological terms and categories he inherits from Magnus Hirschfeld's important 1910 study, "Transvestism: An Investigation into the Erotic Impulse of Disguise." Although Ellis frees the concept from assumptions of pathology, his analysis is limited. In her writing, both fiction and nonfiction, Schreiner returns again and again to the issue and provides the political analysis of dress that the psychologists and sexologists ignore. She feels that current styles of dress are used to exaggerate the differences of men and women that keep women in subjection: "There is not, probably, one man or woman in twenty thousand who is not powerfully influenced in modern life in their conception of the differences, physical and intellectual, dividing the human male and female, by the grotesque exaggerations of modern attire and artificial manners" (*WL,* p. 162). In *From Man to Man,* Rebekah refuses to wear stays although she feels humiliated by the women who laugh at her in the street, and Schreiner writes a letter to Ellis about a "singular scene" she wants to write in which "Veronica goes to look at a man's clothes" (*LOS,* p. 49). She writes to Ellis's sister Louie about her desire for the freedom of male dress: "I want to wear boy's clothes and *will* as soon as I can get other women to join me. Boy's knickerbockers, but not coats, I think they are ugly. A kind of blouse reaching to the knee" (*LOS,* p. 39).

108. Olive Schreiner, *Dreams* (Boston: Roberts Brothers, 1891), pp. 156–57. It is interesting to compare this vision with Havelock Ellis's romantic vision of sexuality that

emphasizes the differences between men and women: "I dream of a world in which the spirits of women are flames stronger than fire, a world in which modesty has become courage and yet remains modesty, a world in which women are as unlike men as ever they were in the world I sought to destroy, a world in which women shine with a loveliness of self-revelation as enchanting as ever the old legends told, and yet a world which would immeasurably transcend the old world in the self-sacrificing passion of human service. I have dreamed of that world ever since I began to dream at all" (see Havelock Ellis, *The Art of Life: From the Works of Havelock Ellis,* ed. Mrs. S. Herbert [1929; reprint, New York: Books for Libraries Press, 1970], p. 17).

109. In fact, she believed that with social, economic, and educational equality between Blacks and Whites, there would be *fewer* interracial relationships. See letter to J. C. Smuts (July 1, 1896) in *OSL,* pp. 286–87.

110. The current debate on the etiology of homosexuality reveals the political pressure on liberals to claim a genetic cause or predisposition (an argument that in most contexts signals a defense of the social status quo) while the conservative voice ironically provides a potentially richer discussion about sexual "choice." It is perhaps the feminist recognition of the dangers of sociobiology that have kept many lesbians from embracing the current scientific research that locates sexual orientation in the hypothalamus, in genes, or in maternal intrauterine stress. For a fuller articulation of this argument, see Mary Elene Wood, "How We Got This Way: Reading the Sciences of Homosexuality," lecture presented November 30, 1993, at University of California at Santa Barbara; and Eve Kosofsky Sedgwick, "How to Bring Your Kids Up Gay: The War on Effeminate Boys," in *Tendencies* (Durham, N.C.: Duke University Press, 1993), pp. 154–64.

111. Vernon February, *Mind Your Colour: The "Coloured" Stereotype in South African Literature* (London: Kegan Paul, 1981).

112. Sheila Jeffreys, *The Spinster and Her Enemies: Feminism and Sexuality, 1880–1930* (London: Pandora Press, 1985), p. 13.

113. See also Schreiner's antiwar allegory/novel *Trooper Peter Halket of Mashonaland* (Boston: Little Brown, 1900) in which Peter, a young man just out of England to make a fortune in South Africa, justifies his own sexual exploitation of and violence against black women as merely one of the ways things are "different" for Englishmen in South Africa. Peter defends his purchase of young black women and his rape of those he finds in the bush with the arguments that "a black woman [isn't] white" and that his behavior is encouraged by the economic and political policies of his leader Cecil Rhodes (pp. 16–40). Mary Dearborn's study of ethnicity in American fiction, *Pocahontas's Daughters* (New York: Oxford University Press, 1986), explores the figure of the mulatto in American fiction. Women writers, she argues, "insistent on the factuality of miscegenation, turned again and again to the mulatto figure, and, in doing so, in effect named the taboo" that threatened the cultural equilibrium of the white-dominated society (p. 150).

114. Gilman, "Black Bodies," pp. 213–16.

115. For a discussion of the mythic stereotypes of black American women, see Alice Walker, "In Search of Our Mothers' Gardens," in *In Search of Our Mothers' Gardens* (New York: Harcourt Brace Jovanovich, 1983); and Deborah Gray White, *Ar'n't I a Woman? Female Slaves in the Plantation South* (New York: W. W. Norton, 1985).

3 / "Great Mistake to Go By Looks"

1. As Rhys wrote to Francis Wyndham on March 29, 1958: "For some time I've been getting down all I remembered about the West Indies as the West Indies used to be.

(Also all I was told, which is more important). I called this 'Creole' but it had no shape or plan...I have no title yet [for the novel that was to become *Wide Sargasso Sea*]. 'The First Mrs. Rochester' is not right. Nor, of course, is 'Creole.' That has a different meaning now. I hope I'll get one soon, for titles mean a lot to me. Almost half the battle. I thought of 'Sargasso Sea' or 'Wide Sargasso Sea' but nobody knew what I meant" (see *The Letters of Jean Rhys*, ed. Francis Wyndham and Diana Melly [New York: Viking, 1984], pp. 153–54; hereafter referred to in text citations and notes as *LJR*).

2. Benita Parry, "Problems in Current Theories of Colonial Discourse," *Oxford Literary Review* 9, nos. 1–2 (1987), p. 29.

3. See Homi Bhabha, "Signs Taken for Wonders: Questions of Ambivalence and Authority under a Tree outside Delhi, May 1817," *Critical Inquiry* 12, no. 1 (autumn 1985), p. 150, and Gayatri Spivak's quotations in Angela McRobbie, "Strategies of Vigilance: An Interview with Gayatri Chakravorty Spivak," *Block* 10 (1985), p. 13: "I am critical of the binary opposition Coloniser/Colonised. I try to examine the heterogeneity of 'Colonial Power,' and to disclose the complicity of the two poles of that opposition as it constitutes the disciplinary enclave of the critique of imperialism."

4. Teresa O'Connor, *Jean Rhys: The West Indian Novels* (New York: New York University Press, 1986), p. 20.

5. Jean Rhys, *Smile Please: An Unfinished Autobiography* (New York: Harper and Row, 1979), pp. 33–34 (quoted in O'Connor, *Jean Rhys*, p. 20).

6. O'Connor (*Jean Rhys*) compares Rhys's sometimes inaccurate statements in her own autobiography with information Louis James found in the Dominica National Archives before it was destroyed in a fire. I rely on O'Connor's and Mary Lou Emery's chronologies of Rhys's life as the most comprehensive (see Emery, *Jean Rhys at "World's End": Novels of Colonial and Sexual Exile* [Austin: University of Texas Press, 1990]).

7. See O'Connor, *Jean Rhys*, pp. 219–21, on the dating of the exercise books, henceforth called the Black Exercise Books.

8. O'Connor, *Jean Rhys*, p. 36.

9. Cited in O'Connor, *Jean Rhys*, p. 30.

10. Carol Ann Howells, *Jean Rhys* (New York: St. Martin's Press, 1991), p. 31. *Quartet* is Rhys's rendition of her romantic and sexual relationship with Ford in those years. (Her husband, under the pen-name Edouard de Nève, subsequently wrote *his* version of the affair, *Barred,* which Rhys translated into English.)

11. Howells, *Jean Rhys*, p. 25.

12. Emery, *Jean Rhys*, p. 11.

13. Pierrette Frickey, introduction to *Critical Perspectives on Jean Rhys* (Washington, D.C.: Three Continents Press, 1990), p. 1.

14. Wally Look Lai, "The Road to Thornfield Hall," *New World Quarterly* 4 (1968), pp. 17–27.

15. Kenneth Ramchand, *Introduction to West Indian Literature* (Middlesex, England: Thomas Nelson, 1976).

16. Kenneth Ramchand, "Terrified Consciousness," *Journal of Commonwealth Literature* 7 (1969), pp. 17. Also reprinted as a chapter of Ramchand's book *The West Indian Novel and Its Background* (1970; reprint, 2d ed., London: Heinemann, 1984).

17. Edward Brathwaite, *Contradictory Omens* (Kingston: Savacou Publications, 1974), pp. 33–38 (quoted in Ramchand, *Introduction,* p. 99).

18. Ramchand, *Introduction,* p. 93.

19. Ibid., p. 95.

20. In 1978 Ramchand wrote in the *Journal of Commonwealth Literature,* "Miss Rhys deserves to be doubly cherished as Elder and Fellow in the house of West Indian fiction"

(cited in Elaine Campbell, "An Expatriate at Home: Dominica's Elma Napier," *Kunapipi* 4, no. 1 [1985], p. 83).

21. Ramchand, *Introduction,* p. 100.

22. O. Dominique Mannoni, *Prospero and Caliban: The Psychology of Colonialism,* trans. Pamela Powesland (London: Methuen, 1956), p. 17 (originally published in 1950 by Editions du Seuil, Paris, under the title *Psychologie de la Colonisation*).

23. Ibid., p. 85.

24. Ibid,, p. 86.

25. Frantz Fanon, *Black Skin, White Masks,* trans. Charles L. Markmann (New York: Grove Press, 1967), pp. 93, 96–97 (originally published in 1952 in French under the title *Peau Noire, Masques Blancs*).

26. Albert Memmi, *The Colonizer and the Colonized* (1957; reprint, Boston: Beacon Press, 1967), p. 88.

27. Conor Cruise O'Brien, *Albert Camus of Europe and Africa* (New York: Viking Press, 1970), p. 11.

28. Quoted in O'Brien, *Albert Camus,* p. 92.

29. Derek Walcott, "The Schooner Flight," from *The Star-Apple Kingdom,* in *Collected Poems, 1948–1984* (New York: Farrar, Straus and Giroux, 1986), p. 346.

30. Mannoni, *Prospero,* p. 105.

31. Memmi, *Colonizer,* p. 3.

32. Mannoni, *Prospero,* p. 108.

33. Parry, "Problems," p. 37; emphasis added.

34. See Elizabeth Nunez-Harrell, "The Paradoxes of Belonging: The White West Indian Woman in Fiction" *Modern Fiction Studies* 31, no. 2 (summer 1985), pp. 281–83.

35. Jean Rhys, *Wide Sargasso Sea* (New York: W. W. Norton, 1966), p. 24; hereafter referred to in text citations and notes as *WSS.*

36. H. Hoetink, *Caribbean Race Relations: A Study in Two Variants* (London: Oxford University Press, 1967).

37. Ibid., pp. 3–31.

38. Ibid., p. 65.

39. Ibid., p. 67.

40. Gloria Anzaldúa, *Border/lands: La Frontera* (San Francisco: Spinsters/Aunt Lute, 1987); Edouard Glissant, *Caribbean Discourse: Selected Essays* (Charlottesville: University Press of Virginia, 1989); Guillermo Gómez-Peña, "Documented/Undocumented," in *Multi-cultural Literacy,* ed. Rick Simonson and Scott Walker (Saint Paul: Graywolf Press, 1988), pp. 127–34. See also Abdul R. JanMohamed "Worldliness-without-World, Homeless-as-Home: Toward a Definition of the Specular Border Intellectual," in *Edward Said: A Critical Reader* ed. Michael Sprinker (London: Basil Blackwell, 1992), pp. 96–120; Emily D. Hicks, *Border Writing: The Multidimensional Text* (Minneapolis: University of Minnesota Press, 1991); Renato Rosaldo, *Culture and Truth: The Remaking of Social Analysis* (Boston: Beacon Press, 1989).

41. Calling *Wide Sargasso Sea* "a novelistic colony," Sandra Drake sees the novel as deliberately derivative, its existence depending on the English classical literary canon. For this reason I have chosen to call the unnamed character in *Wide Sargasso Sea* "Rochester," recognizing Rhys's reworking of Brontë's character. It is important to remember, however, that Rhys deliberately does not call him Rochester, leaving both him and Jane Eyre unnamed and restoring to Antoinette her Caribbean name. Drake argues that while *Jane Eyre* is Rhys's starting point, the conclusion is "a triumph of cultural irony" (see Drake, "All That Foolishness/That All Foolishness: Race and Caribbean Culture as Thematics of Liberation in Jean Rhys's *Wide Sargasso Sea,*" *Critica* 2, no. 2 [fall 1990], p. 99).

42. For an interesting deconstruction in this regard, see Gayatri Spivak's discussion

of "the tangent" to the narrative of *Jane Eyre* represented by St. John Rivers. The story of St. John Rivers's imperialist desires and what Spivak calls his "soul-making" project in Calcutta "escapes the closed circle of *narrative* conclusion" and the closure of the feminist plot (see Spivak, "Three Women's Texts and a Critique of Imperialism," *Critical Inquiry* 12, no. 1 [Autumn 1985], p. 248).

43. Orlando Patterson, *Slavery and Social Death* (Cambridge, Mass.: Harvard University Press, 1982), pp. 62ff.

44. Spivak, "Three Women's Texts," p. 253 (cited in Parry, "Problems," p. 36).

45. Jean Rhys, "Again the Antilles," in *The Collected Short Stories* (New York: W. W. Norton, 1987), pp. 39–41; hereafter the story is referred to in text citations and notes as "AA."

46. Homi Bhabha, "Of Mimicry and Man: The Ambivalence of Colonial Discourse," *October* 28 (spring 1984), p. 130.

47. Fanon, *Black Skin,* p. 18; Bhabha, "Of Mimicry," p. 128.

48. For a summary of Bhabha's, Spivak's, and JanMohamed's positions, see Parry, "Problems," pp. 49–50.

49. Abdul R. JanMohamed, "The Economy of Manichean Allegory: The Function of Racial Difference in Colonialist Literature," *Critical Inquiry* 12, no. 1 (autumn 1985), pp. 60–61.

50. Jean Rhys, "The Day They Burned the Books," in *The Collected Short Stories,* pp. 151–57; hereafter the story is referred to in text citations and notes as "DTBB."

51. Michelle Cliff, *Abeng* (Trumansburg, N.Y.: Crossing Press, 1984), pp. 84–85.

52. Jamaica Kincaid, *Lucy* (New York: Plume, 1991), p. 30.

53. See Bruce King, *The New English Literatures: Cultural Nationalism in a Changing World* (London: Macmillan, 1980), p. 99; and Kenneth Ramchand, *The West Indian Novel and Its Background,* 2d ed. (London: Heinemann, 1983), pp. 63ff.

54. Jean Rhys, *Smile Please: An Unfinished Autobiography* (New York: Harper and Row, 1979), pp. 20–21; hereafter referred to in text citations and notes as *SP.*

55. JanMohamed, "Economy," p. 78.

56. Ibid., p. 79.

57. Lucy Wilson, " 'Women Must Have Spunks': Jean Rhys's West Indian Outcasts," *Modern Fiction Studies* 32, no. 3 (autumn 1986), pp. 439–44. For a discussion of Christophine as "the strongest character of decolonization," see Maria Luisa Nunes, "Becoming Whole: Literary Strategies of Decolonization in the Works of Jean Rhys, Frantz Fanon, and Oswald de Andrade," in *Proceedings of the Xth Congress of the International Comparative Literature Association/Actes du Xe Congrès de l'Association Internationale de Littérature Comparée,* vol. 3 (New York: Garland, 1982), pp. 28–33.

58. Parry, "Problems," p. 39.

59. I owe much of my initial interest in Rhys's use of the figure of the zombi to Sandra Drake, whose article on this theme additionally investigates the African and Afro-Caribbean narrative structure and cosmology in *Wide Sargasso Sea* (see Drake, "All That Foolishness"). Mary Lou Emery has also written a thorough examination of Obeah and Caribbean history in her chapter "*Wide Sargasso Sea:* Obeah Nights," in *Jean Rhys,* pp. 35–62.

60. The zombi is a specifically Caribbean figure created by the magic of Vodou (in Rhys's work, Obeah). Vodou itself is a creolized, syncretic religion, a combination of several West African religions transported to Saint Domingue with the slaves, adapted to the new social and political situation of slavery, and overlaid with Christian symbols introduced by English, French, and Spanish slaveholders. It is the religion and worldview of the greater part of the peasants and the urban proletariat of the republic of Haiti as

well as of members of the Haitian elite. See Claudine Michel, "Tapping the Wisdom of the Ancestors: An Attempt to Recast Vodou and Morality through *The Voice* of Mama Lola and Karen McCarthy Brown," in *The Caribbean: 500 Years of Human Development* (Kingston, Jamaica: University of West Indies Press, forthcoming); Alfred Métraux, *Voodoo in Haiti,* trans. Hugo Charteris (New York: Oxford University Press, 1959), pp. 25–57; James Haskins, *Voodoo and Hoodoo: Their Tradition and Craft as Revealed by Actual Practitioners* (New York: Stein and Day, 1978); Patrick Taylor, *The Narrative of Liberation: Perspectives on Afro-Caribbean Literature, Popular Culture, and Politics* (Ithaca, N.Y.: Cornell University Press, 1989), pp. 95–128. For descriptions of Obeah in seventeenth-, eighteenth-, and nineteenth-century British travel accounts and journals see *After Africa,* ed. Roger Abrahams and John Szwed (New Haven: Yale University Press, 1983), pp. 179–225. Michel discusses the sensationalized and exoticized renderings of the religion Vodou: "Scholars have for years pursued the possibility that the term 'Vodou' is of Dahomean origin, derived from the Fon word for 'God' or 'Spirit.' This is one means by which Vodou has been distinguished from 'Voodoo,' the sign of the fabulous creation of a Euro/American imaginary.... In the United States the word 'Voodoo' is used in a casual and derogatory manner to indicate, on the one hand, anything magic or miraculous or, on the other hand, anything from the deceptive to the downright evil" ("Tapping the Wisdom"). Rhys's representation of "Voodoo," as she calls it, hovers between respect and sensationalism.

61. Elaine Campbell, "Reflections of Obeah in Jean Rhys's Fiction," *Kunapipi* 4, no. 2 (1982), p. 44.

62. Taylor, *Narrative,* p. 102.

63. Maximilien Laroche, "The Myth of the Zombi," in *Exile and Tradition: Studies in African and Caribbean Literature,* ed. Rowland Smith (New York: African Publishing, 1976), p. 54; Drake, "All That Foolishness," p. 110; Taylor, *Narrative,* pp. 109–10.

64. Afro-American novelist Zora Neale Hurston was one of the first ethnographers to study Vodou seriously and to describe the larger social and political meanings of the zombi. In her 1938 study of Jamaican and Haitian "Voodoo," Hurston claims that belief in zombis was not restricted to the lower or peasant classes. Although they did not talk about it openly, the upper classes also had a profound fear of the zombi: "Think of the fiendishness of the thing. It is not good for a person who has lived all his life surrounded by a degree of fastidious culture, loved to his last breath by family and friends, to contemplate the probability of his resurrected body being dragged from the vault — the best that love and means could provide, to set to toiling ceaselessly in the banana fields, working like a beast, unclothed like a beast, and like a beast crouching in some foul den in the few hours allowed for rest and food. From an educated, intelligent being into an unthinking, unknowing beast." Even more threatening to the dominant class is the belief that the power for these transformations rests in the hands of the god Guédé, who is generally associated with the lower class. Métraux's physical description of the zombi includes "their absent-minded manner, their extinguished, almost glossy eyes, and above all...the nasal twang in their voices — a peculiarity which they share with the Guédé, spirits of the dead" (*Voodoo in Haiti,* p. 283 [cited in Laroche, "The Myth of the Zombi," p. 51]). According to Hurston, Guédé is a very powerful god who "is a grave-digger and opens the tombs and when he wishes to do so he takes out the souls and uses them in his service," but he also takes malicious delight in criticizing and ridiculing the dominant society. Although he is an invisible god who talks through the mouths of those he "mounts," he is believed to dress in the apparel of the lower class and to eat roasted peanuts: "So dressed and fed, he bites with sarcasm and slashes with ridicule the class that despises him" (Hurston, *Tell My Horse* [1938; reprint, Berkeley, Calif.: Turtle Island Press, 1981] p. 233).

65. See Helen Jaskoski, "Power Unequal to Man: The Significance of Conjure in

Works by Five Afro-American Authors," *Southern Folklore Quarterly* 38 (June 1974), pp. 91–108.

66. In his study of the social and biological aspects of zombiism Wade Davis notes two kinds of zombis in Haitian folklore. The first is the spirit zombi, a soul that has been bartered to a Bokor (conjurer) but released to "wander the earth until its destined time arrives to return to God." The other kind is the more familiar zombi whose body is sold into slavery. See Wade Davis, *Passage of Darkness: The Ethnobiology of the Haitian Zombi* (Chapel Hill: University of North Carolina Press, 1988), p. 60.

67. Ibid., p. 212.

68. Ibid., pp. 214–15.

69. Thomas Loe uses Davis's account to show that Rhys's allusions to zombification are thoroughly grounded in Caribbean practice and belief. See Loe, "Patterns of the Zombie in Jean Rhys's *Wide Sargasso Sea*," *World Literature Written in English* 31, no. 1 (1991), pp. 34–42.

70. Métraux, *Voodoo in Haiti,* p. 282 (quoted from Laroche's translation in "The Myth of the Zombi," p. 51).

71. Davis, *Passage,* p. 213.

72. Jean Rhys, *Voyage in the Dark,* in *The Complete Novels* (New York: W. W. Norton, 1985), p. 100; hereafter referred to in text citations and notes as *VD.*

73. Mary Lou Emery also notes the double meaning of Annette's use of "marooned" and compares the political status of the Maroons with that of planters' wives. Both, though technically free, maintain that freedom by terms that enslave others. See Mary Lou Emery, "The Politics of Form: Jean Rhys's Social Vision in *Voyage in the Dark* and *Wide Sargasso Sea*," *Twentieth Century Literature* 28, no. 4 (winter 1982), p. 426.

74. *WSS,* p. 154. See also Jean Rhys, *Quartet,* in *The Complete Novels,* p. 182; hereafter referred to in text citations and notes as *Q.*

75. Jean Rhys, *Good Morning, Midnight* (1939; reprint, London: André Deutsch, 1967); hereafter referred to in text citations and notes as *GMM.*

76. Mary Lou Emery identifies Marya as a zombi and, regarding such symbolism, remarks that in *Quartet* "we can see how colonial conflicts of power model the sexual conflicts of even this most European of all Rhys's novels" (*Jean Rhys,* pp. 110, 105).

77. Jean Rhys, "I Spy a Stranger," in *The Collected Short Stories,* p. 248.

78. Rochester's last words recall the despair of Lady Macbeth, who is finally overwhelmed by the enormity of the feelings she has suppressed until after the murder is complete (*Macbeth* 5.1.35–37).

79. Michel, "Tapping the Wisdom."

80. In an excellent article, Lee Erwin also points to this scene as "a refusal by the freed blacks to acknowledge any retracing of that past on the part of the master" (see " 'Like in a Looking-Glass': History and Narrative in *Wide Sargasso Sea*," *Novel: A Forum on Fiction* 22, no. 2 [winter 1989], p. 150). Sandra Drake also argues that Blacks use the Whites' derision of African belief as foolishness "and turn that European assessment to their own protection" ("All That Foolishness," p. 111).

81. Drake "All That Foolishness," pp. 99, 104.

82. Davis, *Passage,* p. 212.

83. Christophine uses traditional conjure symbols such as a hex of powder, candles in multiples of three, and a wine potion; these are described by Loudell F. Snow in "Con Men and Conjure Men: A Ghetto Image," in *Images of Healers,* ed. Anne Hudson Jones (Albany: State University of New York Press, 1983), vol. 2, pp. 45–78.

84. Like Christophine, who both heals and conjures Antoinette, Guédé, the god who sympathizes with the outrages of the poor, is known as both a doctor and root-worker and

the ruler of the spirits of the dead (Hurston, *Tell My Horse,* p. 327). His preparations, like Christophine's, are capable of healing the sick and oppressed and harming the oppressor. Métraux recalls the Maroon hero Macandal, who created powerful poisons which he had slaves use in the kitchens of white plantations throughout Saint Domingue. Historically, slave healers and conjurers have been seen by Whites as sources of danger to slave owners (Métraux, *Voodoo in Haiti,* pp. 46–47). Also see Alejo Carpentier's novel about Macandal and the Maroon rebellion, *The Kingdom of This World,* trans. Harriet DeOnís (New York: Alfred A. Knopf, 1957). Although he was not a practitioner of Vodou, and in fact had a great fear of it, Toussaint-Louverture began his military career as an "herb-doctor" using magic prescriptions (Métraux, *Voodoo in Haiti,* p. 48). In the United States this potentially threatening knowledge of the black herb-doctor increased the discomfort and fear the slave owners of the South had concerning the "strange" practices of black slave-doctors and led to legal restrictions in the black arts of healing. An 1844 Tennessee judicial verdict (*Macon v. State*) prohibited slaves from practicing medicine for fear that they would inspire insurrectionary movements on the part of North American slaves. See Helen Tennicliff Catteral, ed., *Judicial Cases concerning American Slavery and the Negro* (New York: Octagon Books, 1968), vol. 2, p. 520 (cited in Richard Harrison Shryock, "Medical Practice in the Old South," in *Medicine in America: Historical Essays* [Baltimore: Johns Hopkins Press, 1966], p. 63); also see Todd L. Savitt, *Medicine and Slavery: The Diseases and Health Care of Blacks in Antebellum Virginia* (Urbana: University of Illinois Press, 1978): "By 1748 so many blacks claimed to be doctors — some falsely, in order to procure and prepare poisons against their masters or enemies, both black and white — that the colonial legislature prohibited all slaves, on pain of death, from administering medicines without the consent of the owners of both the 'doctor' and the prospective black patient" (p. 175).

85. Christophine's conjuring might also be read as her punishment of Antoinette for bringing such violence (both Rochester's and her own) to the island community. The sentence is commuted at the end by Antoinette's identification with the black community.

86. To please Rochester, Antoinette offers to order another dress in the style he likes — à la Joséphine, made in the Paris of the West Indies, St. Pierre. It is also interesting to note that Josephine was a white Creole from Martinique and, like Antoinette, was the daughter of a plantation family.

87. Abrahams and Szwed, *After Africa,* p. 186.

88. Emery, *Jean Rhys,* pp. 50–52.

89. Métraux, *Voodoo in Haiti,* p. 283 (quoted in Laroche, "The Myth of the Zombi," p. 51).

90. Erwin, "Like in a Looking-Glass," pp. 155–56.

4 / "This Cold Thief Place"

1. Critics such as Helen Tiffin and Erika Smilowitz have pointed out that Rhys creates powerful parallels between colonialism and sexual exploitation; indeed, Rhys exposes colonialism as a particularly pernicious rhetoric and practice for women. See Helen Tiffin, "Mirror and Mask: Colonial Motifs in the Novels of Jean Rhys," *World Literature Written in English* 17, no. 1 (April 1978), pp. 328–41; Erika Smilowitz, "Childlike Women and Paternal Men: Colonialism in Jean Rhys's Fiction," *Ariel: A Review of International Literature* (special edition: Commonwealth Women Writers) 17, no. 4 (Oct. 1986), pp. 93–103.

2. Both authors produced a series of novels relating to this experience. Their first novels are: Samuel Selvon, *Lonely Londoners* (1956; reprint, Harlow, England: Longman, 1985); George Lamming, *In the Castle of My Skin* (New York: McGraw-Hill, 1953).

264 / *Notes to pages 145–155*

3. For example, see Kenneth Ramchand's *An Introduction to the Study of West Indian Literature* (Middlesex, England: Thomas Nelson, 1976); Bruce King, ed., *West Indian Literature* (Hamden, Conn.: Archon Books, 1979). This trend is changing, and Simon Gikandi's recent work *Writing in Limbo* has chapters on Merle Hodge, Paule Marshall, and Michelle Cliff (see *Writing in Limbo: Modernism and Caribbean Literature* [Ithaca, N.Y.: Cornell University Press, 1992]).

4. Merle Hodge, *Crick Crack, Monkey* (1970; reprint, London: Heinemann, 1985), pp. 61–62.

5. Dionne Brand, "I Used to Like the Dallas Cowboys," in *Sans Souci and Other Stories* (Ithaca, N.Y.: Firebrand Books, 1989), p. 115–29; hereafter referred to in text citations and notes as "IUL."

6. For Sandra Drake, the struggle for Antoinette's survival, which represents the survival of the Caribbean as something other than a copy of Britain, is fought and won at the conclusion of the novel. The destruction of Thornfield represents the colonial refusal of European patriarchy and empire and the commitment to indigenous cultural materials instead. See Drake, "All That Foolishness/That All Foolishness," *Critica* 2, no. 2 (fall 1990), p. 100.

7. Mary Lou Emery provides a rich reading of Antoinette's dreams by reading them in the context of Caribbean cultural motifs and theories about the language and logic of dreams. Like Sandra Drake, Emery reads the final dream as Antoinette's spiritual reidentification with black Caribbean culture. See Emery, *Jean Rhys at "World's End": Novels of Colonial and Sexual Exile* (Austin: University of Texas Press, 1990), pp. 53–60.

8. Jean Rhys, "Temps Perdi," in *The Collected Short Stories* (New York: W. W. Norton, 1987), p. 257; hereafter referred to in text citations and notes as "TP."

9. Gayatri Spivak, "Three Women's Texts and a Critique of Imperialism," *Critical Inquiry* 12, no. 1 (autumn 1985), p. 251.

10. Rhys was fond of theatrical metaphors, drawing on her own experience as a chorus girl. Anna, who also becomes a chorus girl in *Voyage in the Dark,* describes her arrival in England: "It was as if a curtain had fallen, hiding everything I had ever known."

11. Benita Parry reads this difference between "belief" and "knowledge" as Christophine's challenge to Rochester and Western empiricism: "'Read and write I don't know. Other things I know.' She walked away without looking back" (*WSS,* p. 161). See Benita Parry, "Problems in Current Theories of Colonial Discourse," *Oxford Literary Review* 9, nos. 1–2 (1987), p. 39.

12. Jean Rhys, "Trio," in *The Collected Short Stories.*

13. Kevin Magarey, "The Sense of Place in Doris Lessing and Jean Rhys," in *A Sense of Place in the New Literatures in English,* ed. Peggy Nightingale (St. Lucia: University of Queensland Press, 1986), p. 55.

14. Teresa O'Connor quotes extensively from the Black Exercise Books that Rhys kept and that are now housed in the McFarlin Library and the University of Tulsa. See Teresa O'Connor, *Jean Rhys: The West Indian Novels* (New York: New York University Press), pp. 4, 25–26. Carol Ann Howells also uses the Black Exercise Books to examine Rhys's relationship with Mr. Howard and the effect this had on her psychologically and her desire to understand this relationship in her writing (Howells, *Jean Rhys* [New York: St. Martin's Press, 1991], pp. 14–20 and 135–38). See also Mary Lou Emery, "Modernism and the Marginal Woman: A Sociocritical Approach to the Novels of Jean Rhys," Ph.D diss. Stanford University, 1982, pp. 16–19.

15. Deborah Kelly Kloepfer examines the absent mother and the pre-Oedipal mother-daughter dyad as central themes in Rhys's work. See her *The Unspeakable Mother: Forbidden Discourse in Jean Rhys and H.D.* (Ithaca, N.Y.: Cornell University Press, 1989).

16. Emery, "Modernism," p. 98.

17. As Emery points out, the prostitute is imagined in racial as well as sexual terms; for instance, in *Voyage in the Dark,* Hester's version of the lady/whore dichotomy actually reveals itself as a lady/"nigger" dichotomy (Emery, "Modernism," p. 75).

18. Jean Rhys, "Let Them Call It Jazz," in *The Collected Short Stories;* hereafter referred to in text citations and notes as "LT."

19. Louise Bennett, "Colonization in Reverse," in *The Penguin Book of Caribbean Verse in English,* ed. Paula Burnett (Harmondsworth, England: Penguin Books, 1986), pp. 32–33.

20. Stella Bowen wrote of Rhys's fundamental distrust of the law: "She regarded the law as the instrument of the 'haves' against the 'have nots' and was well acquainted with every rung of that long and dismal ladder by which the respectable citizen descends towards degradation" (Bowen, *Drawn from Life* [1941; reprint, London: Virago Press, 1984], pp. 166–67). Also cited in O'Connor (*Jean Rhys,* p. 61), who compares Bowen's description of Rhys with Rhys's description of Bowen as Mrs. Heidler in *Quartet.*

In *Wide Sargasso Sea* the law is also on the side not of the right but of the powerful. Christophine is forced out of the conflict with Rochester, and thus out of the text itself, by the threat of Spanish Town police and the "dark jail" (*WSS,* p. 20).

21. Rosalind Miles, *The Fiction of Sex: Themes and Functions of Sex Difference in the Modern Novel* (New York: Barnes and Noble, 1974) p. 98.

22. Stephen Muecke, in an article on the Australian aborigines' confrontation with the English pioneers, contrasts the fluidity of the "nomad" or the migrant worker with the fixity of the state. See Muecke, "The Discourse of Nomadology: Phylums in Flux," *Art and Text* (Winter 1984), pp. 24–40 (cited in Caren Kaplan, "Deterritorializations: The Rewriting of Home and Exile in Western Feminist Discourse," *Cultural Critique* 6 [spring 1987], pp. 187–98).

23. Alice Walker, "Nineteen Fifty-Five," in *You Can't Keep a Good Woman Down* (New York: Harcourt Brace Jovanovich, 1981).

24. George Orwell, *Down and Out in Paris and London* (1933; reprint, New York: Berkeley Publishing, 1959), pp. 147–48.

25. Daphne Patai, *The Orwell Mystique: A Study in Male Ideology* (Amherst: University of Massachusetts Press, 1984), p. 68.

26. Ibid., p. 67. Andrew Gurr points out Doris Lessing's ironic use of the phrase "free woman" to describe the displaced urban women in her fiction. See Andrew Gurr, *Writers in Exile: The Creative Use of Home in Modern Literature* (Sussex, England: Harvester Press, 1981), p. 125. The political resonance of the phrase can be heard when Christophine challenges Rochester's power in *Wide Sargasso Sea* by referring to herself as a "free woman" just before she walks out of the text.

27. Susan Merrill Squier, ed., *Women Writers and the City: Essays in Feminist Literary Criticism* (Knoxville: University of Tennessee Press, 1984). See especially, Susan Merrill Squier, "Tradition and Revision: The Classic City Novel and Virginia Woolf's *Night and Day,*" pp. 114–33; Louise A. DeSalvo, "Every Woman Is an Island: Vita Sackville-West, the Image of the City, and the Pastoral Idyll," pp. 97–113; and Sydney Janet Kaplan, "'A Gigantic Mother': Katherine Mansfield's London," pp. 161–75.

28. Howells, *Jean Rhys,* pp. 26–27; Emery, "Modernism," p. 11. Howells (*Jean Rhys,* chap. 5) provides a compelling reading of *Good Morning, Midnight,* as a self-conscious rewriting of male modernism's representation of the city (Eliot) and of female subjectivity (Joyce).

29. O'Connor, *Jean Rhys,* p. 41.

30. Jean Rhys, "Discourse of a Lady Standing Dinner to a Down-and-Out Friend,"

and "Mannequin," in *The Collected Short Stories;* the latter story is hereafter referred to in text citations and as "M."

31. In Rhys's original draft of the novel Anna dies. She changed the ending under pressure from the publisher, a decision she always regretted.

32. Nancy Casey, "Study in the Alienation of a Creole Woman: Jean Rhys's Voyage in the Dark," *Caribbean Quarterly* 19 (Sept. 1973), p. 99.

33. Peter Wolfe, *Jean Rhys* (Boston: Twayne, 1980), pp. 24, 28.

34. Ibid., p. 16.

35. For example, see ibid., p. 23.

36. Bruce Robbins, "Modernism in History, Modernism in Power," in *Modernism Reconsidered,* ed. Robert Kiely (Cambridge, Mass.: Harvard University Press, 1983), pp. 229–45.

37. Judith Gardiner, for instance, praises Rhys for her own implied criticisms of modernism in *Good Morning, Midnight:* "She does not treat alienation as an existential fact but as the specific historical result of social polarizations about sex, class, and morality" (Gardiner, "Good Morning, Midnight; Good Night, Modernism," *Boundary* 2, no. 1/2 [fall–winter 1982–83], p. 233). Gardiner's comparison of the treatment Rhys receives as a modernist with that the male writers of that tradition receive is suggestive: "When a writer like Joyce or Eliot writes about an alienated man estranged from himself, he is read as a portrait of the diminished possibilities of human existence in modern society. When Rhys writes about an alienated woman estranged from herself, critics applaud her perceptive but narrow depiction of female experience and tend to narrow her vision even further by labelling it both pathological and autobiographical" (p. 247). Simon Gikandi describes Caribbean modernism as differing from "high modernism" in two respects: "It is highly overdetermined by history, which it seeks to confront rather than escape; it is also closely implicated in political and economic theories of modernization" (Gikandi, *Writing in Limbo,* p. 254). It might therefore be useful to read Rhys's fiction in the particular genre of Caribbean modernism.

5 / "With the Logic of a Creole"

1. Jamaica Kincaid, *A Small Place* (New York: Farrar Straus Giroux, 1988), p. 42.

2. Judith Raiskin, "The Art of History: An Interview with Michelle Cliff," *The Kenyon Review* n.s. 15, no. 1 (winter 1993), p. 61.

3. Michelle Cliff, *Abeng* (Trumansburg, N.Y.: Crossing Press, 1984); hereafter referred to in text citations and notes as *A;* idem, *No Telephone to Heaven* (New York: Dutton, 1987); hereafter referred to as *NTH;* idem, *The Land of Look Behind* (Ithaca, N.Y.: Firebrand, 1985); idem, *Bodies of Water* (New York: Dutton, 1990).

4. José Piedra, "Literary Whiteness and the Afro-Hispanic Difference," *New Literary History* 18, no. 2 (winter 1987), pp. 308–9, 313.

5. Virginia R. Domínguez, *White by Definition: Social Classification in Creole Louisiana* (New Brunswick, N.J.: Rutgers University Press, 1986), p. 46.

6. For the history of cases that sought to overturn these mathematical formations of racial identity, see ibid., especially Domínguez's discussion of the Susie Phipps case in which Phipps went to court in 1982 to have her racial status changed from "Colored" to "White." Phipps's racial identity was based on records indicating that her great-great-great-great-grandmother was a "Negress" and on the 1970 Louisiana statute "that made 1/32 'Negro blood' the dividing line between white and black" (p. 2). Michael Omi and Howard Winant also discuss the significance of this case in *Racial Formation in the United States from the 1960s to the 1980s* (New York: Routledge, 1986), p. 57. For the laws that still define

the boundaries of racial categories, see Omi and Winant's book, pp. 268–71, and F. James Davis, *Who Is Black? One Nation's Definition* (University Park: Pennsylvania State University Press, 1991), pp. 9–13.

7. Roberto Fernández Retamar, *Caliban and Other Essays,* trans. Edward Baker (Minneapolis: University of Minnesota Press, 1989).

8. Nancy Stepan, "Biological Degeneration: Races and Proper Places," in *Degeneration: The Dark Side of Progress,* ed. J. Edward Chamberlin and Sander L. Gilman (New York: Columbia University Press, 1985), p. 99.

9. Marianna Torgovnick provides a cultural history of this Western concept of "going native" and the fear of miscegenation in her book *Gone Primitive: Savage Intellects, Modern Lives* (Chicago: University of Chicago Press, 1990).

10. Jean Rhys, "Pioneers, Oh, Pioneers," in *The Collected Short Stories* (New York: W. W. Norton, 1987), pp. 275–84.

11. See also Stuart Hall, "Cultural Identity and Diaspora," in *Identity: Community, Culture, Difference,* ed. Jonathan Rutherford (London: Lawrence and Wishant, 1990), pp. 222–37.

12. Jean Bernabé, Patrick Chamoiseau, and Raphaël Confiant, "In Praise of Creoleness," trans. by Mohamed B. Taleb Khyar, *Callaloo* 13 (1990), pp. 886, 888, 892, 894.

13. Ibid., pp. 896, 901.

14. Iris M. Zavala, "Representing the Colonial Subject," in *1492–1992: Re/Discovering Colonial Writing,* ed. René Jara and Nicholas Spadaccini, Hispanic Issues 4 (Minneapolis: Prisma Institute), pp. 336–37. Zavala describes the visual iconography that accompanied this colonial taxonomy and explains the meaning of some of these signifiers: "An etymological explanation is necessary to grasp the carnival images and the significance of these homologies. *Zambayo* means 'zambaio' or crossed-eyed, and in the sense of Indian or black is 'medically explained' in the sixteenth century by the anatomical singularity of the blacks, portrayed with crossed-legs. Other metonymical freed signifiers, such as *'chamizo,' 'albino,' 'calpamulato,' 'morisco,'* were based on shades of complexion (the *'color quebrado'*); others were zoological, deliberately derogatory — 'coyote,' 'mule,' 'wolf,' 'cow'; while yet others directly alluded to the intricate fluctuations of conceived 'advances' and 'retreats' of the population. Especially where Indian and black blood was dominant, the names denoted scorn, contempt, mockery. Such were the representations of the multiple imperial gaze" (pp. 337–38).

15. Irene Diggs in her study of color classifications in colonial Spanish America interprets *tente en el aire* as revealing neither progress nor regression in color. *Albarrazado* is a classification meaning affected with white leprosy. The *zambo* is "a very ferocious specie of large African monkey with a dog-like head." Diggs explains the metaphors of these labels: "It was not exactly a coincidence that many of the names applied were of zoological origin: mule, coyote, wolf, cow — but rather a genuine expression of the thought of the conquistador: he had only contempt for all those who did not belong to his privileged *casta,* the retainers of wealth and power" (Diggs, "Color in Colonial Spanish America," *Journal of Negro History* 38, no. 4 [Oct. 1953], p. 12; see also pp. 405–8 on "nomenclature").

16. Cliff addresses this in an interview: "I dedicated *Abeng* to Bessie Head and to Jean Toomer who wrote *Cane* and who was light-skinned and who had in his life terrific conflicts about his own racial identification. And I want to acknowledge the damage that is done, or can be done, to and by those of us who are light-skinned" (see Raiskin, "Art of History," p. 60).

17. Domínguez, *White,* p. 90.

18. For instance, see Estelle Freedman and John D'Emilio, *Intimate Matters: The History of Sexuality in America* (New York: Harper and Row, 1988), esp. chap. 5, "Race and

Sexuality"; Olivia Espín, "Cultural and Historical Influences on Sexuality in Hispanic/Latin Women: Implications for Psychotherapy," in *Pleasure and Danger: Exploring Female Sexuality,* ed. Carole Vance (London: Pandora Press, 1984), pp. 149–64; Tómas Almaguer, "Chicano Men: A Cartography of Homosexual Identity and Behavior," in *The Lesbian and Gay Studies Reader,* ed. Henry Abelove et al. (New York: Routledge, 1993), pp. 255–73; Marlon Riggs, *Tongues Untied* (video, 1990).

19. Ann L. Stoler, "Making Empire Respectable: The Politics of Race and Sexual Morality in 20th-Century Colonial Cultures," *American Ethnologist* 16, no. 4 (Nov. 1989), p. 650.

20. Françoise Lionnet remarks that the absence in the English language of a word equivalent to *métis* or *créole* signifies the intense discomfort of non-Whites about ambiguous racial status: "The Anglo-American consciousness seems unable to accommodate miscegenation positively through language. It is a serious blind spot of the English language which thus implies that persons of indeterminate race are freaks" (Lionnet, *Autobiographical Voices: Race, Gender, Self-Portraiture* [Ithaca, N.Y.: Cornell University Press, 1989], p. 14).

21. Michelle Cliff, "Burning Bush," in *Bodies of Water,* p. 77. Cliff cites Elizabeth Alexander's poem "The Venus Hottentot," which similarly gives voice to the black woman "freak" Saartjie Baartman, who was displayed naked in Europe in the early nineteenth century. The poem appears in the collection *The Venus Hottentot* (Charlottesville: University Press of Virginia, 1990). Cliff cites this poem in her essay "Caliban's Daughter: The Tempest and the Teapot," *Frontiers* 12, ·no. 2 (1991), pp. 36–51.

22. Michelle Cliff, "Screen Memory," in *Bodies of Water,* p. 90; Booker T. Washington, *Up from Slavery,* in *Three Negro Classics* (New York: Avon Books, 1965), p. 82. Cited in Diana Fuss, *Essentially Speaking: Feminism, Nature and Difference* (New York: Routledge, 1989), p. 73.

23. See Eve Sedgwick, *Epistemology of the Closet* (Berkeley: University of California Press, 1990), p. 2.

24. Nancy Leys Stepan, "Race and Gender: The Role of Analogy in Science," in *Anatomy of Racism,* ed. David Theo Goldberg (Minneapolis: University of Minnesota Press, 1990), pp. 38–57; Sander L. Gilman, "Black Bodies, White Bodies: Toward an Iconography of Female Sexuality in Late Nineteenth-Century Art, Medicine, and Literature," *Critical Inquiry* 12, no. 1 (autumn 1985), pp. 204–42; Elaine Showalter, *Sexual Anarchy: Gender and Culture at the Fin de Siècle* (New York: Viking Penguin, 1990), esp. chap. 9; Anita Levy, *Other Women: The Writing of Class, Race, and Gender, 1832–1898* (Princeton, N.J.: Princeton University Press, 1991), esp. chap. 5; and Lucius Outlaw, "Toward a Critical Theory of 'Race,'" in *Anatomy of Racism,* ed. David Theo Goldberg (Minneapolis: University of Minnesota Press, 1990), pp. 58–82.

Nancy Stepan examines the way the role of analogy in science determines the "data" that are found. For instance, the race-gender analogy is supported in nineteenth-century science by measurements of skull, jaw, and brain weights. Women's smaller brains and protruding jaws are used to argue that women, like the "lower races," are evolutionarily behind European men. Stepan describes this process where, "by analogy with the so-called lower races, women, the sexually deviate, the criminal, the urban poor, and the insane were in one way or another constructed as biological 'races apart' whose differences from the white male, and likenesses to each other, 'explained' their different and lower position in the social hierarchy" ("Race and Gender," pp. 40–41). This metaphorical linking, while explaining the social power of upper-class white men in biological terms, is also potentially threatening by suggesting that the boundaries between groups are porous. By the mid–nineteenth century, Stepan shows, racial biology thus became "a science of boundaries between groups and the degenerations that threatened when those boundaries were transgressed" (Stepan, "Biological Degeneration: Races and Proper Places," in *Degeneration: The Dark Side of Progress,* ed. Edward Chamberlin and Sander L. Gilman [New York: Columbia University Press, 1985], p. 98).

25. For instance, see Michel Foucault, *The History of Sexuality,* vol. 1, trans. Robert Hurley (New York: Vintage Books, 1978); Jeffrey Weeks, *Against Nature: Essays on History, Sexuality, and Identity* (London: Rivers Oram Press, 1991); Carole Vance, "Social Construction Theory: Problems in the History of Sexuality," in *Homosexuality, Which Homosexuality?* ed. Dennis Altman et al. (London: GMP Publishers, 1989), pp. 13–34.

26. For a more thorough discussion of this connection, see my article "Inverts and Hybrids: Lesbian Rewritings of Sexual and Racial Identities," in *Lesbian Postmodern,* ed. Laura Doan (New York: Columbia University Press, 1994), pp. 156–72.

27. Raiskin, "Art of History," p. 69.

28. Meryl F. Schwartz, "An Interview with Michelle Cliff," *Contemporary Literature* 34, no. 4 (winter 1993), p. 601.

29. As Judith Butler describes lesbian identity: "To say that I 'play' at being [a lesbian] is not to say that I am not one 'really'; rather, how and where I play at being one is the way in which 'being' gets established, instituted, circulated, and confirmed. This is not a performance from which I can take radical distance, for this is deep-seated play, psychically entrenched play, *and this 'I' does not play its lesbianism as a role*" (Butler, "Imitation and Gender Insubordination," in *Inside/Out: Lesbian Theories, Gay Theories,* ed. Diana Fuss [New York: Routledge, 1991], p. 18).

30. Hall, "Cultural Identity," p. 225.

31. Cliff's unflinching insistence on the power of ideology and the ways it works through us is highlighted by a comparison with a more utopian reworking of the race/ sexuality conflation by Gloria Anzaldúa in her collection *Border/lands.* Whereas Cliff reveals the myths of colonial classification systems to suggest possible alliances across difference and the limitations of such alliances, Anzaldúa envisions a collapse of the systems of categorization altogether through the "mestiza and queer consciousness" created by them. For an analysis of this strategy and its historical antecedents, see my article "Inverts and Hybrids."

Antonio Benítez Rojo, even more vehemently than Cliff, is suspicious of such arguments of salvation, even for political reasons: "At the moment that the contradiction is established, a possible reconciliation appears: the syncretic rhythm, the mestizo rhythm, the mulatto text. Such a rhythm, such a text, is not real; it is a *mirage.* In reality, neither the culture nor the literature of the Caribbean are *mestizo,* of mixed blood. They cannot be so because such a mixture is impossible, if by it we mean the condition of having reached a kind of 'unity' or 'totality.' The promise of *mestizaje,* its solution, did not originate in Africa or with any other People of the Sea. We're dealing here with a positivist and logocentric argument, an argument that sees the biological, economic, social and cultural 'whitening' of the Caribbean black as a series of steps toward 'progress,' thus legitimating conquest, slavery, colonization and dependence. In fact, this *mestizaje* is a concentration of conflicts, an exacerbation, brought about by the closeness and density of the Caribbean situation. This literature shouldn't be seen as anything but a system of texts in intense conflict with themselves" (Benítez Rojo, "The Repeating Island," trans. James Maraniss, *New England Review and Bread Loaf Quarterly* 7, no. 4 [summer 1985], pp. 450–51). Cliff refers to this article in her discussion of Caribbean identity in the interview "Art of History," p. 63.

32. Michelle Cliff, "If I Could Write This in Fire, I Would Write This in Fire...," in *The Land of Look Behind* (Ithaca, N.Y.: Firebrand Books, 1985), pp. 72–73; hereafter referred to in text citations and notes as "IICW."

33. Through the character Rachel in *Free Enterprise,* Cliff provides another impor-

tant moment when Jewish, African, and postcolonial diaspora exist in the same frame of reference.

34. Marc Shell, "Marranos (Pigs); or, From Coexistence to Toleration," *Critical Inquiry* 17 (winter 1991), pp. 306–35. Shell writes: "One might think here of the anti-*converso* pamphlet of 1488 that argued that converts were like 'the monstrous animal which carried Mohammed on his back from Jerusalem to Mecca and which, like the *conversos,* belonged to no known species'" (p. 321).

35. Shell, "Marranos (Pigs)," pp. 308–9.

36. In his study of comparative national racial systems, F. James Davis notes the peculiar historical status of Jamaican "mulattoes": "A major motive for manumitting mulattoes was to use them as soldiers to combat rebellions, and they were given strong incentives to remain loyal to the whites and to adopt British culture. All Jamaican 'coloureds' were freed and given full rights in 1830, after which they challenged the slave system and other white policies; yet they worked within the political system rather than rebelling. The free 'coloureds' became Europeanized allies of the British West Indians and achieved a middle status that was to remain distinctly separate from that of unmixed blacks after slavery was ended" (Davis, *Who Is Black?* p. 108).

37. Ngũgĩ Wa Thiong'o, *Decolonizing the Mind: The Politics of Language in African Literature.* Portsmouth, N.H.: Heinemann, 1986.

38. Michelle Cliff, preface to *The Land of Look Behind,* p. 13.

39. Ibid., p. 14.

40. Bernabé, Chamoiseau, and Confiant, "In Praise of Creoleness," p. 895.

41. Edouard Glissant, *Caribbean Discourse: Selected Essays,* trans. J. Michael Dash (Charlottesville: University Press of Virginia, 1989), p. 182.

42. Ibid., p. 12.

43. In her article on Caribbean writers' disruption of the colonial canon, Gay Wilentz remarks on this specific metaphor in English: "The literary language available to [Caribbean writers] reflects the internal domination inscribed in it. For example, the use of 'black' as a negative metaphor in the English language is well documented; formerly colonized black people have felt the need to de-Anglicize and deracialize English..." (Wilentz, "English Is a Foreign Anguish: Caribbean Writers and the Disruption of the Colonial Canon," in *Decolonizing Tradition: New Views of Twentieth-Century "British" Literary Canons,* ed. Karen R. Lawrence [Urbana: University of Illinois Press, 1992], p. 266).

44. Kincaid, *A Small Place,* p. 31.

45. See Maria Helena Lima, "Revolutionary Developments: Michelle Cliff's 'No Telephone to Heaven' and Merle Collins's 'Angel,'" *Ariel* 24, no. 1 (Jan. 1993), p. 42.

46. Jamaica Kincaid, in her scathing analysis of the economic, political, and cultural condition of the so-called independent Antigua in *A Small Place,* also emphasizes the connection between colonialism and tourism. Addressed in the second person to the white/tourist/colonialist/reader, the voice of this text condemns the "ugly human being" a tourist always is for not seeing, let alone understanding, both the poverty and the corruption of the government, a government that, for instance, celebrates the Hotel Training School while letting the damaged library remain unrepaired. In Kincaid's next novel, *Lucy,* the main character talks about her shame in coming from a place North Americans call "fun." *A Small Place* undermines the tourist books that continue to romanticize "the Happy Isles" and the elusive but possible contact between "us" and "real Caribbeans."

47. Paul Gilroy examines not only the transnational nature of black culture in Britain but the slipperiness of the concept of "British culture" itself: "Blacks born, nurtured and schooled in this country are, in significant measure, British even as their presence redefines the meaning of the term.... The penetration of black forms into the dominant culture

mean[s] that it is impossible to theorize black culture in Britain without developing a new perspective on British culture *as a whole*" (Gilroy, *There Ain't No Black in the Union Jack* [London: Hutchinson Education, 1987], pp. 155–56). As Kobena Mercer puts it: "Black film-making not only critiques traditional conceptions of Britishness, which have depended on the subordination of 'other' ethnic identities, but calls the very concept of a coherent national identity into question" ("Recoding Narratives of Race and Nation," in *Black Film, British Cinema,* ed. Kobena Mercer [London: Institute of Contemporary Arts, 1988], p. 5).

48. Benítez Rojo, "Repeating Island," p. 432.

49. William Luis, "Caribbean Cycles: Displacement and Change," *New England Review and Bread Loaf Quarterly* 7, no. 4 (summer 1985), pp. 412–30.

50. Roberto Fernández Retamar also attributes to American movies the dissemination of racist ideology at once denied and perpetrated by white American culture, a culture that would "stigmatize in Hitler what they applauded as a healthy Sunday diversion in westerns and Tarzan films. Those movies proposed to the world — and even to those of us who are kin to the communities under attack and who rejoiced in the evocation of our own extermination — the monstrous racial criteria that have accompanied the United States from its beginning to the genocide in Indochina" (Fernández Retamar, *Caliban and Other Essays,* p. 4).

51. Cliff writes of this ending: "While essentially tragic, I see [the ending] and planned it as an ending that completes the circle, actually triangle, of the character's life. In her death she has achieved complete identification with her homeland. . . . Her death occurs at the moment she relinquishes human language, when the cries of birds are no longer translated by her into signifiers of human history, her own and her people's, but become pure sound, the same music heard by the Arawak and the Carib" (Cliff, "Caliban's Daughter," pp. 45–46).

6 / "Miskien of Gold Gemake"

1. Michelle Cliff, "Caliban's Daughter: The Tempest and the Teapot," *Frontiers* 12, no. 2, p. 38.

2. Zoë Wicomb, *You Can't Get Lost in Cape Town* (New York: Pantheon, 1987); hereafter referred to in text citations and notes as *YCGL.*

3. Hein Willemse, "Die Skrille Sonbesies: Emergent Black Afrikaans Poets in Search of Authority," in *Rendering Things Visible: Essays on South African Literary Culture,* ed. Martin Trump (Athens: Ohio University Press, 1990), p. 370.

4. V. A. February, *Mind Your Colour: The "Coloured" Stereotype in South African Literature* (London: Kegan Paul, 1981), pp. 10, 80, 91, 94.

5. V. A. February points out that Dr. E. Dönges, an Afrikaner cabinet minister, cited these authors as well as Regina Neser, the author of *Kinders van Ishmaël* (February, *Mind Your Colour,* pp. vii, 67).

6. February, *Mind Your Colour,* p. 26.

7. Sarah Gertrude Millin, *God's Step-Children* (London: Constable, 1924); hereafter referred to in text citations and notes as *GSC.*

8. For a discussion of the metaphors of blood in race science, anthropology, and literature with particular attention to Millin's novels, see J. M. Coetzee, "Blood, Flaw, Taint, Degeneration: The Case of Sarah Gertrude Millin," *English Studies in Africa* 23, no. 1 (March 1980), pp. 41–58.

9. Zoë Wicomb, "Another Story," in *Colors of a New Day: Writing for South Africa,*

ed. Sarah Lefanu and Stephen Hayward (New York: Pantheon, 1990), pp. 1–15; hereafter the story is referred to in text citations and notes as "AS."

10. Ian Goldin, *Making Race: The Politics and Economics of Coloured Identity in South Africa* (London and New York: Longman Press, 1987), p. 24.

11. Afrikaners have traditionally preferred the term "Bantu," which means literally "the people," rather than "African," a term that would threaten their own identification as the genuine African population (see February, *Mind Your Colour*, p. 3). In many white texts about South Africa, only the whites are called "South Africans" while all other groups are identified by their racial or tribal labels. For an analysis of texts describing South Africa, see Beverley Naidoo, *Censoring Reality: An Examination of Books on South Africa* (London: ILEA Centre for Anti-racist Education, 1984), p. 12.

12. Goldin, *Making Race,* pp. 25–26.

13. Elsa Joubert, *Poppie Nongena: One Woman's Struggle against Apartheid* (New York: Holt, 1987); originally published in Afrikaans in 1978 under the title *Die Swerfjare van Poppie Nongena.*

14. February, *Mind Your Colour,* pp. 4–7; see also Arthur Suzman, *Race Classification and Definition in the Legislation of the Union of South Africa, 1910–1960: A Survey and Analysis* (Johannesburg: South African Institute of Race Relations, 1960), pp. 354–55.

15. Muriel Horrell, *Legislation and Race Relations: A Summary of the Main South African Laws Which Affect Race Relations* (Johannesburg: South African Institute of Race Relations, 1963), pp. 10–11; February, *Mind Your Colour,* pp. 3–4.

16. Both Trinh T. Minh-ha and Françoise Lionnet have cited this extraordinary report in their own arguments about hybrid identities and *méstissage.* See Trinh T. Minh-ha "Not You/Like You: Post-colonial Women and the Interlocking Questions of Identity and Difference," *Inscriptions* 3/4 (1988), p. 76; Françoise Lionnet, *Autobiographical Voices: Race, Gender, Self-Portraiture* (Ithaca, N.Y.: Cornell University Press, 1989), p. 10, n. 17. Both authors refer to the article "The Crazy Game of Musical Chairs," *Time,* March 9, 1987.

17. In Pierre Hugo, ed. *Quislings or Realists? A Documentary Study of "Coloured" Politics in South Africa* (Johannesburg: Ravan Press, 1978), p. 67.

18. In ibid., p. 79.

19. In ibid., p. 174.

20. Barbara Harlow, *Resistance Literature* (New York: Methuen, 1987); Caren Kaplan, "Resisting Autobiography: Out-law Genres and Transnational Feminist Subjects," in *De/colonizing the Subject: The Politics of Gender in Women's Autobiography,* ed. Sidonie Smith, et al. (Minneapolis: University of Minnesota Press, 1992), pp. 115–38.

21. Karen Press, "Building a National Culture in South Africa," in *Rendering Things Visible,* p. 29.

22. In Kim Heron, " 'The Snob Value' of English," *New York Times Book Review,* May 24, 1987, p. 8. See also the longer review by Bharati Mukherjee, "They Never Wanted to Be Themselves," *New York Times Book Review,* May 24, 1987, pp. 7–8.

23. The Griquas were a mixed-race group, like the self-proclaimed "Bastards," who, alienated from the rural Afrikaner communities, trekked away from European settlements to form frontier communities of their own. See Sheila Patterson, *Colour and Culture in South Africa* (London: Routledge, 1953), p. 182.

24. The Group Areas Act of 1950 set up separate living areas for the different "races" and permitted governmental removal of people from their homes, primarily to make such areas available exclusively to Whites. See "Forced Removals and Bantustans" (Surplus People Project Report), in *The Anti-Apartheid Reader: The Struggle against White Racist Rule in South Africa,* ed. David Mermelstein (New York: Grove Press, 1987), pp. 138–68.

25. At this point Frieda would have had decades of models of black female resistance

had she sought them out. In 1956, fifty thousand women protested the extension of the pass laws to women; in 1959, they participated in the Beer Hall Boycott as part of the "Women's Campaigns." See Cherryl Walker, *Women and Resistance in South Africa* (New York: Monthly Review Press, 1991), p. 193; and Beata Lipman, *We Make Freedom: Women in South Africa* (London: Pandora Press, 1984).

26. Verwoerd was assassinated on September 6, 1966, by a white man who was declared insane. An attempt on Verwoerd's life in 1961 was perpetrated by another white man also declared insane. See T. R. H. Davenport, *South Africa: A Modern History* (Toronto: University of Toronto Press, 1987), pp. 397, 405.

27. February, *Mind Your Colour*, p. 10; Goldin, *Making Race*, pp. 133–34.

28. Harlow, *Resistance Literature*, p. 30.

29. Njabulo S. Ndebele, *Rediscovery of the Ordinary: Essays on South African Literature and Culture* (Johannesburg: Congress of South African Writers, 1991), p. 53. Anthony O'Brien makes a compelling argument that both Ndebele and Bessie Head offer feminist critiques of protest literature "with its gender-coded affinity for the 'public' sphere, and a displacement of the question about power toward the 'private' sphere, traditionally coded female." O'Brien's aside that this feminist move also resuscitates the oral tale is suggestive for my reading of Wicomb's interest in oral storytelling. See Anthony O'Brien, "Literature in Another South Africa: Njabulo Ndebele's Theory of Emergent Culture," *diacritics* 22, no. 1 (spring 1992), pp. 67–85. In response to questions about the writer's relationship to politics, Zoë Wicomb has written: "All writing, whether it deals with revolution or not, occupies a political position. . . . How valid is the term *revolutionary writing* for material that deals directly with the political struggle, when we have no evidence that such work moves people to political action more than, say, writing about hair-straightening?" Shifting her attention from the politics of writing to the politics or reading, she adds: "If our concern then is the social and political impact of writing, it might be more fruitful to focus on what Catherine Belsey calls 'post-Copernican readers' who will reject the authority of the author" (Wicomb, "An Author's Agenda," in *Critical Fictions: The Politics of Imaginative Writing*, ed. Philomena Mariani [Seattle: Bay Press, 1991], pp. 13, 14, 15).

30. Ndebele, *Rediscovery*, p. 65.

31. Michael Vaughan, "Storytelling and Politics in Fiction," in *Rendering Things Visible*, pp. 186–204.

32. Ibid., pp. 198–201.

33. Thulani Davis and Joe Wood, "To Soweto with Love: Black South Africans Respond to the Release of Nelson Mandela," *Village Voice*, February 20, 1990, p. 25.

34. In almost every story of the novel, the issue of payment, exchange, or transaction appears. From actual payment in cigarettes by Mr. Weedon or in coins for the illegal abortion to the metaphorical "transaction" and "currency" of sex in "Behind the Bougainvillea," every relationship is mediated by the terms of capitalism. Even Frieda's bilingual rhyme in "When the Train Comes" turns on gold, the foundational commodity of exchange in colonial South Africa.

35. André Viola comments on Wicomb's inconclusive ironical endings that subvert the expected epiphanies and climaxes of short stories. See André Viola, "Zoë Wicomb's *You Can't Get Lost in Cape Town*: A Portrait of the Artist as a Young Coloured Girl," in *Short Fiction in the New Literatures in English*, ed. J. Bardolf (Nice, France: Proceedings of the Nice Conference of the European Association for Commonwealth Literature and Language Studies, 1989), pp. 231–36.

36. Davis and Wood, "To Soweto with Love," p. 25.

37. Zoë Wicomb, "Nation, Race and Ethnicity: Beyond the Legacy of Victims," *Current Writing* 4 (1992), p. 19. Of interest are other essays Wicomb has written since 1990:

"To Hear the Variety of Discourses," *Current Writing* 2 (1990), pp. 35–44; "Tracing the Path from National to Official Culture," in *Critical Fictions,* pp. 242–50; and "An Author's Agenda," pp. 13–16. See also Johan Deganaar, "How Texts and Their Reception Will Change in the Post-apartheid Era," *Current Writing* 4 (1992), pp. 10–14.

38. Wicomb, "Nation," pp. 19–20.

39. Zoë Wicomb, "Culture beyond Color: A South African Dilemma," *Transition: An International Review* 60 (1993), p. 32.

40. Ibid.

41. Frantz Fanon, "On National Culture," in *The Wretched of the Earth,* trans. Constance Farrington (New York: Grove Press, 1963), p. 240.

42. Edward Kamau Brathwaite, "English in the Caribbean: Notes on Nation Language and Poetry — An Electronic Lecture," in *English Literature: Opening Up the Canon,* selected papers from the English Institute, 1979, ed. Leslie Fiedler and Houston A. Baker Jr. (Baltimore: Johns Hopkins University Press, 1981), p. 21.

Bibliography

I. Olive Schreiner

Barash, Carol, ed. *An Olive Schreiner Reader: Writings on Women and South Africa*. London: Pandora Press, 1987.

Beeton, D. R. *Facets of Olive Schreiner: A Manuscript Source Book*. Craighall, South Africa: Donker, 1987.

———. "In Search of Olive Schreiner in Texas." *Texas Quarterly* 17, no. 3 (autumn 1974), pp. 105–54.

———. *Olive Schreiner: A Short Guide to Her Writings*. Cape Town: Howard Timmins, 1974.

———. "Olive Schreiner and Realism." *Trek* 12, no. 8 (Aug. 1978).

Berkman, Joyce Avrech. *The Healing Imagination of Olive Schreiner: Beyond South African Colonialism*. Amherst: University of Massachusetts Press, 1989.

———. "The Nurturant Fantasies of Olive Schreiner." *Frontiers* 2, no. 3 (1977), pp. 8–17.

———. *Olive Schreiner: Feminism on the Frontier*. St. Albans, Vt.: Eden Press Women's Publications, 1979.

Bishop, Alan. " 'With Suffering and through Time': Olive Schreiner, Vera Brittain and the Great War." In *Olive Schreiner and After*, ed. Malvern van Wyk Smith and Don Maclennan, pp. 80–92. Cape Town: David Philip, 1983.

Blake, Kathleen. "Olive Schreiner: A Note on Sexist Language and the Feminist Writer." In *Gender and Literary Voice*, ed. Janet Todd, pp. 81–86. New York: Holmes and Meier, 1980.

Buchanan-Gould, Vera. *Not without Honour: The Life and Writings of Olive Schreiner*. London: Hutchinson, 1948.

Clayton, Cherry. "Forms of Dependence and Control in Olive Schreiner's Fiction." In *Olive Schreiner and After*, ed. Malvern van Wyk Smith and Don Maclennan, pp. 20–29. Cape Town: David Philip, 1983.

———. "Olive Schreiner: Child of Queen Victoria: Stories, Dreams and Allegories." In *Olive Schreiner*, ed. Cherry Clayton, pp. 192–97. Johannesburg: McGraw-Hill, 1983.

———, ed. *Olive Schreiner*. Johannesburg: McGraw-Hill, 1983.

Colby, Vineta. *The Singular Anomaly: Women Novelists of the Nineteenth Century.* New York: New York University Press, 1970.

Cronwright-Schreiner, S. C. *The Life of Olive Schreiner.* Boston: Little, Brown and Co., 1924.

———, ed. *The Letters of Olive Schreiner 1876–1920.* London: T. Fisher Unwin, 1924.

Davenport, Rodney. "Olive Schreiner and South African Politics." In *Olive Schreiner and After,* ed. Malvern van Wyk Smith and Don Maclennan, pp. 93–107. Cape Town: David Philip, 1983.

Donaldson, Laura E. "(Ex)Changing (Wo)Man: Toward a Materialist-Feminist Semiotics." *Cultural Critique* 11 (winter 1988–89), pp. 5–23.

Draznin, Yaffa Claire, ed. *"My Other Self": The Letters of Olive Schreiner and Havelock Ellis, 1884–1920.* New York: Peter Lang, 1992.

DuPlessis, Rachel Blau. "The Rupture of Story in *The Story of an African Farm.*" In *Writing beyond the Ending: Narrative Strategies of Twentieth-Century Women Writers,* pp. 20–30. Bloomington: Indiana University Press, 1985.

First, Ruth, and Ann Scott. *Olive Schreiner: A Biography.* New York: Schocken Books, 1980.

Fradkin, Betty M. "Havelock Ellis and Olive Schreiner's 'Gregory Rose.'" *Texas Quarterly* 21, no. 3 (autumn 1978), pp. 145–53.

———. "Olive Schreiner — An Opposite Picture." *Contrast* 12, no. 3 (June 1979), pp. 75–88.

Friedlander, Zelda, ed. *Until the Heart Changes: A Garland for Olive Schreiner.* Cape Town: Tafelberg-Uitgewers, 1967.

Friedmann, Marion. *Olive Schreiner: A Study in Latent Meanings.* Johannesburg: Witwatersrand University Press, 1955.

Gordimer, Nadine. "Review of *Olive Schreiner: A Biography,* by Ruth First and Ann Scott." In *Olive Schreiner and After,* ed. Malvern van Wyk Smith and Don Maclennan, pp. 14–19. Cape Town: David Philip, 1983.

Gray, Stephen. *Southern African Literature: An Introduction.* Cape Town: David Philip, 1979.

Heywood, Christopher. "Olive Schreiner and Literary Tradition." In *Olive Schreiner and After,* ed. Malvern van Wyk Smith and Don Maclennan, pp. 58–66. Cape Town: David Philip, 1983.

Jacobson, Dan. Introduction to *The Story of an African Farm,* by Olive Schreiner, pp. 7–23. London: Penguin Books, 1971.

Krige, Uys, ed. *Olive Schreiner: A Selection.* Cape Town: Oxford University Press, 1968.

Lenta, Margaret. "Independence as Creative Choice in Two South African Fictions." *Ariel* 7, no. 1 (Jan. 1986), pp. 35–52.

———. "Racism, Sexism, and Olive Schreiner's Fiction." *Theoria* 80 (Oct. 1987), pp. 16–30.

Lerner, Laurence. "Olive Schreiner and the Feminists." In *Olive Schreiner and After,* ed. Malvern van Wyk Smith and Don Maclennan, pp. 67–79. Cape Town: David Philip, 1983.

Lessing, Doris. Introduction to *The Story of an African Farm,* pp. 1–18. New York: Schocken Books, 1976.

Marcus, Jane. "Olive Schreiner: Cartographer of the Spirit/A Review Article." *Minnesota Review* 12 (spring 1979), pp. 58–66.

Marquard, Jean. "Olive Schreiner's 'Prelude': The Child as Artist." *English Studies in Africa* 22, no. 1 (March 1979), pp. 1–11.

Meintjes, Johannes. *Olive Schreiner: Portrait of a South African Woman.* Johannesburg: Hugh Keartland, 1965.

Monsman, Gerald. *Olive Schreiner's Fiction: Landscape and Power.* New Brunswick, N.J.: Rutgers University Press, 1991.

Morris, Patricia. "Biographical Accounts of Olive Schreiner." In *Olive Schreiner and After,* ed. Malvern van Wyk Smith and Don Maclennan, pp. 3–13. Cape Town: David Philip, 1983.

Paton, Alan. "Trooper Peter Halket of Mashonaland." In *Olive Schreiner and After,* ed. Malvern van Wyk Smith and Don Maclennan, pp. 30–34. Cape Town: David Philip, 1983.

Pechey, Graham. "*The Story of an African Farm:* Colonial History and the Discontinuous Text." *Critical Arts: A Journal of Media Studies* 3, no. 1 (1983), pp. 65–78.

Rive, Richard. Introduction to *English in South Africa* 1, no. 1 (March 1974), pp. 1–29.

———. "New Light on Olive Schreiner." *Contrast: South African Quarterly* 8, no. 4 (Nov. 1973), pp. 40–47.

———, ed. *Olive Schreiner Letters, Volume 1: 1871–1899.* Oxford: Oxford University Press, 1988.

Ross, Robert. "A New Time for the Fiction of Sarah Gertrude Millin and Olive Schreiner." *World Literature in English* 24, no. 2 (1984), pp. 239–43.

Schoeman, Karel. *Olive Schreiner: A Woman in South Africa, 1855–1881.* Johannesburg: Jonathan Ball, 1991.

———. *Only in Anguish to Live Here: Olive Schreiner and the Anglo-Boer War, 1899–1902.* Cape Town: Hamm and Roussca, 1992.

Schreiner, Olive. *Dreams.* Boston: Roberts Brothers, 1891.

———. *An English South African's View of the Situation: Words in Season.* London: Hodder and Stoughton, 1899.

———. *From Man to Man or Perhaps Only. . . .* New York: Harper and Brothers, 1927.

———. *The Story of an African Farm.* 1883. Reprint, Harmondsworth, England: Penguin Books, 1971.

———. *Thoughts on South Africa.* 1923. Reprint, facsimile reproduction, with a foreword by Richard Rive. Johannesburg: Africana Book Society, 1976.

———. *Trooper Peter Halket of Mashonaland.* Boston: Little, Brown and Co., 1900.

———. *Undine.* 1928. Reprint, New York: Johnson Reprint, 1972.

———. *Woman and Labour.* London: T. Fisher Unwin, 1911.

Smith, Malvern van Wyk, and Don Maclennan, eds. *Olive Schreiner and After: Essays on Southern African Literature.* Cape Town: David Philip, 1983.

Stanley, Liz. "Olive Schreiner: New Women, Free Women, All Women." In *Feminist Theorists: Three Centuries of Key Women Thinkers,* ed. Dale Spender, pp. 229–43. New York: Pantheon Books, 1983.

Style, Colin. "Olive Schreiner Today." *Contemporary Review* 244, no. 1419 (April 1984), pp. 204–9.

Visel, Robin. " 'We Bear the World and We Make It': Bessie Head and Olive Schreiner." *Research in African Literatures* 21, no. 3 (fall 1990), pp. 115–24.

Voss, A. E. " 'Not a Word or a Sound in the World about Him That Is Not Modifying Him': Learning, Love, and Language in *The Story of an African Farm.*" In *Olive Schreiner,* ed. Cherry Clayton, pp. 170–81. Johannesburg: McGraw-Hill, 1983.

Wilson, Elaine. "Pervasive Symbolism in 'The Story of an African Farm.' " *English Studies in Africa* 14, no. 2 (1971), pp. 179–86.

Woolf, Virginia. "Olive Schreiner." *New Republic* 18 (March 1925), p. 103.

II. Jean Rhys

Allfrey, Phyllis Shand. "Jean Rhys: A Tribute." *Kunapipi* 1, no. 2 (1979), pp. 23–25.

Angier, Carole. *Jean Rhys: Life and Work*. Boston: Little, Brown and Co., 1990.

Brandmark, Wendy. "The Power of the Victim: A Study of *Quartet, After Leaving Mr. Mackenzie* and *Voyage in the Dark* by Jean Rhys." *Kunapipi* 8, no. 2 (1986), pp. 21–29.

Brown, Bev E. L. "Mansong and Matrix: A Radical Experiment." In *A Double Colonization: Colonial and Post-colonial Women's Writing*, ed. Kirsten Holst Peterson and Anna Rutherford, pp. 68–79. Oxford: Dangaroo Press, 1986.

Bruner, Charlotte H. "A Caribbean Madness: Half Slave and Half Free." *Canadian Review of Comparative Literature* 2, no. 2 (June 1984), pp. 236–48.

Campbell, Elaine. "An Expatriate at Home: Dominica's Elma Napier." *Kunapipi* 4, no. 1 (1985), pp. 82–93.

―――. "From Dominica to Devonshire: A Momento of Jean Rhys." *Kunapipi* 1, no. 2 (1979), pp. 6–22.

―――. "Literature and Transitional Politics in Dominica." *World Literature Written in English* 24, no. 2 (1984), pp. 349–59.

―――. "Reflections of Obeah in Jean Rhys's Fiction." *Kunapipi* 4, no. 2 (1982), pp. 42–50.

―――. "A Report from Dominica, B.W.I." *World Literature Written in English* 17, no. 1 (April 1978), pp. 305–16.

Casey, Nancy. "Study in the Alienation of a Creole Woman: Jean Rhys's Voyage in the Dark." *Caribbean Quarterly* 19 (Sept. 1973), pp. 95–102.

Davidson, Arnold E. *Jean Rhys*. New York: Frederick Ungar, 1985.

Drake, Sandra. "All That Foolishness/That All Foolishness: Race and Caribbean Culture as Thematics of Liberation in Jean Rhys's *Wide Sargasso Sea*." *Critica* 2, no. 2 (fall 1990), pp. 97–112.

Emery, Mary Lou. *Jean Rhys at "World's End": Novels of Colonial and Sexual Exile*. Austin: University of Texas Press, 1990.

―――. "Modernism and the Marginal Woman: A Sociocritical Approach to the Novels of Jean Rhys." Ph.D. diss., Stanford University, 1982.

―――. "The Politics of Form: Jean Rhys's Social Vision in *Voyage in the Dark* and *Wide Sargasso Sea*." *Twentieth Century Literature* 28, no. 4 (winter 1982), pp. 418–30.

Erwin, Lee. " 'Like in a Looking-Glass': History and Narrative in *Wide Sargasso Sea*." *Novel: A Forum on Fiction* 22, no. 2 (winter 1989), pp. 143–58.

Frickey, Pierrette. Introduction to *Critical Perspectives on Jean Rhys*, ed. Pierrette Frickey, pp. 1–16. Washington, D.C.: Three Continents Press, 1990.

Friedman, Ellen G. "Breaking the Master Narrative: Jean Rhys's *Wide Sargasso Sea*." In *Breaking the Sequence: Women's Experimental Fiction*, ed. Ellen G. Friedman and Miriam Fuchs, pp. 117–28. Princeton, N.J.: Princeton University Press, 1989.

Fulton, Nancy J. Casey. "Jean Rhys's *Wide Sargasso Sea*: Exterminating the White Cockroach." *Revista/Review Interamericana* 4 (1974), pp. 340–49.

Gardiner, Judith Kegan. "The Exhilaration of Exile: Rhys, Stead, and Lessing." In *Women's Writing in Exile*, ed. Mary Lynn Broe and Angela Ingram, pp. 133–50. Chapel Hill: University of North Carolina Press, 1989.

―――. "Good Morning, Midnight; Good Night, Modernism." *Boundary 2* 11, nos. 1–2 (fall/winter 1982–83), pp. 233–51.

―――. *Rhys, Stead, Lessing and the Politics of Empathy*. Bloomington: Indiana University Press, 1989.

Harris, Wilson. "Carnival of Psyche: Jean Rhys's *Wide Sargasso Sea*." *Kunapipi* 2, no. 2 (1980), pp. 142–50.

Harrison, Nancy R. *Jean Rhys and the Novel as Women's Text*. Chapel Hill: University of North Carolina Press, 1988.

Howells, Coral Ann. *Jean Rhys*. New York: St. Martin's Press, 1991.

James, Louis. *Jean Rhys*. Critical Studies of Caribbean Writers. London: Longman, 1978.

————. "Sun Fire — Painted Fire: Jean Rhys as a Caribbean Novelist." *Ariel* 8, no. 3 (1977), pp. 111–27.

James, Selma. *The Ladies and the Mammies: Jane Austen and Jean Rhys*. Bristol, England: Falling Wall Press, 1983.

Kloepfer, Deborah Kelly. *The Unspeakable Mother: Forbidden Discourse in Jean Rhys and H.D.* Ithaca, N.Y.: Cornell University Press, 1989.

Leigh, Nancy J. "Mirror, Mirror: The Development of Female Identity in Jean Rhys's Fiction." *World Literature Written in English* 25, no. 2 (1985), pp. 270–85.

Loe, Thomas. "Patterns of the Zombie in Jean Rhys's *Wide Sargasso Sea*." *World Literature Written in English* 31, no. 1 (1991), pp. 34–42.

Look Lai, Wally. "The Road to Thornfield Hall." *New World Quarterly* 4 (1968), pp. 17–27.

Magarey, Kevin. "The Sense of Place in Doris Lessing and Jean Rhys." *A Sense of Place in the New Literatures in English*, ed. Peggy Nightingale, pp. 47–60. St. Lucia: University of Queensland Press, 1986.

Mellown, Elgin W. *Jean Rhys: A Descriptive and Annotated Bibliography of Works and Criticism*. New York: Garland, 1984.

Miles, Rosalind. *The Fiction of Sex: Themes and Functions of Sex Difference in the Modern Novel*. New York: Barnes and Noble, 1974.

Nebeker, Helen. *Jean Rhys: Woman in Passage*. Montreal: Eden, 1981.

Nunes, Maria Luisa. "Becoming Whole: Literary Strategies of Decolonization in the Works of Jean Rhys, Frantz Fanon, and Oswald de Andrade." In *Proceedings of the Xth Congress of the International Comparative Literature Association/Actes du Xe Congrès de l'Association Internationale de Littérature Comparée*, vol. 3, pp. 28–33. New York: Garland, 1982.

Nunez-Harrell, Elizabeth. "The Paradoxes of Belonging: The White West Indian Woman in Fiction." *Modern Fiction Studies* 31, no. 2 (summer 1985), pp. 281–93.

O'Connor, Teresa F. *Jean Rhys: The West Indian Novels*. New York: New York University Press, 1986.

Plante, David. *Difficult Women: A Memoir of Three*. New York: Atheneum, 1983.

Ramchand, Kenneth. Introduction to *Tales of the Wide Caribbean: Stories by Jean Rhys*, pp. 1–21. London: Heinemann, 1985.

————. *An Introduction to the Study of West Indian Literature*. Middlesex, England: Thomas Nelson, 1976.

————. *The West Indian Novel and Its Background*. 2d ed. London: Heinemann, 1984.

Rhys, Jean. *After Leaving Mr. Mackenzie*. In *The Complete Novels*. New York: W. W. Norton, 1985.

————. *The Collected Short Stories*. New York: W. W. Norton, 1987.

————. *Good Morning, Midnight*. 1939. Reprint, London: André Deutsch, 1967.

————. *Quartet*. In *The Complete Novels*. New York: W. W. Norton, 1985.

————. *Smile Please: An Unfinished Autobiography*. New York: Harper and Row, 1979.

————. *Voyage in the Dark*. In *The Complete Novels*. New York: W. W. Norton, 1985.

————. *Wide Sargasso Sea*. 1966. Reprint, New York: W. W. Norton, 1982.

Smilowitz, Erika. "Childlike Women and Paternal Men: Colonialism in Jean Rhys's Fiction." *Ariel* (special edition: *Commonwealth Women Writers*), 17, no. 4 (Oct. 1986), pp. 93–103.

Staley, Thomas F. *Jean Rhys: A Critical Study*. Austin: University of Texas Press, 1979.

Thorpe, Michael. "The Other Side: *Wide Sargasso Sea* and *Jane Eyre*." *Ariel* 8, no. 3 (July 1977), pp. 99–110.

Tiffin, Helen. "Mirror and Mask: Colonial Motifs in the Novels of Jean Rhys." *World Literature Written in English* 17, no. 1 (April 1978), pp. 328–41.

Vreeland, Elizabeth. "Jean Rhys: The Art of Fiction LXIV." *Paris Review* 21, no. 76 (fall 1979), pp. 218–37.

Wilson, Lucy. "'Women Must Have Spunks': Jean Rhys's West Indian Outcasts." *Modern Fiction Studies* 32, no. 3 (autumn 1986), pp. 439–48.

Wolfe, Peter. *Jean Rhys.* Boston: Twayne, 1980.

Wyndham, Francis, and Diana Melly, eds. *The Letters of Jean Rhys.* New York: Viking, 1984.

III. Michelle Cliff

Barnes, Fiona R. "Resisting Cultural Cannibalism: Oppositional Narratives in Michelle Cliff's *No Telephone to Heaven.*" *Journal of the Midwest MLA* 25, no. 1 (spring 1992), pp. 23–31.

Cliff, Michelle. *Abeng.* Trumansburg, N.Y.: Crossing Press, 1984.

———. *Bodies of Water.* New York: Dutton, 1990.

———. "Caliban's Daughter: The Tempest and the Teapot." *Frontiers* 12, no. 2 (1991), pp. 36–51.

———. "Clare Savage as a Crossroads Character." In *Caribbean Women Writers,* ed. Selwyn R. Cudjoe, pp. 263–68. Amherst: University of Massachusetts Press, 1990.

———. *Free Enterprise.* New York: Dutton, 1993.

———. *The Land of Look Behind.* Ithaca, N.Y.: Firebrand, 1985.

———. *No Telephone to Heaven.* New York: Dutton, 1987.

Lima, Maria Helena. "Revolutionary Developments: Michelle Cliff's 'No Telephone to Heaven' and Merle Collins's 'Angel.'" *Ariel* 24, no. 1 (Jan. 1993), pp. 35–56.

Lionnet, Françoise. "Of Mangoes and Maroons: Language, History, and the Multicultural Subject of Michelle Cliff's *Abeng.*" In *De/colonizing the Subject: The Politics of Gender in Women's Autobiography,* ed. Sidonie Smith and Julia Watson, pp. 321–45. Minneapolis: University of Minnesota Press, 1992.

Raiskin, Judith. "The Art of History: An Interview with Michelle Cliff." *The Kenyon Review,* n.s., 15, no. 1 (winter 1993), pp. 57–71.

Schwartz, Meryl F. "An Interview with Michelle Cliff." *Contemporary Literature* 34, no. 4 (winter 1993), p. 595–619.

IV. Zoë Wicomb

Mukherjee, Bharati. "They Never Wanted to Be Themselves (Review of *You Can't Get Lost in Cape Town*)." *New York Times Book Review,* May 24, 1987, pp. 7–8.

Viola, André. "Zoë Wicomb's *You Can't Get Lost in Cape Town:* A Portrait of the Artist as a Young Coloured Girl." In *Short Fiction in the New Literatures in English,* ed. J. Bardolf, pp. 231–36. Nice, France: Proceedings of the Nice Conference of the European Association for Commonwealth Literature and Language Studies, 1989.

Wicomb, Zoë. "Another Story." In *Colors of a New Day: Writing for South Africa,* ed. Sarah Lefanu and Stephen Hayward, pp. 1–15. New York: Pantheon Books, 1990.

———. "An Author's Agenda." In *Critical Fictions: The Politics of Imaginative Writing,* ed. Philomena Mariani, pp. 13–16. Seattle: Bay Press, 1991.

———. "Culture beyond Color: A South African Dilemma." *Transition: An International Review* 60 (1993), pp. 27–32.

———. "In the Botanic Gardens." *Landfall* 44, no. 4 (Dec. 1990), pp. 484–92.

———. "Nation, Race and Ethnicity: Beyond the Legacy of Victims. *Current Writing* 4 (1992), pp. 15–20.

———. "To Hear the Variety of Discourses." *Current Writing* 2 (1990), pp. 35–44.

———. "Tracing the Path from National to Official Culture." In *Critical Fictions,* ed. Philomena Mariani, pp. 242–50. Seattle: Bay Press, 1991.

———. *You Can't Get Lost in Cape Town.* New York: Pantheon Books, 1987.

IV. History, Theory, and Literature

Abrahams, Roger, and John Szwed, eds. *After Africa.* New Haven: Yale University Press, 1983.

Achebe, Chinua. "An Image of Africa: Racism in Conrad's *Heart of Darkness.*" *Massachusetts Review* 18 (1977), pp. 782–94.

Adey, David, et al. *Companion to South African English Literature.* Craighall, South Africa: Donker, 1986.

Allfrey, Phyllis Shand. *The Orchid House.* 1953. Reprint. London: Virago Press, 1982.

Almaguer, Tómas. "Chicano Men: A Cartography of Homosexual Identity and Behavior." In *The Lesbian and Gay Studies Reader,* ed. Henry Abelove et al., pp. 255–73. New York: Routledge, 1993.

Alter, Robert. "Eliot, Lawrence and the Jews." *Commentary* 50 (Oct. 1970), pp. 81–86.

Anderson, Benedict. *Imagined Communities: Reflections on the Origin and Spread of Nationalism.* London: Verso, 1983.

Anzaldúa, Gloria. *Border/lands: La Frontera.* San Francisco: Spinsters/Aunt Lute, 1987.

———. *Making Face, Making Soul/Haciendo Caras: Creative and Critical Perspectives by Women of Color.* San Francisco: Aunt Lute, 1990.

Appiah, Kwame Anthony. "Is the Post- in Postmodernism the Post- in Postcolonialism?" *Critical Inquiry* 17, no. 2 (winter 1991), pp. 336–57.

Arendt, Hannah. *The Jew as Pariah: Jewish Identity and Politics in the Modern Age.* Ed. Ron H. Feldman. New York: Grove Press, 1978.

Auerbach, Erich. *Mimesis.* Trans. Willard R. Trask. Princeton, N.J.: Princeton University Press, 1971.

Auerbach, Nina, ed. *Tulsa Studies in Women's Literature* 6, no. 2 (fall 1987).

Baker, Houston A., Jr. "Caliban's Triple Play." *Critical Inquiry* 13 (autumn 1986), pp. 182–96.

Barker, Francis, et al., eds. *Europe and Its Others.* Vols. 1 and 2 of the Proceedings of the Essex Conference on the Sociology of Literature. Colchester, England: University of Essex, 1985.

Barrett, Michèle. "Representation and Cultural Production." In *Ideology and Cultural Production,* ed. Michèle Barrett et al., pp. 9–24. New York: St. Martin's Press, 1979.

———. *Women's Oppression Today: Problems in Marxist Feminist Analysis.* London: Verso, 1980.

Beard, Linda Susan. "Doris Lessing, African Writer." In *When the Drumbeat Changes,* ed. Carolyn A. Parker and Stephen H. Arnold, pp. 241–60. Washington, D.C.: African Literature Association and Three Continents Press, 1981.

Beer, Gillian. *Darwin's Plots: Evolutionary Narrative in Darwin, George Eliot and Nineteenth Century Fiction.* London: Routledge and Kegan Paul, 1983.

Belsey, Catherine. *Cultural Practice.* London: New Accents, 1980.

Benstock, Shari. *Women of the Left Bank: Paris, 1900–1940.* Austin: University of Texas Press, 1986.

Bernabé, Jean, Patrick Chamoiseau, and Raphaël Confiant. "In Praise of Creoleness," trans. Mohamed B. Taleb Khyar, *Callaloo* 13 (1990), pp. 886–909.

Bhabha, Homi K. "DissemiNation: Time, Narrative, and the Margins of the Modern Nation." In *Nation and Narration,* ed. Homi K. Bhabha, pp. 291–320. New York: Routledge, 1990.

———. "Of Mimicry and Man: The Ambivalence of Colonial Discourse." *October* 28 (spring 1984), pp. 125–33.

———. "The Other Question — Stereotype and Colonial Discourse." *Screen* 24 (Nov.-Dec. 1983), pp. 18–36.

———. "Signs Taken for Wonders: Questions of Ambivalence and Authority under a Tree Outside Delhi, May 1817." *Critical Inquiry* 12, no. 1 (autumn 1985), pp. 144–63.

Bhabha, Jacqueline, Francesca Klug, and Sue Shutter, eds. *Worlds Apart: Women under Immigration and Nationality Law.* London: Pluto Press, 1985.

Boehmer, Elleke. "Motherlands, Mothers and Nationalist Sons: Representations of Nationalism and Women in African Literature." In *From Commonwealth to Post-colonial,* ed. Anna Rutherford, pp. 229–47. Sydney: Dangaroo Press, 1992.

Booth, William. *In Darkest England and the Way Out.* London: International Headquarters of the Salvation Army, 1890.

Boumelha, Penny. *Thomas Hardy and Women: Sexual Ideology and Narrative Form.* Madison: University of Wisconsin Press, 1985.

Bowen, Stella. *Drawn from Life.* 1941. Reprint, London: Virago Press, 1984.

Bradbury, Malcolm, and James McFarlane, eds. *Modernism: 1890–1930.* Harmondsworth, England: Penguin Books, 1976.

Brathwaite, Edward Kamau. *The Development of Creole Society in Jamaica, 1770–1820.* Oxford: Clarendon Press, 1971.

———. "English in the Caribbean: Notes on Nation, Language, and Poetry." In *English Literature: Opening up the Canon,* ed. Leslie Fiedler and Houston A. Baker Jr., pp. 15–53. Selected papers from the English Institute, 1979, n.s., no. 4. Baltimore: Johns Hopkins University Press, 1981.

Brand, Dionne. "Why I Used to Like the Dallas Cowboys." In *Sans Souci and other Stories,* pp. 115–29. Stratford, Ontario: Williams-Wallace, 1988.

Branford, Jean. *A Dictionary of South African English.* Cape Town: Oxford University Press, 1987.

Brantlinger, Patrick. *Rule of Darkness: British Literature and Imperialism, 1830–1914.* Ithaca, N.Y.: Cornell University Press, 1988.

———. "Victorians and Africans: The Genealogy of the Myth of the Dark Continent." *Critical Inquiry* 12, no. 1 (autumn 1985), pp. 166–203.

Brodber, Erna. *Jane and Louisa Will Soon Come Home.* London: New Beacon Books, 1980.

Broe, Mary Lynn, and Angela Ingram, eds. *Women Writing in Exile.* Chapel Hill: University of North Carolina Press, 1989.

Brontë, Charlotte. *Jane Eyre.* 1847. Reprint, Harmondsworth, England: Penguin Books, 1987.

Brown, David Maughan. "The Noble Savage in Anglo-Saxon Colonial Ideology, 1950–1980: 'Masai' and 'Bushmen' in Popular Fiction." *English in Africa* 10, no. 2 (Oct. 1983), pp. 55–77.

Bulkin, Elly, Minnie Bruce Pratt, and Barbara Smith. *Yours in Struggle: Three Feminist Perspectives on Anti-Semitism and Racism.* Brooklyn: Long Haul Press, 1984.

Burnett, Paula, ed. *The Penguin Book of Caribbean Verse in English.* Harmondsworth, England: Penguin Books, 1986.

Butler, Judith. "Imitation and Gender Insubordination." In *Inside/Out: Lesbian Theories, Gay Theories,* ed. Diana Fuss, pp. 13–31. New York: Routledge, 1991.

Carpenter, Edward. *Selected Writings, Vol. I: Sex.* Introduction by Noël Greig. London: GMP, 1984.

Carpentier, Alejo. *The Kingdom of This World.* Trans. Harriet de Onís. New York: Alfred A. Knopf, 1957.

Carr, Glynis. "Caribbean Women Writers: A Bibliography for Teachers." *National Women's Studies Association Newsletter* (1987), pp. 16–18.

Cassidy, F. G., and R. B. LePage, eds. *Dictionary of Jamaican English.* 2d ed. Cambridge: Cambridge University Press, 1980.

Chaudhuri, Nupur, and Margaret Strobel, eds. *Western Women and Imperialism.* Bloomington: Indiana University Press, 1992.

Chesterton, Mrs. Cecil. *In Darkest London.* London: Stanley Paul and Co., 1926.

Cheyette, Brian. *Constructions of "the Jew" in English Literature and Society: Racial Representations, 1875–1945.* Cambridge and New York: Cambridge University Press, 1993.

———. "Jewish Stereotyping and English Literature, 1875–1920: Towards a Political Analysis." In *Traditions of Intolerance: Historical Perspectives on Fascism and Race Discourse in Britain,* ed. Tony Kushner and Kenneth Lunn, pp. 12–32. Manchester: Manchester University Press, 1989.

Clifford, James. "On Ethnographic Self-Fashioning: Conrad and Malinowski." In *Reconstructing Individualism: Autonomy, Individuality, and the Self in Western Thought,* ed. Thomas C. Heller, Morton Sosna, and David E. Wellbery, pp. 140–62. Stanford, Calif.: Stanford University Press, 1986.

Coetzee, J. M. "Blood, Flaw, Taint, Degeneration: The Case of Sarah Gertrude Millin." *English Studies in Africa* 23, no. 1 (March 1980), 41–58.

———. *White Writing: On the Culture of Letters in South Africa.* New Haven: Yale University Press, 1988.

Collins, Merle. *Angel.* Seattle: Seal Press, 1987.

Conrad, Joseph. *Heart of Darkness.* 1902. Reprint, Harmondsworth, England: Penguin Books, 1983.

Cowen, Anne, and Roger Cowen, eds. *Victorian Jews through British Eyes.* Oxford: Oxford University Press, 1986.

Cowley, Malcolm. *Exile's Return: A Literary Odyssey of the 1920's.* New York: Viking, 1951.

Csicsery-Rónay, Istváan, Jr. "The Realistic Historical Novel and the Mythology of Liberal Nationalism: Scott, Manzoni, Eötvös, Kemény, Tolstoy." Ph.D. diss., Princeton University, 1982.

Cudjoe, Selwyn R. *Caribbean Women Writers: Essays from the First International Conference.* Wellesley: University of Massachusetts Press, 1990.

Davenport, T. R. H. *South Africa: A Modern History.* Toronto: University of Toronto Press, 1987.

Davies, Carole Boyce, and Elaine Savory Fido. *Out of the Kumbla: Caribbean Women and Literature.* Trenton, N.J.: Africa World Press, 1990.

Davies, Margaret Llewelyn, ed. *Life as We Have Known It.* 1931. Reprint, New York: W. W. Norton, 1975.

Davin, Anna. "Imperialism and Motherhood." *History Workshop: A Journal of Socialist Historians* 5 (spring 1978), pp. 9–65.

Davis, James. *Who Is Black? One Nation's Definition.* University Park: Pennsylvania State University Press, 1991.

Davis, Thulani, and Joe Wood. "To Soweto with Love: Black South Africans Respond to the Release of Nelson Mandela." *Village Voice,* February 20, 1990, pp. 25–26.

Davis, Wade. *Passage of Darkness: The Ethnobiology of the Haitian Zombie.* Chapel Hill: University of North Carolina Press, 1988.

Dearborn, Mary V. *Pocahontas's Daughters: Gender and Ethnicity in American Culture.* Oxford: Oxford University Press, 1986.

Deganaar, Johan. "How Texts and Their Reception Will Change in the Post-apartheid Era." *Current Writing* 4 (1992), pp. 10–14.

de Lauretis, Teresa. *Alice Doesn't: Feminism, Semiotics, Cinema.* Bloomington: Indiana University Press, 1984.

———. *Technologies of Gender: Essays on Theory, Film, and Fiction.* Bloomington: Indiana University Press, 1987.

Deleuze, Gilles, and Félix Guattari. *Kafka: Toward a Minor Literature.* Trans. Dana Polan. Minneapolis: University of Minnesota Press, 1986.

D'Emilio, John, and Estelle Freedman. *Intimate Matters: The History of Sexuality in America.* New York: Harper and Row, 1988.

Deming, Barbara. *We Are All Part of One Another: A Barbara Deming Reader,* ed. Jane Meyerding. Philadelphia: New Society, 1984.

Derrida, Jacques. "Racism's Last Word." *Critical Inquiry* 12, no. 1 (autumn 1985), pp. 290–99.

Diggs, Irene. "Color in Colonial Spanish America." *Journal of Negro History* 38, no. 4 (Oct. 1953), pp. 403–37.

Domínguez, Virginia R. *White by Definition: Social Classification in Creole Louisiana.* New Brunswick, N.J.: Rutgers University Press, 1986.

Donaldson, Laura E., ed. *Decolonizing Feminisms: Race, Gender, and Empire-Building.* Chapel Hill: University of North Carolina Press, 1992.

Douglas, Mary. *Purity and Danger: An Analysis of the Concepts of Pollution and Taboo.* 1966. Reprint, London: Routledge and Kegan Paul, 1985.

Dowling, William C. *Jameson, Althusser, Marx: An Introduction to the "Political Unconsciousness."* Ithaca, N.Y.: Cornell University Press, 1984.

Drake, Sandra Elizabeth. "The Uses of History in the Caribbean Novel." Ph.D. diss., Stanford University, 1977.

Eliot, George. *Daniel Deronda.* 1876. Reprint, Harmondsworth, England: Penguin Books, 1967.

Eliot, T. S. *The Complete Poems and Plays 1909–1950.* New York: Harcourt, Brace, and Co., 1952.

Ellis, Havelock. *The Art of Life: From the Works of Havelock Ellis,* ed. Mrs. S. Herbert. 1929. Reprint, New York: Books for Libraries Press, 1970.

———. *The Criminal.* London: Walter Scott Publishing Co., 1910.

———. *Studies in the Psychology of Sex.* New York: Random House, 1936.

Emerson, Ralph Waldo. "The American Scholar." In *Selected Essays, Lectures, and Poems,* ed. R. E. Spiller, pp. 63–80. New York: Simon and Schuster, 1960.

Encyclopedia Judaica. Jerusalem: Macmillan, 1971.

Espín, Olivia. "Cultural and Historical Influences on Sexuality in Hispanic/Latin Women: Implications for Psychotherapy." In *Pleasure and Danger: Exploring Female Sexuality,* ed. Carol Vance, pp. 149–64. London: Pandora, 1984.

Esteves, Carmen C., and Lizabeth Paravisini-Gebert, eds. *Green Cane and Juicy Flotsam: Short Stories by Caribbean Women.* New Brunswick, N.J.: Rutgers University Press, 1991.

Fanon, Frantz. *Black Skin, White Masks.* Trans. Charles L. Markmann. New York: Grove Press, 1967. Originally published in French: *Peau Noire, Masques Blancs,* 1952.

———. "On National Culture." In *The Wretched of the Earth.* Trans. Constance Farrington. New York: Grove Press, 1963.

February, Vernon. *Mind Your Colour: The "Coloured" Stereotype in South African Literature.* London: Keegan Paul, 1981.

Ferguson, Moira. *Colonization and Gender Relations from Mary Wollstonecraft to Jamaica Kincaid: East Caribbean Connections.* New York: Columbia University Press, 1993.

Fetterley, Judith. *The Resisting Reader: A Feminist Approach to American Fiction.* Bloomington: Indiana University Press, 1978.

Fiedler, Leslie A. "What Can We Do about Fagin? The Jew Villain in Western Tradition." *Commentary* 7 (May 1949), pp. 411–18.

Fiedler, Leslie A., and Houston A. Baker Jr., eds. *English Literature: Opening Up the Canon.* Selected papers from the English Institute, 1979. Baltimore: Johns Hopkins University Press, 1981.

Figueroa, John, ed. *An Anthology of African and Caribbean Writing in English.* London: Heinemann Educational Books, 1982.

Fishman, Joshua A. "The Lively Life of a 'Dead' Language (or 'Everyone Knows That Yiddish Died Long Ago')." In *Language of Inequality,* ed. Nessa Wolfson and Joan Manes, pp. 207–22. New York: Mouton, 1985.

Fishman, William J. *East End Jewish Radicals, 1875–1914.* London: Duckworth, 1975.

Flynn, Elizabeth A., and Patrocinio P. Schweikart, eds. *Gender and Reading: Essays on Readers, Texts, and Contexts.* Baltimore: Johns Hopkins University Press, 1986.

Forster, E. M. *A Passage to India.* 1924. Reprint, New York: Harcourt, Brace and World, 1952.

Foucault, Michel. *The History of Sexuality.* Vol. I. Trans. Robert Hurley. New York: Vintage Books, 1980.

———. "Politics and the Study of Discourse." *Ideology and Consciousness* 3 (1978), pp. 7–26.

Foulkes, A. P. *Literature and Propaganda.* London: Methuen, 1983.

Fredrickson, George M. *White Supremacy: A Comparative Study in American and South African History.* Oxford: Oxford University Press, 1981.

Freud, Sigmund. *On Creativity and the Unconsciousness.* New York: Harper and Row, 1958.

Frye, Marilyn. "On Being White: Toward a Feminist Understanding of Race and Race Supremacy." In *The Politics of Reality: Essays in Feminist Poetry,* pp. 110–27. New York: Crossing Press, 1983.

Fuss, Diana. *Essentially Speaking: Feminism, Nature, and Difference.* New York: Routledge, 1989.

Garrard, John A. *The English and Immigration 1880–1910.* London: Oxford University Press, 1971.

———. "Parallels of Protest: English Reactions to Jewish and Commonwealth Immigration." *Race* 9, no. 1 (July 1967).

Gartner, Lloyd P. *The Jewish Immigrant in England, 1870–1914.* London: George Allen and Unwin, 1960.

Gikandi, Simon. *Writing in Limbo: Modernism and Caribbean Literature.* Ithaca, N.Y.: Cornell University Press, 1992.

Gilbert, Sandra M. "From *Patria* to *Matria:* Elizabeth Barrett Browning's Risorgimento." *PMLA* 99, no. 2 (March 1984), pp. 194–211.

Gilbert, Sandra, and Susan Gubar. *The Madwoman in the Attic: The Woman Writer and the Nineteenth-century Literary Imagination.* New Haven: Yale University Press, 1979.

Gilman, Sander L. "Black Bodies, White Bodies: Toward an Iconography of Female Sexuality in Late Nineteenth-century Art, Medicine, and Literature." *Critical Inquiry* 12, no. 1 (autumn 1985), pp. 204–42.

———. *Difference and Pathology: Stereotypes of Sexuality, Race, and Madness.* Ithaca, N.Y.: Cornell University Press, 1985.

———. *Jewish Self-Hatred: Anti-Semitism and the Hidden Language of the Jews.* Baltimore: Johns Hopkins University Press, 1986.

Gilroy, Paul. *There Ain't No Black in the Union Jack: The Cultural Politics of Race and Nation.* London: Hutchinson Education, 1987.

Glissant, Edouard. *Caribbean Discourse: Selected Essays.* Charlottesville: University Press of Virginia, 1989.

Goldberg, David Theo, ed. *Anatomy of Racism.* Minneapolis: University of Minnesota Press, 1990.

Goldin, Ian. *Making Race: The Politics and Economics of Coloured Identity in South Africa.* New York and London: Longman, 1987.

Gombrich, E. H. *Art and Illusion: A Study in the Psychology of Pictorial Representation.* New York: Pantheon Books, 1960.

Gómez-Peña, Guillermo. "Documented/Undocumented." In *Multi-cultural Literacy,* ed. Rick Simonson and Scott Walker, pp. 127–34. Saint Paul: Graywolf Press, 1988.

Gooneratne, Yasmine. "Place and Placelessness in the Criticism of the New Literatures in English." In *A Sense of Place in the New Literatures in English,* ed. Peggy Nightingale, pp. 13–21. St. Lucia: University of Queensland Press, 1986.

Gordimer, Nadine. "English-Language Literature and Politics in South Africa." In *Aspects of South African Literature,* ed. Christopher Heywood, pp. 99–120. London: Heinemann Educational Books, 1976.

———. "The Novel and the Nation in South Africa." In *African Writers on African Writing,* ed. G. D. Killam, pp. 33–52. London: Heinemann Educational Books, 1973.

Grand, Sarah. *The Beth Book.* 1897. Reprint, New York: Dial Press, 1980.

Gray, Stephen. *Southern African Literature: An Introduction.* Cape Town: David Philip, 1979.

Greenblatt, Stephen J. "Learning to Curse: Aspects of Linguistic Colonialism in the Sixteenth Century." In *First Images of America: The Impact of the New World on the Old,* vol. 2, ed. Fredi Chiappelli et al., pp. 561–81. Berkeley: University of California Press, 1976.

Griffiths, Gareth. *A Double Exile: African and West Indian Writing between Two Cultures.* London: Marion Boyars, 1978.

Gurr, Andrew. *Writers in Exile: The Creative Use of Home in Modern Literature.* Sussex: Harvester Press, 1981.

Haggard, H. Rider. *She: A History of Adventure.* 1886. Reprint, New York: Airmont Books, 1967.

Hall, Stuart. "Cultural Identity and Diaspora." In *Identity: Community, Culture, Difference,* ed. Jonathan Rutherford, pp. 222–37. London: Lawrence and Wishant, 1990.

Haller, John S., and Robin M. Haller. *The Physician and Sexuality in Victorian America.* Urbana: University of Illinois Press, 1974.

Hammond, Dorothy, and Alta Jablow. *The Africa That Never Was: Four Centuries of British Writing about Africa.* New York: Twayne, 1970.

Hamner, Robert. "Colony, Nationhood, and Beyond: Third World Writers and Critics Contend with Joseph Conrad." *World Literature Written in English* 23, no. 1 (1984), pp. 108–16.

Hannerz, Ulf. "The World in Creolisation." *Africa* 57, no. 4 (1987), pp. 546–59.

Haraway, Donna. *Primate Visions: Gender, Race, and Nature in the World of Modern Science.* New York: Routledge, Chapman, and Hall, 1989.

Harber, Eric. "South Africa: The White English-Speaking Sensibility." *The Journal of Commonwealth Literature* 2, no. 1 (Aug. 1976), pp. 57–71.

Harlow, Barbara. *Resistance Literature.* London: Methuen, 1987.

Hartley, Edward. *Edward Carpenter (1844–1929)*. Sheffield, England: Sheffield City Libraries, 1979.

Haskins, James. *Voodoo and Hoodoo: Their Tradition and Craft as Revealed by Actual Practitioners*. New York: Stein and Day, 1978.

Helfand, Michael S. "T. H. Huxley's 'Evolution and Ethics': The Politics of Evolution and the Evolution of Politics." *Victorian Studies* 20 (1977), pp. 159–77.

Heron, Kim. "'The Snob Value' of English." *New York Times Book Review,* May 24, 1987, p. 8.

Hicks, Emily D. *Border Writing: The Multidimensional Text*. Minneapolis: University of Minnesota Press, 1991.

Hill, Katherine C. "Virginia Woolf and Leslie Stephen: History and Literary Revolution" *PMLA* 96, no. 3 (May 1981), pp. 351–62.

Hodge, Merle. *Crick Crack, Monkey*. London: Heinemann, 1970.

Hoetink, H. *Caribbean Race Relations: A Study of Two Variants*. Trans. Eva M. Hooykass. London: Oxford University Press, 1967.

Holmes, Colin. *Anti-Semitism in British Society, 1876–1939*. London: Edward Arnold Publishers, 1979.

Horrell, Muriel. *Action, Reaction, and Counteraction*. Johannesburg: South African Institute for Race Relations, 1963.

———. *Legislation and Race Relations: A Summary of the Main South African Laws Which Affect Race Relations*. Johannesburg: South African Institute of Race Relations, 1963.

Howes, Barbara, ed. *From the Green Antilles: Writings of the Caribbean*. Introduction by Barbara Howes. New York: Macmillan, 1966.

Hugo, Pierre, ed. *Quislings or Realists? A Documentary Study of "Coloured" Politics in South Africa*. Johannesburg: Ravan Press, 1978.

Hulme, Peter. *Colonial Encounters: Europe and the Native Caribbean 1492–1797*. London: Methuen, 1986.

Hurston, Zora Neale. *Tell My Horse*. 1938. Reprint, Berkeley, Calif.: Turtle Island Press, 1981.

Huxley, T. H. *Evolution and Ethics and Other Essays*. London: Macmillan, 1893.

———. *Man's Place in Nature and Other Anthropological Essays*. London: Macmillan, 1894.

James, Henry. *The American Scene*. 1907. Reprint, New York: Horizon Press, 1967.

JanMohamed, Abdul R. "The Economy of Manichean Allegory: The Function of Racial Difference in Colonialist Literature." *Critical Inquiry* 12, no. 1 (autumn 1985), pp. 59–87.

———. "Humanism and Minority Literature: Toward a Definition of Counter-hegemonic Discourse." *Boundary 2* 12, no. 3—13, no. 1 (spring/fall 1984), pp. 281–99.

———. "Worldliness-without-World, Homelessness-as-Home: Toward a Definition of the Specular Border Intellectual." In *Edward Said: A Critical Reader,* ed. Michael Sprinker, pp. 96–120. London: Basil Blackwell, 1992.

Jaskoski, Helen. "Power Unequal to Man: The Significance of Conjure in Works by Five Afro-American Authors." *Southern Folklore Quarterly* 38 (June 1974), pp. 91–108.

Jeffreys, Sheila. *The Spinster and Her Enemies: Feminism and Sexuality, 1880–1930*. London: Pandora Press, 1985.

Jones, Joseph. *Terranglia: The Case for English as World Literature*. New York: Twayne, 1965.

Joubert, Elsa. *Poppie Nongena: One Woman's Struggle against Apartheid*. New York: Holt, 1987.

Joyce, James. *A Portrait of an Artist as a Young Man*. 1916. Reprint, New York: Viking Press, 1975.

———. *Ulysses*. 1914. Reprint, New York: Random House, 1961.

Kadish, Doris Y. *The Literature of Images: Narrative Landscape from "Julie" to "Jane Eyre."* New Brunswick, N.J.: Rutgers University Press, 1986.

Kaplan, Caren. "Deterritorializations: The Rewriting of Home and Exile in Western Feminist Discourse." *Cultural Critique* 6 (spring 1987), pp. 187–98.

———. "Resisting Autobiography: Out-law Genres and Transnational Feminist Subjects." In *De/Colonizing the Subject: The Politics of Gender in Women's Autobiography,* ed. Sidonie Smith et al., pp. 115–38. Minneapolis: University of Minnesota Press, 1992.

Katz, Wendy R. *Rider Haggard and the Fiction of Empire: A Critical Study of British Imperial Fiction.* Cambridge: Cambridge University Press, 1987.

Kennard, Jean E. *Victims of Convention.* Hamden, Conn.: Archon Books, 1978.

Kincaid, Jamaica. *Annie John.* New York: New American Library, 1983.

———. *Lucy.* New York: Plume, 1991.

———. *A Small Place.* New York: Farrar Straus Giroux, 1988.

King, Bruce. *The New English Literatures: Cultural Nationalism in a Changing World.* London: Macmillan, 1980.

———. *West Indian Literature.* Hamden, Conn.: Archon Books, 1979.

Kipling, Rudyard. *Kim.* 1901. Reprint, New York: Bantam Books, 1983.

Knox, Robert M. D. *The Races of Man.* Philadelphia: Lea and Blanchard, 1850.

LaCapra, Dominic, ed. *The Bounds of Race: Perspectives on Hegemony and Resistance.* Ithaca, N.Y.: Cornell University Press, 1991.

Lamming, George. *In the Castle of My Skin.* New York: McGraw-Hill, 1953.

———. *The Pleasures of Exile.* 1960. Reprint, London: Allison and Busby, 1984.

Laroche, Maximilien. "The Myth of the Zombi." In *Exile and Tradition: Studies in African and Caribbean Literature.* ed. Rowland Smith, pp. 44–61. New York: Africana Publishing, 1976.

Larsen, Nella. *Passing.* 1929. Reprint, New Brunswick, N.J.: Rutgers University Press, 1986.

Lawrence, Karen R., ed. *Decolonizing Tradition: New Views of Twentieth-Century "British" Literary Canons.* Urbana: University of Illinois Press, 1992.

Lessing, Doris. *Going Home.* 1957. Reprint, New York: Ballantine Books, 1968.

———. *The Grass Is Singing.* 1950. Reprint, New York: New American Library, 1976.

———. *In Pursuit of the English.* New York: Popular Library, 1960.

———. *Martha Quest.* 1952. Reprint, London: Granada, 1983.

Levy, Anita. *Other Women: The Writing of Class, Race, and Gender, 1832–1898.* Princeton, N.J.: Princeton University Press, 1991.

Lewald, H. Ernest. Introduction to *The Cry of Home: Cultural Nationalism and the Modern Writer.* Knoxville: University of Tennessee Press, 1972.

Lieven, Elena. "Subjectivity, Materialism, and Patriarchy." In *Women in Society: Interdisciplinary Essays,* ed. the Cambridge Women's Group, pp. 257–75. London: Virago Press, 1981.

Lionnet, Françoise. *Autobiographical Voices: Race, Gender, and Self-Portraiture.* Ithaca, N.Y.: Cornell University Press, 1989.

Lipman, Beata. *We Make Freedom: Women in South Africa.* London: Pandora Press, 1984.

Lorimer, Douglas. "Theoretical Racism in Late Victorian Anthropology, 1870–1900." *Victorian Studies* 13, no. 3 (spring 1988), pp. 405–30.

Luis, William. "Caribbean Cycles: Displacement and Change." *New England Review and Bread Loaf Quarterly* 7, no. 4 (summer 1985), pp. 412–30.

Macaulay, Thomas Babington. "Indian Education, Minute on the 2nd of February, 1835." In *Macaulay, Prose and Poetry,* ed. G. M. Young, pp. 719–30. Cambridge, Mass.: Harvard University Press, 1952.

MacKenzie, John. *Propaganda and Empire: The Manipulation of British Public Opinion 1880–1960.* Manchester: Manchester University Press, 1984.

Mannoni, O. Dominique. *Prospero and Caliban: The Psychology of Colonization.* Trans. Pamela Powesland. 1950. Reprint, London: Methuen, 1956.

Marcus, George E., and Dick Cushman. "Ethnographies as Texts." *Annual Review of Anthropology* 11 (1982), pp. 25–69.

Marcus, Jane, ed. *Virginia Woolf: A Feminist Slant.* Lincoln: University of Nebraska Press, 1983.

Markey, Thomas L. "Afrikaans: Creole or Non-Creole?" *Zeitschrift für Dialecktologie und Linguistik* 49, no. 2 (1982), pp. 169–207.

Martin, Biddy, and Chandra Talpade Mohanty. "Feminist Politics: What's Home Got to Do with It?" In *Feminist Studies, Critical Studies,* ed. Teresa de Lauretis, pp. 191–212. Bloomington: Indiana University Press, 1986.

McClintock, Ann. "The Angel of Progress: Pitfalls of the Term 'Post-Colonialism.'" *Social Text* 10, nos. 2 and 3 (1992), pp. 84–98.

McClure, John. *Kipling and Conrad: The Colonial Fiction.* Cambridge, Mass.: Harvard University Press, 1981.

McRobbie, Angela. "Strategies of Vigilance: An Interview with Gayatri Chakravorty Spivak." *Block* 10 (1985), pp. 9–13.

Meath, Lord. "Anglo-Saxon Unity." *Fortnightly Review* (May 1891).

Memmi, Albert. *The Colonizer and the Colonized.* 1957. Reprint, Boston: Beacon Press, 1967.

Mercer, Kobena. "Recoding Narratives of Race and Nation." In *Black Film, British Cinema,* ed. Kobena Mercer et al. London: Institute of Contemporary Arts, 1988.

Mermelstein, David, ed. *The Anti-apartheid Reader: The Struggle against White Racist Rule in South Africa.* New York: Grove Press, 1987.

Métraux, Alfred. *Voodoo in Haiti.* Trans. Hugo Charteris. New York: Oxford University Press, 1959.

Michel, Claudine. "Tapping the Wisdom of the Ancestors: An Attempt to Recast Vodou and Morality through *The Voice* of Mama Lola and Karen McCarthy Brown." In *The Caribbean: 500 Years of Human Development.* Kingston, Jamaica: University of West Indies Press, forthcoming.

Millin, Sarah Gertrude. *God's Step-Children.* London: Constable, 1924.

Mohanty, Chandra Talpade. "Under Western Eyes: Feminist Scholarship and Colonial Discourses." *Boundary 2* 12, no. 3 (1984), pp. 333–58.

Moi, Toril. *Sexual/Textual Politics: Feminist Literary Theory.* London: Methuen, 1985.

Moore, Gerald. *The Chosen Tongue: English Writing in the Tropical World.* London: Longman, 1969.

————. "The Politics of Negritude." In *Protest and Conflict in African Literature,* eds. Cosmo Pieterse and Donald Munro, pp. 26–42. New York: Africana Publishing, 1969.

Morris, William. "The Earthly Paradise." In *News from Nowhere and Selected Writings and Designs,* ed. Asa Briggs, p. 68. Harmondsworth, England: Penguin Books, 1980.

Mosse, George. *Nationalism and Sexuality: Respectability and Abnormal Sexuality in Modern Europe.* New York: Howard Fertig, 1985.

Muecke, Stephen. "The Discourse of Nomadology: Phylums in Flux." *Art and Text* (winter 1984), pp. 24–40.

Naidoo, Beverley. *Censoring Reality: An Examination of Books on South Africa.* London: ILEA Centre for Anti-racist Education, 1984.

Ndebele, Njabulo S. *Rediscovery of the Ordinary: Essays on South African Literature and Culture.* Johannesburg: Congress of South African Writers, 1991.

New, Elisa. "Killing the Princess: The Offense of a Bad Defense." *Tikkun* 4, no. 2 (March/April 1989), pp. 17ff.

Newton, Judith Lowder. *Women, Power, and Subversion: Social Strategies in British Fiction, 1778–1860.* Athens: University of Georgia Press, 1981.

Newton, Judith, and Deborah Rosenfelt, eds. *Feminist Criticism and Social Change: Sex, Class, and Race in Literature and Culture.* New York: Methuen, 1985.

Ngũgĩ Wa Thiong'o. *Decolonizing the Mind: The Politics of Language in African Literature.* Portsmouth, N.H.: Heinemann, 1986.

———. "The Tension between National and Imperialist Culture." *World Literature Written in English* 24, no. 1 (1984), pp. 3–9.

Nightingale, Peggy, ed. *A Sense of Place in the New Literatures in English.* St. Lucia: University of Queensland Press, 1986.

O'Brien, Anthony. "Literature in Another South Africa: Njabulo Ndebele's Theory of Emergent Culture." *diacritics* 22, no. 1 (spring 1992), pp. 67–85.

O'Brien, Conor Cruise. *Albert Camus of Europe and Africa.* New York: Viking, 1970.

Omi, Michael, and Howard Winant. *Racial Formations in the United States: From the 1960s to the 1980s.* New York: Routledge, 1986.

Orwell, George. *Down and Out in Paris and London.* 1933. Reprint, New York: Berkley Books, 1959.

Outlaw, Lucius. "Toward a Critical Theory of 'Race.'" In *Anatomy of Racism,* ed. David Theo Goldberg, pp. 58–82. Minneapolis: University of Minnesota Press, 1990.

Ozick, Cynthia. *Art and Ardor: Essays.* New York: Alfred A. Knopf, 1983.

———. "Sholem Aleichem's Revolution." *The New Yorker,* 28 March 1988, pp. 99ff.

Parker, Andrew. "Ezra Pound and the 'Economy' of Anti-Semitism." *Boundary* 11, nos. 1–2 (fall/winter 1982–83), pp. 103–28.

Parker, Andrew, et al., eds. *Nationalisms and Sexualities.* New York: Routledge, 1992.

Parry, Benita. *Conrad and Imperialism: Ideological Boundaries and Visionary Frontiers.* London: Macmillan, 1983.

———. "Problems in Current Theories of Colonial Discourse." *Oxford Literary Review* (special edition on colonialism) 9, nos. 1–2 (1987), pp. 27–58.

Patai, Daphne. *The Orwell Mystique: A Study in Male Ideology.* Amherst: University of Massachusetts Press, 1984.

Patterson, Orlando. *Slavery and Social Death.* Cambridge, Mass.: Harvard University Press, 1982.

Patterson, Sheila. *Colour and Culture in South Africa.* London: Routledge, 1953.

Peterson, Kirsten Holst, and Anna Rutherford, eds. *A Double Colonization: Colonial and Post-colonial Women's Writing.* Oxford: Dangaroo Press, 1986.

Piedra, José. "Literary Whiteness and the Afro-Hispanic Difference." *New Literary History* 18, no. 2 (winter 1987), pp. 303–32.

Povey, John. "Landscape in Early African Poetry." In *Olive Schreiner and After,* ed. Malvern van Wyk Smith and Don Maclennan, pp. 116–28. Cape Town: David Philip, 1983.

Pratt, Mary Louise. "Conventions of Representation: Where Discourse and Ideology Meet." In *Georgetown University Round Table on Languages and Linguistics 1982,* ed. Heidi Byrenes, pp. 139–55. Washington, D.C.: Georgetown University Press, 1982.

———. *Imperial Eyes: Travel Writing and Transculturation.* London and New York: Routledge, 1992.

———. "Scratches on the Face of the Country; or, What Mr. Barrow Saw in the Land of the Bushmen." *Critical Inquiry* 12, no. 1 (autumn 1985), pp. 119–43.

Press, Karen. "Building a National Culture in South Africa." In *Rendering Things Visible: Essays on South African Literary Culture,* ed. Martin Trump, pp. 22–40. Athens: Ohio University Press, 1990.

Raiskin, Judith. "Inverts and Hybrids: Lesbian Rewritings of Sexual and Racial Identities." In *Lesbian Postmodern,* ed. Laura Doan, pp. 156–72. New York: Columbia University Press, 1994.

Retamar, Roberto Fernández. *Caliban and Other Essays*. Trans. Edward Baker. Minneapolis: University of Minnesota Press, 1989.

Rich, Adrienne. "Notes toward a Politics of Location." In *Blood, Bread, and Poetry*, pp. 210–31. New York: W. W. Norton, 1986.

Rich, Paul B. *Race and Empire in British Politics*. Cambridge: Cambridge University Press, 1986.

Riemenschneider, Dieter, ed. *The History and Historiography of Commonwealth Literature*. Tübingen: Narr, 1983.

Riggs, Marlon. *Tongues Untied*. Video, 1990.

Riley, Joan. *The Unbelonging*. London: Women's Press, 1985.

Robbins, Bruce. "Modernism in History, Modernism in Power." In *Modernism Reconsidered*, ed. Robert Kiely, pp. 229–45. Cambridge, Mass.: Harvard University Press, 1983.

Robinson, Ronald, and J. Gallagher, with Alice Denny. *Africa and the Victorians: The Official Mind of Imperialism*. 2d ed. London: Macmillan, 1981.

Rojo, Antonio Benítez. "The Repeating Island," trans. James Maraniss. *New England Review and Bread Loaf Quarterly* 7, no. 4 (summer 1985), pp. 430–52.

Romero, Lora. "Vanishing Americans: Gender, Empire, and New Historicism." *American Literature* 63, no. 3 (September 1991), pp. 385–404.

Rosaldo, Renato. *Culture and Truth: The Remaking of Social Analysis*. Boston: Beacon Press, 1989.

Rosenberg, Edgar. *From Shylock to Svengali: Jewish Stereotypes in English Fiction*. Stanford, Calif.: Stanford University Press, 1960.

Rowbotham, Sheila, and Jeffrey Weeks. *Socialism and the New Life: The Personal and Sexual Politics of Edward Carpenter and Havelock Ellis*. London: Pluto Press, 1977.

Said, Edward. "An Ideology of Difference." *Critical Inquiry* 12, no. 1 (autumn 1985), pp. 38–58.

———. *Orientalism*. New York: Pantheon Books, 1978.

Sale, Kirpatrick. *The Conquest of Paradise: Christopher Columbus and the Columbian Legacy*. New York: Plume, 1991.

Salkey, Andrew, ed. *Island Voices: Stories from the West Indies*. New York: Liveright, 1970.

Sandoval, Chela. "US Third World Feminism: A Theory and Method of Oppositional Consciousness in the Postmodern World." *Genders* 10 (spring 1991), pp. 1–24.

Sartre, Jean-Paul. *Anti-Semite and Jew*. Trans. George J. Becker. New York: Schocken Books, 1965. Originally published as *Réflexions sur la Question Juive*, 1946.

Savitt, Todd L. *Medicine and Slavery: The Diseases and Health Care of Blacks in Antebellum Virginia*. Urbana: University of Illinois Press, 1978.

Schipper, Mineke, ed. *Unheard Words: Women and Literature in Africa, the Arab World, Asia, the Caribbean and Latin America*. Trans. Barbara Potter Fasting. London: Allison and Busby, 1985.

Scott, Joan Wallach. "The Evidence of Experience." *Critical Inquiry* 17 (summer 1971), pp. 773–97.

Sedgwick, Eve. *Epistemology of the Closet*. Berkeley: University of California Press, 1990.

Selvon, Samuel. *Lonely Londoners*. Harlow, England: Longman, 1985.

Shell, Marc. "Marranos (Pigs); or, From Coexistence to Toleration." *Critical Inquiry* 17 (winter 1991), pp. 306–35.

Shohat, Ella. "Notes on the 'Post-Colonial.'" *Social Text* 10, nos. 2 and 3 (1992), pp. 99–113.

Showalter, Elaine. *The Female Malady: Women, Madness and Culture in England, 1830–1980*. New York: Pantheon Books, 1985.

———. *Sexual Anarchy: Gender and Culture at the Fin de Siècle.* New York: Viking Penguin, 1990.

Shryock, Richard Harrison. "Medical Practice in the Old South." In *Medicine in America: Historical Essays,* pp. 49–70. Baltimore: Johns Hopkins Press, 1966.

Sinclair, May. *Mary Olivier: A Life.* 1919. Reprint, New York: Dial Press, 1980.

Smith, Lilian. *Killers of the Dream.* 1949. Rev. and enlarged ed. New York: W. W. Norton, 1978.

Smith, Malvern van Wyk. "The Origins of Some Victorian Images of Africa." *English in Africa* 6, no. 1 (March 1979), pp. 12–32.

Smith, Olivia. *The Politics of Language 1791–1819.* Oxford: Clarendon Press, 1984.

Smith, Sidonie, and Julia Watson, eds. *De/colonizing the Subject: The Politics of Gender in Women's Autobiography.* Minneapolis: University of Minnesota Press, 1992

Smith-Rosenberg, Carol. *Disorderly Conduct: Visions of Gender in Victorian America.* New York: Oxford University Press, 1985.

Snow, Loudell F. "Con Men and Conjure Men: A Ghetto Image." In *Images of Healers,* ed. Anne Hudson Jones, vol. 2, pp. 45–78. Albany: State University of New York Press, 1983.

Spivak, Gayatri Chakravorty. "Can the Subaltern Speak? Speculations on Widow Sacrifice." *Wedge* 7/8 (winter/spring 1985), pp. 120–30.

———. "Feminism and Critical Theory." In *For Alma Mater: Theory and Practice in Feminist Scholarship,* ed. Paula A. Treichler, Cheris Kramarae, and Beth Stafford, pp. 119–42. Urbana: University of Illinois Press, 1985.

———. "Imperialism and Sexual Difference." *Oxford Literary Review* 8, nos. 1–2 (1986), pp. 225–40.

———. *In Other Worlds: Essays in Cultural Politics.* New York: Methuen, 1987.

———. "The Rani of Sirmur." In *Europe and Its Others,* vol. 1, ed. Francis Barker et al., pp. 128–51. Colchester, England: University of Essex, 1985.

———. "Three Women's Texts and a Critique of Imperialism." *Critical Inquiry* 12, no. 1 (autumn 1985), pp. 243–61.

Squier, Susan Merrill. *Virginia Woolf and London: The Sexual Politics of the City.* Chapel Hill: University of North Carolina Press, 1985.

———, ed. *Women Writers and the City: Essays in Feminist Literary Criticism.* Knoxville: University of Tennessee Press, 1984.

Stanley, Henry. *Through the Dark Continent.* New York: Harper and Brothers, 1878.

Stepan, Nancy. "Biological Degeneration: Races and Proper Places." In *Degeneration: The Darker Side of Progress,* ed. Edward Chamberlin and Sander L. Gilman, pp. 97–120. New York: Columbia University Press, 1985.

———. *"The Hour of Eugenics": Race, Gender and Nation in Latin America.* Ithaca, N.Y.: Cornell University Press, 1991.

———. *The Idea of Race in Science: Great Britain 1800–1960.* London: Macmillan, 1982.

———. "Race and Gender: The Role of Analogy in Science." In *Anatomy of Racism,* ed. David Theo Goldberg, pp. 38–57. Minneapolis: University of Minnesota Press, 1990.

Stepan, Nancy Leys, and Sander Gilman. "Appropriating the Idioms of Science: The Rejection of Scientific Racism." In *The Bounds of Race: Perspectives on Hegemony and Resistance,* ed. Dominic LaCapra, pp. 72–103. Ithaca, N.Y.: Cornell University Press, 1991.

Stephens, Thomas M. "Creole, Créole, Criollo, Crioulo: The Shadings of a Term." *SECOL Review* 7, no. 3 (fall 1983), pp. 308–9.

Stoler, Ann. "Making Empire Respectable: The Politics of Race and Sexual Morality in 20th-century Colonial Cultures." *American Ethnologist* 16, no. 4 (Nov. 1989), pp. 634–59.

Strobel, Margaret. *European Women and the Second British Empire.* Bloomington: Indiana University Press, 1991.

Suzman, Arthur. *Race Classification and Definition in the Legislation of the Union of South Africa, 1910–1960: A Survey and Analysis.* Johannesburg: South African Institute for Race Relations, 1960.

Talbot, Eugene. *Degeneracy: Its Causes, Signs, and Results,* ed. Havelock Ellis. New York: Scribner's, 1898.

Taussig, Michael. "History as Sorcery." *Representations* 7 (summer 1984), pp. 87–109.

Taylor, Patrick. *The Narrative of Liberation: Perspectives on Afro-Caribbean Literature, Popular Culture, and Politics.* Ithaca, N.Y.: Cornell University Press, 1989.

Thompson, Leonard. *The Political Mythology of Apartheid.* New Haven: Yale University Press, 1985.

Torgovnick, Marianna. *Gone Primitive: Savage Intellects, Modern Lives.* Chicago: University of Chicago Press, 1990.

Trinh T. Minh-ha. "Not You/Like You: Post-colonial Women and the Interlocking Questions of Identity and Difference." *Inscriptions* 3, no. 4 (1988), pp. 71–77.

———. *Woman, Native, Other: Writing Postcoloniality and Feminism.* Bloomington: Indiana University Press, 1989.

Trump, Martin, ed. *Rendering Things Visible: Essays on South African Literary Culture.* Athens: Ohio University Press, 1990.

Tsuzuki, Chushichi. *Edward Carpenter, 1844–1929: Prophet of Human Fellowship.* Cambridge: Cambridge University Press, 1980.

Vaughan, Michael. "Storytelling and Politics in Fiction." *Rendering Things Visible: Essays on South African Literary Culture,* ed. Martin Trump, pp. 186–204. Athens: Ohio University Press, 1990.

Vance, Carol. "Social Construction Theory: Problems in the History of Sexuality." In *Homosexuality, Which Homosexuality?* ed. Dennis Altman et al., pp. 13–34. London: GMP, 1989.

Vicinus, Martha. *Independent Women: Work and Community for Single Women, 1850–1920.* Chicago: University of Chicago Press, 1985.

Walker, Alice. *In Search of Our Mothers' Gardens.* New York: Harcourt Brace Jovanovich, 1983.

———. "Nineteen Fifty-Five." In *You Can't Keep a Good Woman Down,* pp. 3–20. New York: Harcourt Brace Jovanovich, 1981.

Walker, Cherryl. *Women and Resistance in South Africa.* New York: Monthly Review Press, 1991.

Walkowitz, Judith. "Male Vice and Feminist Virtue: Feminism and the Politics of Prostitution in Nineteenth-Century Britain." *History Workshop* 13 (spring 1982), pp. 77–93.

———. "Science, Feminism and Romance: The Men and Women's Club, 1885–89." *History Workshop* 21 (spring 1986), pp. 37–59.

Walvin, James. *Passage to Britain: Immigration in British History and Politics.* Harmondsworth, England: Penguin Books, 1984.

Ware, Vron. *Beyond the Pale: White Women, Racism, and History.* London: Verso Press, 1992.

Washington, Booker T. *Up from Slavery.* In *Three Negro Classics.* New York: Avon Books, 1965.

Watts-Dunton, Theodore. "The Future of American Literature." *Fortnightly Review* (June 1891).

Weeks, Jeffrey. *Against Nature: Essays on History, Sexuality, and Identity.* London: Rivers Oram Press, 1991.

Wilentz, Gay. "English Is a Foreign Anguish: Caribbean Writers and the Disruption of the Colonial Canon." In *Decolonizing Tradition: New Views of Twentieth-Century "British" Literary Canons,* ed. Karen R. Lawrence, pp. 261–78. Urbana: University of Illinois Press, 1992.

Wilk, Melvin. *Jewish Presence in T. S. Eliot and Franz Kafka.* Brown Judaic Studies, no. 82. Atlanta: Scholars Press, 1986.

Willemse, Hein. "Die Skrille Sonbesies: Emergent Black Afrikaans Poets in Search of Authority." In *Rendering Things Visible: Essays on South African Literary Culture,* ed. Martin Trump, pp. 367–401. Athens: Ohio University Press, 1990.

Williams, Eric. *From Columbus to Castro: The History of the Caribbean 1492–1969.* London: André Deutsch, 1970.

Williams, Raymond. "Region and Class in the Novel." In *Writing in Society,* pp. 229–38. London: Verso, 1983.

Wiltsher, Anne. *Most Dangerous Women: Feminist Peace Campaigners of the Great War.* London: Pandora Press, 1985.

Wood, Mary Elene. "How We Got This Way: Reading the Sciences of Homosexuality." Lecture presented November 30, 1993, at University of California at Santa Barbara.

Woolf, Virginia. Introduction to May Llewelyn Davies, *Life as We Have Known It.* London: Leonard and Virginia Woolf, 1931.

———. "Lives of the Obscure." In *The Common Reader,* pp. 146–67. London: Hogarth Press, 1951.

———. *A Room of One's Own.* New York: Harcourt, Brace and World, 1929.

———. *Three Guineas.* London: Hogarth Press, 1938.

———. *The Waves.* 1931. Reprint, Harmondsworth, England: Penguin Books, 1972.

———. "Women and Fiction." In *Collected Essays,* ed. Leonard Woolf, vol. 2. London: Hogarth Press, 1966.

Zangwill, Israel. *Children of the Ghetto: A Study of a Peculiar People.* 1892. Reprint, Philadelphia: Jewish Publication Society of America, 1938.

Zavala, Iris M. *Colonialism and Culture: Hispanic Modernisms and the Social Imaginary.* Bloomington: Indiana University Press, 1992.

———. "Representing the Colonial Subject." In *1492–1992: Re/Discovering Colonial Writing,* ed. René Jara and Nicholas Spadaccini, pp. 323–48. Minneapolis: Prisma Institute, 1989.

Index

Judith Raiskin is assistant professor of women's studies and English at the University of California at Santa Barbara. She is currently at work on the Norton Critical Edition of Jean Rhys's *Wide Sargasso Sea*.